IMPLICIT DIMENSIONS OF CONTRACT

This collection of essays, derived from an international workshop, explores the significance of the implicit understandings and tacit expectations of the parties to different kinds of contractual agreements, ranging from simple discrete transactions to long-term associational agreements such as those formed in companies. An interdisciplinary and comparative approach is used to investigate how the law comprehends and gives effect to the these implicit dimensions of contracts. The significance of this enquiry is found not only in relation to the interpretation of contracts in many different contexts, but more fundamentally in how the social practices involved in making contracts should be analysed and comprehended.

International Studies in the Theory of Private Law

This series of books edited by a distinguished international team of legal scholars aims to investigate the normative and theoretical foundations of the law governing relations between citizens. The context for such investigations of private law systems is set by important modern tendencies in systems of governance. The advent of the regulatory state marks the withdrawal of the state from direct control and management of social and economic activity, and the adoption instead of procedural regulation and co-regulatory strategies that promote the use of private law techniques of ordering and self-regulation in social and economic interactions between citizens. The tendency known as globalisation and the corresponding increases in cross-border trade produce the responses of transnational regulation of commerce and private governance regimes, and these new systems of governance challenge the hegemony of traditional national private law systems. Furthermore, these tendencies towards transnational governance regimes compel an interaction between different national legal traditions, with their differences in culture and philosophy as well as their differences based upon variations in market systems, which provokes questions not only about competing policy frameworks but also about nature and adequacy of different kinds of legal reasoning itself.

The series welcomes a diverse range of theoretical approaches in the examination of these issues including approaches using socio-legal methods, economics, critical theory, systems theory, regulation theory, and moral and political theory. With the aim of stimulating an international discussion of these issues, volumes will be published in Germany, France, and the United Kingdom in one of the three languages.

Editors

Volumes published in German by Nomos Verlagsgesellschaft, Baden-Baden

1. Peer Zumbansen, *Ordnungsmuster im modern Wohlfahrtsstaat: Lernerfahrungen zwischen Staat, Geseelschaft und Vertrag* (2000).
2. Dan Wielsch, *Freiheit und Funktion: Zur Struktur- und Theoriegeschichte des Rechts der Wirtschaftsgesellschaft* (2001).

Implicit Dimensions of Contract

Discrete, Relational and Network Contracts

Edited by
DAVID CAMPBELL
HUGH COLLINS
JOHN WIGHTMAN

·HART·
PUBLISHING

OXFORD AND PORTLAND, OREGON
2003

Hart Publishing
Oxford and Portland, Oregon

Published in North America (US and Canada) by
Hart Publishing c/o
International Specialized Book Services
5804 NE Hassalo Street
Portland, Oregon
97213-3644
USA

Hart Publishing is a specialist legal publisher based in Oxford, England.
To order further copies of this book or to request a list of other publications please write to:

Hart Publishing, Salter's Boatyard, Folly Bridge,
Abingdon Road, Oxford OX1 4LB
Telephone: +44 (0)1865 245533 or Fax: +44 (0)1865 794882
e-mail: mail@hartpub.co.uk
WEBSITE: http//www.hartpub.co.uk

British Library Cataloguing in Publication Data
Data Available
ISBN 1–84113–349–3 (hardback)

Typeset by Hope Services (Abingdon) Ltd.
Printed and bound in Great Britain on acid-free paper by
Biddles Ltd, www.biddles.co.uk

Preface

This collection of essays explores the significance of the implicit understandings and expectations of the parties to different kinds of contracts, ranging from simple discrete transactions to long-term associational agreements such as those formed in companies. An interdisciplinary and comparative approach is used to investigate how the law comprehends and gives effect to these implicit dimensions of contracts. The significance of this enquiry lies not only in relation to the interpretation of contracts in many different contexts, but more fundamentally in how the social practices involved in making contracts should be analysed and comprehended.

The genesis of this collection was in an international workshop held at the London School of Economics in October 2001. The editors are grateful to the *Modern Law Review* for a grant that enabled the participants to attend the workshop, and to the Research Committee of the Cardiff Law School and the ESRC Research Centre for Business Relationships, Accountability, Sustainability and Society for supplemental financial assistance.

We are also grateful to all the participants who commented extensively on the original versions of these papers, and regret that space precludes publication of all those contributions.

David Campbell
Hugh Collins
John Wightman

Contents

List of Contributors

Roger Brownsword, Professor of Law, University of Sheffield

David Campbell, Professor of Law, Cardiff Law School and ESRC Research Centre for Business Relationships, Accountability, Sustainability and Society

Hugh Collins, Professor of English Law, London School of Economics

Simon Deakin, Robert Monks Professor of Corporate Governance, Judge Institute of Management, University of Cambridge

Richard Hobbs, Researcher, Faculty of Law, University of Cambridge

Paddy Ireland, Kent Law School, University of Kent at Canterbury

Stewart Macaulay, Malcolm Pitman Sharp Hilldale Professor, Theodore W Brazeau Bascom Professor of Law, University of Wisconsin Law School

Ian R Macneil, John Henry Wigmore Professor of Law Emeritus, Northwestern University School of Law

David Nash, Research Fellow, Judge Institute of Management, University of Cambridge

Christopher A Riley, Department of Law, University of Durham

Giles Slinger, Associate, AT Kearney and Co, London.

Gunther Teubner, Professor of Law, Johann-Wolfgang-Goethe-Universitat, Frankfurt am Main

William C Whitford, Emeritus Professor Law, University of Wisconsin Law School

John Wightman, Kent Law School, University of Kent at Canterbury

1

Introduction: The Research Agenda of Implicit Dimensions of Contracts

HUGH COLLINS

A CONTRACT CREATES a special form of association between people. Unlike many forms of human relationships such as kinship, friendship, or membership of a community, contracts in all their variety share the qualities of voluntariness and boundedness.[1] The relationship is established through an act of choice, albeit one that is heavily constrained in some instances by economic necessity. The obligations created by this choice appear more determinate and discrete than the responsibilities engendered by other forms of human association. In a sense, contracts reduce complexity in human relationships. Instead of the transaction launching an unspecific and diffuse sense of obligation or loyalty, as might be engendered by a gift, the contract confines expectations and separates itself from those surrounding conventions and norms that may encourage the expectation of indeterminate, wide-ranging obligations. If you want to establish loyalty and commitment, give someone a present, but if you want something in particular, make a contract.

Yet this image of contracts as a discrete, voluntary form of human association presents a distorted picture in some respects. The practice of entering contracts evidently relies upon conventional understandings of the types of conduct that count as making a contract. When I order a cappuccino in my local coffee shop, the significance or meaning of my conduct and that of the server depends upon shared implicit

[1] P Selznick, *Law, Society and Industrial Justice* (New York, Russell Sage Foundation, 1969) 52–62; H Collins, *Regulating Contracts* (Oxford, Oxford University Press, 1999) 13–17.

understandings. Our intention to make an exchange of a cup of coffee for money can only be understood from the context in which the conduct takes place, that is the retail shop, and the broader conventional patterns of people exchanging goods for money in that location. When I visit a friend and ask for a cappuccino, the same request or conduct does not engender the expectation of payment, or indeed many other expectations that may arise in a shop, such as prompt service, high quality coffee beans, and a thermo-insulated cup. Contracts certainly have the distinctive quality of constituting a discrete, voluntary type of relationship, but like other forms of human association, they are nevertheless embedded in conventions, norms, mutual assumptions and unarticulated expectations.[2]

The law of contract provides, among other things, a state guarantee of the binding quality of contractual relations. It insists that contracts should be performed on pain of a state sanction such as payment of compensation. To fulfil this task, the law of contracts must develop techniques for identifying contracts and determining the content of the voluntary obligations that they create. In many instances this job appears deceptively simple. A court may be presented with a written document which describes itself as a contract and which records a set of obligations that have been agreed between the parties, followed by their signatures as a record that agreement was reached. Lawyers tend to think of such a document as the paradigm of a contract, though of course numerically it is far less common than an informal transaction in a shop. Even in such a written contract, however, the tasks of deciding whether the law has encountered a contract and what obligations it engenders are less than straightforward. How is it, for instance, that the signatures on the document amount to proof that an agreement was reached? The practice of signing documents surely relies on a convention that marking one's name in idiosyncratic handwriting signifies a binding record of consent to a transaction. The law recognises this convention and uses it within its reasoning process to provide a conclusive determination of the question of whether an agreement took place, even to the extent of ignoring other evidence that the person who signed the document did not read it or did not appreciate its full meaning, and did not mean to agree to such a transaction.[3] And the significance of the

[2] M Granovetter, 'Economic Action and Social Structure: The Problem of Embeddedness' (1985) 91 *American Journal of Sociology* 481.

[3] *L'Estrange v F Graucob Ltd* [1934] KB 2 KB 394, CA.

convention concerning signatures in legal reasoning can be turned around: a written document that was in fact agreed provides in some instances no valid evidence of a binding transaction without a signature.[4]

Although it is easy to overlook the significance of context and convention in determining whether or not a contract has been made, the relevance of these factors cannot be ignored when the question of the content of the contractual obligations comes to be considered by the legal system. The perennial issue is whether the written document exhausts the obligations of the parties or whether the recorded agreement is supplemented and qualified by implicit undertakings. In the absence of a written document, of course, this issue of the degree to which the voluntary undertaking is isolated from conventional expectations becomes even more central to the task of ensuring that parties respect their contractual obligations.

Thus, any legal system that assumes the role of enforcing contracts must accomplish the central task of developing techniques and processes for determining the legal significance of the contexts and conventions surrounding the social practice of entering into contracts. The underlying problem concerns the recognition and determination of the relevance to the legal process of the implicit understandings and expectations of the participants. In short, the issue is what to make of the implicit dimensions of contracts.

THE POLICY OF COMPETITIVENESS

Before mapping out this field for legal research, it is important to point out that this problem of handling the implicit dimensions of contracts is not merely a challenge for legal technique and an enquiry into contractual justice. The proper recognition of implicit dimensions of contracts is regarded in other branches of the social sciences as a key policy issue in relation to the operation of an efficient and competitive market economy. In contracts of employment, for instance, economic and sociological studies reveal how greater productive efficiency can be achieved through the observance of conventions that augment mutual trust and confidence between employer and employee. Greater productive

[4] Law of Property (Miscellaneous Provisions) Act 1989 s1 (a valid deed requires a signature).

efficiency arises when an employee does not simply do what is required under the contract, but uses skills and knowledge to identify problems and solutions, to make innovations in product design and working methods, and to improve quality. In return for this commitment on the part of the employee, however, the employer needs to do more than to stick by the contract and to treat the worker with respect. The employer has to respond to the implicit expectations of the employee of fair treatment, providing assistance with the development of a career, aiding improvements to the skills and employability and involving the workers in the decision-making process of the enterprise. By observing these requirements of the 'implicit contract' or the 'psychological contract',[5] it is widely believed that an employer benefits from greater efficiency, a more rapid pace of innovation and tighter quality controls.[6] The question confronting policy makers in the field of industrial relations is how to promote these more competitive practices based upon flexible, co-operative employment relations. An important ingredient of this policy agenda is to ensure that the legal system understands the implicit dimensions of this form of contractual relation and provides appropriate and effective support for their development.[7]

A similar policy agenda can be found in studies of commercial transactions, business organisations and market institutions. The recurring questions are how far these economic arrangements depend upon implicit understandings and conventions, and how the efficiency of these institutions might be improved by paying attention to the construction and protection of these implicit dimensions. It is suggested, for instance, that the legal system can make a profound contribution to the creation of trust in inter-firm supply relations, which may help to reduce transaction costs, avoid disputes, improve quality, facilitate the exchange of know-how and be conducive to innovation. To create the necessary long-term supply relations, the parties have to be confident that the legal framework, which comprises the written contract together with the obligations inserted by the law that supplement or qualify that agreement, will support the implicit understanding of

[5] KVW Stone, 'The New Psychological Contract: Implications of the Changing Workplace for Labor and Employment Law' (2001) 48 *UCLA Law Review* 519.

[6] Department of Trade and Industry, White Paper, *Our Competitive Future: Building the Knowledge Driven Economy* (London, 1998); Department of Trade and Industry, *High Performance Workplaces* (London, July 2002).

[7] H Collins, 'Regulating the Employment Relation for Competitiveness' (2001) 30 *Industrial Law Journal* 17.

co-operation and loyalty to the joint economic interests of the parties.[8] The lessons learned from a study of commercial relations may also be applicable to the problem of devising a suitable legal framework for the provision of public services through contractual arrangements formed with private sector companies after a competitive tendering process.[9] These studies also help to direct competition policy, for though recognition of the implicit dimensions of franchises and other long-term contractual relations may restrict competition in some respects, the protection of implicit and anti-competitive expectations through contract law may attract investment, facilitate the development of new products and produce greater consumer choice in the long run.[10]

Underlying these policy oriented approaches, the notion of implicit contracts is used as part of endeavours to understand how successful economic institutions such as firms and markets are established, and why certain patterns of industrial organisation evolve. In the influential research agenda of transaction cost economics,[11] for instance, a central question is why certain economic activities are conducted within firms, whereas others rely on market transactions, and yet other production systems appear to require a kind of hybrid organisation or network? In answering this question by reference to the costs and difficulties of making contracts, the inquiry becomes necessarily interested in how the legal system recognises both the express and the implicit dimensions of contractual arrangements. The metaphor of an 'implicit contract' can be used to explain how the express contracts are supplemented by

[8] S Deakin, C Lane and F Wilkinson, 'Contract Law, Trust Relations, and Incentives for Co-operation: A Comparative Study' in S Deakin and J Mitchie (eds), *Contracts, Co-operation, and Competition* (Oxford, Oxford University Press, 1997) 105; and see other essays in that book.

[9] K Walsh, *et al*, 'Contracts for Public Services: A Comparative Perspective' in D Campbell and P Vincent-Jones (eds), *Contract and Economic Organisation* (Aldershot, Dartmouth, 1996) 212; P Vincent-Jones, 'Hybrid Organization, Contractual Governance, and Compulsory Competitive Tendering in the Provision of Local Authority Services' in Deakin and Mitchie, above n 8, 143; Collins, above n 1, ch 13.

[10] S Deakin, T Goodwin and A Hughes, 'Co-operation and Trust in Inter-Firm Relations: Beyond Competition Policy?' in Deakin and Mitchie, above n 8, 339; S Anderman, 'Commercial Co-operation, International Competitiveness, and EC Competition Policy' in Deakin and Mitchie, above n 8, 392. Competition policy issues also arise in connection with human capital acquired in the performance of contracts of employment: A Hyde, 'A Closer Look at the Emerging Employment Law of Silicon Valley's High Velocity Labour Market' in J Conaghan, RM Fischl and K Klare (eds), *Labour Law in an Era of Globalization* (Oxford, Oxford University Press, 2002) 253; and Stone, above n 5.

[11] OE Williamson, *The Economic Institutions of Capitalism* (New York, Free Press, 1985); O Hart, *Firms, Contracts and Financial Structure* (Oxford, Clarendon Press, 1995).

conventions and institutional practices that serve to reduce transaction costs. The 'implicit contract' modifies the immediate short-term economic interest expressed in the written contract by reference to considerations of long-term economic interest.

The same issues concerning the efficiency of different organisations of productive systems, such as understanding the competitive advantages of hybrid organisations, can be addressed, perhaps even more successfully, from other sociological and economic perspectives. Using agency theory in economics, for instance, it is possible to provide an analysis of how certain long-term contractual arrangements like business format franchises establish a superior system of co-operation through an incentive structure in which both parties act simultaneously as both principals and agents for the other.[12] These studies can also raise critical questions about the merits of these productive organisations. It may be asked, for instance, whether some of the efficiency gains of hybrids and networks over integrated firms derives from their success in repackaging business costs as 'externalities', for which the hybrid or network evades financial or legal responsibility.[13]

Whether oriented by economics or sociology, what these analytical and empirical studies invariably reveal is the practical significance of the implicit dimensions of the economic structure, including the participant's expectations of co-operation and loyalty. The written contracts rarely reveal the dynamics of the co-operative game embedded in the transaction. Long-term contracts often do not so much define a set of discrete obligations as launch a relationship in which incentive structures encourage initiatives and adjustments that will accrue to the joint benefit of both parties.[14] In the language of 'game theory', contractual relations usually form part of a repeated non-cooperative game, where

[12] E Schanze, 'Symbiotic Contracts: Exploring Long-Term Agency Structures Between Contract and Corporation' in C Joerges (ed), *Franchising and the Law: Theoretical and Comparative Approaches in Europe and the United States* (Baden-Baden, Nomos Verlagsgesellschaft, 1991) 67.

[13] H Collins, 'Ascription of Legal Responsibility to Groups in Complex Patterns of Economic Interaction' (1990) 53 *Modern Law Review* 731; G Teubner, 'Piercing the Contractual Veil? The Social Responsibility of Contractual Networks' in T Wilhelmsson (ed), *Perspectives of Critical Contract Law* (Aldershot, Gower, 1997) 211.

[14] D Campbell and D Harris, 'Flexibility in Long-term Contractual Relationships' (1993) 20 *Journal of Law and Society* 166; T Daintith, 'The Design and Performance of Long-term Contracts', in T Daintith and G Teubner (eds), *Contract and Organisation* (Berlin, Walter de Gruyter, 1986) 164; I Macneil, 'Contracts: Adjustment of Long-term Economic Relations under Classical, Neoclassical, and Relational Contract Law' (1978) 72 *Northwestern University Law Review* 854.

the risk of cheating or defection is successfully countered not by the threat of legal sanction but by the incentive provided by the benefits accruing from long-term co-operation and adaptation.[15] The policy question becomes whether legal regulation, as it interacts with non-legal sanctions,[16] facilitates the operation of this implicit incentive structure even though it is not stated expressly in the contract.

A FISSURE IN LEGAL SCHOLARSHIP

Lawyers may not frequently consider such policy issues in identical terms, but they certainly appreciate that contracts have implicit dimensions. Many legal doctrines advert to the presence and significance of implicit understandings between the parties. For example, recognition of implicit dimensions results in the insertion of terms into contracts on the basis of customs of the trade, a course of dealing between the parties, or the unexpressed joint intentions of the parties supported by a business necessity test. Moreover, many commercial contracts express in preliminary statements some of the business expectations that lie behind the transaction. Through these recitals, the parties record the business purpose of the transaction and their implicit expectations of behaviour. More deeply, lawyers appreciate that the practice of entering contracts depends upon mutual trust and confidence. Although a written contract may appear as a guarded delineation of obligations with detailed allocation of risks backed by the threat of legal sanctions, this posture of distrust is misleading, because the willingness to trade must ultimately rely on a disposition to take the risks of disappointment and betrayal.

> Credit, not distrust, is the basis of commercial dealings: mercantile genius consists principally in knowing whom to trust and with whom to deal, and commercial intercourse is no more based on the supposition of fraud than it is on the supposition of forgery.[17]

Although lawyers are aware of the implicit dimensions of contracts, the question of what significance implicit dimensions have and should

[15] LG Telser, 'A Theory of Self-enforcing Agreements' (1980) 53 *Journal of Business* 27; Collins, above n 1, 130.

[16] D Charney, 'Non-legal Sanctions in Commercial Relationships' (1990) 104 *Harvard Law Review* 373.

[17] Bowen LJ, *Saunders v Maclean* (1883) 11 QBD 327, 343.

have in legal reasoning about contracts is controversial. Indeed, the division of opinion on this question can be regarded as a fissure in legal reasoning concerning contracts. On one side of this gulf lies the position that legal reasoning should concern itself primarily with the express aspects of contractual relations. This view argues for the foreclosure of any legal enquiry into the context of a transaction in favour of permitting the express agreement to speak for itself. It is urged that only this legal method will produce the certainty or predictability of legal outcomes which is necessary for commerce to flourish. If judges stray from this narrow path, it is alleged, no one will be sure where they stand, and confidence in contracts as a tool of economic co-ordination will be diminished. This view leads, for example, to a rejection of the insertion of implied obligations into contracts on the basis of broad standards such as reasonableness, and to an insistence that interpretation of contracts should rely on the literal meaning of the words used. This stance can also be defended in policy terms as providing parties to contracts with an incentive to seek maximum clarity in their contracts, to say exactly what they mean, which has the potential benefits of both reducing disputes and improving transparency in markets. The transparency and certainty produced by this legal analysis of contracts are advocated as providing a superior basis for trust in markets. This view is often associated with a 'classical' approach to contracts, with its working assumption that the intended transaction is fully 'presentiated' in the express terms of the contract.[18]

Against that view, and forming the background to the research agenda of this book, the other side of the argument claims not only that it is desirable for legal reasoning to incorporate a recognition of implicit dimensions of contracts in its regulation of transactions, but also, and more fundamentally, that such a process of legal recognition of implicit dimensions is necessary and inevitable in any system of law. In order for legal reasoning to understand and regulate the social practice of making contracts, it has to appreciate that contractual behaviour relies upon several contexts for its meaning and purpose. As well as the explicit agreement between the parties, the participants also conduct themselves by reference to their economic interests in having the deal successfully completed to the benefit of both parties, and by reference to their expected or desired long-term business relationship.[19] In the case of a

[18] Macneil, above n 14; IR Macneil, *The Relational Theory Of Contract* (London, Sweet & Maxwell, 2001) ch 6.

[19] Collins, above n 1, 128–36.

purchase of a cappuccino in a coffee shop, for instance, not only do the parties seek to comply with the express terms of the agreement concerning coffee for payment, but also the parties want a successful outcome in the sense that both feel better off as a result of the transaction, and also, perhaps most crucial of all from the point of view of the shop, that the customer begins as a result of a positive experience to treat the retailer as a reliable and trustworthy source of decent coffee and a place therefore to make regular purchases. This second view insists that the law needs to understand these different and sometimes competing frames of reference of the parties to a contract in order to make sense of contractual behaviour and to provide appropriate support.

In response to the argument that only by sticking strictly to the express terms of the agreement can the law establish certainty and predictability in market transactions, this second view that lays great emphasis on the implicit dimensions of contracts questions whether the classical law's assumption of 'presentiation' really achieves the aim of 'calculability' that it claims.[20] It is not disputed that predictability of legal outcomes is an important goal for the regulation of contracts, though not of course the only goal. The important question is rather whose predictions matter? Lawyers may find legal outcomes more predictable if the legal reasoning sticks closely to an interpretation of the express terms of the contract. But do the businessmen that enter contracts find that those legal outcomes produced by adherence to the text of the standard form contract coincide with their expectations of the outcome of the transaction? There is much evidence of a gap between the lawyer's prediction based upon the express terms of the contract and their clients' prediction based upon implicit understandings and expectations.

> I have had business men in my chambers, when at the bar, who, when a particular point of difference arose, have said how it would be solved according to the customary practices in the trade. 'But', I have interjected, 'that is not what the contract says'. 'Oh. The contract, let me see it', and when his attention is directed to the document which he has signed, and which he is probably considering in any detail for the first time, he is

[20] The criterion of calculability and its connection with formalised law was developed by Weber: M Weber, *Economy and Society* (G Roth and C Wittich, eds) (Berkeley, University of California Press, 1978) ii. 883. Cf DM Trubeck, 'Max Weber on Law and the Rise of Capitalism' (1972) *Wisconsin Law Review* 720; R Cotterell, 'The Development of Capitalism and the Formalisation of Contract Law' in B Fryer *et al* (eds) *Law, State and Society* (London, Croom Helm, 1981) 54.

> apt to say: 'Well I cannot help that; I told you the way things are always done.'[21]

This anecdote is confirmed more systematically by the empirical work concerning the 'non-use' of contracts pioneered by Macaulay.[22] One interpretation of these studies is that enforcement of the express terms of the contract may at least in some instances produce results that surprise and disconcert the parties. Their intentions were not completely expressed in the contract, and so to enforce the terms without modification may make the law produce unpredicted outcomes. So the question becomes whose calculability really matters: the lawyers or the businessmen? Lawyers may take pride in the comprehensive and detailed planning documents that comprise written contracts, but it is surely the value of calculability to businesses and consumers that really matters to help to establish trust in markets, and these documents, when they defeat expectations and cause surprises, only serve to increase wariness of transactions. The disagreement about the significance to be attached to express terms of contracts thus reveals a dilemma about how the law can best achieve one of its primary purposes: to provide support for trust and confidence in markets.

What deepens this fissure in contract scholarship is a disagreement about how justice in relation to contracts should be conceived. The difference between the two views on justice can be simplified as a contrast between procedural and substantive justice. A procedural justice perspective insists that once the parties to a contract have completed a particular procedure, namely the rules for the formation of an express agreement that is legally binding, the enforcement of the outcome of that procedure, the express agreement, should satisfy completely the demands of justice. A substantive justice perspective insists, in contrast, that the completion of the procedure, though vital for fairness, does not exhaust the demands of substantive justice. The written or express agreement, though a significant construction and one to which

[21] P Devlin, 'The Relation between Commercial Law and Commercial Practice' (1951) 14 *Modern Law Review* 249, 266.

[22] S Macaulay, 'Non-Contractual Relations in Business' (1963) 28 *American Sociological Review* 45; S Macaulay, 'The Use and Non-use of Contracts in the Manufacturing Industry' (1963) 9(7) *Practical Lawyer* 13; H Beale and T Dugdale, 'Contracts between Businessmen: Planning and the Use of Contractual Remedies' (1975) 2 *British Journal of Law and Society* 45; RJ Weintraub, 'A Survey of Contract Practice and Policy' (1992) *Wisconsin Law Review* 1; Deakin *et al*, above n 8; B Lyons and J Mehta, 'Private Sector Business Contracts: The Text Between the Lines' in Deakin and Mitchie (eds), above n 8, 58.

considerable weight should be attached, should not be regarded as exhaustive of the voluntary and discrete obligations created by the contract. In addition, the express agreement should be read in context, taking into account the conventions and mutual understandings of the parties, which provide the framework for their agreement. The content of the obligations undertaken should be qualified and extended by reference to these implicit dimensions that refer to economic interests and long-term business relationships. Only by fitting the contract into this broader context can the law ensure that contracts serve beneficial purposes in society.

This contrast between procedural and substantive notions of justice in relation to contracts feeds off deeper political disagreements. The attraction of the procedural conception lies in its apparent fidelity to liberal ideals of respect for individual rights and its avoidance of disruptive welfarist ambitions. The aim of insisting on the procedure is to ensure that the transaction satisfies the requirement of respect for individual autonomy or liberty, so that only voluntary transfers occur. By ignoring any further considerations, the procedural approach eschews any attempt to impose patterns of welfare on society on the ground that such impositions interfere both with individual rights and the utility of markets as opportunities for wealth maximisation. A substantive conception of contractual justice is no doubt more disposed to try to regulate contractual practices so that they achieve an acceptable pattern of welfare. The task of the law is conceived as not merely protecting the rights of individuals, but also of regulating markets, so that as well as producing wealth, markets also lead to fair distributive results.

Whether such a sharp contrast between procedural and substantive notions of contractual justice can be drawn in practice must be doubted.[23] In selecting a fair procedure for the formation of contracts, the legal system evidently tries to respect the rights of individuals, but also surely the fairness of the procedure is tested in practice against the outcomes that it produces. The exact scope of procedural tests such as the law of undue influence is adjusted by reference to the fairness of the results in particular instances. Equally, a substantive conception of justice does not merely examine the welfare implications of legal regulation, but also places considerable emphasis on respect for the

[23] H Collins, 'Distributive Justice Through Contracts' (1992) 45(2) *Current Legal Problems* 49.

rights of individuals. It does not ignore the procedural rules or the integrity of their outcome in the express terms of the contract, but is merely prepared to qualify those processes that ensure respect for rights by having regard to other consequences of the legal regulation. Both conceptions of justice thus seem to have a mixed approach that involves both respect for rights and concern about the welfare effects of legal regulation. The contrast lies in the emphasis placed upon the different elements in the conceptions of justice. This difference can be illustrated in connection with the importance attached by the different notions of contractual justice to the intentions of the parties to the contract.

Both views appeal to the paramount importance of the intentions of the parties as an important ingredient in ensuring respect for the right of individual private autonomy. The procedural version of justice claims that the rules for formation of contracts represent a test for enforceability based upon formal criteria that are elementary and generally known in the community. Once the parties have completed these formal steps, they know, and everyone else knows, including the legal system, that they have made a binding agreement. Furthermore, their express agreement produced by following the requirements of procedural form, such as offer, acceptance and consideration, is the only reliable indication of what agreement they intended to make and the sole matter to which the law should have regard. The express agreement is, in short, the conclusive evidence of the intentions of the parties, because it was produced by following the correct forms. In order to respect the private autonomy of the parties and to do justice between them, a court should not be tempted to intervene by adding or subtracting from the contractual obligations created by adopting the formal process.

In contrast to that view, the substantive approach to justice claims a superior insight into the intentions of the parties. It is argued that the real intentions of the parties must be discovered not only in their express statements but also in the implicit understandings surrounding the transaction. Although these intentions may not have been expressed openly, the context may have rendered that formality apparently superfluous, or perhaps even potentially disruptive of the business relation. The parties followed the forms required for a binding contract in order to signal to each other commitment and trustworthiness, but their expectations of how the transaction should be understood are not confined to the express statements contained in the terms of the agreement. To uncover those latent intentions, legal reasoning must engage in a more elaborate process that examines the context of the transaction in order to discover a complete picture of the parties' intentions and expectations. This elaborate process does not merely fill in gaps left by the express terms of the contract, but also subtracts and qualifies those terms in order to implement the real intentions of the parties. It responds to the striking finding in the Beale and Dugdale study of contractual behaviour that in some instances punctilious reliance on the express terms of the contract contained in a standard form may be regarded as acting in bad faith, because it upsets the expectations of flexibility and mutual adjustment.[24] This substantive justice approach claims superior fidelity to the intentions of the parties precisely because it allows evidence other than the express terms of the contract to determine findings of intention. Both views therefore claim to be attached to a conception of justice that accords deep respect to the autonomy of the parties, but offer competing models of how that respect can best be achieved.

The subject of implicit dimensions in contracts thus strikes at the core of discussions about the law of contract. It poses a dilemma about how the law can best achieve one of its central tasks of providing support for trust and confidence in market transactions. In addition, the examination of implicit dimensions of contracts reveals differences in the relative priorities of rival conceptions of contractual justice.

THEMES

The claim made above about the necessity and inevitability for legal reasoning to encompass the implicit dimensions of contracts is a strong one. It has so many ramifications for the law of contract that no single volume could encompass all its themes, let alone explore satisfactorily the validity of the hypothesis. The essays collected here touch on many themes and overlap in their concerns. By way of an introduction, however, it is possible to locate some central concerns of the authors.

[24] Beale and Dugdale, above n 22, 47.

Ontology and Method

The opening essay by David Campbell and myself sets out to provide a rough map of where and how the idea of the implicit dimensions of contracts becomes a crucial ingredient in legal reasoning. We argue that few legal doctrines relating to contracts, from offer and acceptance to remedies for breach, can be understood and applied without reference to the implicit understandings and expectations of the parties. But the central theoretical claim in the essay concerns legal reasoning with rules designed to interpret events as contractual practices. It consists of the argument that in the application of the central doctrines of contract law, such as offer and acceptance and consideration, legal reasoning must examine the implicit dimensions of the relation. This is an ontological claim in the sense that it is argued that legal reasoning can only apply its abstract concepts to social practices by reflecting on the meaning of those practices to the participants, for only through such reflection can legal reasoning hope to realise the objectives of the rules. Our view of legal reasoning about contracts, especially when it presents itself in the formalist manner of classical legal doctrine, is that it has an incomplete capacity to engage in a suitable appreciation of the implicit dimensions of social practices connected to contracts. This incomplete capacity, it is suggested, harms through inept legal regulation the goal of facilitating voluntary transactions that lead to Pareto optimal outcomes.

This theme of how the law understands contractual practices is taken up in many of the subsequent essays. It informs, for instance, John Wightman's analysis of the formation of 'contractual communities', and lies at the centre of what Ian Macneil calls 'essential contract theory'. But there are major differences between the authors' essays with respect to their proposals for how legal reasoning should develop the capacity for understanding the implicit dimensions of contracts.

In the essay by Stewart Macaulay, for instance, the discussion is oriented around a pragmatic assessment of the costs and benefits of different approaches to legal reasoning about contracts. Many of the other essays consider an economic analysis of how legal reasoning should appraise implicit understandings and expectations, if only to reject this approach as too narrow. Brownsword suggests, in line with his earlier work in contract theory, that ultimately the courts may need an ethical theory of contract to provide a filter for determinations of whether or not legal reasoning should recognise and protect implicit understandings and expectations. Gunther Teubner's essay explores the implications of a controversial normative direction suggested by his earlier work in systems theory. Under this normative orientation, the law's role is to respect and protect the relative autonomy and integrity of social systems. Implicit dimensions of contracts need to be respected for this purpose of ensuring the integrity of contracts as a social institution and a communication system, but at the same time the protection afforded to this social institution should not be permitted to damage other social institutions. In other words, respect for implicit dimensions of contracts should be wary of the consequences of the contractualisation of social life in its entirety. These essays produce no agreed conclusion on how legal reasoning can best approach the task of developing the capacity to incorporate implicit dimensions of contracts into its regulation of contracts. Rather their variety of theoretical and normative perspectives offers an exciting range of possibilities, with the authors only being united by the sense that something needs to be done.

Interpretation

Apart from the procedures related to debt collection, the most common issue that is presented to a court is the determination of the content of the contractual obligations. To answer this question requires a court to try to identify the agreement reached between the parties. That investigation cannot be limited to a straightforward literal reading of the express terms of the contract. Leaving aside oral and highly incomplete agreements, where plainly the law has to construct the detail of the transaction in the event of a dispute, even in lengthy written contracts, the court faces a task of interpretation. The parties may allege that the words used signify a particular obligation when situated in a particular context or trade custom. The parties may also suggest that the express terms need to be qualified or supplemented by the application of implied terms or more general legal standards. Putting these points another way, the courts are routinely asked to articulate and support the implicit understandings and expectations of the parties to the contract. How the courts should approach this task of interpretation, or more realistically of 'construction', is a persistent site of legal controversy.

Most of the essays in this collection touch on this theme concerning the important legal question of the interpretation of contracts, but it forms the focus of enquiry in the next four essays. Stewart Macaulay explores the central issue of the potential divergence between the 'paper deal', that is the express terms of the written contract, and the 'real deal', which comprises the actual expectations of the parties to the contract. Whilst acknowledging and exploring in detail the respective merits of the arguments in favour of and against attaching conclusive force to the paper deal, Macaulay insists that we should recognise how the legal system may lose some of its legitimacy if it ignores the real deal and permits successful participation in the market to depend upon the manipulation of forms or procedures. He urges that one important consideration that is sometimes undervalued by the legal system is enabling the parties to dedicate their efforts to achieve a settlement of a contractual dispute that is compatible with both their needs. He suggests that often recognition of implicit dimensions provides a route towards achieving that goal.

In the next essay, Roger Brownsword takes as his starting-point the 'contextualist' approach to interpretation of contracts advocated by Lord Hoffmann in *Investors Compensation Scheme ltd v West Bromwich Building Society*.[25] In brief, a contextualist approach insists that it is unfair to stand on or give effect to an abstracted or literal interpretation of a contract when the in-context meaning has been or would have been reasonably understood by the promisee. Brownsword argues that the real debate engendered by that case and its progeny is not at bottom about how to establish the meaning of a contract, but rather the role that should be played by normative standards of fairness. The task of protecting the 'reasonable expectations' of the parties is ambiguous because the term 'reasonable' may refer to conventions and practices in the market that have informed the dealings between the parties, or it may refer as well to objective standards of fair dealing. Brownsword argues that the term 'reasonable' necessarily incorporates such objective standards in order to achieve closure in disputes about interpretation of contracts. He recognises that these objective standards could be developed anywhere along a spectrum ranging from an ethic of pure self-interested individualism to an ethic of co-operativism in which each party helps the other to achieve its goals. He also observes that in practice one can detect different standards operating

[25] [1998] 1 All ER 98, HL.

according to such factors as the type of contract, the business relationship and the stage of contractual performance. Brownsword's suggestive conclusion is that it is possible for the law to develop objective standards that are not simply based upon interpretations of business practice but which are based on a Kantian theory of moral entitlements. These entitlements establish basic generic conditions for contracting, such as truth-telling and promise-keeping, which everyone engaged in the practice of contracting is under a duty to respect.

Approaching the problems presented by a contextualist approach from a different angle, John Wightman distinguishes two paradigms of contractual practice, one where a contracting community provides a rich basis for identifying the implicit understandings shared by the parties, and the other where such a contracting community is absent. In this latter category tend to fall consumer purchases of high value items such as cars and specialist services such as plumbers, most of which are apparently governed by the business' standard form contract. He argues that the central problem presented by such standard form contracts is the absence of the customary implicit understandings that typically prevail in commercial contexts, which would enable a court to 'tame' oppressive features of the express terms. In the absence of such joint understandings, the parties are likely to hold divergent expectations. Wightman argues the case for giving interpretive weight to the unilateral reasonable expectations of consumers under these conditions.

In discussions about these issues of interpretation at the workshop which was the genesis of this book, it became apparent from conversations with Americans present that attitudes towards the extent to which courts might ignore the plain meaning of written contracts depended at least in part on conceptions of the judicial role in determining contractual disputes. William Whitford explores the possible differences between the United Kingdom and the Unites States in conceptions of the judicial role and their implications for interpretation of contracts. He explains the origins of these differences, and in particular the greater disposition of American judges to upset apparently determinate written contracts, primarily by reference to the competence and effectiveness of the judiciary and the legislature as institutions of governance.

RELATIONAL CONTRACTS

All the essays mentioned so far acknowledge that in approaching questions of interpretation and other sources of contractual dispute, lawyers need to be sensitive to the differences between discrete and relational contracts. Although scholars disagree on how this contrast should be drawn, even to the extent of doubting whether it can be drawn, some of the elements of the intended distinction are widely accepted. A discrete transaction, such as the purchase of a cappuccino in a shop, contains relatively bounded obligations that are performed more or less instantaneously. In a relational contract, however, such as a contract of employment, a business format franchise, a joint venture, or a partnership, where performance is likely to last for a period of time or perhaps indefinitely, the economic success of the transaction for the parties depends upon a relatively high degree of co-operation, which is often supported by incentive structures that share the profits, and the obligations undertaken by the parties cannot easily be confined to determinate obligations. It is evident that relational contracts are likely to be relatively incomplete in their specifications of the expected obligations, and therefore pose greater problems of interpretation. They may also require a different approach to interpretation, one that recognises how they are highly dependent on implicit understandings between the parties about the expectations of co-operation.

Ian Macneil, to whom the contrast between discrete and relational contracts is often attributed, clarifies what he regards as the central insights of relational contract theory. He argues that relational contract theory insists that understanding and analysis of any transaction requires recognition and consideration of all significant relational elements surrounding a transaction. What is wrong with classical approaches to contract law is their disposition to treat some or all transactions as if they were discrete, with obligations confined to the express terms of the contract, whereas transactions always occur embedded in a relational context. He argues that the disposition of lawyers to commence their analysis of disputes concerning contracts with the express terms is inappropriate, because the prior question is how much weight to attach to the paper deal in view of the relational elements surrounding the document. Macneil also contests a widespread assumption that relational contract theory, or as he now calls it 'essential contract theory',[26] is directed by particular political goals. He argues that it merely provides an analytical method, which can be used for many different purposes, though he acknowledges that unlike some approaches to contract law, essential contract theory does compel a person using this perspective to consider such matters as power, reciprocity and solidarity in contractual relations.

One of the recurrent features of transactions that might be described as relational contracts is that the express terms confer a discretionary power on one or both parties. The contract may provide, for instance, that the power-holder can vary its or the other party's obligations in some respect in its 'absolute discretion'. My own essay explores the rationale for such terms in contracts, and considers how courts should approach the question of whether the discretionary power has been misused by reference to the implicit understandings and expectations of the parties. I argue that the strand that runs through legal regulation of the exercise of discretionary powers in contract is a protection of reasonable expectations based upon an appreciation of the economic and relational dimensions in which the contract is embedded.

Discussions of the relational dimensions of certain types of contracts also form an important aspect of many of the other essays in this collection. In discussions of interpretation, for instance, the authors acknowledge that relational contracts may require different strategies with respect to understanding the context that explains the implicit understandings and expectations of the parties. Similarly, later essays which examine the types of contractual relations found inside companies emphasise how these are often best understood as relational contracts, so that the implicit dimensions of trust and co-operation that are indispensable to the efficiency of these contractual arrangements can be appropriately recognised by legal regulation.

Networks

The term 'networks' signifies a grouping of contractual arrangements between more than two parties with a productive aim that requires the interaction and co-operation of all the parties. Within networks, many of the parties have contractual links, often of a relational type, but there are also many other economic relations present that have not

[26] IR Macneil, 'Contracting Worlds and Essential Contract Theory' (2000) 9 *Social & Legal Studies* 431.

been constructed through an express contract. A common example is a construction project, where the employers of the main contractor may not have direct contractual relations with sub-contractors and the employees of any of the contractors. The idea of a network has also been applied within companies to describe how the relations between the different constituencies such as shareholders, directors, creditors and employees are constructed by a 'nexus' of contracts with the corporate entity, but without direct contractual relations between these different groups. The use of the concept of a network signifies that, although some of these participants may not be directly bound together by express contracts, nevertheless their economic interdependence in practice should be recognised and accommodated within legal reasoning. One graphic metaphor to express this idea is to suggest that all the parties to a network are bound together by implicit contracts.

In his essay, Paddy Ireland explores how this idea of a network of contracts has been employed and manipulated in discussions about corporate governance. He considers, in particular, the implications of regarding directors' fiduciary duties as a type of implicit contract, and the inconsistent treatment of the implicit contractual expectations of other stakeholders such as employees. He argues that contractual theories of the corporation rest in many ways on a denial of the historical changes in the nature of shareholding. They amount to a barely concealed ideology that attempts to justify the efficiency of the current legal structure for the corporate form of business association. In using the idea of contract in order to demonstrate the efficiency of the internal governance arrangements, these contractual theories of the corporation deploy an unsatisfactory concept of contract, which is abstracted from context and ignores the relational and network aspects of productive organisations.

Using the metaphor of implicit contracts, Simon Deakin, Richard Hobbs, David Nash and Giles Slinger explore the practice of take-overs of companies. When a bid is made for the shares of a company, regulations and principles of the common law place constraints on how the incumbent management or directors should conduct themselves. The effect of these rules, the authors argue, is that the directors have to seek the maximum value for their existing shareholders. The side-effect of this practice is that effectively the implicit contracts with other stakeholders, such as employees and the local community, are torn up. Although this regulatory framework has many supporters because it disciplines the management of a company always to act to maximise the value of shares, the authors argue on the basis of their own and other empirical studies that the breach of implicit contracts with other stakeholders may in fact damage the long-term success of the productive enterprise. For example, mass redundancies almost invariably follow a successful takeover bid, with the consequent loss to the firm not only of the considerable human capital represented by the dismissed workforce, but also significant damage to the reputation of the employer as a party that honours implicit understandings concerning employment security and fair treatment. Moreover, the costs to the community of providing economic and social support in the event of mass dismissals are treated by the new owners as much as possible as externalities, so that these social costs are not included in the assessment of whether the take-over of the company produces superior wealth. The authors' work casts doubt on whether this legal framework for the market for corporate control, which fails to acknowledge the significance of respect for implicit contracts in firms, fulfils its goal, namely the most productive use of capital investments.

To the extent that external stakeholders or participants in a network without a direct contractual linkage can obtain legal rights, their claims are usually addressed through the law of tort or delict rather than contract. In claims for pure economic loss brought by third parties, western legal systems have all experienced difficulty in drawing the boundaries of liability. By no means is everyone who is adversely affected by a breach of contract permitted to recover for pure economic loss; only those claimants within some kind of proximate or special relationship can bring a legal action. Even within these relationships, the legal duties must be modified in order to reflect the allocations of risk envisaged in adjacent contractual relations. The problem for the courts and legal theory is to explain the principles on which this type of liability can be incurred. Using institutional economics and the idea of networks, it is possible to suggest reasons for, in effect, devising implicit contracts between parties as part of their co-operative productive relations, which contracts form the basis for liability for pure economic loss. Gunther Teubner builds on that analysis, using systems theory, with particular attention to those instances of claims for pure economic loss against professionals such as surveyors. He suggests that contracts involving professionals employ two systems of communication: first, the ordinary contractual discourse involving private economic interests; and secondly, the discourses of professional expertise, which represent the relationship in terms of the deployment of scientific knowledge, used impartially, to overcome the limitations of other communication systems. Teubner argues that private law should insist that this professional scientific discourse should retain its integrity, without permitting any distortions arising from the other discourse of contractual loyalty. A professional person such as a surveyor or a lawyer must not be permitted to act in a partisan way in favour of his or her client and at the same time induce a reasonable expectation in other participants in the network or project that they can rely upon the professional to exercise his or her expertise in the approved scientific manner. Teubner argues that this reasonable reliance by participants in the project should be protected by professional liability for incompetence and fraud, without any opportunity for the professional to exclude liability to the participants, in order to protect the integrity of the social system of providing scientific expertise.

A fourth essay focussed on networks concerns the relationship between shareholders in small, private companies. In these closely held companies, the shareholders are usually the directors and also expect to participate in management. These expectations may be expressed in contracts or the articles of association of the company, but often the expectations are left implicit, without express contractual protection. In the event of a breakdown of business relations between the shareholders, the corporate form often permits a majority of shareholders to exclude a minority from the business. The essay by Christopher Riley explores how the implicit expectation of participation in the business has been protected in the United Kingdom by using the statutory remedy concerning 'unfair prejudice'. He argues that an economic account of what the courts should regard as unfair tends to underplay the significance of the social context of trust and co-operation within which the relations between shareholders is embedded. Riley charts the shifting attitude of the courts towards the construction of implied contracts concerning management and participation in the business, noting in particular how a recent trend of denying force to implicit understandings fits the economic account, though it may also be explained rather more cogently as a judicial expression of a concern about the damaging effects of the mounting costs of litigation in this field.

Contractual Justice

It was assumed by many of the participants at the seminar that the research agenda of thinking about how the law should respond to the implicit dimensions of contact entailed particular views about contractual justice. This assumption makes a link between, on the one hand, the insistence upon the law giving appropriate weight to reasonable expectations, implicit understandings, and unspoken obligations of loyalty, and on the other hand, a view that contractual justice should be concerned with distributive fairness in the outcomes of contractual practices. In other words, an interest in implicit dimensions is associated with a welfarist view of contractual justice.[27]

The essays in this book reveal that any such necessary connection or association is hard to establish. It seems possible to eschew any welfarist views about contractual justice and yet believe in the importance of implicit dimensions in legal reasoning. For example, it has already been suggested that a liberal or perhaps a libertarian view of contractual justice that seeks to attach exclusionary force to the intentions or will of the parties may discover in the research agenda concerning the implicit dimensions of contracts techniques for establishing the actual intentions of the parties, the 'real deal', which is a more perfect understanding of the will of the parties than can be achieved by confining attention to the express terms contained in the paperwork. Earlier we noted Ian Macneil's similar insistence that a relational theory of contract merely proposed a scientific method for investigation which might be employed using any kind of normative framework or theory of contractual justice.

Yet Macneil also acknowledges that the research agenda of examining the implicit dimensions of contracts raises numerous issues that may not form part of other approaches to contract scholarship. As any person who has set the agenda for a meeting knows, the topics selected tend to steer the conversation in particular directions. In the essay by Deakin *et al*, for instance, by raising the issue of the potential claims of stakeholders under implicit contracts in the event of hostile takeovers, the agenda calls into question both the fairness and the efficiency of the regulatory regime that steers directors of target companies down the route of maximising short-term shareholder value. Although discussion of implicit dimensions of contracts does not entail commitment to any particular view of contractual justice, it inevitably places the question of contractual justice on the agenda and invites critical scrutiny of the standards currently endorsed by the law.

[27] R Brownsword, G Howells, and T Wilhelmsson (eds), *Welfarism in Contract Law* (Aldershot, Dartmouth, 1994).

Furthermore, the research agenda of implicit contracts adds invariably another item for consideration: the capacity and effectiveness of different forms of legal regulation. The assumption of the classical law of contract that clear formal rules of private law provide the most conducive framework for markets to flourish must be questioned when those rules tend to foreclose examinations of implicit understandings and expectations. As Macaulay argues, lawyers need to reflect carefully on whether an exclusive emphasis on the paper deal and the manipulation of formal rules best supports the goal of supporting exchange activities. Other regulatory techniques, such as the imposition of broad standards or the elaboration of detailed default rules, may better serve such purposes as enhancing trust and co-operation between parties to a contract. The research agenda of implicit dimensions of contracts demands an examination of the range of available regulatory techniques in order to determine which method is likely to prove the most effective and efficient in the pursuit of the goals behind the law.

2

Discovering the Implicit Dimensions of Contracts

DAVID CAMPBELL AND
HUGH COLLINS

LAWYERS APPRECIATE THAT there is more to contractual relationships than agreement and consideration. They understand that there are other dimensions to commercial transactions, such as fair dealing, good faith and co-operation. It is now generally acknowledged that the practice of entering into contracts relies upon the presence of trust, implicit understandings and shared conventions established by trade practice. Without using our tacit knowledge of these implicit understandings and expectations, we would not be able to differentiate in social life between taking and trading, and between trading and the exchange of gifts.[1] Despite lawyers' awareness of these implicit dimensions of contracts, legal reasoning has developed only a weak capacity to incorporate these dimensions into its analysis of contracting and into the assistance legal reasoning offers in the resolution of disputes about contracts.

This apparent defect of legal reasoning is a recurrent theme of critiques of the 'classical law of contract'. The classical law, by which is meant the elegant constructions of legal doctrine by jurists and judges of the nineteenth century, is thought by many modern writers to be an inadequate form of legal reasoning about contractual relationships. The classical law's doctrines facilitated an understanding of contracts as a disembedded association between individuals. These doctrines thus marked a break with the legal understanding of economic relationships as being based upon status, loyalty and tradition. They corresponded to the description of the system of economic relationships as a market in which 'faceless buyers and sellers . . . meet . . . for an instant

[1] M Weber, *Critique of Stammler* (New York, The Free Press, 1977) 109; IR Macneil, *The New Social Contract* (New Haven, Yale University Press, 1980) 1.

to exchange standardised goods at equilibrium prices'.[2] In its abstraction from social context, the classical law of contract assumes a 'social' interaction between unsituated individuals who bind themselves to a wholly discrete set of obligations by choosing to employ the legal institution of contract. At its most extreme, the classical law claims that the foundations of markets in individual rational choice, agreement and private property are immutable features of human society.[3]

Many criticisms have been launched against the powerful and seductive doctrines of the classical law of contract. As we say, one persistent theme of those criticisms is that the classical law could not incorporate an adequate acknowledgement of the implicit dimensions of contracts. For example, we see this theme in the contrast drawn between discrete and relational contracts. Relational contracts are different, it is argued, because they rely for their wealth-enhancing properties on a set of diffuse implicit obligations that are not, and cannot be, expressed by formal contractual undertakings.[4] A similar theme emerges in discussions of 'long-term' contracts, which, it is argued, depend upon diffuse obligations of co-operation for their efficiency.[5] In making these criticisms of the classical law, legal scholars make their contribution to a broader criticism of liberal political theory: the classical law of contract reproduces the principal structural contradiction of bourgeois society—a society which has at its heart a denial of its social character.[6]

As we shall argue in detail below, the classical law of contract does not exclude implicit dimensions of contracts from its reasoning altogether. References to implicit dimensions can be inserted by a variety of devices: such as rules that invalidate consent on grounds of misrepresentation and undue influence, the technique of supplementing express terms by implied terms and rules such as mitigation that determine the quantification of damages as a remedy. Our argument, therefore, is not that the classical law could not recognise implicit dimensions of contractual relationships, but rather that its techniques

[2] Y Ben-Porath, 'The F-connection: Families, Friends and Firms and the Organisation of Exchange' (1980) 6 *Population Development Review* 1.

[3] A Supiot, 'The Dogmatic Foundations of the Market' (2000) 29 *Industrial Law Journal* 321, 324.

[4] V Goldberg, *Readings in the Economics of Contract Law* (Cambridge, Cambridge University Press, 1989).

[5] D Campbell and D Harris, 'Flexibility in Long-term Contractual Relationships: The Role of Co-operation' (1993) 20 *Journal of Law and Society* 166, 173.

[6] GWF Hegel, *Philosophy of Right* (Oxford, Oxford University Press, 1956) ss 182–229.

for instantiating these implicit dimensions frequently proved inadequate. The framework of the classical analysis always commences with the assumption that legal reasoning need not incorporate reference to implicit dimensions. As the reasoning proceeds, however, exceptions and qualifications creep in to subvert the exclusive emphasis on the explicit, discrete contractual relationship through references to its social context and the implicit understandings generated by that context. But these insertions of implicit dimensions must always be marginalised or minimised by the classical legal doctrine, for they represent 'dangerous supplements'[7] to classical reasoning, in the sense that an acknowledgement of the pertinence of implicit dimensions threatens the collapse of an analysis that holds itself out as being an instrument of explicit, rational choices. In other words, to be fully operational and to achieve closure in legal reasoning, the manipulation of the classical rules frequently requires reference to the implicit dimensions of contractual relationships, yet these references always threaten to undermine the integrity of the classical discourse.[8]

Before elaborating upon these claims, we need to address the question of why, if this critique of legal reasoning about contracts is correct, it should be a matter of concern to lawyers and others? For some people, the concern may be with the disfunction of the law. If the law seeks to protect and enforce contractual agreements, the recognition that it has a partial and incomplete understanding of those agreements suggests that it fails in many instances to achieve its goals by enforcing not the agreement of the parties in all its relevant dimensions but a truncated perception of that agreement. From another functional perspective, the law of contract promotes and controls the social practice of entering self-regulated transactions, and misunderstandings of this practice create the risk that legal regulation will either fail adequately to support the practice when required or misdirect its controls so that they are ineffective. For others, the concern may be that the law's

[7] For an explanation of the use of this term used by Jacques Derrida in connection with contract law, see H Collins, 'The Decline of Privacy in Private Law' (1987) 14 *Journal of Law and Society* 91.

[8] On the strategies the classical law has used to try to rein in the implications of these dangerous supplements see D Campbell, 'The Undeath of Contract: A Study in the Degeneration of a Research Programme' (1992) 22 *The Hong Kong Law Journal* 20. Ian Macneil has long argued that the law actually used in practice and actually envisaged by competent scholars is 'neo-classical' rather than classical: IR Macneil, 'Contracts: Adjustment of Long-term Economic Relations Under Classical, Neo-classical and Relational Contract Law' (1978) 72 *Northwestern University Law Review* 854.

misunderstanding of contractual agreements causes it to promote inefficient (ie not Pareto optimal) outcomes. Most lawyers would be content with voicing the concern that one is not doing justice if the law frustrates the reasonable expectations of honest men.[9]

Our general aim in this essay is to map out many of the occasions when the traditional doctrines of the law of contract require legal reasoning to take into account an understanding of implicit dimensions of contractual relationships that cannot be discovered in the express words or terms of the agreement. Our discussion ranges over the conventional categories of formation of contracts, the content of obligations, and remedies for breach of contract. Our further purpose is to reveal how the need to incorporate recognition of the implicit dimensions of contracts into legal reasoning is at once essential to, but disruptive of, traditional contract law doctrine. This disruptive tendency is revealed both by silences when legal reasoning avoids any reference to implicit dimensions yet depends upon them to produce an intelligible outcome, and by attempts to confine by arbitrary lines the extent to which implicit dimensions should be considered.

FORMATION OF CONTRACTS

The legal requirements for the formation of contracts that there should be a bargain (consideration and intention to create legal relations) produced by voluntary consent (agreement) focus attention on the explicit dimensions of the contractual relationship. Have the parties both expressed the wish to enter into the same transaction, and does their express agreement satisfy the criterion that both parties expect to enhance their wealth by its performance? In addition, further rules concerning fraud and coercion determine the validity of consent to the contract.

Within all these legal rules, it is the equitable controls over the validity of consent which refer most openly to the implicit dimensions of contractual relationships, and we hazard the suggestion that this openness is a characteristic feature of equitable interventions in the law of contract. The doctrine of undue influence permits the court to examine the prior social relationship between the parties to discover whether

[9] Lord Steyn, 'Contract Law and the Reasonable Expectations of Honest Men' (1997) 113 *Law Quarterly Review* 433.

one party has exercised unfairly some kind of dominant influence over the other. Although there are many kinds of undue influence, a frequent element comprises the abuse of a prior relationship of confidence, which is a situation where the weaker party reposes trust in the other to the extent of being guided about the merits of entering transactions. A court relies on a finding of a relationship of confidence to conclude that this implicit dimension created the risk that the explicit contract was not a wealth-enhancing transaction for the weaker party.

Similarly, the equitable technique of invalidating express agreements for 'innocent misrepresentation' demands an appreciation of the implicit dimensions of the relationship. In order to distinguish false statements of fact, which permit the weaker party to avoid the contract, from statements of opinion, which do not, the court has to place the statement in its context. If the misrepresentor is in a better position to have complete information and has superior expertise in evaluating that information, a statement is more likely to be regarded as one of fact rather than opinion. In other words, it is the quality of the relationship within which the contract is made and the existence of dependence that determines whether false statements trigger the legal response of invalidating the express agreement. Once equity opens the door to an examination of the relationship between the parties, however, the crucial problem becomes how to prevent this exploration of implicit dimensions from threatening to disrupt the enforcement of a wide range of contracts that satisfy the formal common law requirements. How can the courts both respond to the social reality of relationships of dependence on expertise and relationships of confidence and avoid the conclusion that ordinary consumers in their dealings with large businesses such as banks must be protected against any disadvantage or disappointment? The solution lies in the attempt to draw arbitrary lines between different situations, such as those instances where a presumption of undue influence applies; but this solution invariably breaks down when confronted by the variety of possible relationships that might be abused.

Although equitable techniques provide fairly transparent methods for inserting the implicit dimensions of contracts into legal reasoning, the common law rules regarding formation of contracts also depend at least in some instances on unacknowledged references to implicit dimensions of contracts. Consider, for instance, the problem of knowing whether the parties have reached an agreement and the objective test that is employed for the resolution of disputes.

> If, whatever a man's real intention may be, he so conducts himself that a reasonable man would believe that he was assenting to the terms proposed by the other party, and that the other party upon that belief enters into the contract with him, the man thus conducting himself would be equally bound as if he had intended to agree to the other party's terms.[10]

When there seems no real 'meeting of the minds', though at least one party believes the parties have entered a contract, the classical law appeals to the reasonable man's perception of the other's actions. Conduct which can reasonably be interpreted by reference to conventional understandings as signifying consent will be regarded as consent to a contract, even if there was in fact no subjective intention to make an agreement. The use of the word 'reasonable' in the quotation requires the court to consider not what the promisee actually believed, but rather what a person might think about the conduct viewed in its context. This man is reasonable because he is aware of the context of the transaction, the typical expectations of the traders and their implicit understandings. The reasonable man interprets the other's conduct as a series of signs, which have that particular meaning owing to the context of social conventions and practices surrounding the contractual behaviour. The objective test of agreement is not merely an evidentiary rule, but rather a switch from a search for the individual preferences of the parties, when the failure of the individual to meet social standards of clarity leaves those preferences equivocal, to an examination of conduct and its significance in the light of implicit understandings and expectations.

We can detect a similar concealed reliance on implicit dimensions of contractual relationships in the operation of the doctrine of consideration. In those cases which prove troublesome because it is unclear whether what was envisaged was an exchange or merely some form of conditional donative promise, the doctrine of consideration can operate as a test of legal enforceability only by incorporating reference to the implicit dimensions of the relationship between the parties. The courts delve into the implicit dimensions of the relationship between the parties in order to determine whether to imply a request for something in exchange for the promise. In *Combe v Combe*,[11] for instance, the issue was whether a husband's promise to pay an annuity to his wife on their separation was binding. The husband had not explicitly

[10] Blackburn J, *Smith v Hughes* (1871) LR 6 QB 597.
[11] [1951] 2 KB 215, CA.

requested that the wife should refrain from claiming her legal entitlement to maintenance in return for the annuity. The question was whether that request could be implied in the circumstances. The trial court found such an implicit understanding, but the Court of Appeal reversed this conclusion. Either view depends upon an interpretation of the parties' unarticulated expectations about the present and future nature of their relationship. The fact that the wife was wealthy seems to have tipped the Court of Appeal towards an interpretation of the relationship as being one in which there was no firm expectation of continuing economic support from the husband, since the wife could live comfortably on her independent means.

Shadwell v Shadwell[12] provides another illustration of how the doctrine of consideration achieves closure only by resorting to implicit understandings. An uncle promised his nephew, in view of his forthcoming marriage, a regular income until he prospered at the Bar. The evidence disclosed no explicit request to marry or to pursue a career at the Bar in return for the money. At the explicit level of contractual relationships, there was therefore no consideration to support the uncle's promise. At an implicit level, however, we can discern the operation of a convention that wealthy relatives might seek to encourage young men to marry and settle down by making it financially possible or even advantageous for them to do so. With this convention in mind, the court (by a majority) could understand that the uncle had made an implicit request, a request that could remain silent because the social convention was understood; and, indeed, the request perhaps *needed* to remain silent in order to suppress any explicit acknowledgement of the commercial character of the bourgeois marriage. This implicit dimension of social convention (and hypocrisy about that convention) seems to have been the crucial element in the determination of the legal outcome in favour of the nephew.

One last example of the use of implicit dimensions of contractual relationships in order to resolve basic questions concerning the formation of obligations takes us outside a strict definition of contracts. When neither party can seriously contend that an express agreement was reached, perhaps because negotiations were continuing, the classical law insisted that no contractual obligations could have arisen. Any claim for a remedy for breach of an obligation in these circumstances had to be presented through such doctrines as equitable estoppel for

[12] (1860) 9 CBNS 159.

misplaced detrimental reliance or restitution for benefits conferred. The classical law drove out notions of implied contracts or quasi-contracts because such devices contradicted its insistence upon express choices of explicit bargains as the foundation of and justification for contractual obligations. Leaving this field of pre-contractual negotiations to be handled by doctrines of equitable estoppel and restitution produced the unfortunate consequence that legal reasoning failed to direct its attention to the most important source of the claim for compensation, namely the existence (or otherwise) of implicit understandings between the parties to the negotiations that obligations had arisen as a result of their interaction.

The implicit dimension of mutual understandings and expectations can be inserted back into legal reasoning, but only with difficulty. In equitable estoppel, the issue of whether there was an implicit agreement or tacit understanding has to be dealt with as the question of whether the detrimental reliance was reasonable. In restitutionary claims, the enquiry into an implicit understanding is truncated into the question of whether the goods or services were freely accepted. Once it is appreciated how much the classical law relating to the formation of contracts depends upon unacknowledged reference to the implicit dimensions of contractual relationships, this doctrinal analysis of pre-contractual negotiations that distances itself from any reference to these dimensions appears unsatisfactory. The law absolutely requires cognitive openness to the presence of the implicit understandings that are the necessary context of any contractual obligations. Although the doctrinal path may be too embedded to be overturned, our argument suggests that a doctrinal analysis framed in terms of implied contracts may offer a better approach to the field of pre-contractual negotiations, one which appreciates the significance of the implicit understandings of the parties in generating obligations.

CONTENT OF CONTRACTUAL OBLIGATIONS

Our central argument that legal reasoning about contracts must engage with the implicit dimensions of contractual relationships despite any protestations to the contrary is perhaps less controversial in connection with the law's assessment of the content of contractual obligations. In many cases, recent cases in particular, the courts openly acknowledge that in order to interpret a written document they must examine these implicit dimensions of the relationship, that is the 'matrix of fact'.[13] Similarly, the insertion of implied terms into contracts frequently relies upon references to implicit understandings and expectations. Terms implied in fact search for the implicit understandings that guided the formal expression of the contract. Terms implied by reference to custom and usage place the agreement in its normal business context, inserting a conventional rule or expectation of the particular trade or business. Terms implied by law represent a generalisation about the normal expectations of the parties when making a standard type of contractual agreement. On all these occasions, legal reasoning restores the context that was supposed to be excluded by the classical law's emphasis on the express agreement.

Much the same effect is achieved in other legal systems through the use of general clauses in the civil codes. General clauses are typically stated in normative language, such as a general principle of good faith to which the parties ought to conform. At first sight, the articulation of such a principle might be regarded as the imposition of external moral ideals. But we think that this would be to misunderstand the operation of general clauses. Although the general principle may be coloured by the moral ideals of the society at large, in its detailed application the general clause inserts the implicit understandings and expectations of the parties' specific epistemic community into the binding contractual undertakings. Teubner argues persuasively, for instance, that the good faith clause in the German Civil Code permits courts to insert business custom and convention into express agreements, thus qualifying or supplementing contracts by reference to what already was implicit in the business relationship.[14]

Interpretation

Many of the subsequent essays in this volume examine the role of implicit expectations in the interpretation of contracts. Without trespassing excessively on their territory, we can briefly state that our argument includes the contention that in any interpretation of contracts, whether they are discrete bilateral contracts, relational

[13] Lord Wilberforce, *Reardon Smith Line Ltd v Hansen-Tangen* [1976] 1 WLR 989, HI.

[14] G Teubner, 'Legal Irritants: Good Faith in British Law or How Unifying Law Ends Up in New Divergences' (1998) 61 *Modern Law Review* 11, 25.

contracts, or networks of contracts that form a productive organisation, legal reasoning must engage with the implicit dimensions of the relationship in order to make sense of the express contractual agreement. In other words, the option of sticking to the literal meaning of the contract except in some cases such as ambiguity, which is sometimes described as formalism,[15] is not, we would argue, in reality available. Thus the 'new contextualism' associated with recent judgments of Lord Hoffmann[16] is, we contend, nothing new, but merely an explicit recognition of a legal method for interpretation that has often been suppressed. There are two, rather different, kinds of argument to support that contention.

The first argument relies on theories of meaning and Wittgenstein's concept of a language game. It is the same argument used by Lon Fuller against HLA Hart in their famous debate about vehicles in the park. The point of the analysis of language games is that the meaning of words depends upon how they are used in different kinds of communication exercise. The question is what kind of language game is represented by a written contract? We might regard the document as a record or description of the reciprocal undertakings of the parties. If so, this description should be interpreted according to the ordinary uses of words, that is the conventional or dictionary definitions, because this kind of language game relies upon those meanings for the purposes of description. Thus, for controversies about the word 'vehicle', we should resort to the dictionary to settle the dispute. In contrast, if we regard the document as a record of instructions to each party, designed to implement a purpose such as the completion of a sale of goods, the language game changes into one that determines meaning by reference to purpose. The meaning of a word like vehicle then depends upon the intention, purpose, or expectation of the parties to the contract. If the parties were engaged in a transaction for the hire of a car, the word vehicle should be interpreted to mean a car and nothing else. Fuller argued, convincingly in our view, that for the purpose of statutory interpretation, this latter approach was the appropriate language game. The same conclusion should apply to the construction of contractual documents, for they represent an attempt at self-regulation by the parties. But in order to use this language game of examining the

[15] See the essay by Macaulay in this volume.

[16] *Investors Compensation Scheme Ltd v West Bromwich Building Society* [1998] 1 WLR 896, H; *Mannai Investments Co Ltd v Eagle Star Life Assurance Co* [1997] AC 749, HL; see the essay by Brownsword in this volume.

purpose of the parties to the contract, it is essential to place the formal agreement in the context of the implicit understandings surrounding the scope and purpose of the agreement. Thus, this first argument insists that meaning can be correctly attributed to contractual documents only by reference to the purpose of those documents, which necessarily relies upon the implicit dimensions of contracts. To rely upon literal meaning, that is conventional dictionary definitions, is to misunderstand the language game or communication system employed in written contracts.

A second argument for supporting the claim that interpretation of contracts requires reference to the implicit dimensions of contracts is that a careful observation of the practice of the courts reveals that they invariably resort to references to implicit understandings. We might label an approach that purports to eschew the implicit dimensions 'the literal approach' to construction, for it claims merely to look at the words used by the parties in the documents and nothing else. An approach that examines implicit understandings could be labelled, in contrast, the 'intentions of the parties' approach, for it acknowledges that it must discover those intentions from the context of the relationship as well as the formal document. What we find on close examination of the legal reasoning is that neither approach is used on its own. Judges always invoke the other method of interpretation as qualifiers, or, perhaps more accurately, as dangerous supplements. When a court adopts the literal approach, the dictionary definition of words will be confined by reference to the absurdity of the result, which seems to be an invocation of the presumed intentions of the parties to rule out certain meanings. The purposive method of interpretation places limits on meaning by reference to conventional limits on the meaning of words, which are ascertained by asking what a reasonable promisee would have understood the words to mean.

The reason why these qualifications represent dangerous supplements is that, if taken to their logical conclusion, each qualifier (ie absurdity or reasonable promisee) would in fact destroy the foundations of the method. Thus, a literal method that chooses between available meanings by reference to the intentions of the parties could be said in fact to collapse into a purposive approach. Similarly, a purposive approach that purports to follow the joint intentions of the parties, but then proceeds to rule out possible intentions by reference to conventional meanings, could be said to collapse into a literal approach.

The presence of these dangerous supplements, requiring the employment of different language games to deal with them, suggests that when interpreting contracts the courts appreciate that they should not deracinate the formal written document from the implicit undertakings that arise from the context of entering into a transaction. The problem is rather one of playing off explicit and implicit understandings against each other; explicit understandings must be qualified by implicit understandings, and vice-versa. Methods of interpretation of contracts provide procedures or arguments for handling this process, but never produce a method for terminating the process. The meaning of explicit undertakings must depend upon implicit undertakings, and implicit undertakings have to be understood by reference to explicit undertakings.

If this 'critical' analysis of the practice of interpretation of contracts seems too quick with the vast judicial learning on the subject, it may be worth looking at some more concrete examples of the dangerous supplements at work. For example, judges often commence the process by asserting that their task is to ascertain the 'joint intention' of the parties. This principle of construction invokes a purposive approach which permits implicit understandings to be incorporated. But then two further moves are immediately made which undercut the purposive approach. The first is to assert that the actual intentions of the parties, if not communicated, should be ignored—that is the objective approach to interpretation, which returns priority to explicit undertakings interpreted by conventional meanings. The second is to say that the court must discover the common or joint intentions, and since these may well have been at odds, the court must ascertain these intentions from the words of the contract, which amounts to a reversion to a literal interpretation.

If, on the other hand, judges launch the enquiry into the meaning of a contract with an assertion that the task is to interpret the words used by the parties in the contract, which is an invocation of a literal approach, we find two similar moves designed to reinsert the implicit dimension. The first move is to invoke the understanding of the reasonable man familiar with the context:

> The fact that the words are capable of a literal application is no obstacle to evidence which demonstrates what a reasonable person with knowledge of the background would have understood the parties to mean, even if this compels one to say that they used the wrong words.[17]

[17] Lord Hoffmann, *Mannai Investments Co Ltd v Eagle Star Life Assurance Co* [1997] AC 749, 779.

The second move is to discount 'unreasonable results' produced by the literal meaning, the unreasonableness depending, of course, on an interpretation of the implicit understanding:

> The fact that a particular construction leads to a very unreasonable result must be a relevant consideration. The more unreasonable the result the more unlikely it is that the parties can have intended it, and if they do intend it the more necessary it is that they should make that intention abundantly clear.[18]

If either of these arguments for asserting that the process of interpretation of formal contractual documents necessarily relies upon the implicit dimensions of contracts is correct, we have established that legal reasoning cannot avoid reference to the implicit dimensions of contracts for the purpose of construing formal contracts. To seek to avoid implicit dimensions, a court would either have to misunderstand the language game of self-regulation through contractual documents, or to deviate from the normal practice of interpretation in which a literal approach is always harnessed to the dangerous supplement of purposive interpretation.

Planning Documents

Given this view that implicit dimensions of contractual relationships provide an essential ingredient in the interpretation of contracts, a deeper question arises for legal reasoning about written contracts, namely how much significance should be attached to a written contract, ie the planning documents, or what Macaulay calls the 'paper deal'?[19] How far does the recognition of implicit dimensions of contractual relationships lead one down the road of diminishing the significance of the planning documents to the legal enquiry about the content of contractual obligations?

The written contract is usually produced by lawyers for the parties to a transaction. It serves the evidentiary function of recording the explicitly negotiated aspects of the deal. It also serves a cautionary function in the sense that the parties may be induced to reflect carefully on their commitments before signing a written contract. But the parties to the contract will have already agreed these elements of the transaction at

[18] Lord Reid, *Wickman Machine Tools Sales Ltd v L Schuler AG* [1974] AC 235, 251.
[19] See the essay by Macaulay in this volume.

least in outline. What the formal contractual document adds to the transaction, which the parties may not have discussed in any detail, is the allocation of risks, together with specification of remedial devices in the event of breach of contract. In other words, what the lawyer typically adds to the transaction is detailed planning with respect to contingencies and remedies for breach. This view of the formal contract as a planning document opens up the possibility of two sources of divergence between the express terms and implicit understandings.

The first potential source of divergence concerns the primary obligations or commitments under the contract. The formal contract records the main elements of the proposed economic transaction, such as the price and the goods or services required. But the formal contract is unlikely to record every point of detail of the expectations of the parties with respect to the transaction. The law can often insert these expectations by the device of terms implied in fact; without such a term the contract would lack business efficacy. On the sale of a particular car, the formal contract records the price and describes the car, but the formal document is unlikely to specify explicitly that the seller should also deliver at least one set of keys to the car. Without such an obligation, however, the transaction loses its economic point; few people buy a car just to observe it from the outside, with no intention of driving it. The law can insert the obligation to deliver a set of keys as an implied term.

Beyond simple cases of this kind, however, the formal contract may not record explicitly other kinds of conventions or expectations which at least one party presupposed in reaching the economic deal. As in *Sagar v Ridehalgh and Son Ltd*,[20] an employer might hire a worker to produce goods on a piece-work basis, assuming that the employer's practice of refusing to pay for defective goods applies to the transaction, though without recording that rule in the formal contract or communicating it to the worker. If the worker objects to deductions from his wages for defective pieces, which version of the economic transaction should apply: the employer's implicit understanding or the formal agreement? In this case, the transaction has business efficacy on either version, so it is necessary to adopt a different method of reasoning in order to resolve the dispute. Either the legal system can refuse to look beyond the formal agreement, or it can try to situate the agreement in the context or social practice. If the latter is chosen, the

[20] [1930] 2 Ch 117.

law faces the difficulties of discovering the practice accurately, and of deciding whether or not it may be used to qualify the express agreement.

The second source of potential divergence between the planning documents and the implicit understandings of the parties are in the terms governing risk allocation and remedies. Here it seems much less likely that the parties will have actively considered these issues in detail. In bargaining about the transaction, they concentrate on such matters as price and quality, not on what will happen if things go wrong. We may then observe a divergence between what the formal contract states should happen if some contingency occurs, and what the parties actually expect to happen when it does. For example, the formal contract may precisely allocate the entire risk of late delivery of goods to the seller, so that the buyer is entitled to terminate the contract the moment that the due date has passed. The expectation of the seller and the buyer, however, may be rather that some leeway will be given, that some contingencies may provide an excuse, or that the obligation of the seller is confined to the payment of compensation for any reliance losses (in the form of a reduction of the price). The divergence between formal agreement and implicit expectations arises in this instance because the parties to the contract have not ensured that the formal document (in the small print at the end expressed in lawyers' jargon, eg time is of the essence) precisely corresponds to their expectations, no doubt for the very good reason that they do not expect such problems to arise. Perhaps even more significantly, the parties may also have an implicit expectation that neither will rely upon the small print of the contract in any case, but rather try to work out a mutually satisfactory solution. An example of this behaviour in found in *Mitchell (George) (Chesterhall) Ltd v Finney Lock Seeds Ltd*, where it was found that, when dealing with regular customers, the seed merchant rarely insisted upon the limitation clause in the written contract.[21] Here the problem of divergence is not simply that the planning document does not accurately record all the expectations of the parties, but also that it actually inserts provisions to which the parties have not really agreed despite their formal signatures on the document.

These two sources of potential divergence between planning documents and the implicit understandings of the parties thus pose rather different problems for the legal system. In the case of the former, the

[21] [1983] 2 AC 803.

planning documents are arguably incomplete in their specification of the commitments. The problem is whether to *supplement* the formal agreement, and if so, by reference to what other kinds of sources of obligations. In the case of the latter source of divergence, the planning documents are arguably inaccurate in their expression of the commitments. The problem now is whether to *override* or *qualify* the formal agreement, and if so, by reference to what sources of implicit understandings.

In response to both of these types of problem there is always strong support among lawyers for giving priority to the planning documents and for discounting the significance of any implicit understandings. In favour of this attitude it can be said that the planning documents provide relatively clear guidance about the content of the obligations of the parties, and this facilitates dispute resolution. In addition, if the law discounts other evidence about the content of the obligations, it provides an incentive for the parties to say what they mean, which may avoid disagreements in the future. In the long run this policy might not only avoid the cost of disputes, but also lead to more optimal transactions in the sense that, as a result of spelling out the details of the transaction, the price can more accurately reflect the value of the deal to the parties.

A more controversial argument in favour of giving the planning documents an exclusive role in determining contractual obligations is to insist that the purpose of the law is not to enforce the intentions or expectations of the parties, which in any case may conflict or be indeterminate, but rather to enforce the self-regulation of the parties, which is contained in the planning documents. This argument is possibly supported by the 'objective' approach of the common law to the determination of the existence and content of contractual obligations; it is not the intention of the parties that matters, but how a reasonable person would interpret their words and conduct. A reasonable person, it might be urged, could place significant weight on the planning documents, but could not reasonably attach much significance to the other party's unexpressed intentions. And an objective approach rules out reliance upon one's own unexpressed expectations and understandings. The objective approach to the interpretation of contracts tends to protect reasonable reliance rather than the joint intention of the parties. Emphasising the role of contract law as supporting self-regulation through planning documents also tends to emphasise the protection of reasonable reliance at the expense of the will of the parties.

We can make several points which weigh against these considerations. First, the pressure on parties to business transactions to record everything in detail in the planning documents plainly increases the costs of entering into transactions. Secondly, we must doubt whether the parties have the competence to assess whether the planning documents accurately reflect their expectations in every respect, because those documents are often expressed in technical legal terminology. The parties might even need to hire another lawyer to assess whether their lawyers had accurately expressed their intentions in the planning documents, again adding to transaction costs (were it possible at all). Thirdly, we must doubt whether even the most gifted draftsman would be able to reduce the subtlety of some implicit expectations to a form of words or a rule to govern the transaction. There is always likely to be a problem that express terms are too 'coarse' in the sense that their provision for a contingency, though complete in the sense of dealing with the problem, does not reflect all the appropriate qualifications. Thus, the pressure on the parties to increase the complexity of the planning documents will never completely eliminate unwelcome divergence from implicit understandings. Fourthly, if a general aim of the law of contract is to enforce the agreement reached by the parties, we should not ignore evidence about the content of the agreement merely because it was not formally recorded. It may be appropriate in some instances to ignore other evidence, if, for example, the parties have agreed that the written document is their entire agreement. But such deliberate statements indicate a special state of mind, which is unlikely to be present in most transactions. Fifthly, contracts provide a special mechanism through which the parties can augment and qualify obligations owed to other persons, but they are always located in the surrounding pattern of obligations which are presupposed in the transaction. For example, a sale presupposes a system of ownership of goods, and a contract to perform a service is nested in reciprocal duties of care. In the absence of detailed knowledge of the law, the parties to a transaction will not make a sharp distinction between those surrounding obligations which have legal sanctions and those which represent mere social conventions. Another way to make this argument is to suggest that the surrounding obligations describe the extent to which the parties implicitly place reliance upon each other beyond the formal document. To the extent that the law of obligations should aim to protect reasonable reliance, it is important to take into account these other obligations in determining the full scope of the contractual undertakings. To examine the planning documents in isolation as the determinant of obligations runs the risk of ignoring this surrounding pattern of obligations and their implications for the accurate understanding of what the contractual commitments were between the parties.

These arguments for and against attributing weight to the planning documents do not produce a conclusive result. Instead, our conclusion is that the weight that should be attached to the written record or paper deal must itself ultimately depend on the context and the implicit understandings surrounding the transaction. At one extreme, we may find a complex financial transaction involving a loan and security, where the documents purport to describe exhaustively the undertakings, the allocation of risks, and the remedies available, capping this off with an 'entire agreement' clause. In this context, arguments for legal support for implicit understandings and expectations may be regarded as weak, though not necessarily excluded altogether (eg estoppel by convention, interpretation of technical terms). At the other extreme, the document may be brief, not attempting to be a piece of comprehensive self-regulation, and the context may be a frequent pattern of trading between the parties in the same line of business. In such instances, there seems to be a compelling case for legal recognition of the implicit dimensions of the contract to be discovered in the customs of the trade and the pattern of dealing between the parties. The difference between these contexts lies ultimately in the implicit dimensions of the contractual relationship. We might say that, in effect, in the former context there is an implicit contract that the planning document should have paramount importance, whereas in the latter context the implicit understanding is rather that the paper deal is merely an incomplete memorandum of a transaction that is largely constructed on the basis of implicit expectations. In this latter context, we should also conclude that we should not give too much weight to those clauses in the planning document which have been fabricated by lawyers without the explicit guidance of their clients, since if we were to do so, we would be judging the quality of the lawyers, not supporting the transaction agreed between the parties.

REMEDIES

To complete this outline map of the necessary role played by the implicit dimensions of contractual relationships in legal reasoning, we turn finally to the body of legal doctrine concerned with remedies for breach of contract. The most important feature of these remedies is that they normally do not insist on the performance of the primary obligations under the contract. Leaving aside the peculiar case of debt, literal enforcement of primary obligations is an unusual remedy available only when the normal remedy, of payment of compensatory or expectation damages when the claimant has a 'duty' to mitigate her or his loss, is judged inadequate. The explanation for this preference for compensatory damages is that, between good faith parties, the purpose of providing a remedy is not the overt one of, as it were, unilateral vindication of the claimant's rights[22] under the contract but the implicit one of co-operating to deal with the effects of the breach according to 'the principle of joint-cost minimisation'.[23] By shifting from the primary obligation to perform to the secondary obligation to provide a remedy, the law gives the defendant the opportunity to choose between different ways of satisfying the claimant's expectation, and, of course, he or she will normally choose the cheapest. But, the crucial point we now wish to emphasise, this can work only if there is an implicit dimension of co-operation by the claimant in the handling of the breach.

As we have discussed the way that the rules about remedies give effect to co-operation at great length elsewhere,[24] we will here discuss only the two legal doctrines which have a particularly important role in inserting consideration of this implicit dimension of co-operation into the handling of breach. The first is the duty to mitigate loss. Joint-cost minimisation works because the mitigation rules give the claimant a great incentive to take reasonable steps to minimise his or her losses because failure to do so will result in the court refusing to award compensation for those avoidable but unavoided, and therefore excessive, losses. The question of what amounts to reasonable steps seems to us to depend heavily on implicit understandings and business conventions. We are fortunate in this context in having available a study by Beale and Dugdale of what are regarded in one line of business as reasonable steps or the implicit conventions of contractual relationships

[22] H Collins, *Regulating Contracts* (Oxford, Oxford University Press, 1999) 330–8.

[23] GJ Goetz and RE Scott, 'The Mitigation Principle' (1983) 69 *Virginia Law Review* 967, 972–3.

[24] H Collins, *The Law of Contract*, 3rd edn (London, Butterworths, 1997) ch 17; D Harris *et al*, *Remedies in Contract and Tort*, 2nd edn (London, Butterworths, 2002) ch 1.

concerning the handling of breach of contract.[25] A common problem was breach through late delivery. In the following quotation we have inserted numbers in square brackets to assist the discussion:

> the buyer is similarly entitled to damages for consequential loss caused by late delivery, but it appeared that such consequential losses were seldom claimed and almost never paid . . . The reason for this general position does not appear to be the difficulty of claiming such losses . . . It seemed that the situation was caused by an interplay of related commercial facts and practices. On the one hand [1] buyers were expected to guard against delay by planning schedules so that deliveries could be late without causing loss; on the other hand [2] sellers were bound by an 'unwritten law' that the buyer must be notified in advance of any likely delay, to enable the buyer to reschedule (only one contract required this). If this could not solve the problem the buyer might well have [3] alternative sources of supply or [4] be able to use other materials. Even if the buyer did suffer a loss it was [5] generally recognised that the seller should not be liable for delays which were not his fault, and it seemed to be the general view that it was [6] far safer to refuse any claim for consequential loss for fear of creating a precedent. Finally [7] in some cases it would not be possible to claim serious consequential losses from a small supplier without the risk of bankrupting him. Thus, although there was potential scope for making a claim in a few cases, it was almost unknown for such a claim to be paid.[26]

Beale and Dugdale describe a repertoire of responses to delay in performance which match in function some aspects of the formal legal remedies but in other respects rely upon implicit understandings that demand co-operation according to implicit conventions. Stages [5] and [6] represent implicit understandings and expectations, which may qualify the express agreement, and certainly depart from strict legal rights. Stages [1], [2], [3] and [4] seem to be equivalent to the position the parties would be left in by the operation of the mitigation rule combined with the unavailability of specific performance, except that what amounts to reasonable steps to minimise loss is rendered more determinate by the 'unwritten laws' of the trade. The further limit on taking action presented by stage [7], the threat of driving the defendant into bankruptcy, is a formal limit on taking contractual action in one sense (the formal rules being those of insolvency), but it is also an implicit understanding about the limits of contractual commitment whatever

[25] H Beale and T Dugdale, 'Contracts Between Businessmen: Planning and the Use of Contractual Remedies' (1975) 2 *British Journal of Law and Society* 45.

[26] *Ibid*, 54.

the terms of the contract. When a court has to decide the question whether the claimant violated the duty to mitigate loss, it is all these factors that are taken into account, with the test of reasonableness allowing the claimant a margin of appreciation with respect to the application of the implicit conventions in the circumstances.

A second technique for inserting implicit understandings into the determination of remedies is the doctrine of remoteness of loss. The courts answer the question whether the defendant should be liable for all the claimant's losses by use of the doctrine of remoteness. A line is drawn on the measure of recovery, so that some losses flowing from the breach of contract are said to be too remote to be recoverable. This result can be restated in the language of risk: the defendant did not accept the risk of certain kinds of losses. If the contract makes no explicit provision about the type of risk under consideration, the court has to infer this allocation of risk from some other material. We suggest that this context is an aspect of the implicit dimensions of the contract.

Attempts to elucidate the meaning of the doctrine of remoteness, and specifically of the phrase 'reasonable contemplation', by abstract speculation on the literal meanings of the words have produced a pointless logomachy in the leading cases.[27] A clearer justification for the limits on recovery may be produced by reference to the implicit understandings and expectations of the parties that may have evolved in a course of dealing or may be set by usage of trade.[28] For example, when a carrier delays delivery of goods to a market where they will be resold, the implicit understanding may be that the carrier should bear the risk of a fall in the market price of the goods, provided that the carrier is aware that the goods are of the kind that will be resold on a market. Whether or not that represents the understanding in the shipping business is in principle a question of fact that could be explored by the court by examining normal compensatory practices. It may be that the lawyers in the higher courts have gained experience in this trade themselves through experience in litigation and settlement, and have become aware of the relevant implicit understandings. In the absence of such knowledge, the problem cannot be solved by resort to general standards of fairness or

[27] *Hadley v Baxendale* [1843–60] All ER 461; *Victoria Laundry v Newman* [1949] 2 KB 528 and *The Heron II* [1969] 1 AC 350.

[28] *Monarch Steamship v Karlshamns Oljefabriker* [1949] AC 196; *British Columbia Saw Mill v Nettleship* (1868) 3 CP 499 and *Montevideo Gas v Clan Line* (1921) 8 Ll LR 192.

the like, for in the allocation of risks in commercial contracts the touchstone is not fairness but the efficient allocation of insurable risks. It would be better for the court to discover evidence of practice, perhaps revealed in the insurance arrangements, in order to determine the application of limitations on recovery of damages.

Many formal contracts make explicit provision for remedies through such devices as deposits, security, liquidated damages and limitation clauses. Although these agreed remedies are normally legally valid, the courts have wide and vague powers to control the exercise of such contractual rights on the basis of standards such as reasonableness and unconscionability. In order to exercise such indeterminate powers and to justify their application, the courts seem to rely to a considerable extent upon an investigation of the implicit dimensions of contracts, that is the implicit expectations and understandings of the parties. For instance, in *Mitchell (George) (Chesterhall) Ltd v Finney Lock Seeds Ltd*,[29] when the seed merchants supplied the farmer with the wrong type of seeds but sought to rely on a limitation of damages clause to defeat a claim for loss of profits, the court held the limitation clause to be unreasonable and unfair. The House of Lords invalidated the limitation clause in part because the admission by the seed merchant that it did not always insist upon its standard form limitation clause suggested that an implicit understanding of the trade was that the defendants would limit compensation, but not to the full extent of the clause, in the light of the circumstances such as the degree of fault of the defendants and whether or not the claimant was a valued customer. We suggest that similar references to implicit dimensions of contractual relationships plays a vital role in the other instances of judicial control of agreed remedies. A forfeiture is 'reasonable' if it conforms to the customs of the trade. A liquidated damages clause is not an invalid penalty if it produces outcomes that conform to the reasonable expectations of the parties about the appropriate level of compensation. The technique for leading the courts to ascertain those implicit understandings is the legal requirement that the contractual estimation of loss should be 'genuine'.

JUSTIFICATION FOR INCORPORATION OF IMPLICIT DIMENSIONS

Our discussion of formation, content and remedies has been directed towards identifying those techniques employed by legal reasoning for

[29] [1983] 2 AC 803.

inserting implicit dimensions of contractual relationships into its determinations. Although the classical law ostensibly eschews these implicit dimensions, we have pointed to many instances where more or less covertly the implicit dimension plays a crucial role in legal reasoning. We noted that at times legal reasoning senses just how subversive of classical orthodoxy can be the judicial reliance on implicit dimensions, yet we also argued that often in those same instances the legal process could not exclude implicit dimensions without lapsing into unfounded decisions or even incoherence. In stressing the significant role played by the implicit dimensions of contractual relationships in legal reasoning, we have touched only briefly on the normative question whether this practice is desirable. The question is whether courts should be encouraged to use legal reasoning that consciously and explicitly inserts implicit dimensions of contract relationships into determinations of contractual disputes.

As a matter of principle, it is argued that the courts are properly reluctant to rewrite contracts in ways that they might regard as more reasonable, or to satisfy what may be regarded as a reasonable expectation which has not been protected by an express contractual agreement. The courts should not exercise such powers because they will interfere with freedom of contract. And freedom of contract in general enhances the utility of contracts as a welfare-enhancing mechanism The reasons why we reject this argument of principle are both that mere or exclusive reliance on the express terms of the contract is not a practical alternative; and, secondly, if, as the principle of freedom of contract maintains, the job of the law is to enforce the agreement of the parties, this task can only be achieved by looking at the 'real deal', which is not necessarily the same as the written contract. Assuming that respect for freedom of contract has the alleged desirable utilitarian consequences or at least ensures respects for individual rights, it does not follow in our view that legal reasoning should eschew reference to the implicit dimensions of contractual relationships. On the contrary, by incorporating implicit dimensions into legal analysis, by recontextualising private law, the legal system can achieve a greater capacity for upholding freedom of contract and its consequent benefits.

We do not subscribe, however, to the view that contract law should be governed by a version of efficiency that places freedom of contract on a pedestal. In many contracts, the need for co-operation and adaptation in order to achieve efficient production and competitiveness can only be met by contracts that are incomplete by design supplemented by implicit obligations of co-operation and protection of reasonable expectations. These kinds of long-term, relational and network contracts require from time to time legal support to protect against disappointment, and this support must entail giving legal effect to these implicit obligations if it is to help the parties to secure the efficiency gains of their transaction.

As well as arguments of principle for and against the incorporation of implicit dimensions of contractual relationships in legal reasoning, pragmatic considerations about the costs and benefits of this practice need to be considered. The main pragmatic reason to discourage the courts from engaging with the implicit dimensions of contracts is that they do not have ready access to information that might determine what these implicit understandings and expectations may have been. This information can only be discovered by secondhand and conflicting evidence about the state of mind of the parties or investigations of customs of the trade that may be uncertain and far from uniform. Instead of embarking on such a speculative enquiry, a court may be better advised to stick to the letter of the contract and send a warning to the market that parties should look after their own interests more carefully in the formation of contracts. This awareness of the possibility, indeed likelihood, of 'radical judicial error'[30] is currently being made the basis of a strong renewed defence of formalism in contract interpretation.[31] Not only does such a warning seem unlikely to be effective in many contexts, such as consumer standard form contracts and contracts of employment, but also it seems difficult for formalism, even accepting that it can be presented in more sophisticated versions,[32] to avoid dependence on some sort of idea that there is a literal sense available from the wording of a contract, a possibility that we have sought to deny. A correct judicial appreciation of implicit dimensions is certainly not guaranteed, but the option of ignoring those dimensions and confining attention to the express terms of a written contract seems destined to guarantee some judicial mistakes about the bargain that the

[30] EA Posner, 'A Theory of Contract Law Under Conditions of Radical Judicial Error' (2000) 94 *Northwestern University Law Review* 749.

[31] RE Scott, 'The Case for Formalism in Relational Contract' (2000) 94 *Northwestern University Law Review* 847.

[32] TC Grey, 'Langdell's Orthodoxy' (1983) 45 *University of Pittsburgh Law Review* 1 and TC Grey, 'The New Formalism', Stanford Public Law and Legal Theory Working Paper No 4, Stanford Law School, 1999; D Kennedy, *A Critique of Adjudication (fin de siècle)* (Cambridge (USA), Harvard University Press, 1997) 105: Langdellian formalism is a 'theory with no known American proponents'.

parties wanted. These arguments about pragmatism are considered in greater detail in the next essay in this volume by Stewart Macaulay, so we will not pursue them further here.

We therefore defend the proposition that the courts should incorporate examinations of implicit dimensions of contractual relationships on two grounds: there is no alternative intelligible method of legal reasoning, and even if there were, the practice would be justified in any case, subject only to pragmatic considerations of cost, on the basis of welfare-maximisation, efficiency and respect for the rights of individuals. We are conscious that many issues have been left unresolved. How determinate is the notion of implicit dimensions of contracts? At times we have spoken of customs of the trade as an example of implicit dimensions of contracts, but at others the whole social context of the agreement, including conventions of meaning in language, have been invoked as the implicit dimension of contractual relationships. Another question is how we can best analyse these implicit dimensions? Is it helpful to follow economic analysis to try to explain their presence as further agreements (implicit contracts), or does this analysis deprive the social context of what makes it social? Yet a further problem is how can legal reasoning discover the implicit dimensions of contracts. Legal reasoning works best with evidence and proven facts, but the incorporation of implicit dimensions of contracts requires a reliance upon unspoken assumptions, 'unwritten laws' of the trade, and signs which acquire their meaning through unrecorded habits and conventions. To some extent these questions are addressed in the subsequent essays in this book, but no doubt this research agenda leaves much for further discussion on another occasion.

3

The Real and the Paper Deal: Empirical Pictures of Relationships, Complexity and the Urge for Transparent Simple Rules

STEWART MACAULAY*

ASSUME THAT CONTRACT law matters, at least in some subset of all the situations where people consider making or do make contracts. Also assume that contract law should rest to a large extent on choice or responsibility for misleading others about one's choices. Making these assumptions, we must be concerned with how the legal system deals with the expectations of the parties. One approach is formal. Judges can limit themselves to dealing with only the formal expressions of the parties—the paper deal. They need ask only whether the parties signed or accepted a document, and if they did, what is the 'plain meaning' of the words they used. Sometimes, writings labeled 'contract' do capture many if not most of the expectations of those who sign them.

Often, however, the paper deal will not reflect the real deal: a writing can be inconsistent with the actual expectations of the parties. Courts frequently have sought to protect such actual expectations despite the presence of a writing that does not mention them or even one that is inconsistent with them. However, establishing real

* I have discussed the issues considered in this article with my Wisconsin colleagues, John Kidwell and William Whitford, and I have learned much from them. David Campbell commented on a draft of this article, and it is much better as a result. All mistakes are mine; I did not take all the good advice offered.

expectations often is very difficult. Courts face what Richard Danzig has called 'the capability problem.'[1] Some expectations, for example, are only tacit assumptions—what I would have said if I had thought about a question that I did not think about. Even if the parties did have real expectations that they did not express in their written document, we must worry that today's testimony about them will be self-serving and fabricated to make the case come out the right way. Also, proving the real deal often will be very costly. The parties must convey a commercial context to a judge or to jurors. They may come to the task with little, if any, knowledge of the part of the business world in question. Experts can inform them, but experts are not free.

If we want our courts to carry out the expectations of the parties to contracts, both those that they express in writing and those that are left unrecorded or even unspoken, we must accept a contract law that rests on standards rather than on clear, quantitative rules. Contract law then will talk of 'good faith', 'duties of co-operation', or 'within limits set by commercial reasonableness.'[2] Others have written much about what standards are most appropriate.[3]

However, there are objections to writing contract law in the qualitative fashion that seems necessary that are so well known that we can call them classic. Furthermore, there are also classic responses to these

[1] Richard Danzig, *The Capability Problem in Contract Law* (Mineola, New York, Foundation Press, 1978).

[2] See, eg, Uniform Commercial Code §2–311(1): 'An agreement for sale which is otherwise sufficiently definite . . . to be a contract is not made invalid by the fact that it leaves particulars of performance to be specified by one of the parties. Any such specification must be made in good faith and within the limits set by commercial reasonableness.'

[3] David Campbell, 'Reflexivity and Welfarism in the Modern Law of Contract' (2000) 20 *Oxford Journal of Legal Studies* 477, 497, notes that much American writing on contracts, except that of Ian Macneil, criticises classical contract law but fails to set out a rival theory. I have said: 'people should not attempt to write about contracts until they have studied Macneil.' Stewart Macaulay, 'Relational Contracts Floating on a Sea of Custom? Thoughts About the Ideas of Ian Macneil and Lisa Bernstein' (2000) 94 *Northwestern University Law Review* 775, 776. Nonetheless, I am skeptical about whether anyone can create a complete rival theory applicable to all kinds of contracts without a good deal of oversimplification. I also doubt that any such grand rival theory could be sold to the judges and lawyers who would have to put it into practice. See Jay M Feinman, 'Relational Contract Theory in Context' (2000) 94 *Northwestern University Law Review* 737. I would be pleased to be proven wrong. My contribution, if any, will be only to look at proposals and arguments advocating positions and to ask whether they seem compatible with business practices about which I know something. Pointing out over-generalisations and questionable assumptions is still valuable work.

objections.[4] In this paper I will ask whether we can do more than just reprise these old songs and hear one group of scholars, judges and lawyers sing one song while another group whistles the other. We can clarify our choices by examining each from a law and society perspective—that is, by asking how the law in action appears from the point of view of business people and their lawyers. Moreover, we can gain a little ground in at least one limited subset of contract cases if we focus on judges in such disputes serving as agents of settlement. With all of its flaws, such coerced co-operation may be the least bad solution in many situations.

I will review briefly some of the reasons why the paper deal often does not reflect the real deal or the implicit dimension of contract. I will consider the somewhat chaotic responses American courts have given to the problem. I will look at what relational contract theory suggests courts should do and what a concern about the rule of law offers. My conclusion is not startling: we cannot have our cake and eat it too. There are costs and benefits flowing from focusing on the paper deal and from focusing on the real deal. The twentieth century history of American contract law and scholarship reflects cycles of privileging one judgement about those costs and benefits and then rejecting it and adopting another. Finally, I will suggest that in a limited subset of all contract cases, we should be content with almost any approach that leads to settlements that give expression, more or less, to relational norms and values.

THE GAP BETWEEN THE REAL DEAL AND THE PAPER DEAL

Things are easier for some parties and courts if the legal system focuses entirely on any written document that the parties have signed or accepted. If legal agencies do this consistently, corporate lawyers, for example, need worry less about what their client's sales people say or do. However, this approach requires courts to close their eyes to real expectations resting in the implicit dimensions of contract and significant reliance on them. Contracts are always more than the contract document. We have long known the many reasons for this: Words do not have a fixed meaning that every speaker of the language will translate

[4] The best discussion of these classic pro and con arguments is Duncan Kennedy, 'Form and Substance in Private Law Adjudication' (1976) 89 *Harvard Law Review* 1685.

the same way. We create the meaning of written language by bringing to the words some measure of context, background assumptions, our experiences, and, too often, our bias, ignorance and stupidities.[5]

Also, it is very hard to bring the future to the present and provide that X will happen if event Y takes place.[6] Our ability to predict the future is limited, and even careful business people often leave gaps in written contracts. The world changes and surprises us: Wars break out in places where we do not expect them; or our contract may have dealt with a war but left open what happens when the indirect effect of a major terrorist attack makes performance much more costly; OPEC drives up energy costs unexpectedly; new technologies, often involving computers, change things so that an older contract no longer makes sense.

Even when we can foresee that it is possible that something might happen, there are limits on the time that we can or should spend on trying to provide for all contingencies in our contracts. In most instances, it would not pay to hire enough people with the skill needed to review what is printed in fine print on the back of various sellers' forms such as proposals, acknowledgement of orders and invoices. A firm that is filling thousands of purchase orders every week could not afford to take the time to negotiate all the details of every transaction. Moreover, as Tom Palay notes: 'looking beyond the [written] contract is important because parties who have, or anticipate, strong relational ties with their contracting opposites are not particularly worried about initial terms of agreement.'[7] In many situations careful contract negotiation signals distrust when the situation calls for a business marriage.

[5] See Professor Linzer's discussion of *Shore v Motorola*, in Peter Linzer, 'Rough Justice: A Theory of Restitution and Reliance, Contracts and Torts' (2001) *Wisconsin Law Review* 695, 764–72. The price of the position I take in this article is that I have to accept that sometimes judges will use their discretion to reach results that I think are outrageous. *Shore v Motorola* was for me an unhappy example.

[6] By the 'real deal' I mean both those actual expectations that exist in and out of a written contract and the generalised expectation that a trading partner will behave reasonably in solving problems as they arise. My experience talking with business people suggests that reading written contracts clauses to one another seldom would be seen as a reasonable way to solve problems. There may be situations where applying the letter of a written document would be a reasonable way to cope with a contract problem, but I suspect that these situations are a very limited group of all contract problems. Also, there are situations where parties do not expect the other to act reasonably for the mutual benefit of the relationship. Again, I would expect this to be a very limited group of cases because some trust is needed before most people will make contracts.

[7] Thomas M Palay, 'A Contract Does Not a Contract Make' (1985) *Wisconsin Law Review* 561, 562.

Furthermore, we must remember that business corporations are collections of people and their activities are seldom tightly co-ordinated. Those who negotiate the deal often are not the people who draft the written document recording it. Still others must perform the contract. This opens the possibility that, for example, a firm's lawyers may have different assumptions and expectations than its purchasing agents, sales people and engineers.

Strategy may be involved too. If I want a clause that says if event X takes place, then consequence Y will follow, you may demand something in exchange that I do not want to give you. When I anticipate this, it may be better to avoid raising the issue in negotiations and hope that the matter can be resolved if event X ever takes place.

Lawyers deal with many of these problems by fabricating detailed standard form contracts that typically are written in legal or technical language that 'is not meant to be read, still less to be understood.'[8] The written document, however, may be seen by purchasing agents, sales personnel and engineers as a formality created only to please the whims of the lawyers. It is also possible that parties will write or accept a flat, unqualified contract clause but assume that there are exceptions or qualifications that are not worth the effort to spell out in advance. In short, there are many reasons why the paper deal will fail to capture the real deal. As a matter of fact, there is a 'text between the lines.'

The performance of contractual obligations often will be prolonged in time and require the active co-operation of both parties. Situations may change during the time that one or both parties are attempting to perform or it may become clear that the written language is an inadequate guide to performance. While parties can modify their written contract, often they do not engage in an explicit renegotiation. Rather, they make adjustments as they attempt to cope with the demands of the original agreement and the new situation. Sometimes we can say that when the parties signed a written agreement, they intended their contract to be adjusted in light of continually changing circumstances. In some kinds of contracts, cancellation for convenience or broad impossibility/frustration clauses are common. Sometimes the written contract provides that if event X happens, 'the contract shall be equitably adjusted.' Often, however, we can suspect that those who signed the written document never thought about the possibility of changes

8 The phrase is Lord Justice Devlin's. See *McCutcheon v David MacBrayne, Inc* [1964] 1 WLR 125.

beyond a general tacit assumption that both sides would proceed in good faith.

AMERICAN LAW: RULE AND COUNTER-RULE, CORE AND PERIPHERY

The Law: Something Less than Certainty and Perfect Predictability

How does or should contract law respond to any gap between the paper deal and the real deal? Let me briefly sketch some of the approaches taken by American courts or advocated by American writers.[9] I offer American law and writing only as an example which I know. I do not presume that they should be a model for the rest of the world.

People can respond to a problem by denying that it exists. We could point to many judicial opinions that talk about the plain meaning of a written contract without ever considering how they know that this is what the parties meant. This is the strongest version of the parol evidence rule.[10] There is an old American expression that tells us that 'if it looks like a duck, waddles like a duck and quacks like a duck, it is a duck!' Sometimes an objective theory of contracts gives us, essentially, the duck test. If I signed a writing, you are entitled to rely on my agreement to the plain meaning of the words written, typed or printed. Sometimes this position is reinforced by a tort-like duty to read and understand which can transform contract law's claim to rest on choice into pure magic. Also, there is an assumption, often unstated, that all the parties' rights and duties must be traced back to the specific provisions of their written agreement. Courts say that they will not make a contract for the parties. However, when judges want to impose contractual liability, implied conditions and strange readings of contract language rationalise the enforcement of what judges think parties ought to have done. Sometimes, of course, implied conditions and strange readings rationalise a judge's refusal to enforce the bargain that the parties made.

[9] See Jay M Feinman, 'The Significance of Contract Theory' (1990) 58 *Cincinnati Law Review* 1283.

[10] See John D Calamari and Joseph M Perillo, 'A Plea for a Uniform Parol Evidence Rule and Principles of Contract Interpretation' (1967) 42 *Indiana Law Journal* 333; William C Whitford, 'The Role of the Jury (and the Fact/Law Distinction) in the Interpretation of Written Contracts' (2001) *Wisconsin Law Review* 931.

Lawrence Friedman pointed out that American contract law in the late Nineteenth and early Twentieth Centuries was grounded in abstraction; it offered rules assumed to be applicable whether the parties were rich or poor and without regard to the subject matter of the transaction. The rules purported to be unchanging over time. However, when faced with the demands of a developing economy, American courts used tools such as waiver and estoppel and construction of language to bend specific rules into conforming with standards of higher generality.[11] Often careful study would reveal that contract law featured a rule opposed by a counter rule with no principled way of knowing when one or the other would apply. American law, for example, tells us that it is not duress to threaten to do what you have a legal right to do.[12] Yet a wrongful although not illegal threat can be duress.[13] These two statements of the law do not live together happily.

The legal realists had a fine time dropping bombs on ideas about plain meaning and abstraction. The more you know about language, the less comfortable you are with ideas that any collection of words has but one complete and clear meaning apart from context. Recognising this, Professor Corbin would reduce doctrines such as the parol evidence rule to a possibility that seldom would apply. Parol evidence is to be excluded when the parties intended their writing to be the final expression of their agreement. Corbin, however, argued that such an intention about finality was a fact to be proved by any relevant evidence that was credible. He thought that judges should not blind themselves to everything but the text of a writing. Justice Roger Traynor of the Supreme Court of California wrote this form of realism into the law of his state, at least for a time.[14] A California judge was not to look for the plain meaning. He or she could look to evidence of intention other than the text of a written contract even when the words did not seem to be ambiguous.

[11] Lawrence M Friedman, *Contract Law in America: a Social and Economic Case Study* (1965).

[12] See eg, *Wurtz v Fleischman* 97 Wis.2d 100, 293 N.W.2d 155 (1980).

[13] Restatement (2d) Contracts §176(2)(c) tells us that a threat is 'improper if the resulting exchange is not on fair terms, and . . . what is threatened is otherwise a use of a power for illegitimate ends.' See Claire Dalton, 'An Essay in the Deconstruction of Contract Doctrine' (1985) 94 *Yale Law Journal* 997, 1032–36, for a criticism of this approach. Dalton sees the Restatement as evading the real but difficult questions about what are 'illegitimate ends' for the use of power.

[14] See eg, *Masterson v Sine* 68 Cal.2d 222, 436 P.2d 561 (1968); *Pacific Gas & Elect Co v GW Thomas Drayage & Rigging Co* 69 Cal.2d 33, 442 P.2d 641 (1968).

To a great extent, legal realism was written into American law when Professor Karl Llewellyn became the Reporter for Article 2 of our Uniform Commercial Code. Article 2 became the law in almost all American states by 1965. In Llewellyn's Code, much turns on the concept of 'agreement.' Section 1–201(3) defines this concept as 'the bargain of the parties in fact as found in their language or by implication from other circumstances . . .' The phrase 'bargain of the parties in fact' would seem to call for enforcing the real deal rather than holding people to any asserted plain meaning of the documents which they signed or accepted. The Code also attempts to cut back the idea that contracts must be defined with certainty.[15] Llewellyn celebrated what he called the grand style of common law judging.[16] Judges working in the grand style did not apply rules mindlessly. Rather, drawing on their situation sense, rules served only as guides to judgement.[17]

However, the Code is not pure Llewellyn but a compromise between the legal realism of the academics who produced the first drafts and the traditional views of the commercial lawyers who forced revisions.[18]

[15] Section 2–204(1) says '[a] contract for sale of goods may be made in any manner sufficient to show agreement, including conduct by both parties which recognizes the existence of a contract.' We can have an enforceable contract although the price is uncertain, quantity is defined only as 'requirements' and nothing is said about the date for performance.

[16] See Karl N Llewellyn, *The Common Law Tradition: Deciding Appeals* (Boston, Little Brown, 1960) 64–72; William Twining, *Karl Llewellyn and the Realist Movement* (London, Wiedenfeld and Nicolson, 1973) 210–245.

[17] For example, Section 1–102(1), Official Comment 1, says: 'The Act should be construed in accordance with its underlying purposes and policies. The text of each section should be read in the light of the purpose and policy of the rule or principle in question, as also of the Act as a whole, and the application of the language should be construed narrowly or broadly, as the case maybe, in conformity with the purposes and policies involved.' Section 1–205, Official Comment 1, says: 'The measure and background for interpretation are set by the commercial context, which may explain and supplement even the language of a formal or final writing.'

[18] See Allen R Kamp, 'Downtown Code: A History of the Uniform Commercial Code 1949–1954' (2001) 49 *Buffalo Law Review* 359, 361, 392: '[T]he present Code is a product of two conflicting visions of what commercial law should be—one, a regulatory system based on self-regulation by the trade, judicial supervision according to commercial norms, and legislative dictate, as opposed to one based on an autonomous business world operating under a regime of unregulated contract . . . Llewellyn's views and his original program for the Code grew out of the matrix of the collectivist mentality of the 1930s . . . Llewellyn was once part of an academic avant guard, a supporter of FDR [President Roosevelt] in his court-packing plan, a folk dancer, a student of Boas' anthropology, part of a 1930s radical, collectivist milieu.' See also, Allen R Kamp, 'Between-The-Wars Social Thought: Karl Llewellyn, Legal Realism, and the Uniform Commercial Code in Contex' (1995) 59 *Albany Law Review* 325; Allen R Kamp, 'Uptown Act: A History of the Uniform Commercial Code: 1940–49' (1998) 51 *Southern Methodist University Law Review* 275; Allen R. Kamp, 'Increasing Complexity in Commercial Law: The Failure of the Uniform Commercial Code' (1991) 10 *Corporate Counsel Review* 59.

Llewellyn was not free to innovate at will. He had to obtain the blessing of the American Law Institute and the National Conference of Commissions on Uniform State Law. Moreover, the Code had to be passed by state legislatures, most of which had many members who were lawyers trained in the conventional wisdom. Article 2 has, for example, a parol evidence rule and a Statute of Frauds. In the hands of a judge holding traditional views, there are ways to read the Code that can serve as a road back to the familiar territory of the common law of contracts. In making this move, it helps to ignore the definitional sections of the statute. As a result, Article 2 often preserves aspects of the classic common law approaches but seeks to change the common law enough to deal with modern conditions. It can be considered an example of 'neo-classical contract.'[19] In short, many of the tools needed to seek the implicit dimensions of contract are in Article 2, but even judges who read statutes carefully do not have to use these tools.[20]

Scholarly Reaction: Modern Challenges to Code Methods

In the last decade or two, some American scholars have questioned the approach of Article 2 of the Uniform Commercial Code as a means of achieving its announced ends. It was, they say, sold as a uniform law, but it fails to produce uniform results. In its contextual approach, every case is different. Llewellyn had defended his open textured qualitative provisions in Article 2 by saying that the common law method would, over time, provide enough certainty. Courts would give meaning to concepts such as 'unconscionability' or 'commercial reasonableness' by deciding a series of cases involving specific facts. Patterns would emerge and judges and scholars would be able to discern working rules. Moreover, Llewellyn thought that judges could be informed of the usages of trade in order to give content to Article 2's frequent reference to reasonable commercial behavior.

[19] In the right hands, however, Art 2 offers an opportunity for an application of a relational theory of contract to specific problems. See Ian R Macneil, 'Restatement (2d) of Contracts and Presentation' (1974) 60 *Virginia Law Review* 589; Richard E Speidel, 'Article 2 and Relational Sales Contracts' (1993) 26 *Loyola of Los Angeles Law Review* 789.

[20] See Amy H Kastely, 'Stock Equipment for the Bargain in Fact: Trade Usage, "Express Terms," and Consistency Under Section 1–205 of the Uniform Commercial Code' (1986) 64 *North Carolina Law Review* 777.

Many have challenged Llewellyn's justifications for the way that Article 2 of the UCC is drafted. Here I will look at two writers whose work I admire, Dean Robert Scott and Professor Lisa Bernstein. Both do empirical work, and both are sensitive to making theories about contract accord with business practice. Dean Scott has questioned whether more than 30 years experience with the Code has done much to make its qualitative standards clear to lawyers. He has studied American courts dealing with these general norms.[21] Scott accepts that most contractual transactions are relational. However, he argues 'the state's primary substantive role in uniformly enforcing commercial contracts is to regulate incomplete contracts efficiently.'[22] This involves two often inconsistent tasks: Courts must 'correctly (or uniformly) interpret . . . the meaning of the contract terms chosen by the parties to allocate contract risk.' They also must create 'broadly suitable default rules and/or . . . [label] widely used contract terms and clauses with standard meanings.' He argues that uniformity requires not just that the same substantive standards be adopted by all American states. For all of the advantages of uniformity, courts in all states must apply those standards in predictable ways. He finds that Article 2 of the Uniform Commercial code fails to give reliable and predictable interpretations of contractual text. Llewellyn's theory about courts developing consistent readings of and reactions to contract terms incrementally over time has not proved accurate. Dean Scott asserts:

> While the Code was explicitly designed to incorporate evolving norms into an ever-growing set of legally defined default rules, incorporation as such has simply not occurred. To be sure, courts have interpreted contracts in which context evidence has been evaluated together with the written terms

[21] Robert E Scott, 'Rethinking the Uniformity Norm in Commercial Law: A Comparative Analysis of Common Law and Code Methodologies' in Jody S Kraus and Steven D Walt (eds) *The Jurisprudential Foundations of Corporate and Commercial Law* (2000) 149, 166 n 68; Robert E Scott, 'The Case for Formalism in Relational Contract' (2000) 94 *Northwestern University Law Review* 847. See also, Robert E Scott, 'Conflict and Cooperation in Long-Term Contracts' (1987) 75 *California Law Review* 2005; Robert E Scott, 'A Relational Theory of Default Rules for Commercial Contracts' (1990) 19 *Journal of Legal Studies* 597. Compare Omri Ben-Shahar, 'The Tentative Case Against Flexibility in Commercial Law' (1999) 66 *University of Chicago Law Review* 781. For an earlier, and very well done, presentation of the arguments against flexibility in the Code, see Arthur I Rosett, 'Contract Performance: Promises, Conditions and the Obligation to Communicate' (1975) 22 *UCLA Law Review* 1083.

[22] Scott, 'Rethinking the Uniformity Norm in Commercial Law: A Comparative Analysis of Common Law and Code Methodologies' *loc cit* 149, 150.

> of the contract. . . . But while such judicial decisions affirm the institutional bias toward contextualizing contract, the fact-specific nature of the contract dispute leaves, in virtually every case, little opportunity for subsequent incorporation as tailored defaults. . . . A systematic examination of the litigated cases interpreting the 'reasonableness' standards of Article 2 reveals that courts have consistently interpreted these statutory instructions not as inductive directions to incorporate commercial norms and prototypes but rather as invitations to make deductive speculations according to 'Code policy' or other noncontextual criteria.[23]

Scott's conclusions are not surprising. Insofar as courts try to apply general relational norms to particular transactions, they are seeking goals other than uniformity of application. Scott's solution to the uniformity problem is a return to formalism, a plain-meaning approach to interpretation and a strict parol evidence rule. Often, for reasons that I have indicated, this will defend written text at the cost of defeating actual expectations and the implicit dimensions of contract. To a great extent, any differences between my judgements and those of Professor Scott turn on how much we value predictable results when there are disputes. He seems ready to trade having courts seek the assumptions of the parties for something approaching certainty. He says:

> [T]he efficient regulation of contract does not require that every relational norm be judicialized or that the legal mechanism operates efficiently viewed on its own terms, but rather that it operates efficiently in concert with social norms of trust, reciprocity, and conditional cooperation that also regulate relational contracts. Under the formalist approach, these norms would not be legally enforceable contract terms . . . but they nevertheless would be enforced by social sanctions that would effectively constrain the parties' incentives to exploit changed circumstances strategically.[24]

I, on the other hand, am content with a contract law where lawyers can make probabilistic judgements about likely outcomes if, at the same time, we can enforce duties of co-operation and good faith. I would be

[23] *Ibid* 164.

[24] Scott, 'The Case for Formalism in Relational Contract' above n 21, 861. See, also, Robert E Scott, 'Comment' (2002) 52 *Hastings Law Journal* 700: '[T]here are powerful normative forces in relational contracts and . . . they regulate a great deal of the relationship . . . and . . . therefore legal default rules serve a minor but very important purpose as kind of a nuclear umbrella. . . . [T]here's a difference between Contract as an institution, which is synthetic and relational, and Contract Law which is simple, formal, classical . . . We have a set of rules for umbrella legal enforcement, and then a set of informal social norms that are better if not judicialized.'

very uncomfortable with a contract law that attempted to apply a plain meaning rule and a strict parol evidence rule to every situation.[25] In a great many cases, this would ignore actual expectations and allow the lawyers for the side that got to do the drafting to create a license for its sales people to lie and mislead. I would be more comfortable with Dean Scott's approach if it were limited to cases where bargainers were represented by lawyers and the language of the writing was subject to negotiation.[26]

Scott acknowledges that '[o]ne who argues for a return to acontextual modes of interpretation has to concede, and I do, that there are real costs to a return to the common law approach.'[27] This is well said. Yet there is another point: I am still enough of a legal realist to doubt whether courts would or could abandon a contextual approach to giving meaning to language and behaviour. Just as some writers are skeptical about whether courts can apply a realist approach, we can be equally skeptical about whether courts can be truly formal and close their eyes to everything but the words on a piece of paper. Even the classic formalist parol evidence rule allowed contextual evidence if terms were 'ambiguous.' In the hands of many judges, this opens the door to a case-by-case policy approach. Would the advocates of near-certainty abandon this exception? Could they abandon it if they wanted to do so without reducing contract interpretation to an empty ritual? Or put in Chief Judge Richard Posner's words:

[25] Parties in specific industries or trades can minimise the risk of having agreements interpreted in light of an expanded consideration of context if this is what they want. They can withdraw from the public courts by providing for arbitration. Insofar as they can influence or control who will do the arbitrating, they can opt for an expert who will bring an expanded view of context because of his experience. Or they can opt for a person who approaches written contracts very literally. Professor Daintith suggests that the presence of arbitration clauses in contracts does not necessarily suggest that parties expect conflict. '[E]xperience shows that parties do not in fact resort to arbitration as a mode of settlement [in the iron ore market]. Incorporation of an arbitration clause, I would suggest, shows only that the parties wish to avoid the possibility that a dispute will come before the ordinary courts.' Terence Daintith, 'The Design and the Performance of Long-Term Contracts', in G Teubner and T Dainntith (eds) *Contract and Organisation* (Berlin, W de Gruyter, 1986) 164. For a criticism of the move to arbitration that is so common today, see Chris A Carr and Michael R Jencks, 'The Privatization of Business and Commercial Dispute Resolution' (2000) 88 *Kentucky Law Journal* 183.

[26] This was the approach of the United States Court of Appeals for the Seventh Circuit in the early 1980s. See *Binks Manufacturing Co v National Presto Industries, Inc* 709 F.2d 1109 (7th Cir. 1983); *Air Line Stewards and Stewardesses Assoc v Trans World Airlines* 713 F.2d 319 (7th Cir. 1983). Given that court's tendency to ignore its own precedents, the status of these decisions is uncertain. See Linzer, n 5 above.

[27] Robert E Scott, 'Is Article Two the Best We Can Do?' (2001) 52 *Hastings Law Journal* 677, 687.

> [It is] an embarrassment for a theory of judicial legitimacy that denies that judges have any right to exercise discretion. A choice among semantically plausible interpretations of a text, in circumstances remote from those contemplated by its drafters, requires the exercise of discretion and the weighing of consequences. Reading is not a form of deduction; understanding requires a consideration of consequences . . . The broader principle . . . is that if one possible interpretation of an ambiguous statement would entail absurd or terrible results, that is a good reason to adopt an alternative interpretation.[28]

Furthermore, if we really wanted certainty and predictability, we would have to wipe out such doctrines as waiver and estoppel. We would have to do without doctrines such as substantial performance or requirements that breaches be material in order to trigger rights to call off contracts. We would have to make very clear any rules that required aggrieved parties to give notice that they considered the contract to be breached. Furthermore, I cannot imagine anything such as the doctrines of mistake, impossibility and frustration being expressed in certain terms that did not require judgement. Perhaps others can imagine judges closing their eyes to context, but my imagination will not carry me that far. Even the most formalist judge will read the paper deal knowing that it describes a sale of machinery, a bank loan, a franchise under which one party gains rights to sell new cars and so on. Such a judge probably will have his or her own experiences that will colour the way that he or she understands the language used as applied to the situation before the court. Moreover, such a judge, or his or her law clerk, will have read some or all of the record on appeal, and usually it is filled with context. This is not to say that a formalist judge cannot write an acontextual opinion. However, decision and rationalisation are different matters.

Moreover, the possibility of minting useful default rules that would eliminate almost all uncertainty strikes me as questionable. I can imagine some relatively certain default rules.[29] I suspect, however, that in

[28] Richard A Posner, 'What Am I? A Potted Plant?' *The New Republic*, 18 Sept 1987, 23. Posner continues, saying: 'There has never been a time when the courts of the United States, state or federal, behaved consistently in accordance with . . . [legal formalism]. Nor could they, for reasons rooted in the nature of law and legal institutions, in the limitations of human knowledge, and in the character of the political system.'

[29] For example, when a contract made in Madison, Wisconsin speaks of the price as a specified number of dollars, American law would tell the judge to read this as United States dollars and not Australian dollars. Yet the case gets harder when the parties deal over the Internet and one is in Madison and the other is in Sydney.

creating default rules for many situations courts would feel a need to use some general terms calling on judgement in application. For example, suppose the parties failed to provide for the time of performance. I accept that it might be very useful to know for sure whether the seller would have to perform a day, a week or a month after the contract was signed. Nonetheless, can we imagine being satisfied with a rule that provided that all contracts made without a fixed date for delivery had to be performed within a week after they were signed? The rule would *look* certain, but there is not much more that could be said for it. Courts could gain certainty by refusing to enforce any contract that did not specify a date for performance. Yet this would make many bargains unenforceable even when it was clear that a seller's failure to deliver had continued far beyond any reasonable time for performance. I would find this too much to pay for whatever benefits near certainty would bring.

Furthermore, I can imagine many situations where there would be good arguments for both sides as we tried to apply these brave new clear default rules to the particular facts of the case. It is not news that even certain rules do not necessarily yield certain results as applied, particularly in an adversary system that rewards lawyers for putting a self-serving spin on situations. And jurors and judges can pretend that facts exist, or do not exist, as a means to defeat a result seemingly dictated by the clearest rule of substantive law that the most skilled drafter can fashion. This may not be playing the game, but those of us who read briefs and excerpts from the record as well as appellate opinions have so often been startled when appellate judges get to where they want to go by fudging the facts that we really should no longer be surprised.

Scott, as well as others such as Bernstein, argue that business people may honour relational norms and sanctions while a relationship is underway, but when it breaks up, they may want 'end-game norms' to apply.[30] These end-game norms often appear in written formal contracts, but parties may pay little attention to them as they perform. During the life of a relationship, for example, a buyer may accept delayed deliveries. Once the parties reach the end-game when the relationship is not going to continue, the buyer may wish to insist on the

[30] See 'A Relational Theory of Default Rules for Commercial Contracts' above n 21, 615: 'The parties, in essence, have learned to behave under two sets of rules: a strict set of rules for legal enforcement and a more flexible set of rules for social enforcement.'

written contract's fixed delivery dates to justify ending or limiting its obligations to the seller. The point is similar to one that Professor Fuller made in his 1947 casebook:

> The practice actually followed in the settlement of claims by companies which employ a standard form for transacting business is often much more liberal than might be inferred from the terms of the contract they ask their customers to sign. . . . The companies . . . seek a contractual margin of safety within which they can exercise their own discretion free from the threat of litigation. . . .[31]

Once a relationship comes to the end-game, reading a written contract literally sometimes may seem appropriate. For example, this often will be the case when the contract deals with borrowing money. I think that most people understand that money lenders can be expected to turn to the text of financing instruments when the time comes to call in a loan. Sometimes, however, turning to a writing at the end-game would only disappoint expectations created during the process of attempting to maintain a relationship. Courts had good reasons for fashioning the doctrines of waiver, interpreting contracts by the course of performance and rules that require an aggrieved party to give the other notice that s/he thinks that there has been a breach of contract. We cannot assume that parties always intend one set of rules for performance and another for resolving disputes before courts.[32] This would seem particularly true when a written document was signed as a formality signifying commitment but not read nor understood by those who negotiated it.

Professor Lisa Bernstein has engaged in a grand empirical study of commercial custom.[33] Llewellyn, in drafting Article 2 of the UCC,

[31] Lon L Fuller, *Basic Contract Law* (St Paul, West Publishing Co, 1947) 213. He continues: 'To obtain a proper perspective of the whole question, one must also consider whether trial in court, especially before a jury, is an efficient and just means of settling disputes involving small sums.'

[32] See Stewart Macaulay, 'Relational Contracts Floating on a Sea of Custom? Thoughts About the Ideas of Ian Macneil and Lisa Bernstein' (2000) 94 *Northwestern University Law Review* 775, 794–96.

[33] See Lisa Bernstein, 'The Questionable Empirical Basis of Article 2's Incorporation Strategy: A Preliminary Study' (1999) 66 *University of Chicago Law Review* 710; Lisa Bernstein, 'Merchant Law in a Merchant Court: Rethinking the Code's Search for Immanent Business Norms' (1996) 144 *University of Pennsylvania Law Review* 1765. For my largely favourable comments on Bernstein's work, see Stewart Macaulay, 'Relational Contracts Floating on a Sea of Custom? Thoughts About the Ideas of Ian Macneil and Lisa Bernstein' *loc cit.* Compare Richard Epstein, 'Confusion About Custom: Disentangling Informal Customs from Standard Contractual Provisions' (1999) 66 *University of Chicago Law Review* 821.

again and again turned to business practices to give content to the qualitative standards found in his rules. After interviewing many business people, Bernstein does not find much trade usage that would be useful to courts in deciding particular cases. Customs are vague, and they often differ from place to place. Published codes of trade practice often are far more political than empirical, reflecting power struggles in trade associations rather than the expectations of typical members of the trade.

Bernstein's judgement about usage will often be right. Yet there are some customs and practices that can give meaning to the words in an agreement. Seldom, however, can judges just pick up the quaint native customs of business people and plug them into contracts without interpretation. Customs often are vague and qualified by imprecise exceptions. At best, such a custom may influence a court's judgement but not decide the case. Judges and jurors can be informed about community standards by expert witnesses. Of course, a critic may object that experts can be bought to testify to just about anything. Of course, we can hope that legal decision-makers can ward off biased claims in light of what makes sense in a commercial setting, at least in most cases.

Llewellyn had a different argument for the qualitative approach of Article 2 of the UCC. Judges might not be able to rely on trade usage because none existed or none could be proved. There also might be no established default rule because courts would not have worked one out incrementally through a series of cases. Nonetheless, Llewellyn argued that judges could rely on their 'situation sense'[34]—informed intuition—and the policies expressed and implied in the Code, and, perhaps, in the legal culture of their time.[35] He thought that typically judges would reach a defensible result, although they might not explain it well. In America there are many roads to a judgeship, but some judges will have some background in business as a result of their practice before they took the bench. In many cases, the practice of law itself involves participating in a small business, and this experience could

[34] See Twining, above n 16, 225: 'A judge in a commercial case who can see the facts in the way businessmen would see them, as well as from the lawyer's point of view and from the point of view of the "mores" of the community as a whole, has grasped "wisdom." '.

[35] Llewellyn, above n 16, 4. Leon Trakman develops this idea and argues that judicial discretion will not be capricious because of the inherent controls in the common law system apart from the rules of contract law. See L Trakman, 'The Effect of Illegality in the Law of Contract: Suggestions for Reform' (1977) 55 *Canadian Bar Review/La Revue due Barreau Canadien* 627, 652–54.

affect attitudes and assumptions. Lawyers argue legal rules, but they know that appeals to 'common sense' can reinforce their technical claim.

Would an informed intuitive policy approach produce complete uncertainty? Llewellyn argues that it would produce 'reckonability' rather than uncertainty. Farber and Matheson note:

> Courts often resort to conclusory language in finding that a manifestation rises to the level of a promise . . . [R]elationships and surrounding circumstances do not speak for themselves. They must be interpreted by judges on the basis of expectations likely to arise between similarly situated parties. The conclusory tone follows because we are being told what we ought to already understand as members of the community.[36]

Lawyers might not know for sure how a particular case would be resolved, but, as members of the community of commercial lawyers, they would have a good idea of the probabilities. They would be aware that some cases were close ones with good arguments for both sides. These they could consider settling, and these situations might provoke changes in drafting, negotiation or both in the future. Those who advise American corporations are not helpless in the face of demands for such things as 'commercial reasonableness' and avoiding 'unconscionability.' They can help clients change behaviour so that there is little question about running afoul of such qualitative standards. They can advise clients about the risks, and clients can decide to take the chance that a court might disapprove of certain practices. Lawyers might even get their clients to tone down advertising that creates expectations that they cannot satisfy.

If the burden on business flowing from a particular application of a rule were great enough, business interests could seek legislation to clarify or reverse the offending reading of the law. Their lawyers could redraft standard language to make it more likely that they would win the next time the problem comes before the courts. In some situations, they could move the game from the courts to arbitration and select their own judges and rules.

Clearly, any intuitive approach to the qualitative standards found in Article 2 will not serve the purposes that Dean Scott specifies in his writings. It will not give us uniformity in the application of the law nor produce clear default rules. Nonetheless, Llewellyn's whole approach

[36] Daniel A Farber and John H Matheson, 'Beyond Promissory Estoppel: Contract Law and the "Invisible Handshake"' (1985) 52 *University of Chicago Law Review* 903, 915 n 45.

should prompt us to ask how much uniformity we need and what price are we willing to pay for it? Dean Scott's study suggests that courts have not defined general standards or worked out specific rules very often. They just announce conclusions without offering much by way of explanation. Yet we can ask whether American contracts decisions leave an experienced business lawyer at sea with no land in sight. It would be hard to answer this question by an empirical study because of the vagueness of the question. Nonetheless, the lawyers with whom I talk continue to draft contracts and to interpret them for clients. Many of them are confident that they can predict what courts are likely to do with a contract problem. Again, there may be types of contracts or particular situations where more certainty would be highly valuable and where other-than-legal relational norms and sanctions are all that we need. However, giving content to this idea requires that we look at the realities of various types of business transactions in detail before we make judgements about the need for greater certainty and clarity, the power of relational norms and sanctions and the costs of a flexible judicial approach. The problem is to avoid over-generalisation.

This is but a quick sketch of debates in the American contract field. Yet it should make clear that not everyone accepts that courts should pursue the implicit dimensions of contract. Moreover, American contract law has not been certain and perfectly predictable.

'THE RULE OF LAW', TRUST AND ECONOMIC DEVELOPMENT

Concern for the 'rule of law' could inhibit courts from searching for the implicit dimensions of contract.[37] Hendley observes that the phrase 'has become a trendy political slogan around the world.'[38] However,

[37] For excellent discussions of the idea of the rule of law, see William C Whitford, 'The Rule of Law' [2000] *Wisconsin Law Review* 723; Frank Lovett, 'A Positivist Account of the Rule of Law' (2002) 27 *Law and Social Inquiry* 41; Martin Krygier, 'The Rule of Law' in Neil J Smelser and Paul B Bates (eds), *International Encyclopedia of the Social and Behavioral Sciences* (Amsterdam, Elsevier, 2001) 13403. Stephen Lubben examines claims that an approach to contract interpretation resting on qualitative standards is the same as the German free law movement that the Nazi's found useful. Not surprisingly, he is very skeptical of such a position. See Stephen J Lubben, 'Chief Justice Traynor's Contract Jurisprudence and the Free Law Dilemma: Nazism, the Judiciary, and California's Contract Law' (1998) 7 *Southern California Interdisciplinary Law Journal* 81. See also Edward L Rubin, 'Discretion and Its Discontents' (1997) 72 *Chicago Kent Law Review* 1299.

[38] Kathryn Hendley, 'The Rule of Law and Economic Development in a Global Era' in Austin Sarat (ed) *The Blackwell Companion to Law and Society* (forthcoming).

she notes that the content of the phrase and the means to achieve this goal are most uncertain. Ohnesorge has reviewed the various publications of international organisations, political leaders and scholars who deal with the concept.[39] He finds that those who are not lawyers tend to assume that the rule of law is a condition of a society which is governed by a complete and functioning legal system. A society either is characterised by the rule of law or it is not. These writers assume that legal rules are 'not subject to significant indeterminacy, and that these are sufficient to provide single correct solutions without resorting to principles, policies or purposes.'[40] They also assume that the rule of law is useful because the more the future can be made predictable, the easier it is to plan and take risks in a capitalist society. Under this view of the rule of law, the outcome of contract disputes should be predictable. Contract law would deter breaches and provide compensation when a party failed to perform. However, judges often will differ about the implications of words and behavior in context. This means that seeking the implicit dimensions to a contract would insert uncertainty into the system because the courts would have to exercise judgement about what was implied but not expressed. This is to be avoided.

Ohnesorge notes that legal scholars tend to see the rule of law only as an aspiration. A society honours the rule of law when a high number of its characteristics are met a high percentage of the time. These scholars have read many cases where the rules and their application to the facts were debatable. They are skeptical about whether single correct solutions exist for the kinds of cases that are filtered into appellate courts. Legal realism and experience have taught lawyers that the outcome of particular cases can never be perfectly certain. Nonetheless, as we have seen, some legal scholars seek to increase the predictability of what courts will do with contract disputes.

The formal classical model of contract law has an illustrious history. We find traces of this version of the rule of law in Shakespeare's *The Merchant of Venice*. As you recall, Antonio has breached a contract, and, under its terms, he owes Shylock a pound of flesh. Several characters look for a way out, but others argue that the economy of Venice depends on the certain and predictable enforcement of contracts. Even Antonio himself rejects a suggestion that the judge should not enforce

39 John Ohnesorge, 'The Rule of Law, Economic Development, and the Developmental States of Northeast Asia', Christoph Antons (ed) in *Law and Development in East and Southeast Asia* (London, Routledge Curzon, 2003) 91.

40 *Ibid.*

the bargain. He says that if the course of the law is denied, it will 'impeach the justice of the state'. This will harm the 'trade and profit of the city'. Of course, Shakespeare finds a way out of the dilemma, but it involves at least claiming to enforce the letter of the contract in the most formal sense. Shylock could take his pound of flesh, but he could not take a drop of blood. Shakespeare's court refused to look at the implicit dimension of that contract.

We also find traces of the classic model of the role of contract in the writings of the great sociologist Max Weber. Weber argued that capitalism and increasing 'formal rationality' go together. David Trubek tells us that Weber thought only a formal system of law can be predictable enough to support economic activity.[41] Law seeking substantive ends leads to particularistic decisions. Such decisions make it impossible for business people to know in advance the right answers to legal questions. Formal justice, Weber argues, enhances individual opportunities, promotes self-determination and helps assure individual freedom.[42] Trubek notes that Weber also argues, perhaps paradoxic-

[41] David M Trubek, 'Reconstructing Max Weber's Sociology of Law' (1985) 37 *Stanford Law Review* 919. See, also, David M Trubek, 'Max Weber's Tragic Modernism and the Study of Law in Society' (1986) 20 *Law and Society Review* 573. See, also, David Campbell, 'Truth Claims and Value-Freedom in the Treatment of Legitimacy: The Case of Weber' (1986) 13 *Journal of Law and Society* 207.

[42] On the other hand, a group of scholars has told us that economic conditions throughout the world are better in nations that have legal systems based on the common law than in nations with legal systems based on European continental codes. Florencio Lopez-de-Silanes, Rafael La Porta, Andrei Shleifer and Robert Vishny reached this conclusion in a study conducted for the National Bureau of Economic Research. See Richard Morin, 'Unconventional Wisdom: New Facts and Hot Stats from the Social Sciences' *The Washington Post* 1 Nov 1998. The current version of the paper is 'Courts: The Lex Mundi Project' revised March 2002. It is available at <http://post.economics.harvard.edu/faculty/shleifer/papers.html>. More recently, David Wessel, 'Capital: The Legal DNA of Good Economics, Wall Street Journal' 6 Sept 2001, relies on Andrei Shleifer's work to show: 'Rule-laden civil-law countries aren't well-adapted to cope with change: the case-law approach makes common-law countries inherently more flexible.' This turns Weber on his head. However, these scholars tell us that the legal culture of the continent allows legal and governmental officials to intervene in the market, applying vague rationalisations for regulation. This explanation is consistent with Weber's observations. Of course, we can look at such studies skeptically. Even if we accept the correlation between a legal culture based on common-law approaches and economic success, we can question just how much the common-law systems contribute to that success. American, British and Indian legal officials do intervene in the market, and substantive rationality can be found in each of their legal systems. It was not too long ago that we marveled at the German and Japanese economic miracles. Taiwan, South Korea and Japan all are civil law systems and economic successes. It is hard to believe that the more recent economic difficulties of these nations can be explained by the absence of the common-law tradition in these countries. There are many more likely suspects. Compare Philip J McConnaughay, 'Rethinking the Role of Law and Contracts in East-West Commercial Relationships'(2001) 41

ally, that formal thought in law may actually defeat the intent of transacting parties, and benefit those with power and wealth. In fact, Weber suggested that completely formal thought may be impossible.

Many scholars have been critical of the approaches to development championed by the World Bank and the International Monetary Fund, which have included the rule of law as a key component.[43] The larger criticisms focus on the presumption that private actors in markets unchecked by regulation produce the greatest good. As Silbey remarks,

> [l]aw is relegated to . . . [a] . . . subordinate role as a background figure providing context but little determinative action . . . [T]he market narrative is a parable about lowering expectations about what collectivities can or should do. It thus asks us to limit our conceptions of justice to a contentless efficiency.[44]

Conceding that many of the ideas captured by the phrase 'rule of law' are valuable, other critics question whether it is enough to enact particular laws or to adopt a formalist approach. Creating a rule of law with substance is not a mere technical matter. Legal institutions rest on a larger legal culture.[45] In Campbell's words: 'An effective contract law requires an ethically endorsed framework for co-operation between involved parties which cannot be reduced to technical predictability.'[46]

Accepting that nations in transition to market economies need laws governing property, contract and bankruptcy, must courts abandon searching for the implicit dimensions of contract and operate in as formalist a way as possible? First, we could argue again that contract law

Virginia Journal of International Law 427, 432: 'The much-heralded worldwide "harmonization" of commercial law . . . does not necessarily also herald its Westernization; certain aspects of non-Western commercial traditions—for example, principles of accommodation and adjustment to future contingencies—are both consistent with core characteristics of the rule of law, and susceptible of reasonable articulation in commercial laws and contracts.'

[43] See, eg Joseph E Stiglitz, *Globalization and Its Discontents* (2002) 139, 160–61, 208–09; Ha-Joon Chang, *Joseph Stiglitz and the World Bank: The Rebel Within* (2001) 96

[44] Susan S Silbey, '"Let Them Eat Cake:" Globalization, Postmodern Colonialism, and the Possibilities of Justice' (1997) 31 *Law and Society Review* 207. See also Udo Reifner's remark: 'While in former times capitalist nations used priests, soldiers and merchants to convince less developed peoples to adhere to their system, we can now rely on the convincing forces of the IMF, World Bank, BERD and other financial institutions where nations cue up to be accepted as members.' U Reifner, 'The Vikings and the Romans—Contract Law and Social Economy' 6 (paper presented at the Conference on Perspectives of Critical Contract Law, Tuusula, Finland, 7–10 May 1992).

[45] See Hendley, n 38 above.

[46] David Campbell, 'What is Meant by "the Rule of Law" in Asian Company Law Reform?' in Roman Tomasic (ed) *Company Law in East Asia* (1999) 11.

plays but a minor role in a limited subset of situations.[47] As a result, courts are free to argue their decisions in terms of substantive rationality; any loss in predictability just will not matter much. Whatever theories say about the efficiency of clear rules, American contract law often is uncertain, featuring a rule neatly matched by a counterrule. Often there is, as Duncan Kennedy has pointed out, what seems to be a hard rule but it is encircled by a periphery of soft exceptions.[48] American legal procedure is costly and subject to procedural games such as discovery abuse and what seems to be endless delays. We have a relatively easy system of bankruptcy that can serve to wipe out or modify drastically contractual obligations.[49] Nonetheless, even with this kind of uncertain contract law in action, America has enjoyed great economic success. What is predictable is that contracts in the United States will be carried out in an acceptable fashion. When Americans make a contract, it is not certain that it be performed to the letter of its text or performed at all. Yet, it is a good bet that the parties will perform acceptably.

In my 1963 study of business practices related to contract, I note that 'business units are organized to perform commitments . . .'[50] Most simply, someone in the seller's organisation must have a reason to stop goods that have been ordered from being delivered to the buyer. Someone in the buyer's organisation must have a reason to stop the standard procedure for paying bills. In the absence of a reason to the contrary, commitments are honoured as a matter of course. Documents are needed to establish that there is a commitment. Sales people must communicate with financial people so that they will approve credit, to engineering people so that they will design and make the goods and to shipping people so that they will package and deliver them. Of course, there can be mistakes, but most of the time mistakes are discovered and corrected. Contract law may play some subtle and indirect role in all of this. Business people do know that there are such things as actions for breach of contract. They also know that their

[47] See Chong Ju Choi, 'Contract Enforcement Across Cultures' (1994) 15 *Organizational Studies* 673; Peter H. Solomon, Jr, 'The Limits of Legal Order in Post-Soviet Russia' (1995) 11 *Post-Soviet Affairs* 89.

[48] See Kennedy, above n 4, 1700–01, 1737.

[49] See, eg, Lynn M LoPucki and William C Whitford, 'Venue Choice and Forum Shopping in the Bankruptcy Reorganization of Large, Publicly Held Companies' [1991] *Wisconsin Law Review* 11. Compare Robert Hillman, 'Contract Excuse and Bankruptcy Discharge' (1990) 43 *Stanford Law Review* 99.

[50] Stewart Macaulay, 'Non-Contractual Relations in Business: A Preliminary Study' (1963) 28 *American Sociological Review* 55, 63.

reputation with their trading partner is valuable, and they do not knowingly do things that would damage it without a good reason. Most of the time, I would guess, avoiding breach of contract litigation is not something that business people spend much time thinking about. Insofar as this is true, the style of contract analysis used by judges will not matter much to people who are not law professors.[51]

Some scholars have argued that contract law plays a real and essential role in market economies. The case for formal approaches to maximise predictability importantly turns on one's position about such an economic role. Douglass North, for example, argues that relational contract sanctions work in simple transactions but complex contracts require formal drafting and the possibility of legal enforcement.[52] Farber stresses the potential costs of relying on informal relational sanctions. He contends:

> [I]nformal incentives [to gain acceptable contract performance] are costly; to the extent that inadequate legal incentives cause excessive use of informal incentives, economic efficiency suffers . . . Customers will tend to deal with sellers with whom they have dealt before and will tend not to engage in a widespread search for sellers. As a result, their willingness to shop for better prices can decrease. Furthermore, entry by new sellers becomes more difficult, because a reputation for reliability cannot be immediately established. Although these effects on behavior are difficult to quantify, they nevertheless represent real costs, because they impede the market's movement toward equilibrium.[53]

Johnson, McMillan and Woodruff surveyed about 1,500 privately owned manufacturing firms in Poland, Slovakia, Romania, Russia and Ukraine.[54] They found that

> while informal relationships are the main basis for our firms' contracting, the formal institutions also foster contracting . . . [W]orkable courts encourage firms to take on new partners. It is by making it easier for new firms to enter that having workable courts improves on relational contracting and boosts overall productivity.

[51] To repeat, in some areas of business people do write contracts while carefully considering contract law. My point is simple, obvious but often overlooked: we should not overgeneralise from what is appropriate in particular areas to all contracts.

[52] Douglass C North, *Institutions, Institutional Change and Economic Performance* (Cambridge, Cambridge University Press 1990) 56–60.

[53] Daniel A Farber, 'Reassessing the Economic Efficiency of Compensatory Damages for Breach of Contract' (1980) 66 *Virginia Law Review* 1443, 1465–66.

[54] Simon Johnson, John McMillan and Christopher Woodruff, 'Courts and Relational Contracts' (2002) 18 *Journal of Law, Economics and Organization* 221.

Deakin, Lane and Wilkinson[55] argue that contract law plays an important role in fostering trust, but they expand the idea of contract law to include both the legal and the other-than-legal norms external to the contract that create a stable framework for the process of exchange and the presence of a sense of trust between the parties.

While there is substance in all of these arguments, each can be questioned. These qualifications and doubts suggest that contract law may play a role only in a limited subset of cases. North's suggestion that relational contract is confined to simple transactions runs counter to experience, particularly in Asia.[56] We can find many complex contracts made and performed in situations where the chance of an effective legal remedy for breach is low or non-existent. Indeed, a long-term complex contract often defeats a court's abilities to provide meaningful remedies for breach.[57] Relying on long-term continuing relationships can involve costs, as Farber suggests. However, Professor Okun pointed out that there are also gains.[58] He distinguishes auction markets from

[55] Simon Deakin, Christel Lane and Frank Wilkinson, ' "Trust" or Law? Toward an Integrated Theory of Contractual Relations between Firms' (1994) 21 *Journal of Law and Society* 329.

[56] See eg, Jane Kaufman Winn, 'Law and Relational Practices in Taiwan' (1994) 28 *Law and Society Review* 193; Frank K Upham, 'Comment—Speculations on Legal Informality: On Winn's "Relational Practices and the Marginalization of Law' (1994) 28 *Law and Society Review* 233; Ohnesorge, n 39 above.

[57] See eg *Bethlehem Steel Corp v Litton Industries Inc,* 507 Pa 88, 488 A.2d 581 (1985). Litton made an elaborate complex contract with Bethlehem to supply an innovative self-unloading ore boat at a price subject to an escalator clause. Litton gave Bethlehem an option to buy five additional vessels within five years. The prices of the ore boats purchased under the option were to be subject to escalation based upon a 'mutually agreed' price index. When Bethlehem tried to exercise the options, the parties were unable to agree on an escalator clause. The trial judge found that there was no enforceable contract. He said that the lack of a price indicated that the parties did not intend the options to be legally enforceable, and, even if they had intended to make such contracts, the court could not fill the gap and write an escalator clause based on the parties' agreement. An intermediate appellate court affirmed, as did the Supreme Court of Pennsylvania. Eleven appellate judges considered the case. Six found that the record supported the trial court's decision that no contract had been formed for the additional ore boats; five dissented and would have reversed. The majority said that a court could not fashion an escalator clause for the transactions covered by the option. It seemed to require that the basis for such a clause be found in the parties' agreement or trade usage. The dissenters thought that the trial court should have fashioned a reasonable option clause not limited to what it could find in the express agreement and trade usage. It was not clear how the dissenters would have the trial court fashion a reasonable escalator clause. Apparently, it was to use its discretion and make its own judgements about what a reasonable clause would provide.

[58] Arthur Okun, *Prices and Quantities: A Macroeconomic Analysis* (Washington DC, Brookings Institution 1981) 89, 134–78.

what he calls 'consumer markets', but his use of the term 'consumer' differs from the way most contracts professors would use it. In an auction market supply and demand affect prices directly, and we often get the benefits of competition. However, in what he calls consumer markets, buyers do not invest what would be needed to find a dependable seller offering the lowest price. Products sold in these markets usually are not standardised. Relying on long-term relationships minimises the costs of shopping and trying out products. Often the seller's reliability is highly valuable to the buyer who will not be able to procure a substitute quickly enough to avoid large losses. Okun concludes that whether the costs outweigh the gains is unclear. Often contract law enforced through the courts could do little to offset the losses a breach might cause. Awarding the increased costs of getting substitute goods elsewhere will not work because either there are no substitutes available or they cannot be made and shipped in time. There may be little, if any, evidence of whether there would have been profits had there been no breach or the dollar amount of those profits.

Finally, it is unclear whether some blend of contract law enforced through courts and informal sanctions for breach creates the trust needed for a market economy. Generally, I agree with Deakin, Lane and Wilkinson that many factors unite to support the trust necessary for people to make plans and take risks. Indeed, if business people think that there is an efficient and effective system of contract law, it would not matter if they were wrong as long as they do not discover the truth through bitter experience. However, I have some reservations about what business people think that the law could do for them if a supplier failed to perform a contract or a buyer failed to pay. A few years ago, I responded to Deakin and his colleagues, saying:

> I suspect that contract law contributes to trust most for those who know the least about it. My guess is that it operates as a vague threat that should be avoided in all but a few situations. As I argued in 1977:
>
> The contract litigation process may also maintain a vague sense of threat that keeps everyone reasonably reliable . . . For this process to operate, it is not necessary that business managers understand contract norms and the realities of the litigation process. Perhaps all that is needed is a sense that breach may entail disagreeable legal problems.[59]

[59] Stewart Macaulay, 'Crime and Custom in Business Society' (1995) 22 *Journal of Law and Society* 248, citing Stewart Macaulay, 'Elegant Models, Empirical Pictures, and the Complexities of Contract' (1977) 11 *Law and Society Review* 508, 518–20. Compare Iris Bohnet, Bruno S Frey and Steffen Huck, 'More Order with Less Law: On Contract

If Deakin, Lane and Wilkinson would define contract to include all of the legal devices that support secured transactions—real estate mortgages, structures that support buying machine tools, jet aircraft, automobiles and other expensive items 'on time' and the like—their position would seem even stronger. Secured transactions are where I think effective law matters most. However, even with this expansion, we must remember that the institution of secured financing also rests on other-than-legal tools such as credit ratings and ways of communicating information, rumours and gossip about the financial health of individuals and corporations.[60] Even here creditors write off a percentage of their loans as uncollectible and sometimes find their security of only marginal value. To some extent, the credit system works because the cost of these bad debts can be included in the overall price for credit.

Daintith suggests that business people in the iron ore industry distinguish written agreements from letters and memoranda. However, what is important to them is the formality itself and not legal enforceability. In other words, a formal written contract can have symbolic power. He explains the attachment to contractual form as follows:

> First, the LTC [long-term contract] facilitates the dealings of buyer and seller with important third parties. It reassures lenders . . . It offers tidy answers to governments anxious for a fair return on their natural resources.
>
> Second, it provides a fairly comprehensive set of parameters for the parties' regular—or irregular—dealings and discussions. If problems arise, say on a matter like quality, the LTC offers a series of elements—price, quantity, shipping, etc—which, at least at the beginning of the negotiation are fixed points of reference . . .
>
> Third, and most important, the LTC creates a privileged trading relationship between the parties, which is of great importance in times of difficult markets, of glut or scarcity, in the sense that it reinforces, by rendering unambiguous, each party's claim to remain in business relations with the

Enforcement, Trust and Crowding' (2001) 95 *American Political Science Review* 131; Arne Bigsten *et al*, 'Contract Flexibility and Dispute Resolution in African Manufacturing' (2000) 36 *Journal of Development Studies* 1.

[60] See Ronald J Mann, 'Information Technology and Non-Legal Sanctions in Financing Transactions' (2000) 98 *Michigan Law Review* 2494.

> other. It thus gives better, but not absolute, security to the trading position of each party.[61]

All in all, I doubt that courts seeking the implicit dimensions of contract would exert much influence on most business persons' assumptions about whether contract law might influence the other party's decisions about performing the bargain. Most business people do not stay up nights reading appellate opinions about contract law. Most of them seldom face contract litigation. A trade publication might tell them something about a case involving an unusual newsworthy situation, but such a story would be read in light of the business person's own experiences. My guess is that only a business person burned by a judicial opinion that 'makes no sense' in his or her own case would lose his or her faith that most contracts will be performed and that contract law might make some contribution at the margin.

The American economy has been successful over the past half century, but we have lived with an uncertain contract law. In America we have gone from classic formalism, with many counter rules such as waiver, to Llewellyn's Article 2 of the Uniform Commercial Code. Article 2, to a great extent, called for 'judging in the grand style' and celebrated Weber's substantive rationality. Conservative judges appointed by President Reagan and like-minded governors have moved us toward a kind of formal rationality.[62] However, formalism always has proved to be unstable, at least in the United States. Our judges and scholars have never been comfortable with certain rules that produce results that are hard to stomach. Moreover, there are enough wild cards in our contract law that any judge who wants to evade a clear formally rational rule in a particular case can rationalise his or her decision with a nicely aged precedent.

[61] Daintith, n 25 above, 187–88. Compare Edward L Rubin, 'The Nonjudicial Life of Contract: Beyond the Shadow of the Law' (1995) 90 *Northwestern University Law Review* 107 ('There is a vast world of commercial relations—of contractual relations—waiting outside the judiciary's narrow chambers . . . [When Grant Gilmore told us that Contract is Dead, he meant] that we must venture forth into that world if we want to avoid the charnel house of intellectual irrelevance.')

[62] Compare Ralph James Moody, 'The New Conceptualism in Contract Law' (1995) 74 *Oregon Law Review* 1131, with Robert A Hillman, 'The "New Conservativism" in Contract Law and the Process of Legal Change' (1999) 40 *Boston College Law Review* 879.

Ronen Shamir[63] has examined Max Weber's arguments about formally rational and substantively rational styles of law in United States history. He sees a never-ending series of cycles:

> [T]he interplay between ideally formal and ideally substantive law corresponds to the interplay between periods of stability and reform in the political arena . . .
>
> Autonomous law is discarded when its internal tensions and inconsistencies can no longer be sustained. But in order to institutionalize and permanently root desired reforms, a reawakening of formal rationality, as a means of ensuring stability, security and predictability, is again called for. In the sphere of the economic market, this means that the same old capitalists may dominate again after such 'radical' changes as, say, the Wagner Labor Relations Act. In the legal sphere, this means that legalistic orientations and strict formal procedures regain their power, albeit under new conditions. It is by invoking Weber's analysis that we may grasp the cycle of *formal rationality—internal contradictions—substantive rationality—substantive rationality—routinization—formal rationality*. Social change and progress appear, when they do, in the form of a spiral ascent: important and radical changes are introduced through substantive rationality; once in place, formal rationality, albeit on a new 'progressive' level, reappears.[64]

One reason for the instability and cyclic movement from formal to substantive rationality and then back again, is the way that we rationalise contract law. Despite almost a century of celebrating an objective theory and hundreds, if not thousands, of cases talking about a duty to read, contract still is supposed to rest on choice. Academic writers can brush aside the phrase 'the meeting of the minds', but courts still mention it constantly because it does express an important rationalisation widely accepted in society for contractual liability. When larger organisations deal with smaller organisations or with consumers, they use contract documents that resemble the statutes of private governments. Often it would be irrational to attempt to read these documents. Usually people ignore them and rely on norms present in relational contracts.[65] These private governments raise the text of the printed

[63] Ronen Shamir, 'Formal and Substantive Rationality in American Law: A Weberian Perspective' (1993) 2 *Social and Legal Studies* 45.

[64] *Ibid*, 63–65.

[65] Macneil observes: '[N]o one can honestly say that consumers *ought* to read long documents of this kind. The many courts which over the years have casually or not so casually said that ignore the fact that if consumers actually did such a foolish thing the modern economy would come to a screeching halt.' Ian R Macneil, 'Bureaucracy and Contracts of Adhesion' (1984) 22 *Osgoode Hall Law Journal* 5, 5–6. Macneil argues that you cannot legitimate holding people to such contracts by either choice or fault. Rather, the legitimacy

form contract only when trouble arises and when means more appropriate to relationships have failed. Whatever the efficiency claims for treating the document as if it had been freely agreed to and a reflection of the party's contract, often the element of choice is just too attenuated for the comfort of a judge writing an opinion. Sometimes, we can suspect, second class choice is accompanied by a contract clause that, as applied to the particular case, just does not seem fair judged completely intuitively. Most of us will not worry about whether the expectations of a lawyer who tried to draft a license for sales people to lie will be defeated if a court seeks the real expectations of the one tricked.

Importantly, this is American legal history. As I have emphasised, despite, or because of, the imprecise and often conflicting nature of our contract law, the American economy has been successful. Those who would argue for a limited judicial role, formal and clear rules and technical predictability can claim only that things might have been even better had we had a very different kind of contract law. Whether a different kind of contract law would have been beneficial is a difficult empirical question. It involves assumptions about when and how the nature of contract doctrine will matter to those who deal in a market economy. However, clearly there is room for a contract law with strong elements of flexibility and qualitative norms in many areas of business. Such a law is not wildly uncertain. As Llewellyn said,

> For the fact is that the work of our appellate courts all over the country is reckonable. It is reckonable first, and on a relative scale, far beyond what any sane man has any business expecting from a machinery devoted to settling disputes self-selected for their toughness. It is reckonable second, and on an absolute scale, quite sufficiently for skilled craftsmen to make usable and valuable judgments about likelihoods, and quite sufficiently to render the handling of an appeal a fitting subject for effective and satisfying craftsmanship.[66]

Yet it is also true that in some situations more formality and relatively clear default rules may be justified. However, we have only begun to look for those areas. One factor pointing in this direction is when parties are represented by lawyers, the document reflects real negotiation

must come from holding people to be bureaucrats in organisations performing consumer functions such as the Ford Motor Company. This way the justification is the same as holding us to many relationships which we enter not knowing the details of what we will be called on to do, such as military service, working for a law firm and marriage.

[66] Llewellyn, n 16 above, 4.

and parties and lawyers worried at the outset about the consequences of failure of performance and disrupting events such as wars, depressions and terrorism. Perhaps paradoxically another area might be consumer transactions where one side almost certainly will not be represented by lawyers. Clear rules here might cut the costs of consumers seeking remedies; consumers can seldom afford to battle about reasonableness and unconscionability when the product in issue cost only a few thousand dollars.[67]

'AND NOW FOR SOMETHING COMPLETELY DIFFERENT': IAN MACNEIL AND RELATIONAL CONTRACT THEORY

If we are concerned about implied contracts and the text between the lines, the new formalists are not the only American scholars whom we should consider. Ian Macneil has, for over 30 years, championed relational contract theory.[68] He contrasts long-term continuing relationships with the discrete transactions often assumed by earlier writers and many common law judges to be the form of all contracts. Empirically, many of us have shown that the continuing relationship is extremely common.[69] Relationships have their own normative systems

[67] See William C Whitford, 'Contract Law and the Control of Standardized Terms in Consumer Contracts: An American Report' (1995) 3 *European Review of Private Law* 193, 203, 207. In some American states, however, consumers can make effective use of small claims courts and various administrative tribunals. Here qualitative standards might help consumers because the decision-making tends to be intuitive. Many American suppliers of consumer goods have attempted to avoid this type of informal dispute resolution by providing for compulsory arbitration in their standard form contracts. Sometimes arbitration is an alternative form of dispute resolution selected in good faith; often, however, it is just a ploy to ward off claims when the manufacturer selects the arbitrator and names a place for arbitration far from most consumers.

[68] See IR Macneil, *The Relational Theory of Contract: Selected Works of Ian Macneil* (2001); David Campbell, 'Ian Macneil and the Relational Theory of Contract' in *ibid*, 3; David Campbell and Donald Harris, 'Flexibility in Long-term Contractual Relationships: The Role of Co-Operation' (1993) 20 *Journal of Law and Society* 166.

[69] See eg Macaulay, n 50 above; Stewart Macaulay, 'Elegant Models, Empirical Pictures, and the Complexities of Contract' (1977) 11 *Law and Society Review* 507; Stewart Macaulay, 'An Empirical View of Contract' [1985] *Wisconsin Law Review* 465; Hugh Beale and Anthony Dugdale, 'Contracts Between Businessmen' (1975) 2 *British Journal of Law and Society* 45; Britt-Mari Blegvad, 'Commercial Relations, Contract, and Litigation in Denmark: A Discussion of Macaulay's Theories' (1990) 24 *Law and Society Review* 397. Daniel Jutras, 'The Legal Dimensions of Everyday Life' (2001) 16

backed in complex ways by sanction systems. Most simply, if parties are to continue the relationship, this may call for many adjustments of rights and duties over time. The risk of losing the relationship usually is a powerful sanction. Insofar as contract law rests on reasonable expectations and reliance, the relational nature of a transaction calls for a different kind of contract law. Such a law would recognise the implicit dimensions of contracts.

Macneil draws an analytic distinction between discrete and relational contracts. Discrete contracts are abstract statements of the total obligation. The parties bring the future to the present and enter a contract that will define their obligations to each other. Context is unimportant. The parties may not have dealt before, and there is no assurance that they will deal again. Relational contracts, typically, are not specific and precise allocations of risk. They involve complex transactions, and often it is hard to determine when they begin and are to end. They are agreements to co-operate to achieve mutually desired goals.

In a well-known passage, Gordon tells us that in relational contracts:

> parties treat their contracts more like marriages than like one-night stands. Obligations grow out of the commitment that they have made to one another, and the conventions that the trading community establishes for such commitments; they are not frozen at the initial moment of commitment, but change as circumstances change; the object of contracting is not primarily to allocate risks, but to signify a commitment to co-operate. In bad times parties are expected to lend one another mutual support, rather than standing on their rights; each will treat the others insistence on literal

Canadian Journal of Law and Society 45, summarises in English, JG Belley, 'Le Contrat entre Droit' (1998) *Économie et Société*, which was published only in French. Jutras says:

> Belley studied ALCAN, and he tells the story of a transformation of the economic culture of corporations, from the traditional culture of relationships of trust, confidence and interdependence to a modern, technocratic culture of quality control and co-ordination, driven by fixed objectives of growth. Previous scholarship had emphasised the importance of implicit norms and personal bonds of trust in long-term commercial contracts. Belley underlines the unresolved tension created in those contracts by the introduction of the depersonalised logic of expert system and explicit parameters of production. Supply contracts at ALCAN are very much explicit, but Belley's research shows that the behaviour of parties in circumstances of uncertainty is guided by unspoken shared assumptions that make up underlying cultures of the contract. There is a plurality of such cultures, which together provide structure and depth to the terms of interaction between ALCAN and its suppliers. Next to the juridical culture of the explicit contract, there is, in particular, an economic cultureof profitability and pragmatism, at once traditional (resting on interpersonal bonds of trust) and modern (resting on the cold technocratic comfort of expert systems). Furthermore, the process of explicit articulation of the terms of co-operation necessarily affects the implicit culture of the relationship.

> performance as willful obstructionism; if unexpected contingencies occur resulting in severe losses, the parties are to search for equitable ways of dividing the losses; and the sanction for egregiously bad behavior, is always, of course, refusal to deal again.[70]

All human exchanges, Macneil asserts, involve norms. Some are internal to the exchange; others are external. Some norms are more appropriate to discrete transactions. For example, implementation of planning and obligations limited to the boundaries of consent fit more discrete deals. Other norms fit relational ones better. Here values such as maintaining the integrity of roles within the relation and maintaining the relationship itself are all important. Furthermore, more complex relationships can call for harmonising the arrangement with the surrounding social matrix. However, Macneil's theory recognises that norms and sanctions can be applied by legal and other-than-legal institutions and organisations. There are costs to imposing norms by formal legal means. Sometimes it makes sense to pay this price; often it does not.

When we turn from theoretical constructs to looking at the world of buying and selling, we discover that matters are not so neat as a spectrum ranging from the discrete to the relational. We can debate whether there are any real world discrete transactions: parties must have some sort of relationship in order to have at least the minimum of trust needed to bargain. Even in close relationships, moreover, parties usually do not leave everything to be worked out as they go. Moreover, sometimes the parties will structure a transaction as if it were a discrete one despite its relational elements. Sometimes the party with greater power wants a relationship based on trust and co-operation but also wants to reserve the power to hold the other to the letter of a written document when it is to its advantage.

What does this mean for law? Several writers have called for a new relationally based system of contract doctrine.[71] Courts would look to

[70] Robert Gordon, 'Macaulay, Macneil, and the Discovery of Solidarity and Power in Contract Law' [1985] *Wisconsin Law Review* 565, 569.

[71] See the debate between Peter Linzer, Steven J Burton and Jonathan Eddy in (1988) *Annual Survey of American Law* 137. Whitford says: 'Macneil believes the legal system needs to take radically different approaches to relational contracts than it traditionally has. In dealing with disputes, he favors greater reliance on procedures oriented toward mediation and less emphasis on adversary processes looking toward adjudication. In regulating contracts, he counsels greater reliance on proactive administrative agencies that can take account of the many third-party interests at stake and less reliance on courts able to apply regulatory rules only when a disadvantaged party initiates a court procedure.' William C

standards based on Macneil's rich classificatory scheme of internal and external contract norms. Feinman suggests that such an approach would look less like typical doctrinal method and more like policy analysis.[72] Other scholars have worried whether courts would be capable of supervising the good faith of those in a relationship, and whether, if courts tried to do this, it would create major problems for those trying to plan what risks to assume and which to avoid. Trebilcock, for example, argues that Macneil's relational approach cannot 'yield determinate legal principles' because it 'entails a highly amorphous sociological inquiry that seems well beyond the competence of courts in case-by-case adjudication.'[73] The key phrase in Trebilcock's criticism is 'determinate legal principles'. Macneil's writings raise the question whether a court could deal with a highly relational contract by using determinate legal principles. However, Macneil would accept that in some situations courts should treat what are in fact relational transactions *as if* they were discrete. When such a fiction is appropriate, determinate legal principles might be appropriate. The hard part, as I have said, is deciding when courts should honour the work of a corporate lawyer which she has labelled 'contract' when there is only second class consent, if that.

Would a relational approach be 'well beyond the competence of courts in case-by-case adjudication?' If we think that any trial in an adversary system is more than a comforting ritual, we might ask why the principles of relational contract theory are any more difficult or amorphous than, for example, deciding whether to impose the death penalty or to remedy Microsoft's violation of the antitrust laws by breaking up the corporation. This is not to deny that flexible approaches often present daunting problems for lawyers and judges. There is a capability problem, and high cost barriers stand before putting on a case to be judged by standards such as reasonableness. Yet there is no reason to presume that courts will always get it wrong, apart from one's faith in an anti-government ideology.

Whitford, 'Ian Macneil's Contribution to Contracts Scholarship' [1985] *Wisconsin Law Review* 545, 551.

[72] Jay M Feinman, 'Relational Contract Theory in Context' (2000) 94 *Northwestern University Law Review* 737.

[73] Michael J Trebilcock, *The Limits of Freedom of Contract* (Cambridge, Mass., Harvard University Press 1994) 141–42.

A Limited Trace of Optimism: The Real Deal Resting on Relational Norms Can be Supported by Courts Inducing Settlements Rather than Announcing Judgments.

Perhaps we should not conclude too quickly that the moral of my story is damned if you do and damned if you don't. While there is more to law than just legal rules, doctrine can matter. I applaud the efforts of those attempting to give us better conceptual tools. We will, however, do better if we attempt to fashion doctrines more or less suited for specific types of contracts rather than trying to fabricate one grand contract law. Nonetheless, doctrine rests on assumptions about the society and its proper organisation. Brownsword tells us:

> There are two plausible ethics for contract law, individualism and cooperativism. . . . It is not easy for contract doctrine (whether through notions of good faith, unconscionability, reasonableness, loyalty, legitimate expectation, or whatever) to hold strictly to either of these ethics in their most robust form. Doctrinal adherence to individualism will often seem out of touch with business practice (where compromise, adjustment, and partnering and the like govern dealings); but, equally, doctrinal adherence to cooperativism can put too great a strain on the idea of a common enterprise (at any rate, in the sense of an identity of interest).[74]

But Americans always want to have their cake and eat it too: We want both individualism and co-operativism at the same time. We bounce back and forth through cycles where we emphasise one and then the other. Yet it is a question of emphasis: words rationalising individualism are still there when our legal culture accepts more co-operativism. The one safe statement about American contract law in action is that it is messy.

In some situations, there is no reason to think that courts will not be able to do as well in a contract case as they do in any other type of case. If we impose duties of co-operation or tell a court to give a remedy 'if injustice can be avoided only by enforcement of the promise',[75] our legal system often will reach at least acceptable results. Assuming that cost barriers permit, lawyers may be able to show judges what would be fair in a particular commercial context. The judges and the lawyers involved might never define 'fair' in a precise fashion that would satisfy

[74] Roger Brownsword, 'Individualism, Co-operativism and an Ethic for European Contract Law' (2001) 64 *Modern Law Review* 628, 630.

[75] Contracts scholars will recognise that the quoted phrase is a key passage in the American Restatement (2d) Contracts §90.

a critic or offer answers to judges and lawyers in future cases. Nonetheless, all involved might accept that the results seemed to fall within an intuited zone of fairness. This process, however, might be very costly because it could require an exploration of the full commercial context. Of course, there is a risk that the judges might get it wrong, and cost barriers to proving the full context of a transaction would likely increase that risk. However, there is no reason to presume that the process always will be unduly costly or judges will always get it wrong. Perhaps if we conclude that there is a problem in a type of case such as those involving consumers, we should advocate flat rules for those kinds of situations.

We can consider an example both of what can be done and some of the limitations. An Ohio trial court filled substantial gaps in a long-term contract in *Oglebay Norton Co v Armco Inc*.[76] The firms had close long-term continuing relations: Oglebay Norton ran iron ore boats on the Great Lakes, and it managed the Eveleth iron ore mining operation in Minnesota. Armco was a major steel producer, and it owned one third of the Eveleth operation. Armco had a seat on Oglebay Norton's board of directors. In 1957, the firms entered a contract that required Oglebay to have adequate shipping capacity available for Armco. Armco was to use this shipping capacity if Armco wished to transport iron ore from mines in the Lake Superior district to Armco's plants in the lower Great Lakes region. Armco was to pay 'the regular net contract rates for the season as recognized by the leading iron ore shippers in such season.' If there were no such regular net contract rate,

> the parties shall mutually agree upon a rate for such transportation, taking into consideration the contract rate being charged for similar transportation by the leading independent vessel operators engaged in the transportation of iron ore from the Lake Superior District.

During the next 23 years, the parties modified the contract four times. They continued to extend its duration until it finally ran until 2010. In 1980, they agreed that Oglebay Norton would upgrade its fleet to give self-unloading capability to each vessel used to haul Armco ore. To help pay for this large capital investment, Armco agreed to pay an additional 25 cents per ton shipped in the self-unloading vessels. From 1957 to 1983, Oglebay Norton based the price charged to Armco on the rate published in *Skillings Mining Review*, a trade journal that gathered this information. In 1983, Armco, as was true of all American steel producers, had

[76] 52 Ohio St.3d 232, 556 N.E.2d 515 (1990).

suffered heavy losses because of competition from foreign steel mills. The *Wall Street Journal* reported that 'Armco had a $295 million loss in 1983, bringing total losses for the last three years to about $1.3 billion.'[77] Armco negotiated lower rates from Oglebay Norton for 1983. The parties, however, were unable to negotiate a rate for 1984 and 1985. Oglebay Norton billed Armco for ore shipped, but Armco rejected this bill and paid much less than Oglebay had demanded. To further complicate matters, after 1985, *Skillings Mining Review* no longer published rates for shipping iron ore on the Great Lakes.

In 1986, Oglebay Norton sued for a declaratory judgment. 'After a lengthy bench trial,' the trial court made findings of fact and law. It found that the parties had intended to make a binding contract although the shipping rates were not settled. In such a case, the rate is a reasonable price. The court found a rate for the 1987 season. To do this, it listened to the testimony of a person who was an economic and financial expert about freight rates on the Great Lakes. It had data about what Armco had paid in the past few years, and information about the rates that Oglebay Norton had quoted as the price for carrying Armco ore. It had evidence of what one of Armco's competitors had paid. The trial court selected a rate that fell within the range of rates in evidence. Finally, the trial court ordered the parties to negotiate rates during the rest of the life of the contract. If they could not reach agreement, the parties were ordered to ask the court to appoint a mediator and to co-operate in mediation. The Supreme Court of Ohio affirmed this decision.

We can notice several things about the *Oglebay Norton* case. The reasonable rate was not a thing that existed in the world that could be just picked up and plugged into the contract. The trial court had to exercise judgement and create the rate based on information in the record. We do not know anything about the expert who testified at trial. How did he know what was being charged for Great Lakes shipping of this cargo? In 1996, a magazine story pointed out that there was not much competition among shipping companies because the steel companies owned their own fleets or were closely associated with particular operators of ore boats. The story commented:

> Rates in the laker trade are difficult to get ahold of. Published rates are nothing more than a starting point, and with such an incestuous relationship between shippers and carriers, no one talks about what they actually pay.[78]

[77] *Wall Street Journal* 28 March 1985.

[78] Paul F Conlye, 'A Long Season Ends for Great Lakes Fleet' *Journal of Commerce* 29 February 1996, 18.

Oglebay Norton tried to subpoena information about rates from independent vessel operators and captive fleets, but the trial court quashed these subpoenas before trial because Oglebay had no right to this proprietary information. Thus, the court had to use its judgement without precise information when it established a rate. Nonetheless, there is no reason to think that there was anything drastically wrong with the price that the court set.

American contracts scholars might find the order to negotiate and then mediate future freight rates surprising. The contract had about 22 more years to run, and the court sought to support the relationship as best it could. If we assume that the relationship would continue more or less as it had in the past, the court's approach seems reasonable. Oglebay Norton, after all, had invested in self-unloading ore boats at Armco's request. The contract had not been in effect long enough after this major investment so that the extra payment per ton of iron ore would have covered this expense. The mediator could have reinforced a duty to negotiate in good faith.

We do not know how well this structure worked. We know that the parties continued a business relationship at least until 1995, because Oglebay Norton's Annual Report for that year stated that it had supplied advanced technology for Armco's new continuous casting mill. However, all the effort of the Ohio courts probably failed to keep the Great Lakes shipping relationship alive in anything like its former state. Throughout the 1980s, the American steel industry faced great financial difficulty. In 1989, Armco sold much of its carbon steel making capacity to a joint venture it formed with a Japanese steel company. We can suspect that Armco had fewer, if any, requirements for hauling ore on the Great Lakes. Armco focused on making stainless steel:

> Armco buys domestic steel and limited amounts of imported steel—including Japanese steel—to convert into pipe and tube at its downstream plants. Armco used to make the steel itself but now makes exclusively specialty steels. . . .[79]

In 1992, Armco bought about two thirds of its now reduced requirements of ore from the Eveleth facility managed by Oglebay, but it bought the rest at a much cheaper price from Brazil. The Brazilian ore was shipped on barges up the Mississippi River to the Ohio River and

[79] Thomas W Gerdel, 'Oglebay Norton Lays Off 140 at Ore Mine' *Cleveland Plain Dealer* 11 December 1992, E-1.

then to Armco's plants. This ore did not come under the contract with Oglebay Norton.

Instead of having to negotiate a price, with any disputes subject to mediation, it seems likely that Armco changed its way of doing business so that it needed much less, if any, ore hauled from mines in the Lake Superior region on the Great Lakes. When issued, the court's order to negotiate and mediate seemed reasonable enough. After just a few years, the changes at Armco seemed to have meant that Armco no longer had as many requirements for carrying ore on the Great Lakes. But this was a risk that Oglebay Norton assumed when it made a requirements contract. If our speculation is right, the court's order made sense as long as a requirements contract made sense. The court could not change the decline of the American steel industry.

Macneil has pointed out that there are situations where it is in the interest of the parties, and even perhaps of the economy as a whole, where the law should treat parties *as if* their relationship was discrete and entirely contained within the borders of a written document. The task is to identify such situations. One approach is to submit such documents to a regulatory agency for approval, such as is often done with insurance policies. This seems to be a sensible solution as long as we are confident that the regulatory agency will not be captured by trade associations that make campaign contributions. We have long distinguished consumer transactions from those between merchants. Yet even this leaves me uneasy; it seems too crude. Some transactions between businesses have many elements of a consumer transaction. Often a franchise agreement is one-sided and written by the more powerful party. Often these agreements or amendments to them are hard to read and understand. Perhaps courts can approach documents such as franchises as if the relationships involved were discrete. They may be able to do this because those involved can gain legislation that calls for a more relational approach to the legal rights of the parties. Courts can avoid the difficulties involved in a relational approach unless a legislature determines that it is worth the costs of attempting to reinforce the norms of co-operation. Yet, here too, we would be more comfortable if we had more faith in our American legislatures as something other than places where law is sold to the highest bidder.[80]

[80] Special interest pressure has even moved from the public legislative arena to the National Conference of Commissioners on Uniform Laws, the group that proposes revisions to the Uniform Commercial Code. See Richard E Speidel, 'Introduction to Symposium on Proposed Revised Article 2' (2001) 54 *Southern Methodist University Law*

Whatever our success in identifying places for treating relationships as if they were discrete, we must remember that it is not just a question of legal doctrine. Doctrine does not have little legs so that it can hop down from law books and enforce itself. Doctrine is delivered in an extremely expensive system for which someone must pay. Often the reason that a transaction broke down is that one side lost the ability to perform because it ran out of money. A claim in bankruptcy often is not worth the effort. Even when there is little risk of bankruptcy, suing someone usually destroys relationships and invites retaliation.

We might be happier if we took a lawyer's perspective and saw the game as one involving acceptable, if not ideal, settlements. While not all cases can be nor should be settled, more often than not the 'least bad' solution is a compromise fashioned in light of the situation facing the parties at the time of the dispute. Many, if not most, settlements fall beneath the radar screen of contract scholars. Publishers do not deliver reports of these cases to our door or to our computer. The parties often want their settlement to be secret. However, parties do invoke the legal system as part of a strategy to produce settlements. When co-operative approaches fail, letters can be written on an attorney's letterhead in order to make an implicit threat. Complaints may be filed in court, and negotiations may be commenced if summary judgment is not granted. Sometimes, however, cases involving large sums of money may proceed far down the path to a final judgment affirmed on appeal and still be settled. Furthermore, sometimes the settlement provokes the parties to resume their relationship, although often with a modified balance of power. This may be a way, if not the most common way, that the ideas of relational contract are implemented in the American legal system.

What appears to be a final judgment at the trial level may be only a step toward settlement. The judgment may affect the balance of power between the parties, but often it will not take effect as written. For example, the judge in *Aluminum Corporation of America v Essex Group Inc*,[81] rewrote an escalator clause to express what he saw as the actual risk distribution between the parties. This was an implicit dimension of this relationship. The opinion was highly controversial, but none of the academic writing about it considered the final outcome

Review 787; Richard E Speidel, 'Revising UCC Article 2: A View from the Trenches' (2001) 52 *Hastings Law Review* 607; Alan Schwartz and Robert E Scott, 'The Political Economy of Private Legislatures' (1995) 143 *University of Pennsylvania Law Review* 595.

[81] 499 F. Supp. 53 (WDPa 1980).

of the case. ALCOA and Essex entered a toll conversion contract in 1967 that was to run until 1983. In form, this was a services rather than a sales contract. ALCOA would convert Essex's ore into molten aluminum, and Essex would receive it in this form. Essex made the contract when it decided to expand its manufacturing of aluminum wire products. The court said:

> The long term supply of aluminum was important to assure Essex of the steady use of its expensive machinery. A steady production stream was vital to preserve the market position it sought to establish. The favorable price was important to allow Essex to compete with firms like ALCOA which produced aluminum and manufactured aluminum wire products in an efficient, integrated operation.[82]

ALCOA had drafted an escalator clause to set the price for the aluminum that it processed. The escalator was tied in part to the federal government's Wholesale Price Index-Industrial Commodities. The WPI-IC failed to reflect an unexpected rapid increase in the cost of electric power. 'Electric power is the principal non-labor cost factor in aluminum conversion, and the electric power rates rose much more rapidly than did the WPI-IC.'[83] Moreover, there was a sharp increase in the demand for aluminum. Essex did not use the material delivered by ALCOA in the manufacture of wire products. Instead, it resold millions of pounds on the market. In June of 1979, the cost to Essex of the ALCOA product was 36.35 cents per pound, but Essex was reselling on the market at more than 73 cents per pound.

The court found that ALCOA was excused from performing the contract under the doctrines of mutual mistake, impossibility and frustration. The court decided that while ALCOA necessarily had taken some risk in entering the contract which it thought that it had covered by its escalator clause, the actual result was not within the zone of risk that it had assumed. The escalator did not serve to create a price that would give ALCOA 'the minimum return of one cent per pound which the parties had contemplated.'[84] However, the court thought it unfair to excuse ALCOA entirely from its obligations under the contract. It said:

> To decree rescission in this case would be to grant ALCOA a windfall gain in the current aluminum market. It would at the same time deprive Essex of

[82] 499 F. Supp. 53 (WDPa 1980), at 58.
[83] *Ibid.*
[84] *Ibid*, 66.

> the assured long term aluminum supply which it obtained under the contract and of the gains it legitimately may enforce within the scope of the risk ALCOA bears under the contract.[85]

The court decided that the contract price would be the smallest produced by one of three ways of computing it, including the original formula found in the written document. Importantly, one method was 'the price which yields ALCOA a profit of one cent per pound of aluminum converted.' Unless the price of aluminum fell significantly, the judge had transformed the agreement into a cost plus a percentage of profit contract. However, ALCOA was not freed of all obligations under the contract. Also, Essex could not continue to resell its aluminum to other users of the product at the market price while paying only the very low contract price.

For my purposes, the important thing to notice is that the judge's formula was never put into effect. The parties settled after Essex appealed and the appellate court had heard oral argument. As part of the settlement, the original contract remained in effect until 31 December 1981. It was extended for five years beyond the end of 1981. During the balance of time remaining from the date of the settlement to the new termination date, ALCOA would sell to Essex at a favourable price, but not one as favourable as Essex enjoyed through 1981. We can see the ultimate resolution of the dispute as very relational. The parties continued their relationship and provided for a transition bringing it to an end. Essex, to a large extent but not entirely, had to stay in its role under the original allocation of risks. It was buying aluminum in order to make aluminum wire products. It was not entitled to act as a middleman, capturing the gains from low cost sheets of aluminum which it could sell on the market. Essex had some duty to pay attention to ALCOA's interests. Rather than maximising its own return, the implicit dimension of the relationship required Essex to co-operate to accommodate their mutual interests.

What was the contribution of Judge Teitlebaum in achieving such a relational end? Essentially, he acted as a mixture of mediator and arbitrator. He found what he saw as a fair solution on the basis of the facts presented to him. When mediators offer their solutions to a problem, often it triggers successful negotiations. The mediator's solution is where the bargaining begins, and it may be very useful to the parties who are constrained by negotiation tactics. However, Judge

[85] *Ibid*, 84.

Teitlebaum's solution was more than just a suggestion. It would take effect unless the parties found a better one. Of course, Judge Teitlebaum's revised escalator clause might not take effect if Essex were able to persuade an appellate court to overturn it. ALCOA had won a victory, but it rested on an opinion that certainly pushed the envelope. If the appellate court were staffed by judges who had faith in classic contract law, ALCOA could lose. Yet Essex could not be sure that it could get Judge Teitlebaum's revisions overturned, and it faced both delay in resolving the matter and the costs of the appellate process. It might appeal, wait, and invest a great deal in lawyers' fees, only to have Judge Teitlebaum's opinion affirmed. It was even possible that the appellate court would have reversed the trial court but written an opinion that would make Essex worse off than the Teitlebaum escalator clause.

Did Judge Teitlebaum reach a good solution? Our appraisal must turn on our judgement as to whether ALCOA took the risk in this contract of having Essex go into competition with ALCOA in the general market for sheets of aluminum. If we see the contract in substance as one calling for ALCOA to supply Essex's requirements of the raw material needed to manufacture aluminum wire products with its expensive machinery, the implied dimension of this contract seems clear enough. It is hard to see why ALCOA should be burdened with the risk of supplying Essex with ridiculously low priced aluminum which Essex could sell in competition with ALCOA's own sales in that market. While Judge Teitlebaum may have been mistaken in the formula that he imposed on the parties, they were not stuck with it. They were able to fashion one that they thought would better their situation.[86]

[86] Attempts to rework the obligations of parties in a complex relationship can burden courts and litigants. For example, in *BP Exploration Co v Hunt*, [1979] 1 WLR 783, aff'd [1982] 1 All ER 925, the court dealt with a qualitative statute that gave little more direction than calling for compensation for benefits conferred and allowing retention of some or all of a down payment if the court 'considers it just to do so having regard to all the circumstances of the case.' See the Law Reform (Frustrated Contracts) Act 1943 (6 & 7 Geo. 6, c. 40). The case involved a complex transaction in the oil industry. Nelson Bunker Hunt owned a concession in Libya. BP Exploration agreed to develop the concession, and the two were to share equally the oil produced. Hunt was to pay for his share of the development costs from his share of the oil produced. The concession was expropriated, and the court had to consider offsetting claims.

Justice Goff wrote a 67-page opinion. He noted there:

> [I]n addition to difficult and novel questions of law, the case involves substantial questions of fact and of accounting procedure. The sums involved are enormous; BP's claim was advanced in a number of alternative ways, the sum claimed varying from

The next two examples involve Westinghouse's attempt to become the dominant corporation in supplying nuclear power plants. We have to put ourselves back to those wonderful days when the peaceful atom was going to supply endless clean power. However, fossil fuels were cheap, and nuclear power plants were expensive. Westinghouse had to convince reluctant utility executives to invest in what was being sold as cutting edge technology. In the first group of cases, Westinghouse sweetened the deal to sell reactors by promises to supply fuel at a fixed price which was far above the market when they made the contracts. The utility executives felt comfortable because the fuel could never cost more than the price fixed in the contract, but it was likely to cost a great deal less. An international cartel formed to fix uranium prices, and it succeeded for a time. Now Westinghouse was being called on to supply fuel at extremely high prices. The newspapers of the time said that Westinghouse simply could not buy all the fuel it had promise to supply at the cartel price. Westinghouse notified its utility customers that it would not supply the fuel, but it claimed to be excused under the Uniform Commercial Code's impossibility provision. Section 2–615(1) grants an excuse 'if performance as agreed has been made impracticable by the occurrence of a contingency the non-occurrence of which

nearly$45,000,000 to nearly $230,000,000. Furthermore, allegations made by Mr Hunt related to the manner in which BP developed the oil field led to an investigation of almost the entire history of the exploration, appraisal, and development of the field, and the production of oil from the field. This investigation required a substantial body of evidence, much of it technical; and the documents before the court, which were very largely concerned with these allegations by Mr Hunt were very numerous—I was told that there were over 15,000 documents in court. Many of these were of a technical nature; and in any event they represented only the tip of the iceberg of documents disclosed on discovery. Only by reason of the good sense and restraint shown by counsel on both sides, and the efficiency of their instructing solicitors, was it possible for a so substantial piece of litigation to be kept under control and for the hearing to take no longer than 57 days.

After this elaborate procedure, and without much explanation, the judge accepted BP's claim that half the benefit was attributable to its actions and half to Hunt's. This served to make the final judgment something of a rough split-the-difference compromise. Donald Harris, David Campbell and Roger Halson, *Remedies in Contract and Tort* 2nd edn (London, Butterworth, 2002) 246–54, are, 'with greatest respect,' very critical of this decision. They judge it 'thoroughly painstaking but . . . undeniably unsatisfactory . . .' Perhaps the only way to defend the process and the result is to notice that Nelson Bunker Hunt is a Texas oil man. While more conventional wealthy people might have worked out a settlement with BP Oil, only a 'shoot-out at the okay corral' would satisfy him. The process can be viewed as an elaborate social ritual for the privileged. It is highly unlikely that any American federal court would have invested this amount of time and effort in any contract case today.

was a basic assumption on which the contract was made . . .'[87] The cases were consolidated before United States District Judge Robert Merhige, Jr. Judge Merhige was known as a settling judge who wanted the parties to solve the problems rather than litigate. The day the trial opened, he told the many lawyers assembled in his courtroom, 'I don't ever expect to finish these cases. . . . I expect [them] to get settled.'[88]

Judge Merhige's biographer[89] tells us:

> In an attempt to facilitate settlement discussions, Merhige and his wife hosted cocktail parties in their home for the lawyers *and* the corporate executives. It may not have been a crucial factor, but the social contact did facilitate discussions in a context other than confrontational litigation. Westinghouse Chairman Robert E. Kirby finally agreed to become involved in the negotiations and made personal contact with the chief executive officer of each utility. The jawboning paid some immediate benefits when six of the thirteen utility companies reached a settlement with Westinghouse before the conclusion of the trial. The other utilities, however, remained adamant . . .
>
> Utilizing his expertise in alternative dispute resolution, Merhige offered each party a carrot and a stick. The utilities received an important bargaining chip with Merhige's recognition that Westinghouse was subject to some liability. By warning the utilities that they would not receive the full damages they sought, Merhige significantly strengthened Westinghouse's bargaining position. . . . He increased the pressure on the parties to negotiate by announcing that the court would meet and confer with counsel in an effort to assist them in reaching an agreement . . .
>
> Merhige once again increased the pressure to compromise by escalating the length and frequency of the negotiation conferences. Out-of-town lawyers were astonished when the judge insisted that they come to court on weekends, early mornings and late evenings. At one point, Merhige threat-

[87] The Official Comment is perplexing. On the one hand, it tells us: 'a rise or a collapse in the market [is not] in itself a justification [for not performing], for that is exactly the type of business risk which business contracts made at fixed prices are intended to cover.' This would seem to favour the utility buyers. On the other hand, the Comment continues: 'But a severe shortage of raw materials or of supplies due to a contingency such as war, embargo, local crop failure, unforeseen shutdown of major sources of supply or the like, which either causes a marked increase in cost or altogether prevents the seller from securing supplies necessary to his performance, is within the contemplation of this section.' Obviously, Westinghouse liked this last part but wanted to downplay the first.

[88] Pappas, 'Westinghouse, Utilities Under Pressure to Settle Uranium Suit Before Court Does' *Wall Street Journal*, 2 June 1978, 32.

[89] Ronald J Bacigal, *May It Please the Court: A Biography of Judge Robert R Merhige, Jr.* (Lanham, Maryland, University Press of America, 1992).

ened to have counsel work on 'Saturdays, Sundays, and some days that aren't even on the calendar'. . .

Lewis Booker, liaison counsel for the utilities . . . said that Judge Merhige was very astute in recognizing that the parties and the experts could negotiate on matters that a judicial verdict could not cover. For example, the utilities could agree to accept a turbine generator in lieu of damages, but Merhige would have been powerless to order that. His verdict would necessarily have been limited to computing dollar damages. . . .[90]

Judge Merhige appointed a law school dean as a special master to assist the parties in reaching an adjustment of the respective claims. Merhige required the parties to file proposals for settlement. In most cases, the settlements reached did not require Westinghouse just to pay cash to its customers as damages. Rather, the settlements involved a combination of cash and services. Often Westinghouse agreed to provide services maintaining the nuclear reactors and supply replacement parts at a deeply discounted rate. In the Texas Utilities Services Inc case, the settlement was contained in a 350 page agreement. It was estimated to be worth $80 million to the utility, but the out of pocket cost to Westinghouse was only $27 million. Westinghouse assigned some of its claims against the uranium cartel to its customers as another way of sharing potential gains and losses. Most of the settlements reinforced the relationships between Westinghouse and its customers who had a Westinghouse nuclear reactor to run for many years.

Again observers who knew something about nuclear energy thought that Westinghouse had settled all of the utilities cases for about half of what they had claimed.[91] Stewart reports: '[i]f Westinghouse and the utilities had simply split their differences in 1975, before resorting to litigation, the result would have been about the same.'[92] However, the parties could not have done this without going through something like the process that took place in and out of Judge Merhige's courtroom. Many utilities were hesitant to settle without establishing that they had given nothing away. At the time of this litigation, these power companies were regulated, and a regulatory commission would have to be satisfied with the settlement. Moreover, some of Westinghouse's customers hesitated to settle early in the process because they did not want utilities that negotiated later to get larger amounts and make the

90 *Ibid*, 145, 146–47.

91 See James B Stewart, *The Partners: Inside America's Most Powerful Law Firms* (New York, Warner Books, 1983) 153.

92 *Ibid*, 198.

pioneers look as if they had sold out too cheaply. The law school dean was able to help manage the work with the large group of buyers and keep the pressure on both sides to solve the problem. The dean was a mediator who always had the power of the trial judge as a potential sanction.

The settlements at least attempted to further the interests of both seller and buyers. Westinghouse managed to avoid the crushing liability that a literal application of its many contracts with customers would have imposed. Yet Westinghouse was able to keep alive relationships that might prove to be profitable. The utilities kept alive the relationship so that there would be someone who could service and maintain the reactors. We cannot be sure, but it seems that this outcome was better than the utilities could have gained had they been able to win judgments enforcing their contract rights. It is likely that all this would have done was force Westinghouse into bankruptcy, and as unsecured creditors the utilities would not have done well in such a proceeding. The liaison counsel for the utilities told Judge Merhige's biographer:

> The overall feeling by everyone was that justice had really been done. The utilities got what they needed to continue operations, while Westinghouse was able to avoid bankruptcy, keep its plants running and its people employed . . .[93]

In the next example, Westinghouse closed its deal with Florida Power and Light Company by offering another sweetener in the negotiations that ultimately provoked litigation.[94] Westinghouse promised to remove the spent rods of uranium from FP&L's holding ponds into which the rods were placed. Westinghouse had planned to recycle these rods, but no commercial recycling was available in the United States. The United States Government represented that such reprocessing would be available, but it never brought this about. Once again, the case was tried by Judge Merhige. This time he issued a decision holding that Westinghouse was not excused under Section 2–615(1) of the

[93] Bacigal, n 89 above, 148. See also Campbell and Harris, n 68 above, 172: 'Once freed from the panic of the oil crisis and the competitive suspicion and hostility into which the mutually destructive idea of holding Westinghouse to its contracts or of Westinghouse abandoning its buyers led, a sensible co-operative adjustment to the changed circumstances took place.'

[94] See *Florida Power and Light Co v Westinghouse Electric Corp* 517 F. Supp. 440 (E. D. Va. 1981).

UCC. FP&L had asked for a decree of specific performance ordering Westinghouse to remove the rods. Judge Merhige said:

> [W]hile the court is fully cognizant of the difficulty of fashioning a sufficiently specific decree should the parties be unable to reach agreement, and should the Court conclude that specific enforcement is appropriate considering various other factors, the Court believes that, with the assistance of the parties, a workable and appropriate decree would be achieved.[95]

The judge then granted the parties 90 days in which to attempt to agree on a settlement. The parties were directed to select experts to aid the court. The judge said: 'both parties are urged to use the initial time period in an intensive attempt to reach agreement rather than in preparing to further litigate the issue of remedy.'[96]

The parties failed to reach agreement.[97] Nonetheless, they had appointed a committee of nuclear engineers who studied the situation. These engineers determined that it was possible to rerack the nuclear facility's holding ponds. As a result, all the rods that would be produced during the designed life of the plant could be stored there. The reactors would not have to shut down when the ponds were full. FP&L would not have to buy power to substitute for that generated by this plant. Westinghouse agreed to do the reracking at no cost to FP&L. Judge Merhige decided that there should be an equitable allocation of the interim costs of storing the spent rods. After the dispute arose, Congress had passed a statute that called for the construction of a permanent storage facility for all nuclear waste. While then it looked as if the problem might be solved after the litigation ended, Americans are still battling about what to do with nuclear waste. Judge Merhige also allocated the other costs. He took into account that while utility customers elsewhere had paid high rates for electricity produced by fossil fuels, FP&L's customers had not. His allocation was roughly an equal division of various costs.[98]

[95] *Ibid*, 461.

[96] *Ibid*, 462.

[97] See *Florida Power and Light Co* v *Westinghouse Electric Co* 597 F. Supp. 1456 (E.D. Va. 1984).

[98] Judge Merhige's opinion resolving Westinghouse's liability was reversed in *Florida Power and Light Co* v *Westinghouse Electric Corp*, 826 F.2d 239 (4th Cir. 1987). However, because of the way the parties appealed the case, much of Judge Merhige's compromise settlement remained in place. The process served to provoke discovery of the engineering solution—reracking the cooling ponds—to the major problem in the case.

Again, we see something of a relational approach to the problems. By convening a panel of engineers, the judge managed to produce a technical solution to a major part of the contract problem. The final result reinforced the continuation of the relationship. The decision required both sides to co-operate in the future.

Which approach is better? Will we get more and better settlements if trial judges rewrite contract clauses that might or might not be overturned on appeal? Will we get more and better settlements if a judge takes over negotiations and presses the parties to work out a deal? The answer again is not clear. My guess is that sometimes one will work best, but other times a different approach is called for. One important factor in the first of the disputes about Westinghouse's contracts was the large number of parties who faced governmental regulation. For many reasons, no utility wanted to get a settlement that was clearly less favourable than those gained by other utilities in similar positions. Judge Merhige's control over the entire process may have co-ordinated matters so that no settlement would appear very much better than the others. There were only two large corporations involved in the ALCOA case, and so Judge Teitlebaum was free to issue an opinion and leave it to the parties to accept it, appeal, settle or settle after the appellate process suggested that each side had to worry about the appellate court writing an opinion that one of the parties might not like as well as Judge Teitlebaum's revised escalator clause.

Can we rely on settlement negotiations to provoke relational sanctions to all contracts problems? Clearly not.[99] As Galanter and Cahill note:

> Settlement is not intrinsically good or bad, anymore than adjudication is good or bad. Settlements do not share any generic traits that commend us to avoid them per se or to promote them. This does not mean that some settlements are not preferable to some adjudications—and to other settlements . . . [T]here is, we would suppose, great variation in the quality of settlements from one disputing arena to another and within such arenas.[100]

[99] Consumer protection almost certainly requires a different approach. It is my impression that the United Kingdom is well ahead of all but a few American states. See Susan Bright, 'Winning the Battle Against Unfair Contract Terms' (2000) 20 *Legal Studies* 331; Meryll Dean, 'Unfair Contract Terms: The European Approach' (1993) 56 *Modern Law Review* 581 (1993).

[100] Marc Galanter and Mia Cahill, '"Most Cases Settle": Judicial Promotion and Regulation of Settlements' (1994) 46 *Stanford Law Review* 1339, 1388.

Often efforts at settlement cannot begin until the summary judgment hurdle has been cleared. American conditions and culture allow one party before summary judgment motions have been decided to run up the costs of litigation in order to discourage the other. Settlement should be easier when both parties are wealthy, so that one party will not have an incentive to try to induce the other to quit the litigation because of continuing court costs.

Sometimes litigation is a pure salvage operation. The parties are not interested in continuing their relationship. Settlement then becomes a question of costs and benefits. By settling, the parties reduce or eliminate uncertainty and contain costs. Things are in their control rather than in the control of judges and jurors. It may make more sense to litigate and take one's chances that any judgment recovered could be satisfied. Having conceded this, still we cannot forget that settlements also can produce compromises that keep relationships alive. The effort to settle can force the parties to co-operate and seek common interests.

We should notice how similar this coercive mediation approach is to what takes place in bankruptcy in the United States. To a great extent, in bankruptcy the parties are pushed to accept some sort of compromise to remedy the debtor's inability to perform many contracts. We get little predictability if we move from contract to bankruptcy, and the original contract controls then only if one party took a secured interest in the right form and recorded it. Those who write about contracts often fail to consider this remedy—bankruptcy—for multiple breaches of contract. Yet the most formal approach to relational contracts will have limited impact if firms facing difficulty often use bankruptcy. Any theory about the role of contract law must include the functions of bankruptcy or it will be seriously incomplete.

Dean Scott clearly recognises that most cases are settled, but he argues that clear rules will provoke more settlements. He argues that categorical binary contract rules may be effective complements to the more flexible extra legal mechanisms that regulate adjustment of ongoing relationships.[101] My colleague William Whitford has offered several propositions about relational contracts.[102] Whitford says:

> —As contracts become more relational, the parties will comply less frequently with formalities (including the parol evidence rule). Hence, a strict

[101] Robert E Scott, 'Conflict and Cooperation in Long-Term Contracts' (1987) 75 *California Law Review* 2005.

[102] William C Whitford, Unpublished Memorandum.

> enforcement strategy with respect to formalities is more likely to raise issues about protection of reasonable reliance with respect to relational than discrete contracts.
>
> —As contracts become more relational, it becomes more difficult for courts to apply sensibly doctrine that requires courts to make qualitative judgments about a course of conduct. Courts lack the capacity to understand complex relations between all the affected parties.
>
> —As contracts become more relational, there is an increasing tendency of the parties to value non-material aspects of the relation (continuation of the relation, maintenance of harmony and respect, etc.). Courts have no effective way to protect these expectations, and hence they tend to over commodify the relation—that is, they try to compensate in money for that which is really not commensable this way.

What do Whitford's hypotheses mean for settlement? Dean Scott suggests that legally imposed adjustments may create perverse incentives that undermine the stability of the co-operative equilibrium of contracting parties.[103] When stakes are large, the chance that a court may rework the distribution of risk in a contract may be enough to offset possible future rewards for co-operative behaviour. Even the threat of going to court to seek relief may affect how the parties readjust matters. Scott concedes that we do not know how judicial activity affects decisions about co-operation and readjustment. He concludes:

> [T]he relational context is a complex environment of many regulatory systems, including individualized and patterned responses, legal and social norms, and ex ante and ex post bargains. The challenge for contract law is to construct a legal apparatus that complements these forces. As a first step, we must abandon the assumptions of legal centrism and acknowledge our incomplete understanding of contractual relationships and of the linkages between legal rules and social norms.[104]

Scott will be right in some cases. If courts seek to impose relational contract norms in a legal proceeding, as Macneil stresses, this may not produce good faith and co-operation. The very fact that the parties have shifted from the vocabulary of contractual partners to adversaries in litigation may undercut trust and reciprocal obligations. Furthermore, one side may see incentives to gamble that it will win big in litigation. Scott certainly is right that those who think about contract law must abandon assumptions about legal-centrism and think about linkages

[103] Scott, n 98 above, 2051.
[104] *Ibid*, 2053–54.

between legal rules, social norms and the urge that many who are sued have to fight back.

Nonetheless, sometimes legal uncertainty could be a factor provoking parties to spend more effort seeking a settlement. Litigation usually is expensive and unpleasant. Business people must turn over a large measure of control to lawyers, and many resist this. Even the threat of having a lawyer for the other side take a deposition might be enough to deter some business people from taking the legal route; few business people would enjoy being cross-examined at trial. My judgement is that in all but unusual situations, flexible doctrine will provoke settlements. The only way to determine how the doctrine applies to the particular facts of the case would be to litigate until some courts provide an answer. While lawyers may be able to predict what courts will do, they cannot guarantee that their clients will win. Even if they win, lawyers cannot guarantee that the legal rules dealing with contracts damages and an inability to satisfy a judgment will not leave a claimant with but a Pyrrhic victory. Settlements are under the control of business people and their lawyers. Unless money is no object and there is a point of principle, rational business people will salvage what they can by settlement and avoid throwing good money after bad in the litigation game.

Moreover, as we have seen in the *ALCOA* and *Westinghouse* cases, litigation can produce settlements. A judge, such as Judge Teitlebaum, who rewrites a contract based on his own view of what is demanded by relational norms may provoke the parties to rededicate their efforts to find a compromise that is more compatible with their needs. A judge, such as Judge Merhige, who participates actively in settlement negotiations may be able to act as a mediator backed up by his power as a judge to discipline lawyers and even the parties.

CONCLUSION

Clearly, contract documents often fail to capture the real deal between the parties. There are many arguments rationalising treating documents in such situations *as if* they were the complete expressions of the contracts made by the bargainers. This may avoid giving courts discretion so that we reduce the risk of arbitrary action by judges. This may even reduce the risk of decisions based on bribery. This may avoid sending courts on missions that often they cannot carry out because of the very real capability problem. Taking this approach to writings may cut the costs of goods and services so that we may have computers, airplanes, compact disks, machine tools and microwave ovens at lower prices. In some, but not all, situations these arguments have merit. Nonetheless, all of them assume that it is worth running the real risk of defeating actual reasonable expectations of bargainers in the service of some more important end.

We might at least focus the issues if we were to accept that there is a text between the lines in most contracts, and if we do not attempt to implement this implicit text, we are denying reasonable expectations. If we are willing to take an 'as if' approach, we then must ask whether reputational sanctions are enough to support most ongoing transactions. Sometimes a formal approach that treats a contract as if it were a discrete transaction may be justified, but we must be sure that we consider all the costs of this approach. We might decide that there is a high cost in legitimacy if the legal system comes to symbolise that contract rests on manipulations of forms and courts reject the substance of the real deal of the parties. At the very least, if our courts allow those who draft written contracts to impose terms inconsistent with expectations and the implicit dimensions of contract, we can expect reformers to demand that the law police those bits of private legislation that masquerade as contracts so that they are fair.

4

After Investors: *Interpretation, Expectation and the Implicit Dimension of the 'New Contextualism'*

ROGER BROWNSWORD*

1. INTRODUCTION

ACCORDING TO LORD Hoffmann, writing about the construction of contractual documents in *Investors Compensation Scheme Ltd v West Bromwich Building Society*,[1] '[a]lmost all the old intellectual baggage of "legal" interpretation has been discarded.'[2] What this betokens is a new 'contextualism' in place of an abstracted 'literalism'. Whilst the latter is wedded to application of the plain, natural and ordinary meaning of the language used by the contractors, the latter seeks out

> the meaning which the document would convey to a reasonable person having all the background knowledge which would reasonably have been available to the parties in the situation in which they were at the time of the contract.[3]

* A draft of this paper was presented at an MLR-sponsored seminar at the LSE in October 2001. I am grateful to those who participated at the seminar for their comments, and especially to Sarah Worthington and Peter Vincent-Jones who presented their interpretation of what Peter helpfully described as my 'excavation of contextualism'. If the layers of the excavation are now more clearly visible, it is due in no small part to their promptings.

[1] [1998] 1 All ER 98. In similar terms, see, too, the speeches of both Lord Hoffmann and Lord Steyn in *Mannai Investments Co Ltd v Eagle Star Life Assurance Co Ltd* [1997] 3 All ER 352 (this latter case dealing specifically with contractual notices).

[2] *Investors Compensation, loc cit*, 114.

[3] *Ibid.*

Contextualist interpretation, then, draws on three elements: the meaning of a contract is that which would be conveyed to (i) a reasonable person, (ii) put in the situation of the parties at the time they made their agreement, and (iii) who is informed by the background knowledge that they would have had at that time. In short, contracts are to be interpreted in a way that keeps faith with the reasonable expectations of the contracting parties.[4]

Even though, as Lord Hoffmann admits, the contextualism that he outlines is more in the nature of a consolidation of existing judicial practice rather than an initiation of change, his Lordship's speech—to borrow Professor McLauchlan's apt description—'is rapidly becoming the bible for the Courts in contract interpretation disputes'.[5] Moreover, if the deepest thought that we have about the purpose of contract law (and its application in the courts) is that the reasonable expectations of contractors should be protected and respected, then Lord Hoffmann's declaration of contextualism must be viewed as a progressive statement.[6] Granted, to open up the process of contractual interpretation to contextual considerations is not a costless exercise.[7] Nevertheless, if we think that the protection of reasonable expectation

[4] In *Total Gas Marketing Ltd v Arco British Ltd* [1998] 2 Lloyd's Rep 209, 221, Lord Steyn (albeit without relying explicitly on *Investors Compensation*) put the key ideas together in the following way: '[questions of interpretation] must be considered in the light of the contractual language, the contractual scheme, the commercial context and the reasonable expectations of the parties.'

[5] DW McLauchlan, 'The New Law of Contract Interpretation' (2000) 19 *New Zealand Universities Law Review* 147.

[6] According to McLauchlan, n 5 above, 'Lord Hoffmann's principles represent a sensible liberalisation of the law relating to contract interpretation' (at 164). He also says, quite rightly, that few surely would deny that 'the primary purpose of the law of contract is to give effect to the reasonable expectations of the parties to an agreement' (at 166). See, too, Johan Steyn, 'Contract Law and the Reasonable Expectations of Honest Men' (1997) 113 *Law Quarterly Review* 433; and, with regard to the recent legislative reform of the privity doctrine in English law, Roger Brownsword and Dale Hutchison, 'Beyond Promissory Principle and Protective Pragmatism' in Peter Kincaid (ed), *Privity* (Aldershot, Ashgate, 2001) 126.

[7] Cf Sir Christopher Staughton, 'How Do the Courts Interpret Commercial Contracts?' [1999] *Cambridge Law Journal* 303, 307: 'It is hard to imagine a ruling more calculated to perpetuate the vast cost of commercial litigation.' This criticism, however, is particularly directed at the second of Lord Hoffmann's guiding principles where he says that the background may include '*absolutely anything* which would have affected the way in which the language of the document would have been understood by a reasonable man' (emphasis added). For Lord Hoffmann's response to this criticism, see *BCCI v Ali* [2001] 1 All ER 961, 975 (para 39), where his Lordship explains that he was simply emphasising that 'there is no conceptual limit to what can be regarded as background'.

is the end of contract law, and if contextualism is a more effective means than its rivals to that end, then Lord Hoffmann's approach in *Investors* must be on the right track.

If there is a fundamental problem with the new contextualism, it is a problem that stems from the driving idea of reasonable expectation. Relative to what precisely is a particular contractor's expectation 'reasonable'?[8] Here, we must distinguish between 'practice-based' and 'entitlement-based' expectations. In the case of the former, expectations are claimed (and judged) to be reasonable (or not) relative to recognised standards, that is, to those standards that are explicitly declared or implicitly accepted in practice. In the case of the latter, expectations are claimed (and judged) to be reasonable (or not) relative to certain standards irrespective of whether such standards are explicitly declared or implicitly accepted in practice. In other words, in a practice-based approach an expectation is reasonable only because it is accepted as reasonable; in an entitlement-based approach, it is because an expectation is reasonable that we should accept it as reasonable. To illustrate the distinction between these two bases of expectation and the relationship between them, consider the simple case of a promise. A promisee might claim to reasonably expect that a promisor will keep his promise. On what basis might we judge whether the promisee's expectation is reasonable? If the claim is practice-based, we are looking for a (contingent) recognition or acceptance of the idea that promises are binding; and the promisee needs to lock the promisor into the relevant group that, for the time being at least, so recognises or accepts this idea. If, on the other hand, the claim is entitlement-based, recognition or acceptance by the promisor and promisee or others is neither necessary nor sufficient; this claim rests on the proposition that promises are categorically binding.[9]

How does the distinction between 'practice-based' and 'entitlement-based' expectations bear on the new contextualism? In principle, contextual interpretation could be guided by either approach to reasonable expectation. In *Investors* itself, the emphasis on the background knowledge of the contractors coupled with their situation at

[8] A question sharply put in Peter Kincaid, 'Privity and Private Justice in Contract' (1997) 12 *Journal of Contract Law* 47, 51.

[9] Having said this, even if practice is not the basis for the claim itself (ie that promises are categorically binding), the application of the standard might be practice-sensitive to the extent that different groups might have different understandings about the particular settings and signals that give rise to a 'promise'.

the time of contracting points fairly strongly towards an ostensibly practice-based approach. So understood, the reasonable man is implicated only in order to put the practice-based pieces together in a plausible way. Against this, the reasonable man might be involved as an independent standard-setter (in other words, as the source of entitlement-based expectations), in which case the reasonable man rather than the parties' background knowledge and contracting situation would become the dominant consideration.

These introductory remarks prompt three general sets of questions. First, if the new contextualism is in line with the underlying premise that contract law is essentially for the protection of practice-based expectations, then how well can we do in delivering interpretations of contracts that accord with the parties' reasonable (practice-based) expectations? Can we maintain the integrity of this approach when the particulars of practice are unclear or when we resort to default rules? Secondly, can we make any sense of the idea of the reasonable man as an independent standard-setter and, with that, of a contextualism that is in line with an entitlement-based approach to reasonable expectation? Thirdly, if we take on board the idea of entitlement-based reasonable expectation, does it mean that the expectations generated inter-subjectively between the parties or in other practice-based ways are irrelevant? Does it mean that the new contextualism is seriously misconceived?

These are large questions to which it is difficult to give a complete response in just one paper. In what follows, most of what is said responds to the first two sets of questions; and the main lines of my response, as far as I am able to take it, are as follows:

(i) Practice-based contextualism (as per *Investors Compensation* and its partner case *Mannai Investments*) has not only a very obvious corrective dimension (see (ii) below) but also a much less obvious (but much more significant) normative dimension (see (iii) below).

(ii) According to the corrective dimension of contextualism, a party is not allowed to stand on an extra-contextual meaning of a contractual term when, in the particular context, its meaning should have been perfectly well understood by that party.[10] Thus, context can correct for meaning and literalism is rejected.

[10] Notice the normative dimension already implicit in corrective contextualism—namely the silent normative premise that it is not reasonable to rely on an extra-contextual meaning (ie, that such reliance would offend principles of fair dealing). Notice also that this principle of fair dealing might be argued to arise as a matter of entitlement rather than on the basis of practice-based acceptance.

(iii) According to the normative dimension of contextualism, where a question of fair dealing arises between the contractors, that question is to be resolved by reference to the accepted (practice-based) transactional ground rules constituting the particular contractual context.

(iv) In both *Investors Compensation* and *Mannai Investments*, corrective contextualism displaces literalism but it does not get to the heart of the dispute. The fundamental question is not one of the intended meaning of the contract but of the standards of fair dealing that should apply. In both cases, this normative issue is the one that really divides the Law Lords.

(v) In both *Investors Compensation* and *Mannai Investments*, normative contextualism runs into difficulties because the practice-based particulars do not yield a clear answer.

(vi) Faced with such a difficulty, there is a temptation to import a standard of reasonableness in order to resolve the case. If the imported standards are practice-based, albeit not based in the particular practice (context) in which the dispute is located, then a more complex version of contextualism is in play and it needs to be fully explained. If the imported standards are not practice-based (for example, if they reflect a judge's personal convictions as to entitlement), then the integrity of new contextualism is compromised—in fact, new contextualism is abandoned.

(vii) To keep faith with new contextualism, a more productive move might be to seek guidance, not in specific accepted standards of fair dealing but in the culture that shapes the disposition of contractors, whether embedded in their particular relationship or in the general trading milieu. Crucially, is this a culture in which one expects (reasonably expects) others to act in an adversarial or a co-operative way? If we can identify an ethic of individualism or co-operativism that guides practice, normative contextualism might not yet be exhausted.

(viii) If practice simply resists such an analysis, the final resort for new contextualism is to adopt a default ethic. In principle, one might operate with contextualism loaded with an individualistic default position or contextualism loaded with a co-operative default position.

(ix) We have now reached the outer limits of contextualism and the boundary-setting default position invites justification. The obvious candidates would seem to be either economic efficiency or some entitlement-based theory of reasonable expectation.[11]

(x) Whichever non practice-based theory one resorts to at the margins of contextualism, one must expect its logic to run on in to the core of the project. In other words, whatever non practice-based steps one takes to achieve closure on the context, a tension is set up. Hence, if an entitlement-based theory of reasonable expectation is used to support, say, a co-operative default position, a fully coherent approach to the construction of contracts will involve using that theory of reasonable expectation to inform our reading of the context in all cases and not just exceptionally.

The paper is divided into four principal sections. In the first two of these sections, we unpack and elaborate the idea of contextualism (as a practice-based approach) to draw out the way in which the implicit ground rules of fair dealing are central to this strategy. This takes us into a consideration of the contrasting cultures associated with individualistic and co-operative ethics as indicative features of particular contracting contexts before turning, in the fourth section, to entitlement as a radically different approach to reasonable expectation.

2. THE NEW CONTEXTUALISM

In *Investors*, Lord Hoffmann makes no claim to be articulating a radically new or original approach to the interpretation of contracts. As his Lordship observes, it was Lord Diplock in *The Antaios*[12] who said that:

> if detailed semantic analysis of words in a commercial contract is going to lead to a conclusion that flouts business common sense, it must be made to yield to business common sense[13]

Before that, it was Lord Wilberforce who talked about the need for interpretation of commercial contracts to be guided by the 'factual

[11] For a range of possibilities, see CA Riley, 'Designing Default Rules in Contract Law: Consent, Conventionalism, and Efficiency' (2000) 20 *Oxford Journal of Legal Studies* 367.

[12] [1985] AC 191.

[13] *Ibid*, 201.

matrix' associated with the particular contract.[14] Moreover, we might detect a certain similarity between the approach in *Investors* and the contextualism brought by Lord Steyn to the implication of terms in commercial contracts.[15] There are apparent echoes, too, of Lord Reid's famous remark in *L Schuler AG v Wickman Machine Tool Sales Ltd*, to the effect that '[t]he more unreasonable the result the more unlikely it is that the parties can have intended it'[16] as well as of Simon Brown LJ's more recent observation in *Lancashire County Council v Municipal Mutual Insurance Ltd*,[17] that commercial contracts are to be construed in accordance with the principle that 'the more unreasonable the result of a given construction, the readier should the court be to adopt some less obvious construction of the words.'[18]

In order to bring the new contextualism clearly into focus, we need to distinguish it from the literalism that it purports to have overtaken, and then we must be clear about the way in which the distinction between practice-based and entitlement-based approaches to reasonable expectation cuts across both literalism and contextualism.

(i) Literalism and Contextualism Distinguished

Literalism treats the words of a contractual agreement as having an abstracted life, or meaning, of their own. To the extent that context must be supplied, it is minimal. Where literalism works, it will generate a plain, or ordinary, or natural meaning which is then taken to represent the contracting parties' meaning. There are two ways in which

[14] See *Reardon Smith Line Ltd v Hansen-Tangen, Hansen-Tangen v Sanko Steamship Co* [1976] 3 All ER 570, 575: '[w]hat the court must do must be to place itself in thought in the same factual matrix as that in which the parties were'. His Lordship recognised, however, that this was not a straightforward exercise. Thus, shortly before his famous reference to the factual matrix, Lord Wilberforce said (at 574):

> No contracts are made in a vacuum: there is always a setting in which they have to be placed. The nature of what is legitimate to have regard to is usually described as 'the surrounding circumstances' but this phrase is imprecise: it can be illustrated but hardly defined. In a commercial contract it is certainly right that the court should know the commercial purpose of the contract and this in turn presupposes knowledge of the genesis of the transaction, the background, the context, the market in which the parties are operating.

[15] See eg *Mosvolds Rederi A/S v Food Corpn of India* [1986] 2 Lloyd's Rep 68.

[16] [1974] AC 235, 251.

[17] [1996] 3 All ER 545, 552.

[18] But, one wonders, are these echoes of an entitlement-based theory of reasonableness?

literalism might not work: one is where the language suffers from some ambiguity, the other is where the application of the plain meaning produces a result that is wholly unacceptable. Literalism must have a strategy for dealing with both these problems and the stock move is to draw on some idea of reasonableness (or, at any rate, the avoidance of manifest unreasonableness). For example, in *Segovia Compania Naviera SA v R Pagnan & Fratelli*,[19] a charterparty provided that the charterers could order the vessel to any port in the United States of America that was to the east of the Panama Canal. The vessel was ordered to New Orleans. However, this port like a number of others in the US Gulf is actually to the west of the Panama Canal. To avoid such an unacceptable outcome, the charterparty was read as meaning that the vessel could be ordered to any port that would be approached in the ordinary course of things from the Caribbean, rather than the Pacific, end of the Canal.

Contextualism, by contrast, treats the words of a contractual agreement as taking their meaning from the context in which the agreement was made. There are a number of issues here about the breadth of this context—for example, about whether the pre-contractual negotiations or previous dealings between the parties are a material part of the context. However, such nice points need not detain us. The fundamental feature of contextualism is that it seeks out the meaning that fits best with the context. The two problems faced by literalism come out rather differently in contextualism. Ambiguity is not so much a linguistic as a contextual problem.[20] As for outcomes that are wholly unreasonable, ex hypothesi, this cannot happen where the context itself supplies the standard of reasonableness, for the meaning that best fits the context will necessarily square with contextual ideas of reasonableness.

In *Mannai Investments Co Ltd v Eagle Star Life Assurance Co Ltd*,[21] where Lord Hoffmann prefigured the key aspects of his approach in *Investors*, he sketched his understanding of the relevance of context in the following helpful way:

[19] [1977] 2 Lloyd's Rep 343. Cf *Total Gas Marketing Ltd v Arco British Ltd* [1998] 2 Lloyd's Rep 209, where the House of Lords gave an intended long-term commercial contract a literal reading but with Lords Steyn and Hope expressing reservations about the consistency of the outcome with the parties' reasonable expectations (see further n 30 below). For solid support for the House's approach, see Davenport (1999) 115 LQR 11.

[20] Another difficulty detected by Sir Christopher Staughton. See further section 3 below.

[21] n 1 above.

> The meaning of words, as they would appear in a dictionary, and the effect of their syntactical arrangement, as it would appear in a grammar, is part of the material which we use to understand a speaker's utterance. But it is only a part; another part is our knowledge of the background against which the utterance was made. It is that background which enables us, not only to choose the intended meaning when a word has more than one dictionary meaning but also. . .to understand a speaker's meaning, often without ambiguity, when he has used the wrong words.[22]

Context (or background), thus, can assist our understanding at more than one level. First, at a level of general orientation or focus, it enables us to select the relevant intended meaning—for example, when the words are, say, 'civil service', context enables us to take this as a reference to a mode of public administration or to a mode of marriage ceremony. Secondly, assuming that our general orientation is appropriate, there is a level of corrective effect that context can supply—for example, when we are talking about public administration, context will enable us to recognise 'silver service' as a slip of the tongue when 'civil service' is what is actually intended. When we say that literalism implies a minimal use of context, this amounts to saying that context is supplied (i) only so far as is necessary to give a general *orientation* to our understanding (thus resolving the problem of ambiguity) and then (ii) only, for *corrective* purposes, where the plain meaning leads to a result that is unacceptable.[23] What is distinctive about contextualism, as against literalism, is that the *corrective* effect of context is applied much more robustly as well as being fully integrated into the process of construction. Again, Lord Hoffmann is very clear about the robustness of this approach. Having said that we can draw on the context to appreciate that when Mrs Malaprop talks about 'an allegory on the banks of the Nile' she is actually intending to say 'an alligator on the banks of the Nile' (or, even more correctly perhaps, a crocodile on the banks of the Nile), Lord Hoffmann continues:

> [T]he reason for the mistake does not really matter. We use the same process of adjustment when people have made mistakes about names or descriptions or days or times because they have forgotten or become mixed up.[24]

Hence, in *Mannai* itself, where a tenant purported to give notice to determine leases on 12 January 1995, when (to comply strictly with the

[22] *Ibid*, 376.

[23] As Lord Hoffmann says in *Mannai*: it is doubtful whether it is conceptually possible 'to interpret the use of language without the aid of any background' (*ibid*, 377).

[24] *Ibid*, 375.

terms of the leases) the tenant should have specified 13 January 1995, it mattered little why this mistake had been made. The critical point, as the majority ruled in *Mannai*, was that the landlord, receiving the notice, would have realised, *in this particular context*, that the tenant was intending to give notice in accordance with the terms of the lease and that a slip had been made in specifying 12 January rather than 13 January. We will return to this case in a moment but, before we do so, we must briefly pick up the distinction between practice-based and entitlement-based approaches to reasonable expectation.

(ii) **Practice-based and Entitlement-based Approaches to Reasonable Expectation**

The idea of reasonable expectation is much less pronounced in literalism than in contextualism. Even so, reasonableness as it appears in literalism could be either practice-based or entitlement-based. For our purposes, however, it is the way that this distinction maps on to contextualism that is more relevant. The paradigm of contractual interpretation that is announced in *Investors* is one of contextualism tied to practice-based reasonable expectation. In principle, though, contextualism could operate with an overriding standard of entitlement-based expectation in which what is accepted or recognised in practice governs only so long as it is consistent with entitlement-based standards. Of course, if practice is not to serve as the reference point for reasonable expectation (which, by definition, is just the case with entitlement-based standards) and if one is disinclined to believe that reasonable expectations are somehow part of the natural order, then it remains to be seen whether a defensible basis for entitlement is available. Nevertheless, the more problematic a practice-based approach becomes, the more seriously we might consider the possibility that an entitlement-based approach is the way out of the difficulty—at any rate, we might entertain such a possibility unless a return to literalism is thought to be a real option. However, as we shall see, it is an answer that comes at a price; because, once entitlement-based standards are explicitly in play, it is in their nature to regulate practice-based standards and they may start turning practice inside out.

(iii) From Contextual Interpretation to Contextual Standards

In the *Mannai Investments* case, the tenants purported to determine the leases by giving due notice. As we have said, however, they slipped up and served a notice which, on its face, stated the wrong date for termination. Nevertheless, it was clear that the landlord understood that there had been a slip and that it was the tenants' intention to determine in accordance with the terms of the leases. With Lords Hoffmann and Steyn, in the majority, saying that no reasonable party in the landlord's position would misunderstand the tenants' intentions, who could possibly disagree with the view that, the slip notwithstanding, the notice was effective to determine the leases?

Yet, Lord Goff, for one, disagreed with the majority view. Recalling his Lordship's celebrated concern that the courts should act so as to oil the wheels of commerce,[25] why should he take such an apparently anti-contextual line? In fact, Lord Goff's position can be read as being every bit as contextual as that of his majority counterparts. According to Lord Goff, it is well settled that 'it is enough that the notice should be so expressed to expire in accordance with the terms of the clause'[26]; and, likewise, that:

> if the person giving the notice specifies the actual date but out of caution also specifies, in the alternative, the end of the period at which the notice is required under the clause to take effect, the alternative so given will be effective to save notice if the actual date so given should prove to have been mistaken.[27]

Hence, 'it is a commonplace for notices to quit to take this form, which avoids the trap into which the tenant fell in the present case.'[28] Summing up, Lord Goff says:

> I start from the position not only that the established meaning is clear and well known, but also that the trap which the tenant fell into in the present case is easily avoided by adopting the familiar stratagem of invoking, as an alternative to the specified date, a date identifiable by reference to the terms of the clause itself.[29]

[25] Famously, see The Rt Hon Sir Robert Goff, 'Commercial Contracts and the Commercial Court' [1984] *Lloyds Maritime and Commercial Law Quarterly* 382.

[26] See *Mannai*, 359.

[27] *Ibid.*

[28] *Ibid.*

[29] *Ibid*, 363.

To appreciate fully how Lord Goff's reading of the context differs from that of Lord Hoffmann, the important question is not whether the former agrees with the latter that, given the background, the landlord must reasonably have understood that the tenant was trying to determine the leases in accordance with their terms. The question is whether, even if the landlord so understood the tenants' intentions (which we can assume the landlord did), the notice should be treated as effective. For the majority, once it was clear that the landlord understood the spirit and intent of the notice, the fact that the letter of the notice did not strictly comply was not a barrier to its effectiveness. However, for Lord Goff, the fact that the letter of the notice did not strictly comply indicated that the notice was not effective and that, as his Lordship put it, the tenant had fallen into a well-known trap in this field of commerce.

Now, here we come closer to the core of the matter. Supporters of the majority view in *Mannai*, will want to say that it would defeat the reasonable expectations of the tenants if their notice was caught by the trap. Yet, by reference to whose standards of reasonableness do they say this? If this is relative to the practice-based standards of those who are regular players in this field of commerce, then they can vindicate the majority view if the facts are with them. On the other side, supporters of Lord Goff will want to respond in kind by arguing that practice-based standards are actually with them (trap and all); and, again, the defence of this position depends on what the facts are. Let us suppose that the settled position as Lord Goff describes it also includes a settled understanding that, if a tenant falls into the trap, then the landlord can legitimately take advantage of the tenant's slip. If this is the case, then the majority fail to keep faith with the parties' reasonable (practice-based) expectations after all. But, could the majority not contend that, the practice notwithstanding, the very idea of a 'trap' is unreasonable and that expectations should not be tied to such an unreasonable practice? Indeed, they could, and perhaps they should. However, to which standards of reasonableness is this view of expectation now anchored? Are we moving to some other (secondary) context where such a standard is accepted; or are we invoking some a priori entitlement-based view of reasonable expectation (for example, to take an arguable principle, that where A has actually understood B perfectly well, B can reasonably expect A to be estopped from disclaiming or denying such understanding)?

The slippage in *Mannai Investments* from the question of (so to speak) the pure meaning of the contract (given its context) to the construction of the contract in the light of the rules of fair dealing accepted in that particular sector is hardly new. Even (or especially) in *Reardon Smith Line Ltd v Hansen-Tangen*, where the idea of the factual matrix was conceived, we see the same two inter-acting dimensions to contextual interpretation. As a matter of the pure meaning of the relevant contracts, the issue was whether references to the shipyard and yard number were essential to the description of the vessel (which, as tendered, was compliant with its contractual description in all other respects); but, as a matter of fair dealing, the issue was whether it would be contrary to the parties' reasonable expectations for the charterers to reject the vessel for non-compliance with this part of the contract 'description'. What was perfectly clear was that the charterers (and sub-charterers) were desperate to find a way out of the contract because, following the oil crisis of 1974, the market had collapsed. Putting oneself in the factual matrix of this contract, one could say either that the charterers could not reasonably regard the references to the shipyard and yard number as material to the description of the vessel (these references simply identified the particular vessel), or that it was contrary to accepted standards of fair dealing for the charterers to purport to reject the vessel, which was precisely the vessel that they had contracted for, simply because the market had changed. Whichever way one prefers to put it, contextualism tells us that it would defeat reasonable expectations to allow the charterers to reject in these circumstances. Moreover, once we are into the context in order to keep faith with the parties' reasonable expectations, it makes no sense to restrict the inquiry to their linguistic conventions; we are committed, too, to taking account of their understanding of the groundrules of fair dealing. In short, the factual matrix is also a normative matrix.[30]

[30] This also comes through strongly in *Total Gas Marketing Ltd v Arco British Ltd* n 4 above. Briefly, the point of interpretation in *Total Gas* arose in connection with an intended long-term agreement for the supply of gas. The supply agreement was said to be 'conditional on' the seller executing an Allocation Agreement with Aramco (who operated the relevant terminal through which the gas would be supplied); and, as construed, this condition was to be met before the first delivery date (which date was to be nominated by the seller). The seller duly nominated 31 October 1996 as the first delivery date; but the Allocation Agreement was not executed until a few days later. With gas prices on the open market being cheaper than under the supply agreement, the buyers contended that the sellers' failure to meet the terms of the 'condition' released them from the agreement. The House of Lords unanimously ruled in favour of the buyers. However, both Lord Steyn and Lord Hope took a contextual approach which gave them pause as to this ruling. At p 223, Lord Hope expressed his concerns as well as uncovering the normative aspect of the matrix at some length:

> The bargain was struck against the background of a market for gas which had proved in the past to be extremely volatile. Substantial changes in the open market price of this

(iv) Taking Stock

In the light of this analysis, we can say that the new contextualism is a practice-based paradigm within which the background informs the meaning of the contract (for the purpose of both general focusing and correction) as well as supplying the ground rules of fair dealing applying to the parties' transaction. On the one side, this new contextualism is bounded by old-style literalism (which takes a minimalist approach to context) and, on the other side, by a rival entitlement-based contextualism (the shape of which has yet to be identified). We can also see the possibility of, so to speak, a substituted form of contextualism in which reference is made to a secondary context when the standards that are recognised within the primary context are judged to be unacceptable. Whether the substitution involves a sideways move to an alternative context, or reliance on an overlapping context, or the exclusionary impact of a superior context, the burden of explanation for new contextualists is now a considerable one.[31]

3. HARDER CASES FOR PRACTICE-BASED CONTEXTUALISM

Contextualism, as we have seen, construes contracts by placing the interpretative question in the context in which the parties themselves are situated. Where contextualism is practice-based, the language of the contract takes its meaning from the conventions accepted by the

> commodity would be bound to affect the value of the investment by either party in the transaction. One of the purposes of an agreement of this kind is to eliminate the risk of having to carry the burden of such price changes. It is no secret that the reason why the buyer wishes to terminate the agreement is that the market has now turned in its favour. It can obtain gas elsewhere more cheaply than it would have been required to take gas from the Trent reservoir under the agreement. No doubt it will seek to renegotiate a fresh bargain with the seller for the supply of the Trent gas at a more favourable price. The buyer is not to be criticised if the wording of the agreement permits this course. But the Court should be slow to lend its assistance. Commercial contracts should so far as possible be upheld. This is especially so where the party who seeks to preserve the contract has incurred expenditure after it was entered into with a view to performing it in the future over a period of many years. . . . It is disappointing to find that in this case it has not been possible to construe the agreement in such a way as to provide the seller with the protection which it was designed to achieve.

[31] As, we can take it, Lord Hoffmann would be one of the first to admit: see his lecture, 'Anthropomorphic Justice: The Reasonable Man and his Friends' (1995) 29 *The Law Teacher* 127, esp 134.

parties and relative to which their (reasonable) expectations are formed. Ideal-typically, the dispute is resolved by drawing on the linguistic conventions employed by the parties (so that A can say to B, 'You, B, knew what I, A, meant—even if others would not have done so'). However, where the interpretative issue arises because of some underlying question of fair dealing, context takes on a further function, namely to bring the practice-based rules of fair dealing into play. Once again, ideal-typically, this will generate a decision that is true to the parties' reasonable expectations.[32] What, though, if the context (at one level or another) is not sufficiently clear and precise to enable the issue to be dealt with cleanly?[33] What about the position in the *Investors* case itself?

The general background to the litigation in *Investors* is well-known. In the late 1980s, financial advisers in conjunction with a number of building societies marketed so-called 'home income plans'. Typically, these plans were sold to elderly homeowners who hoped to realise income by mortgaging their homes. Unfortunately, these income plans proved to be disastrous investments as a result of which those who invested in such plans had claims (in negligence and for breach of statutory duty under the Financial Services Act 1986) against their financial advisers as well as possible claims against the building societies and solicitors who had dealt with the mortgages. Where investors had unsatisfied claims against financial advisers belonging to the Financial Intermediaries, Managers and Brokers Regulatory Association (FIMBRA), they could seek compensation under a scheme set up by the 1986 Act. This scheme was administered by a management company, the Investors Compensation Scheme Ltd (the ICS).

The particular context for the litigation in *Investors* was that a number of investors, having come to grief after receiving advice about home income plans from a firm called Fisher Prew-Smith, had claimed compensation under the statutory compensation scheme which generally covered between half and three-quarters of their losses. Under the terms of the compensation scheme, the ICS treated the investors' claims as having been assigned to the company and it commenced action

[32] For specification of an ideal-typical case, see John Wightman, 'Good Faith and Pluralism in the Law of Contract' in Roger Brownsword, Norma J Hird and Geraint Howells (eds), *Good Faith in Contract: Concept and Context* (Aldershot, Dartmouth, 1999) 41, esp 43–44.

[33] See eg, Hugh Collins, *Regulating Contracts* (Oxford, Oxford University Press, 1999) 143–44.

against the relevant building society, the West Bromwich Building Society. However, the investors, too, proceeded against the building society. Faced with competing claims for damages, by the ICS and by the investors, the building society raised the question of whether (and, if so, to what extent) the investors' claims had been assigned to the ICS.

For the most part, the provisions of the standard form claims agreement made between the investors and the ICS were drafted in the best legalese. However, an accompanying explanatory note tried to put matters more straightforwardly. This note, having dealt with the assignment of claims against Fisher Prew-Smith, then (in para 4) said that it was to be agreed that 'ICS should be able to use any rights which you now have against anyone else in relation to the claim.'

This seemingly general assignment of third party claims was mirrored in the claims agreement under which the investors agreed to 'assign absolutely to ICS each and every Third Party Claim and the benefit thereof . . .' Section 3(b) of the same claims agreement, however, provided for an exception to the assignment of third party claims. According to section 3(b), the investors did not assign

> Any claim (whether sounding in rescission for undue influence or otherwise) that you [ie the investor] have or may have against the West Bromwich Building Society in which you claim an abatement of sums which you would otherwise have to repay to that Society in respect of sums borrowed by you from that Society in connection with the transaction and dealings giving rise to the claim (including interest on any such sums).

Once section 3(b) was brought into the equation, the question was how wide a sweep of claims had been reserved by the investors. Had they reserved 'any claim' against the building society in which they sought a reduction of the amounts due under the mortgage loans (as the investors submitted), or had they reserved a narrower range of claims sounding in rescission (as the ICS contended)? The majority of the House, led by Lord Hoffmann, ruled that section 3(b) should be understood as reserving only the narrower band of claims (as if section 3(b) was reorganised to read 'Any claim sounding in rescission (whether for undue influence or otherwise)'). Lord Lloyd dissented, holding that the broader reading argued for by the investors was both more natural and more plausible.

As in *Mannai*, the difference of opinion amongst their Lordships in *Investors Compensation* is not at all a simple case of the majority taking a contextualist approach while the minority applies a literal interpretation. Far from it—the factual matrix matters greatly to both sides.

As Lord Hoffmann reads the situation, it would be very odd (indeed, commercially ridiculous) for the ICS to compensate the investors but not then to take an assignment of the investors' claim to compensation from the Building Society. Even though the out-of-context meaning of section 3(b) would clearly be that 'any claim' was reserved, the documents were to be read in context, particularly in the light of the explanatory note which, designed for the lay reader, stated very clearly that all third party claims were to be assigned to the ICS. Against this reading, Lord Lloyd not only defends the Court of Appeal's literalism (in rejecting the ICS's construction as impossible) against the withering remarks of Lord Hoffmann, he resists the critical suggestion that the investors' interpretation was commercially absurd. As Lord Lloyd points out, the investors had not been *fully* compensated by the ICS and so they had a perfectly good reason for advancing claims against the Building Society. Thus:

> It is common ground that [the] investors have retained rights of some kind against WBSS. That being so it would seem to me as likely as not, commercially, that the agreement would provide for the investors to retain the whole of their rights against WBSS, including the right to claim damages in reduction of their loans. Such a consequence cannot be regarded as 'ridiculous' or 'extraordinary' or 'very unreasonable'.[34]

If we assume that both the majority and the minority in *Investors Compensation* accept the axioms of contextualism, then they cannot reject out of hand the idea that section 3(b) might be reconstructed in the way that the ICS contended for. However, it should only be so reconstructed if that would convey the meaning that a reasonable investor would have gathered in such a situation. For Lord Hoffmann to suggest that the reasonable investor would have been guided by the explanatory notes is unconvincing; just as it would be unconvincing to insist that the reasonable investor would have been guided by section 3(b). Recall the simple test: if A (here, ICS) can say to B (here, the investors), 'You, investors, knew full well what we, ICS, meant—even if others would not have so understood our meaning', then the investors cannot plead blissful ignorance or misunderstanding based on literalism. Plainly, though, where (as in this case) we are not dealing with a clear slip of the pen which would be detected and corrected by the addressee (or, for that matter, by the addressee's legal advisers who, no doubt, would be equally confused), *corrective* contextualism alone

[34] n 1 above, 107.

cannot deliver a plausible answer. What is doing all the work here is their Lordships' reading of what would be a reasonable person's view of fair dealing where investors were compensated. Would it be, as Lord Hoffmann assumes, that the ICS should take over any compensatory claim? Surely the investors could not *reasonably* expect anything different to this. Or, would it be, as Lord Lloyd assumes, that the investors might *reasonably* expect to hold on to their claims (at any rate to the extent of their under-compensation by the ICS)?

Their Lordships found contextualism taking them into similar interpretative problems in *Bank of Credit and Commerce International SA v Ali*.[35] In this case, following reorganisation by the bank, a number of employees (including one Mr Naeem) were made redundant. Mr Naeem's basic redundancy package, amounting to £7,138, purported to settle in full all known claims arising from the termination of his employment. However, the bank offered Mr Naeem the option of receiving a further payment, equivalent to one month's salary of £2,772, if he would sign a general release (on ACAS form COT 3). Having talked this through with an officer from ACAS, Mr Naeem duly signed in July 1990. The general release provided:

> The Applicant [Mr Naeem] agrees to accept the terms set out in the documents attached in full and final settlement of all or any claims whether under statute, Common Law or in Equity of whatsoever nature that exist or may exist and, in particular, all or any claims rights or applications of whatsoever nature that the Applicant has or may have or has made or could make in or to the Industrial Tribunal, except the Applicant's rights under the Respondent's [the bank's] pension scheme.

About one year later, application was made to wind up the bank and it became clear that the business had been carried on in a dishonest and corrupt manner. In the wake of the collapse of the bank, one of the questions to arise was whether the bank's ex-employees might be entitled to so-called stigma damages; but it was not until 1998 that the House of Lords ruled that such claims were sustainable in principle.[36] In turn, this gave rise to the question whether, if Mr Naeem were now to seek stigma damages, his claim would be barred by the general release that he had signed eight years earlier and at a time when a claim for stigma damages was not, as such, known to English law. Their Lordships, contextualists all, were divided, holding 4 to 1 (with Lord

[35] [2001] 1 All ER 961.

[36] See *Mahmud v Bank of Credit and Commerce International SA* [1998] AC 20.

Hoffmann dissenting) that the release properly interpreted did not bar such an unknown claim.

As in *Investors Compensation*, the question in *BCCI v Ali* concerned the extent of one contracting party's surrender of claims (whether by assignment or by release). In *BCCI v Ali*, context gave several leads as to the scope of the surrender—the release surely related to claims that Mr Naeem might have arising from his employment with the bank, or (more narrowly) to claims arising from the termination of his employment with the bank; and, as Lord Hoffmann emphasised, the context in which the release was agreed was not one of a dispute or the compromise of a claim. Nevertheless, this did not quite get to the heart of the matter. If the context was to be decisive, it had to settle whether a reasonable person in Mr Naeem's position would have understood that he was signing away the possibility of pursuing a claim against the bank for compensation (a) in relation to facts which were not then generally known and/or (b) where the claim pleaded was of a kind which would only be recognised in English law some years later. For Lord Hoffmann, the business sense of the release in *BCCI v Ali*—very much as his Lordship sees the business sense of the arrangement in *Investors Compensation*—was that 'unknown claims' must have been swept up. Thus:

> The reasonable man is bound to ask himself: what was it [the bank] paying for? If it was intended that the release should be confined to claims within the contemplation of the parties, it was getting no consideration whatever. Why did it bother to insist on the forms being signed? In my view, one of the first principles of construction is to try to give some business sense to the agreement. To exclude unknown claims makes the release nonsensical. Nor do I think it is realistic to attribute to the parties an intention to make fine distinctions between different kinds of unknown claims; for example, between those which were conceivable but not conceived of and those which (perhaps because of what was then thought to be the law) were not even conceivable.[37]

Quite clearly, though, Lord Hoffmann is enriching the context somewhat in order to deliver this reading of the release. If (practice-based) contextualism is the governing approach, giving the agreement 'some business sense' is only appropriate if commercial practice within the particular context so indicates. Similarly, it is the particular context that determines what makes sense and what is a nonsense, not some

[37] n 35 above, 977 (para 47).

imported principle of construction. Crucially, Lord Hoffmann's contention that it would be unrealistic to suppose that the parties would distinguish between conceivable and (at the time) inconceivable claims is unconvincing unless it is grounded in the context in which Mr Naeem signed the release. In that context, Lord Bingham surely offers the only realistic assessment when he says that neither party could 'have supposed that such a claim [for stigma damages] lay within the realm of practical possibility.'[38] This being so, whose risk was it that the law might change in Mr Naeem's favour?[39] The majority's response was put most explicitly by Lord Nicholls:

> I consider these parties are to be taken to have contracted on the basis of the law as it then stood. To my mind there is something inherently unattractive in treating these parties as having intended to include within the release a claim which, *as a matter of law*, did not then exist and whose existence could not then have been foreseen. This employee signed an informal release when he lost his job, in return for an additional month's pay. The ambit of the release should be kept within reasonable bounds.[40]

Once again, the context is substantially enriched, this time with notions of what is inherently unattractive coupled with keeping the scope of the release within reasonable bounds. But, whose ideas of what is inherently unattractive, whose ideas of reasonable bounds, whose reasonable expectations are we now relying upon?

Once more, let us take stock. We started with contextualism as a corrective to literalism. In this respect, whereas *Mannai Investments* is a relatively easy case, both *Investors Compensation* and *BCCI v Ali* are already problematic (because there is no extra-contextual meaning to be corrected by a clear contextual understanding). However, even in *Mannai Investments*, once we are into the context for linguistic understanding, we are also into it for expectations anchored in the standards of fair dealing recognised within the particular context. At

[38] [2001] 1 All ER 961, 970 (para 19).

[39] Conversely, whose risk was it that the law might change in favour of the *bank*? Suppose that a subsequent, wholly unanticipated, change in the law revealed that the bank had over-compensated Mr Naeem. Would the bank be entitled to a refund? Granted, prior to the decision of the House of Lords in *Kleinwort Benson Ltd v Lincoln City Council* [1998] 4 All ER 513, to have read the contract in favour of the bank in this way might have struck one as contrary to reasonable expectation. In principle, though, we might see some unfairness in the bank trying to allocate the risk of any change in the law, whether favourable to Mr Naeem or to the bank, to Mr Naeem. I am indebted to my colleague, Rob Bradgate, for developing this point in this direction.

[40] n 35 above, 974 (para 35).

this normative level, all three cases—*Mannai Investments*, *Investors Compensation* and *BCCI v Ali*—are hard cases for contextualism. Quite simply, the problem is that, in none of these cases does the particular context offer unequivocal standards of reasonableness to inform the reasonable person's understanding of the contractual documents. Of course, in such cases, we can enjoin judges to scrutinise each aspect of the context; but the reality is that, in hard cases, even hard looks have their limitations.[41] What we find in these cases is that the context is peppered with references to what would be ridiculous, unrealistic, nonsensical, and inherently unattractive and the like in order to induce a particular resolution of the question. In some cases, one suspects that a priori ideas of reasonableness are being imported (in line with an entitlement theory); in other cases, one supects that an enlarged or secondary context is being deployed in order to draw on practice-based standards of reasonableness; but, in all cases, there seems to be some supplementation or subversion of normative contextualism.[42]

At this stage of the analysis, two thoughts occur. One is the thought that we might be able to derive further assistance from the context (and, thus, keep faith with normative contextualism) if we focus more on the culture represented by the contractors' relationship (or the milieu in which they contract) rather than specific standards of fair dealing. The other thought is that, if the parties' relationship or the setting in which they contract resists such a cultural analysis, then it looks as though the contextualist project might need to develop a defensible default position in order to respond to hard cases. We take up these thoughts in the next section.

4. FAIR DEALING: CONTEXT AND CONTRACTING CULTURE

One way of addressing the puzzle in *Investors Compensation* is to consider how the parties to the compensation agreement actually related to

[41] Some processes of inquiry may prove more effective than others. For example, arbitration might be more effective than court-based procedures in identifying accepted rules of fair dealing in a sector. See Collins, n 33 above, ch 8.

[42] In *BCCI v Ali*, n 35 above, the courts recognised the possibility of a fall-back position should a contextual approach lead to a wholly unacceptable interpretation: namely, that the bank might be precluded from reliance on the release by the doctrine of unconscionability. Although this was not really an issue for the House of Lords, this was the ground on which two members of the Court of Appeal (Chadwick and Buxton LJJ) allowed Mr Naeem's appeal.

one another. Did they relate as robust individualists or did they approach the transaction in a more co-operative spirit? If the former, we should have no problem about the investors standing firm on their favoured reading of section 3(b) and insisting on the broad protection of their claims. If, by contrast, the law supports the latter perhaps the investors should yield to the ICS. Similarly, if we think about the situation in *Mannai Investments* in fair dealing terms of this kind, we might suppose that allowing a fellow contractor to fall into a trap is the sort of conduct that would be more consistent with an individualist rather than a co-operative ethic of contracting. This line of thinking suggests that, as new contextualists, we should be looking to the culture that informs the contractors' relationship as well as the background culture of the particular contracting community. Essentially, is it the cultural disposition that one contracts on an individualist or a co-operative basis?

(i) The Basic Ethic of Contract Law

Generally, there is no more important question for contract law than to determine its basic ethic. In particular, where the cornerstone concept of contract is that of reasonable expectation, the law needs to establish the basis on which contractors meet to deal with one another and, with this, the basis on which expectations are judged to be reasonable or not. The two plausible starting positions in this regard are an ethic of individualism and an ethic of co-operativism.[43] In its most robust version, individualism places no requirement on contractor A to pay any regard to fellow contractor B's economic interests. Contractor A is permitted to pursue its own economic interests, even if in doing so there is an economic cost to B (and vice versa). By contrast, co-operativism requires contractor A to pay some level of regard to fellow contractor B's economic interests; and, in its most robust form, this ethic requires contractor A to treat contractor B's economic interests as equal to its own (and vice versa). It is not easy for contract doctrine (whether through notions of good faith, unconscionability, reasonableness, loyalty, legitimate expectation, or whatever) to hold strictly to either of these ethics in their most robust form. Doctrinal adherence

[43] See Roger Brownsword, *Contract Law: Themes for the Twenty-First Century* (London, Butterworths, 2000) 15–22.

to individualism will often seem out of touch with business practice (where compromise, adjustment, and partnering and the like govern dealings);[44] but, equally, doctrinal adherence to co-operativism can put too great a strain on the idea of a common enterprise (at any rate, in the sense of an identity of interest).

The relationship (and choice) between individualism and co-operativism is nicely illustrated by the important recent case of *Baird Textile Holdings Limited v Marks and Spencer plc*.[45] In that case, there was no dispute about the conspicuously co-operative relationship between the parties. Baird had been a principal supplier to Marks and Spencer for 30 years and, in practice, there was a considerable degree of horizontal integration between the businesses. Even Marks and Spencer's director for procurement attested that the relationship with suppliers, such as Baird, was symbiotic—if not a partnership in the strict legal sense, business was most definitely conducted in a spirit of co-operation.[46] Not surprisingly, then, Baird were aggrieved when, without warning, Marks and Spencer notified them that, as from the end of the current production season, all supply arrangements were to be determined. In response, Baird argued that they were entitled to a reasonable period of notice (some three years) during which time they could make the necessary adjustments to their business. Such an entitlement, Baird argued, arose either under an implicit contract or by way of an estoppel. If there had been an express framework contract governing the relationship between the parties and including a termination clause, Baird might have argued that, in the light of the prevailing co-operative culture, the notice period should be extended to reflect the duration of the dealings between the parties—and this would have been an interesting test case for contextualism. However, in the absence of such an express contract, Baird relied on the co-operative culture to argue for an implied contract. The Court of Appeal took their bearings from individualistic thinking in order to reject this argument. As Mance LJ put it:

[44] There is now a very considerable local literature, including David Campbell and Peter Vincent-Jones (eds), *Contract and Economic Organisation* (Aldershot, Dartmouth, 1996); Simon Deakin and Jonathan Michie (eds), *Contracts, Co-operation and Competition* (Oxford, Oxford University Press, 1997); and Collins n 33 above. Seminally, though, see Stewart Macaulay, 'Non-Contractual Relations in Business' (1963) 28 *American Sociological Review* 55; and 'Elegant Models, Empirical Patterns, and the Complexities of Contract' (1977) 11 *Law and Society Review* 507.

[45] [2001] EWCA Civ 274.

[46] *Ibid*, para 4.

> It is evident that Baird felt, quite rightly, that it had achieved a long and very close relationship, an informal business 'partnership', with M & S, and that it could, as a practical matter, rely on this and M & S's management's general goodwill and good intentions. But managements, economic conditions and intentions may all change, and businessmen must be taken to be aware that, without specific contractual protection, their business may suffer in consequence. I do not think that the law should be ready to seek to fetter business relationships, even—and perhaps especially—those as long and as close as the present, with its own view of what might represent appropriate business conduct, when the parties have not chosen, or have not been willing or able, to do so in any identifiable legal fashion or terms themselves.[47]

So, even in a co-operative context, individualistic thinking can reassert itself, either because there is no explicit contractual protection for the party seeking to extend the relationship or because (for instance, in a case such as *Schuler v Wickman*)[48] there is an explicit contractual reservation for the party seeking to terminate it.

In *Baird Textiles*, one of the reasons for rejecting the argument based on an implied contract amounts to the following: (i) terms are not to be implied into a contract unless it is strictly necessary to do so; (ii) the test for implying a contract cannot be less demanding than that for implying a term into a contract; so (iii) the test for implying a contract must be at least as demanding as the necessity test for implied terms. Notoriously, though, the necessity test presupposes a context of adversarial dealing; and, it only makes sense in a case such as *Baird Textiles* if we suppress the co-operative context in which the parties dealt for 30 years.

Given Lord Ackner's support for an adversarial ethic in *Walford v Miles*,[49] as well as considerable academic resistance to good faith,[50] we should perhaps not be too surprised at the outcome of *Baird Textiles*. However, it sounds a warning for contextualists: not only must literalism be displaced, contextualism must also address a readiness to revert to classical type—namely, the reversion to an individualist ethic where

[47] *Ibid*, para 76.

[48] [1974] AC 235.

[49] [1992] 2 AC 128. At 138, Lord Ackner said that 'the concept of a duty to carry on negotiations in good faith is inherently repugnant to the adversarial position of the parties when involved in negotiations'.

[50] See, eg, Michael Bridge's well-known strictures against good faith in 'Good Faith in Commercial Contracts' in Brownsword, Hird, and Howells (eds), n 32 above, 139. Recently, however, there have been signs that the balance of academic opinion might be shifting, see, eg, several of the papers in Angelo DM Forte (ed), *Good Faith in Contract and Property Law* (Oxford, Hart Publishing, 1999).

the context, even if co-operative in spirit, leaves room for doubt about the details of agreed standards of fair dealing.

If we want to find out more about contract doctrine operating with co-operative premises, English law is hardly the best place to look. We can turn, therefore, to the more co-operative regimes of contract law that we find elsewhere in Europe, specifically by drawing on Reinhard Zimmermann and Simon Whittaker's major study of good faith in European contract law (good faith, of course, being intimately connected with the idea of reasonable or legitimate expectation).[51]

(ii) The Limits of Co-operativism

Briefly, we should remind ourselves that, in its classical expression, English contract law has little room for co-operativism. The governing ethic, as vividly illustrated in *Arcos Ltd v EA Ronaasen and Son*,[52] is a robust individualism. In *Arcos*, because timber prices were falling, the buyers were keen to find a way out of the contract that they had made with the timber sellers.[53] Initially, when the shipping documents were tendered, the buyers purported to refuse them on the ground that the timber was not shipped 'during the Summer' as the contract provided. Having argued this without success at the ensuing arbitration, the buyers then purported to reject the timber when it arrived in London, this time on the ground that it did not correspond with its contractual description (and, indeed, although the timber delivered was perfectly suitable for its intended purpose, it was fractionally out from the contract specification). Plainly, the buyers were looking for a breach in order to realise the economic opportunity afforded by the falling market. Did such behaviour by the buyers defeat the sellers' reasonable expectations? The House of Lords saw no unfairness in the buyers taking advantage of the sellers' breach in this way. Indeed, Lord Atkin said explicitly that he accepted that it was permissible for a buyer to rely on a breach of condition in order to withdraw for collateral economic reasons on a falling market:

[51] Reinhard Zimmermann and Simon Whittaker (eds), *Good Faith in European Contract Law* (Cambridge, Cambridge University Press, 2000). The material in the next sub-section of the paper draws on my 'Individualism, Cooperativism and an Ethic for European Contract Law' (2001) 64 *Modern Law Review* 628.

[52] [1933] AC 470.

[53] Compare the scenario discussed above in the *Reardon Smith* case.

> If a condition is not performed the buyer has a right to reject. I do not myself think that there is any difference between business men and lawyers on this matter. No doubt, in business, men often find it unnecessary or inexpedient to insist on their strict legal rights. In a normal market if they get something substantially like the specified goods they may take them with or without grumbling and a claim for an allowance. But in a falling market I find the buyers are often as eager to insist on their legal rights as courts of law are to maintain them. No doubt at all times sellers are prepared to take a liberal view as to the rigidity of their own obligations, and possibly buyers who in turn are sellers may also dislike too much precision. But buyers are not, as far as my experience goes, inclined to think that the rights defined in the code [ie the Sale of Goods Act] are in excess of business needs.[54]

Applying the logic of Lord Atkin's view of fair dealing, and to put the boot on the other foot, if the *sellers* in *Arcos* had known that timber prices were about to fall, it would not have been unfair for them to have kept this information to themselves and to have allowed the buyers to have contracted in ignorance. To some extent, the attitude of English contract law has changed. For example, the courts in cases such as *Reardon Smith*[55] and *Hong Kong Fir Shipping*[56] betray a reluctance to allow a 'literal' (but trivial) breach of contract to be used as a pretext to escape from a losing contract, and section 4 of the Sale and Supply of Goods Act 1994 now provides that where a business buyer would otherwise have the right to withdraw for breach of the implied terms in sections 13–15 SOGA, this right will not be available where 'the breach is so slight that it would be unreasonable for [the buyer] to reject'—and, one assumes, that in 2003, the result of *Arcos Ltd v EA Ronaasen and Son* would be different.

Turning to Zimmermann and Whittaker's study,[57] we find 30 hypotheticals designed to test the limits of good faith (and contractual co-operation) in European contract law. Case 6 looks as though it might be helpful. It runs as follows:

> George owes Harry fifty heavy bags of flour. On the appointed day he drives to Harry in order to deliver them. After he has unloaded the bags, it turns out that he has only brought forty-nine rather than fifty of them. Will he be able to deliver the fiftieth bag later that day or will he have to reload and take

[54] [1933] AC 470, 480.
[55] Above n 14. But cf the *Total Gas* case, above n 40.
[56] *Hong Kong Fir Shipping Co. Ltd v Kawasaki Kisen Kaisha Ltd* [1962] 2 QB 26.
[57] Above n 51.

back the forty-nine bags in order to deliver all fifty bags at one and the same time?

With the exception of Ireland, where the law 'puts a premium on certainty in relation to business dealings, despite the occasional inconvenience caused to the parties',[58] the consensus is that the buyer is not entitled to reject delivery of the 49 bags. Ideas of good faith, abuse of right, proportionality, and de minimis figure in the national responses; and, in the case of England and Scotland, the qualifying provisions of the 1994 legislation (mentioned above) preclude the buyer rejecting for the shortfall where it is so slight as to be unreasonable for him to do so. In other words, various doctrinal resources are deployed to articulate the idea that rejection would be contrary to the reasonable expectations of the supplier. However, with the facts of the hypothetical so thinly specified, one immediately wonders how rejection by Harry might be a plausible scenario. On the face of it, it makes no sense for Harry, who has 49 of the 50 bags, to insist on George reloading the bags and redelivering all 50 as per the contract. Why should Harry so insist? One possibility is that Harry is acting in a way that is totally perverse (an example of 'malicious bad faith' as the French report puts it,[59] in which case, we would not expect contract law to encourage such behaviour). Or, it might be that these parties deal with one another regularly and Harry, sensing that George is taking the benefit of Harry's custom somewhat for granted, chooses this occasion to register his larger concerns about George's diligence. Or, it might be that Harry will suffer some logistical inconvenience and cost unless all 50 bags are delivered in one go (for example, the Belgian report speculates that Harry might have to open his warehouse for a second time). A familiarity with the common law of contract, however, suggests that none of these possibilities is the most likely reason for Harry to insist upon strict performance. The most likely scenario is that Harry, with a view to playing the flour market, is using George's failure as a pretext to escape from the contract. In which case, we want to know whether the agreed result (Ireland apart) that Harry is not entitled to reject the delivery actually made by George is based on (i) a consideration of the reasons that Harry has for rejecting the delivery and (ii) a common view that Harry would not be acting in line with good faith and fair

[58] *Ibid*, 299.
[59] *Ibid*, 295.

dealing (ie with George's reasonable expectations) if his rejection was a pretext to take advantage of open market flour prices.

So far as the first point is concerned, a number of the reports indicate that, in saying that Harry has no ground for rejecting the delivery, it is assumed that he has no legitimate reason for insisting upon all 50 bags being delivered at the same time.[60] The Italian report, having said that the principle of good faith forbids chicanery, continues:

> This means that Harry should have had a good reason for refusing to accept delivery of the forty-nine bags. Yet, the facts as they are described do not disclose why Harry behaved as he did. In the absence of a good reason, however, his refusal to take delivery of the bags is unjustified, and will be considered an example of *mora creditoris*.[61]

The agreed result with regard to case 6, therefore, assumes that Harry has no legitimate interest or good reason for refusal. This is not insignificant, because it suggests a division between those legal systems that treat a contractor's reasons for action as relevant to questions of fair dealing and those that do not (as seems to be the case with Ireland in case 6). However, it falls short of shedding light on the second point. Whilst we know that some legal systems are operating with a distinction between good reasons and bad reasons, between interests that are legitimate and those that are not, this bears only on the form of doctrinal thinking within these systems. We do not yet know what (substantively) counts as a good or bad reason; we do not know whether Harry would be seen as breaching principles of good faith and fair dealing if his rejection was a pretext to take advantage of open market flour prices; and, more generally, we do not know how far the pursuit of one's own economic advantage is regarded as legitimate (ie as in line with reasonable expectation).

Another of the hypotheticals, case 3, which involves breaking off negotiations in order to take advantage of a better offer elsewhere, explicitly raises the question of the pursuit of one's own economic interests. The scenario here is as follows:

> Falstaff & Co., a large firm of accountants, enters protracted negotiations with the owner of an office block, Hal & Sons, with a view to renting space

[60] See, eg, Germany (*ibid*, 293), Greece (293), Austria (294), Spain (296), and The Netherlands (297) and, by implication, the reports from Sweden and Finland which speak respectively of the fiftieth bag being of 'essential importance' (303) and of 'material importance' (303).

[61] *Ibid*, 296–97.

> for their new office in Everdale. In the course of these negotiations, Falstaffs ask for various work to be done on the premises, including the installation of the wiring necessary for their computer and communications systems. Just before an appointment fixed by the parties for signing the contract, Falstaffs find equally suitable premises in Everdale on offer at a lesser rent and refuse to go any further with Hal & Sons. What claim or claims do Hal & Sons have?

This is a textbook case of pre-contractual reliance by Hal & Sons raising the question of whether Falstaffs' economic opportunism violates local rules of good faith and fair dealing. The German report comes down against Falstaffs. In favour of Falstaffs, it is accepted that 'freedom of contract entails that every contracting party has the right to withdraw from contractual negotiations before a contract has actually been concluded'[62]; and, moreover, not only may 'a better offer . . . be regarded as a good reason for Falstaff & Co. to give preference to a competitor' but also in general 'the standard for accepting a good reason to break off negotiations must not be pitched too high'.[63] On the other hand,

> where [as in Falstaffs' case] negotiations have extended over a long period of time and where the one party has requested the other to incur precontractual expenses, a better offer from another party cannot justify termination of the negotiations.[64]

In a similar vein, the Austrian report says that the relationship between the parties has become so close that Falstaffs can only pull out 'for good cause, such as for a reason which would be significant enough to allow the cancellation of a contract which has actually been concluded'.[65] On the facts, no such reason exists: Falstaffs 'have simply found a better offer elsewhere'.[66] These ingredients are also evident in the Italian report such that, freedom of contract notwithstanding, where one party induces the other to rely on the anticipated contract being concluded, the former cannot then pull out 'for no serious reason'.[67] And, although 'the existence of a more attractive deal offered by a third party . . . may be considered by the courts to be a good reason to refuse to go ahead with a contract to which the negotiations

62 *Ibid*, 237.
63 *Ibid*.
64 *Ibid*.
65 *Ibid*, 239.
66 *Ibid*.
67 *Ibid*, 245.

relate',[68] the reliance induced by Falstaffs would probably mean that their refusal to conclude the contract with Hal would be seen as contrary to good faith (ie as defeating reasonable expectations). For the Nordic countries, the key to what we are looking for is the requirement of 'loyal behaviour'[69]. According to the Swedish report, Hal & Sons have incurred pre-contractual expenses at their own risk. However, in the joint report from Denmark and Norway, it seems that loyalty might at least require Hal & Sons to be given a reasonable opportunity to make a fresh offer in the light of the third party's offer to Falstaff.

These few remarks suffice to tell us that where a legal system makes a judgement about fair dealing by reference to a party's reasons for action, its background picture of good faith and reasonable expectation is likely to be a complex mosaic. At most, the reports on case 3 give us a few pieces. Elsewhere in Zimmermann and Whittaker's study, there are a few more clues but also more questions. For example, in case 7, which concerns the termination of a lease for late payment of the rent, the German report says that good faith is not infringed 'if the opportunity to terminate the lease suits the lessor, for instance because he has found a lessee who is prepared to pay a higher rent'.[70] Yet, one wonders, why is this different from case 3? Both hypotheticals involve leases but does the fact that one involves a commercial lease, the other a non-commercial lease, render the contexts materially different? Again, some of the reports on case 14 are to the point. In this case, which is one of a trio dealing with termination (the others being 23 and 24),[71] Ian contracts to supply components to a car manufacturer, Hamish. In order to perform the contract, Ian incurs considerable expense but then, seven months into the contract, Hamish gives notice

[68] *Ibid*, 246.

[69] *Ibid*, 254.

[70] *Ibid*, 306.

[71] Cases 23 and 24 involve long term de facto co-operative relationships built, legally speaking, on the renewal of 12-month fixed term contracts which specify a one-month notice period to terminate. After more than 40 years of trading, the question is whether one-month's notice (as per the express terms of the contract) is sufficient. A regime of contract law at the individualistic end of the spectrum (such as English contract law) will treat the express term as decisive and the de facto co-operative relationship as irrelevant. A regime of contract law that adopts a more co-operative ethic will treat the de facto relationship as relevant to the parties' reasonable expectations and modify the notice period accordingly (in Zimmermann and Whittaker's study, it is the Swedish, Finnish and Belgian regimes, closely followed by the Greek and Dutch, that are at this end of the spectrum). The comparison with the Court of Appeal's approach in *Baird Textiles* is too obvious to call for comment.

to terminate (which, as the hypothetical goes, he is entitled to do under a legislative provision). The hypothetical gives no indication as to Hamish's reasons for terminating the contract—respondents are channelled towards the fact of Ian's reliance and the question of whether he has any good faith protection over and above the statutory notice period. Nevertheless, the joint report from Denmark and Norway (i) assumes that 'the termination was not made on entirely illegitimate grounds',[72] (ii) echoes the point made in relation to case 3, that where the reason for termination (or withdrawal from negotiation) is to take advantage of a better offer then the opportunity to make a revised offer should be given, and (iii) says that, on different facts, where

> the termination by the buyer was not the result of pure market evaluations, etc., but had definite overtones of disloyalty, it is not impossible that the courts might set aside the termination. . . .[73]

Finally, in response to case 11 (which involves a purchaser, who regrets making a purchase, seeking to rescind for the seller's fraud, even though the fraud does not actually reduce the value of the contract), the Austrian report picks up on the point that the purchaser is seeking (illegitimately) to rescind the contract 'for reasons which have nothing at all to do with the other party's fraudulent conduct'.[74]

Piecing together these fragments, we can say that, where a question of fair dealing (and consistency with reasonable expectation) is raised before at least some legal systems in Europe, reasons are relevant in the sense that the contractor must act for what the particular legal regime treats as a good reason, or for the protection of the contractor's legitimate interests, or in line with the duty of loyalty. However, the extent of co-operativism within such legal regimes remains unclear and, even where there is a developed jurisprudence, there is still scope to speculate about the finer details of this ethic.[75]

[72] *Ibid*, 415.

[73] *Ibid*, 416.

[74] *Ibid*, 365.

[75] See eg the Finnish report to case 17 (where a bank mistakenly credits its customer) which remarks that 'although loyalty is recognised as a general principle of Finnish contract law, its scope in judicial practice is unclear' (*ibid*, 468).

(iii) Practice-based Contextualism and the Contractual Culture

What does this detour via Zimmermann and Whittaker's comparative survey tell us about the new contextualism? Or, at any rate, what does it tell us when we recall that, for the purposes of new contextualism, practice is the basis of reasonable expectation?

First, we must establish the relevant 'context'. It could be a context that is special to the contractors or it could be drawn more widely with the boundaries set by reference to some larger group or community of which the contractors are members or by reference to some sector or sectors of cognate trades or businesses. There are also geographical and jurisdictional issues to be resolved in relation to fixing the relevant context.[76] At all events, having identified the relevant context, this now encloses the relevant practice. If reference to the particulars of this practice yields a clear and settled understanding on the material question of fair dealing, normative contextualism can deliver an answer to the question of contractual interpretation that led us off in this direction. If not, then we face the problem that we had before we started talking about dispositions and default positions.

Assuming that we face such a problem, then, secondly, we must consider whether the context (however identified) is characterised by a distinctive culture of individualistic or co-operative dealing. If we can identify a specific relational (as in *Baird Textiles*) or general contextual disposition to co-operate (or not), then we can be guided by this disposition when we address the contested issue of fair dealing. This might or might not give us a clear steer. In *Baird Textiles* itself, where the parties were so to speak involved in an 'end game', the Court of Appeal assumes that it is no longer possible or appropriate to apply co-operative thinking to the (winding down of the) relationship. Thus, we find Mance LJ saying:

> When the suggested long-term contract is put in these terms [ie as pleaded by Baird], it becomes clear that it would, in case of any dispute, involve the court writing a 'reasonable' contract for the parties, after making a complete review of their situations, needs, abilities and expectations. It could only become relevant to seek to identify the impact of such long-term obligations in a situation where actual co-operation had broken down or one or the

[76] As globalisation takes hold, this difficulty will, in one respect, become more acute. However, where regional harmonisation takes place, this will ease the problem. See the concluding comments in Collins, n 33 above.

> other party wanted to reduce its commitment to the minimum. So the court would be expected to undertake the exercise in the very situation where the parties' actual behaviour could no longer serve as a guide to the answer. I agree with the Vice-Chancellor that this is not an exercise that the court can or should undertake, or, indeed, which the parties can objectively be taken to have intended.[77]

It has to be conceded that 'end games' are particularly problematic for contextualism because it is possible that neither the particular ground rules nor the culture of fair dealing is sufficiently articulated to govern such situations. Even if the culture is clearly co-operative in relation to ongoing relationships, it might take a different view of how partners should relate to one another during the dismantling of a relationship. Putting matters more generally, one thing that the Zimmermann and Whittaker study demonstrates is that, even where legal regimes are geared for co-operation, loyalty, good faith and the like, the scope and extent of a contractor's co-operative responsibilities might well remain moot (at which point, adjudicators might well have to resort to handing down a decision as a matter of best impression). Having said this, it could be worse for contextualism because we might find that there is no clear background disposition one way or the other—in which case, the contextualist problem runs deeper.

Thirdly, if we have to address this deeper problem, the obvious response is to adopt a default position. This default position would be set somewhere on the spectrum between unqualified individualism and complete co-operativism and it would act as a beacon for the interpretation of contracts (and for judgements as to reasonable expectation) unless practice clearly indicated some different standard of fair dealing (which, in this problematic scenario, we are assuming practice does not). Again, on the basis of what we find in the Zimmermann and Whittaker study, we should not be over-confident that the jurisprudence of co-operativism will be sufficiently well-developed to yield ready answers to all our questions—but, unless co-operativism is truly unworkable, this is a poor excuse for a reversion to individualism.

If it takes the adoption of a default position to keep the contextualist project intact, we might not wish to agonise about which default position would be optimal. However, for a project that is so strongly committed to the principle of protecting reasonable expectation, it would be hard to resist entertaining the idea that the default position

[77] n 45 above, para 68.

itself should be grounded in some deeper theory of reasonable expectations (whether expressed in the form of general principle, particular standards, or contractual ethic). If such thoughts are to be entertained, we are moving into the territory of an entitlement-based theory.

5. AN ENTITLEMENT BASED THEORY OF REASONABLE EXPECTATION: PLAUSIBILITY AND POTENTIAL

Is it the least bit plausible that we can reasonably expect others to act in certain ways for reasons other than the fact that our expectation is based on, and encouraged by, their practice (or the fact that certain standards are commonly accepted, or the like)? In other words, are any standards of fair dealing reasonably to be expected a priori?

Consider the case of a promise which, if not the whole story in contract law, is at least an important aspect of contracting. Is A's expectation that B will keep a promise made to A *reasonable* because (i) A has dealt with B before and knows that B is a man of his word, or (ii) because, although A has not dealt with B before, A has dealt with C and D (who are in the same group as B or in the same line of business) and A knows that they are men of their word, or (iii) because, although A has not dealt with B before, A knows that in the community to which A and B belong the principle of pacta sunt servanda is recognised, or (iv) because the binding force of a promise cannot be coherently or rationally denied (ie promises simply are categorically binding)? Reasons (i)–(iii) are practice-based; reason (iv) is entitlement-based. Practice, as we have seen, can have its limitations; but is anything stronger (such as entitlement free of practice, commitment or convention) plausible?

To respond to such a question, of course, calls for a book, let alone a paper, let alone a paragraph or two. Nevertheless, let me try to remove one major source of scepticism, after which a few indicative comments must suffice. This paper, after all, is primarily about the limits and the implicit dimensions of new contextualism.

When Jeremy Bentham famously contended that the idea of natural rights was a nonsense and that the only rights (or entitlements or reasonable expectations) that we have are those that we positively recognise and accept, he seemed to allow for only two possibilities: (i) rights existing as part of the natural order (or in a state of nature, or as part of the moral furniture of the universe or whatever) and (ii) rights as positively recognised and accepted in practice. Unless we subscribe to the idea of a sixth sense (of moral intuition), the first option looks implausible and we are seemingly left with practice-based contingencies. Indeed, contextualism beckons. However, there is a third option, stemming from Kant rather than Bentham. This is the idea that as rational and purposive beings, we are committed (logically) to certain binding principles of action. Following such an approach, promises would be treated as categorically binding not because that is just the way things are in the moral world but because, as rational beings, we cannot coherently deny that we are bound by our promises. Controversial though this approach is, it seems to me to have the best prospects of giving us a defensible account of our non practice-based entitlements.[78]

The starting point for this preferred strategy is the idea that those who engage in contracting are agents with particular transactional purposes. As agents, they must recognise that they cannot function without a degree of protection and respect for their freedom and well-being. No matter what an agent's particular purpose, there are certain conditions that must be in place if there is to be any prospect of successful action. Where an agent's particular purposes necessitate interacting with others, truth-telling and promise-keeping are conditions of this kind. Such generic conditions carry over into transactional contexts; however, it is arguable that the generic conditions applicable to contracting agents are richer than the conditions applicable to agency in general. Just how rich these conditions are is something that we will return to but, first, we need to see how the idea of entitlement-based rights emerges as a plausible idea within this scheme of thinking.

What contracting agent, CA, must will, as a contracting agent, is that others do not interfere with the necessary conditions for successful contracting in general (the generic contracting conditions) when this is against the will of CA. Ideally, CA must will that there should be a culture of respect for these generic contracting conditions. Moreover, each and every contracting agent, as a contracting agent, must will the very same thing. It follows that there is a realistic prospect of enlightened contracting agents reaching a background compact to respect one another's generic contracting conditions. And, in this way, one might talk about a *hypothetical* practice-based compact, agreed by rational

[78] See eg Roger Brownsword, 'From Co-operative Contracting to a Contract of Co-operation' in Campbell and Vincent-Jones (eds) n 44 above, 14.

contracting agents, and relative to which expectations are judged to be reasonable or otherwise. This, however, leaves open the possibility of free-riding (and, anyway, does not yet get us to a full-blown entitlement theory). How can we establish that even those contractors who are minded to take advantage of the compact without also respecting it (at least when they can get away with it) are bound by the requirement of respect for the generic contracting conditions?

If we can establish that would-be free-riders are nevertheless bound, we presuppose that CA (free-riding inclinations notwithstanding) must accept a duty to respect the generic conditions of fellow contracting agents; and this will hold most convincingly if CA must acknowledge the appropriateness of the demand made by others for respect. In short, this will hold most convincingly if CA must accept that others are entitled to have CA respect their generic contracting conditions. But, then, if CA must judge that others are so entitled, CA must certainly judge that CA himself is entitled to the respect of others. Thus, the critical move that must be made in CA's reflection on the generic contracting conditions is that CA is entitled to have others respect these conditions (specifically for the benefit of CA himself). If CA must so judge then we can go smoothly through to CA having to accept that other contracting agents have the same entitlement; and, in the community of contracting agents, we now have a rationally grounded theory of entitlement that does not rest contingently on acceptance of certain standards in practice.

Yet, why should CA be compelled to make such a judgement about CA's own entitlement to respect? Quite simply, if CA does not make such a judgement then this is tantamount to CA reasoning that it is permissible for others to fail to respect CA's generic contracting conditions even though CA must will that these conditions are respected. The only way for a contracting agent to resolve this contradiction is by accepting that (relative to CA's own contracting interests) unwilled interference of this kind is not permissible and, thus, that CA does have an entitlement (again, judged relative to CA's, and only to CA's, contracting interests).

There is one other point that should be made. A steadfast amoralist will resist being drawn into the rhetoric of entitlement or any of its cognates. The amoralist CA will certainly want others to respect his generic contracting conditions, may threaten others if they look as though they might interfere against his will, and may even plead with others not to interfere against his will. However, the language of entitlement is not part of the amoralist's vocabulary. If, relative to the amoralist's own interests, eschewing the language of entitlement is counter-productive and contradictory, amoralism must give way. For our purposes, however, there is no such philosophical battle to be fought.[79] The audience that we are addressing is already comfortable with the idea of entitlement, albeit entitlement that is driven by practice-based recognition. If, as suggested above, contracting agents are logically bound to recognise that there are entitlements associated with the very conditions of contracting and their participation as agents in a contracting community, then the idea of entitlement-based expectations is at least plausible.

Even if the idea of entitlement-based reasonable expectations is plausible, it remains to be seen what those expectations are. Putting the question in terms of an entitlement-based default position, is it the reasonable expectation that fellow contractors will be disposed to co-operate or not? This is, again, a large and difficult question and this is not the occasion to pursue it. However, it is trite that the forces that set contract in motion—the move from 'taking to trading' as Hugh Collins puts it[80]—are either that B has something that A desires (and cannot otherwise obtain) or that what A desires cannot be achieved without B's co-operation. Either way, for exchange or joint venture, A needs to do a deal with B. It is also trite that, without trust between A and B, the deal either will not happen or will happen in a defensive and less than optimal form. What these primitive remarks imply is that the generic conditions of contract need to establish a basis for trust between contractors and, in this light, a co-operative default position makes a lot of sense.[81] It follows that an entitlement-based co-operative default position is not implausible and that one can begin to see the shape of a contextualism in which entitlement-based reasonable expectations would run from a co-operative default position.

This, it should be said, would not necessarily preclude the possibility of contractors agreeing in some settings to waive the benefit of co-operation in favour of a more adversarial approach to dealing (adversarial contract would, as it were, be one game that might be played by

[79] For some possible lines of response to the amoralist, see eg, Bernard Williams, *Morality* (Cambridge, Cambridge University Press, 1972) ch 1 (The Amoralist).

[80] n 33 above.

[81] From a philosophical perspective, see David Gauthier, *Morals by Agreement* (Oxford, Clarendon Press, 1986); from a socio-economic perspective, see Deakin and Michie n 44 above; and see, too, Collins n 33 above, ch 5.

agreement). For example, one might hold that in the commercial property market (as in *Mannai Investments*), the parties freely waive the benefits of co-operative dealing. Moreover, waivers might be withdrawn and co-operative relations re-introduced in some cases (eg, in exceptional longer term dealing in otherwise non-co-operative settings). Suffice it to say that when and how such waivers and their withdrawals might be operative would be for the background entitlement-based theory to specify. And, as I have suggested elsewhere, one of the principal challenges for contract theorists today is to model a regime of reasonable expectation with these layers of complexity fully worked out.[82]

6. CONCLUSION

The new contextualism centres on the (latent normative) idea that it is inappropriate (unfair) to stand on, or give effect to, a non-contextual (abstracted) interpretation of a contract where the in-context meaning has been received and understood (or at least would have been understood by a reasonably competent addressee). This immediately raises the question, though, of whose standards of fairness govern. Whose standards, for instance, determine that literalism is inappropriate? Is it the standards accepted by the contractors who populate the particular context or recognised by parties in some secondary context? Or, is it some standard of fair dealing (and interpretation) that is grounded independently of practice? If it is the latter, the practice-based version of contextualism is undone with its opening corrective move. Assuming, however, that it is the former, then the new contextualism is safe so long as the particular context discloses this particular rule as one of the accepted standards of fair dealing.

Where the particular context does not yield a clearly accepted rule on the point of fair dealing that is at issue, we might be able to formulate an appropriate rule by drawing on the culture that informs the parties' relationship or that constitutes the contractual community as one of individualists or co-operators. If this does not resolve the question (which starts as a question of construction, becomes one of fair dealing, and now becomes one of culture), then contextualism seems to have exhausted its resources. Closure now requires the specification of a default position.

[82] See Brownsword, n 43 above; and similarly see Collins, n 33 above, ch 2.

In response to this requirement, to get the cork back into the contextualist bottle, one might think about resorting to a default position that takes up the idea of an entitlement-based theory of reasonableness. Once this move is made, however, the new contextualism that starts by aligning itself with practice-based reasonable expectations turns itself into an entitlement-based approach to reasonable expectation that now shapes, structures and gives substance to the context—in other words, the effect of replacing the cork in the bottle is also to replace the contents. Although the wine in this particular bottle is something of an unknown quantity, we already know that it is likely to be as complex, challenging, and subtle as that which it is replacing.

5

Beyond Custom: Contract, Contexts, and the Recognition of Implicit Understandings

JOHN WIGHTMAN

IN AMERICAN CONTRACT law, and the rich academic literature which engages with it, there has long been a recognition of the significance of the implicit understandings which can swirl around the processes of negotiation, modification and performance. The roots of this recognition are many, but they include the work of Karl Llewellyn, the contextual orientation of the Uniform Commercial Code which he influenced,[1] and the differing contributions of Ian Macneil and Stewart Macaulay. Macneil shifted the emphasis from the discrete, one shot contract, with the terms spelt out in full at the moment of formation (presentiation), to the contract which emerges around a relation, where much may be left open and the process of commitment gradual rather than sudden, as the parties establish understandings as their relationship evolves.[2] Macaulay has demonstrated that the performance of contracts is frequently governed by the parties' own understandings which are at variance with the letter of contract terms which they have

[1] On Llewellyn's influence see W Twining *Karl Llewelleyn and the Realist Movement* (London, Weidenfeld and Nicholson, 1973) 270–301. Contextual provisions of the UCC include 1–203 (obligation of good faith) and 1–205 (course of dealing and course of trade); for a History of the formation of the UCC, see AR Kamp 'Downtown Code: the History of the UCC 1949–1954' (2001) 99 Buffalo *Law Review* 359.

[2] See generally Macneil, IR 'The Many Futures of Contract' (1974) 47 *University of Southern California Law Review* 691; 'Contracts Adjustments of Long-term Economic Relations Under Classical, Neoclassical, and Relational Contract Law' (1978) 72 *Northwestern University Law Review* 854; *The New Social Contract* (New Haven, Yale University Press, 1980).

signed, and that these understandings are heavily shaped by the customs and practices of the trading communities in which they operate.[3]

Although these insights are familiar, probably hackneyed, to American contracts lawyers, in English law, and its traditionally more homogenous literature, the role of implicit dimensions has received much less attention. Without a general doctrine of good faith, or other general context-based provisions such as those contained in the UCC, most academic commentary published in the UK has shown little interest in mining the rich seams of issues which Macaulay, Macneil and others after them have opened in the US.[4] Stirrings of greater academic interest are evident, as is a greater consciousness on the part of some leading judges of the role of context in making sense of contracts.[5]

However, the fact that significant judicial and academic interest in contextual and relational issues is relatively recent does not mean that English contract law has been oblivious to the implicit understandings of the parties. In chapter 2 in this volume Campbell and Collins argue that many of the doctrines of orthodox English contract law can be understood as drawing on implicit understandings of the parties. This conclusion is in line with that of more traditional scholars who have argued, for example, that English contract law contains the resources to respond to relational contracts[6] and that a good faith doctrine is unnecessary because its function can be discharged by other doctrinal tools, for example implied terms.[7]

[3] S Macaulay, 'Non-contractual Relations in Business' (1963) 28 *American Sociological Review* 55; 'Elegant Models, Empirical Pictures, and the Complexities of Contract' (1977) 11 *Law and Society Review* 507; 'An Empirical View of Contract' [1985] *Wisconsin Law Review* 561; 'Relational Contracts Floating on a Sea of Custom? Thoughts about the Ideas of Ian Macneil and Lisa Bernstein' (2000) 94 *Northwestern University Law Review* 775.

[4] There are of course notable exceptions, of which Beale and Dugdale's is probably the best known: M Beale and T Dugdale, 'Contracts Between Businessmen: Planning and the Use of Contractual Remedies' (1975) 2 *British Journal of Law and Society* 45. This article must come high in any table of the most cited (UK) law journal articles in the last 25 years, yet there has been until quite recently astonishingly little empirical research which has followed in their footsteps. Substantial studies have now emerged, although it is striking that much of the work has focussed on the contractual arrangements within the public sector, rather than on mainstream commercial contracting. See especially the essays in the second part of D Campbell and P Vincent Jones (eds) *Contract and Economic Organisation* (Aldershot, Dartmouth, 1996), and also S Deakin and J Mitchie (eds) *Contracts, Co-operation, and Competition* (Oxford, Oxford University Press, 1997).

[5] See text at n 19 below.

[6] E McKendrick 'The Regulation of Long Term Contracts in English Law' in J Beatson and D Friedmann (eds) *Good Faith and Fault in Contract Law* (Oxford, Clarendon Press, 1995).

[7] MG Bridge, 'Does Anglo Canadian Contract Law Need a Doctrine of Good Faith?' (1984) 9 *Canadian Business Law Journal* 385.

Campbell and Collins' argument also receives indirect support from the traditional pride which many of the most respected judges have taken in being responsive to exigencies of commercial convenience.[8] English contract law may be less showy than American law, but it has traditionally preferred (*pace* Lord Denning) to work unobtrusively by adapting existing doctrines and taking into account commercial expectations without doctrinal upheaval—or at least that may be how some would put it.

It is thus possible that the greater recent emphasis on the openness of English law to the importance of the context of the parties may be as much a change in self description as a significant shift in underlying reality. However, even if one can, at a general level, identify some broad brush tendency to recognise implicit understandings stemming from the parties' context, much remains to be clarified about the detail and incidence of such developments. I do not minimise the significance of these issues, but my own focus here is in one sense a jump beyond the debate about the recognition of implicit understandings in English law.

I intend to move on from this engagement and take as established, for present purposes, that implicit understandings *are* a vital part of the machinery of existing English contract law, despite the law being expressed in language that sometimes gives the opposite impression. I want in one sense to flip the issue over. Rather than demonstrate how doctrine which is structured using agreement-based concepts is dependent on absorbing implicit dimensions, I propose to take this more or less for granted and ask the next question: if contract doctrine *is* often dependent on incorporating the implicit dimensions of the parties' relationship, what happens when those understandings are non-existent, or generated in ways other than those typical in mainstream commercial contracts?

My starting point is thus to suggest a generalisation: that the extent and nature of implicit understandings are not constants across all kinds of contracts, but vary signifcantly according to context. Can we get

[8] See for example: Lord Devlin, 'The Relation Between Commercial Law and Commercial Practice' (1951) 14 *Modern Law Review* 249; Lord Goff, 'Commercial Contracts and the Commercial Court' [1984] *Lloyds Maritime and Commercial Law Quarterly* 382; Lord Steyn, 'Contract Law: Fulfilling the Reasonable Expectations of Honest Men' (1997) 113 *Law Quarterly Review* 433, and also the judicial pronouncements of Lord Diplock (eg *Antaios Cia Naviera SA v Salen Rederierna AB* [1985 AC 191, 201) and Lord Wilberforce (eg *New Zealand Shipping Co Ltd v AM Satterthwaite* [1975] AC 154, 167); see also R Brownsword, *Contract Law: Themes for the Twenty-First Century* (2000) 124–143.

further than saying this is a plausible generalisation? One approach might be to embark on empirical research across different kinds of contracting contexts.[9] Among other problems, this would need a selection of contexts, and thus criteria for selection. On the other hand, a substantial body of empirical work has now accumulated, and reported cases have at least some value as evidence of practice. The path I have chosen is to attempt to get some purchase on the *general* issues about the varying incidence and nature of implicit understandings by identifying two models of contractual relations. After exploring in section 1 the different senses in which implicit is used, in section 2 I construct a model of contracting practice—the contracting community model—which I argue covers most of the situations where implicit understandings are routinely recognised in the law of contract. This is an ideal type; it is intended to present a simplified but coherent picture of how implicit understandings may emerge, so that elements which favour the emergence of implicit understandings can be more clearly identified.

In section 3, I construct a second model, the personal consumption model, which is intended to highlight some features of contractual relations which do not foster the emergence of customary implicit understandings. In Section 4 I explore some of the implications for contracting practice and contract law where customary implicit understandings are not developed, and look at other types of contract relation which do not exhibit these kinds of understandings.[10]

1. MEANINGS OF 'IMPLICIT'

Neither 'implicit dimension' or 'implicit understanding' is a term of art, in either the law or the literature about contracting practice. Either could be treated as a residual category, defined by what is left after express agreement has been removed—thus it could be defined as 'all

[9] The direction of the enquiry in some respects resembles that of B Lyons and J Mehta's 'Private Sector Business Contracts—text Between the Lines' in S Deakin and J Mitchie (eds) *Contracts, Co-operation, and Competition* (Oxford, Oxford University Press, 1997), in which they sought, by empirical investigation, to test Williamson's theory of contract types.

[10] The exploration of these issues involves looking at contracting practice as well as contract law, and I refer to some of the well known empirical studies and to other sources that shed light on contracting practice. But I am conscious that some of the claims made are ultimately empirical ones which, although I believe they are plausible in the light of what we know, require further empirical investigation.

the knowledge, practices and norms pertaining to contracting which are not express.' However, this includes matters of which the parties to any exchange will typically be wholly unaware—notably things such as the regulatory structure which controls the way certain products or services are made or traded. These may accurately be described as part of the social institutions of exchange, but lack any element of understanding or awareness, which arguably is usually included in usages of 'implicit'.

By 'implicit', I will mean the knowledge, practices and or norms pertaining to contracting in general (or an individual transaction) of which the parties to a particular contract are actually aware, (or can, in the circumstances, reasonably be expected to be aware), but which are not typically rendered express in their contracting activity. However, by saying the parties are 'aware' I do not mean to convey that they must be consciously deliberating (albeit silently) at the moment of contracting: 'aware' includes assumptions about knowledge practice and norms which the parties bring to the contractual relationship. In one sense, implicit dimensions includes all the assumptions about the operation of transactions which are needed to endow the transaction with meaning. It useful to make a number of preliminary distinctions, initially by identifying three kinds of implicit understandings.

First, there are the implicit understandings stemming from a shared language, knowledge of the social institution of money, currency, and a shared 'market mentality'[11] ('general understandings'). The market mentality includes many tacit understandings about buying and selling, about the nature of private ownership, about money and modes of payment, the banking system, expectations of interest and the like. These provide the minium social institutions for exchange in developed societies, and are general, in that they are not specific to any species of transaction; they are very widespread in societies with long established market economies.

Secondly, there are those implicit understandings which emerge over time between the parties to a particular contract—'inter-party understandings'. For example, in an employment contract, understandings may evolve which stem from specific behaviour of the parties. These are distinct from the general understandings because they relate to behaviour rather than background knowledge. Moreover, these understandings

[11] K Polanyi, 'Our Obsolete Market Mentality' in K Polanyi (ed), *Primitive, Archaic and Modern Economies* (Boston, Beacon Press, 1968).

need not actually emerge during the span of any contract which is the subject matter of any dispute. They may be built up as part of a long-term trading relationship, which itself may be composed of frequent but relatively discrete contracts. Understandings laid down in this way will often take on meaning in the context set by the third type of implicit understandings.

The third type consist of implicit understandings about how commercial relations in a particular sector are carried on, in particular the practices and norms with which participants need to become familiar if they are to participate in the sector ('customary understandings'). It is this sense of implicit understanding that the empirical work of Macaulay and others has brought home most forcefully, in that much of that empirical work paints a picture of contracting as an activity where parties actions are shaped by informal understandings as much, (and often more than) the letter of their contract, even if cast in written form. It is customary understandings which, I will argue, are typically drawn upon in contract doctrine.

Although these three senses of implicitness can be differentiated, they are obviously related. General understandings are a necessary platform for both customary understandings and inter-party understandings. Most importantly, customary understandings provide the framework within which the parties deal and the baseline for one-off adjustments, including those reached by inter-party implicit understandings.

So far, the discussion of implicit understandings has assumed that these are shared between the parties. However, I do not propose to treat it as a necessary characteristic of 'implicit' that the understandings are shared, and will examine situations where there are unvoiced understandings which are held by one side only. For example, it is common in consumer contexts for the supplier to know much more of the background context in which the parties deal than the consumer, and the consumer may equally make assumptions or harbour expectations which are not shared by the supplier. Where understandings are divergent in this way, they can still play an important role in conferring meaning on the contracting process, and (I will argue) have potential significance in legal determination.

The existence of implicit understandings (whether shared or divergent) is often signalled when we use the language of reasonable expectation. This expression tends to be used to mean more than merely saying that one party's expectations are a mirror image of whatever the contract terms provide. It includes expectations which are more widely grounded, which may be based on implied terms, but equally may be based on aspects of the background context which confers meaning on the parties dealings. Overall, I am treating 'implicit understandings' as including all the background assumptions about the transaction and its course that the parties bring to the contract.[12]

2. THE CONTRACTING COMMUNITY MODEL OF CONTRACTUAL RELATIONS

The Features of the Contracting Community Model

The contracting community model refers to contractual relations which occur within a market sector where there are established practices for carrying on trade which any firm wishing to participate in the trade will normally have to take part in. There are three basic features.

First, there is specialist knowledge about the 'physical nature' of the 'products' being traded.[13] This is primarily knowledge of the substance of the product or service, and will typically include technical knowledge relating to its construction and performance specification, and this will include knowledge of alternatives available in the sector. Equivalent dimensions of knowledge are also developed in the case of fungibles such as grain, coffee etc.[14]

Secondly, there is specialist knowledge of the way the trade is carried on, such that knowledge of these practices is necessary to participate effectively in the sector. This knowledge of how the product or service in question is typically traded will include aspects such as in what units

[12] This is not because I am taking some view of what the correct meaning is, but rather because implicit understandings have a function in many commercial contracts which I argue is left unperformed in contexts where the understandings are arrived at in different ways. See section 4 below.

[13] I am using 'product' as a generic term to include all things which are traded, including services, labour, intellectual property rights, and by 'physical nature' I mean the inherent characteristics of the product.

[14] Lisa Bernstein's empirical work (especially on commodities markets) is replete with examples of this specialist knowledge, despite the fact she argues against the automatic incorporation of custom in adjudication. See 'The Questionable Empirical Basis of Article 2's Incorporationist Strategy' (1999) 66 *University of Chicago Law Review* 710 and 'Merchant Law in a Merchant Court: Rethinking the Code's Search for Immanent Business Norms' (1996) 114 *University of Pennsylvania Law Review* 1765; see text at n 34 below.

it is traded, the pricing structure and arrangements for payment, quality control, what legal instruments (financial and otherwise) are used. Most of the fields of commerce with which contract lawyers become familiar from case law are about contracting communities in this sense—shipping, the international sale of commodities, insurance, construction and so forth. Typically, these sectors have developed social institutions of exchange which play a key role in mediating and structuring exchange behaviour, a notable example being the bill of lading.

The third feature is knowledge of the practices that are used when hitches in performance arise. This knowledge is based on knowledge about the physical attributes of the product or service, including what can go wrong with these products/services in general. But it also includes knowledge about how hitches such as shortfalls in the quality or quantity of goods or services are actually handled, or how late payment or other late performance is regarded. The actual techniques used to handle resulting disputes may vary greatly across different sectors, so that in some cases dispute resolution is almost always informal, with rare recourse to the terms of contracts, while in others arbitration or litigation may be a much nearer prospect.[15] Whichever approach tends to be adopted, the present point is that knowldge of what tends to happen when performance miscarries in some way is part of the contracting community model.[16]

For these features to obtain, there will need to be a number of contractors who are repeat players, although it is not necessary that the contractors always contract with parties known to them. The key element for a contracting community to generate these features is its social organisation, so that the practices themselves are shaped, and knowledge of them disseminated, through interaction.[17] Market

[15] Compare, for example, Beale and Dugdale's study (n 4 above) with that of M Bridge on grain contracts in commodities markets: 'Good Faith in Commercial Contracts' in R Brownsword, NJ Hird and G Howells (eds) *Good Faith: Concept and Context* (Aldershot, Dartmouth, 1999) 139.

[16] This is not to say that, where customary implicit understandings exist, they will provide a constant, homogenous backcloth for every contract. The point is that these are the understandings which the parties expect in the absence of arrangements to the contrary, some elements of which will be normal in most contracts. It is arguable that it is precisely this background of shared implicit understandings which enable the parties to focus attention on the detail of matters which they wish to expressly negotiate .

[17] A contracting community of this type may also be further integrated by the role of a trade association, or groups of trade associations.

relations are the social relations which construct, preserve and renew these understandings.[18]

Although the three features above are described in terms of matters of fact, the understandings about trade practice, including the handling of miscarried performance, may harden into generalised expectations whenever they are so much a part of doing business in a sector that those in that sector assume others will (unless announced otherwise) conform with the usual practices; in that sense these understandings may have a normative dimension. These implicit understandings are, in terms of the meanings of 'implicit' discussed above, shared and customary. They provide a kind of normative and cognitive grid within which exchange relations are carried out.

The Contracting Community Model and the Law

I have described the features of the contracting community model mainly in terms of contracting behaviour, rather than in terms of the content of contract doctrine. However, the customary implicit understandings in the contractual relationships covered by the contracting community model are clearly detectable in contract doctrine. Perhaps the most striking, and significant example, can be seen in the law relating to the construction of contracts.

The understanding of construction which is now embraced by leading Law Lords places great weight on understanding contract terms in the whole context in which they are set. The views of Lord Wilberforce expressed in *Reardon Smith Line Ltd v Hansen-Tangen*[19] have been influential:

> No contracts are made in a vacuum: there is always a setting in which they have to be placed. The nature of what is legitimate to have regard to is usually described as 'the surrounding circumstances' but this phrase is imprecise: it can be illustrated but hardly defined. In a commercial contract it is certainly right that the court should know the commercial purpose of the

[18] A feature which may (but not necessarily) accompany this matrix of factual and normative understandings is a high degree of trust. By trust, I mean the voluntary exposure to the risk of opportunistic behaviour by the other party. Where firms are known to one another, either because of previous dealings or reputation, there may be high levels of trust shown in the performance of the other; this may be evident in, for example, the granting of extensive credit, the co-operative handling of difficulties, etc; see further the text at n 45 below.

[19] [1976 1 WLR 989, 995.

> contract and this in turn presupposes knowledge of the genesis of the transaction, the background, the context, the market in which the parties are operating. . . . [W]hat the court must do must be to place itself in thought in the same factual matrix as that in which the parties were. All of these opinions seem to me implicitly to recognise that, in the search for the relevant background, there may be facts which form part of the circumstances in which the parties contract in which one, or both, may take no particular interest, their minds being addressed to or concentrated on other facts so that if asked they would assert that they did not have these facts in the forefront of their mind, but that will not prevent those facts from forming part of an objective setting in which the contract is to be construed.

More recently, Lord Hoffmann, in passages that have been widely quoted, has re-emphasised Lord Wilberforce's contextual approach. In the *Investors Compensation Scheme v West Bromwich Building Society*[20] he said:

> Interpretation is the ascertainment of the meaning which the document would convey to a reasonable person having all the background knowledge which would reasonably have been available to the parties in the situation in which they were at the time of the contract. [This] includes absolutely anything which would have affected the way in which the language of the document would have been understood by a reasonable man.

And in *Mannai Investment Co Ltd v Eagle Star Life Assurance Co Ltd*:[21]

> The meaning of words, as they would appear in a dictionary, and the effect of their syntactical arrangement, as it would appear in a grammar, is part of the material which we use to understand a speaker's utterance. But it is only a part; another part is our knowledge of the background against which the utterance was made. It is that background which enables us, not only to choose the intended meaning when a word has more than one dictionary meaning, but also . . . to understand a speaker's meaning, often without ambiguity, when he has used the wrong words.

[20] [1998] 1 WLR 896, 912.

[21] [1997] AC 749, 775. See also Lord Steyn at 771:

> In determining the meaning of the language of a commercial contract, and unilateral contractual notices, the law therefore generally favours a commercially sensible construction. The reason for this approach is that a commercial construction is more likely to give effect to the intention of the parties. Words are therefore interpreted in the way in which a reasonable commercial person would construe them. And the standard of the reasonable commercial person is hostile to technical interpretations and undue emphasis on niceties of language.

This contextual approach is used to displace an apparent meaning not just where the words in question are ambiguous on their face, but also where (as in *Investors*) they have a clear meaning but one which did not make much commercial sense, and where (as in *Mannai*) the words have a clear meaning which the reasonable recipient would realise was not intended.

Although this contextual approach has received renewed prominence in recent years, the reference to aspects of the background to the contract that was not made express can be detected in other parts of the law of contract. For example, the use of context was clear in law on the construction of exception clauses as far back as the nineteenth century. Where written contracts contained onerous terms, attempts were made to construe the offending express term with reference to the 'main object' or purpose of the contract. This had clear affinities with the modern contextual approach, as is made clear in Lord Halsbury's judgment in the leading case of *Glynn v Margetson*:[22]

> Looking at the whole of the instrument, and seeing what one must regard . . . as its main purpose, one must reject the words, indeed whole provisions, if they are inconsistent with what one assumes to be the main purpose or object of the contract . . . Mercantile men when they do business in this form . . . recollect that a business sense will be given to business documents, and that therefore they are not under peril of leaving it absolutely to the shipowner himself to do what he will with the cargo.[23]

The 'main object' was not found in the express terms of the contract, but was deduced from the surrounding circumstances.[24] The terms used in these passages do, I think, demonstrate a focus on the shared understandings which are based on the knowledge of those familiar with the contracting contexts in which the parties operate—what I am calling customary implicit understandings.[25]

[22] [1893] AC 351, 357. A ship was carrying oranges from Malaga to Liverpool, and under the bill of lading the ship was permitted to visit almost any port in Europe or Africa. The House of Lords held that the clause could not permit the ship to call at any port because it had to be read subject to the main object of the contract.

[23] *Ibid*, 357 and 359.

[24] See B Coote, *Exception Clauses* (London, Sweet and Maxwell, 1964) for a discussion of the case law on deducing the 'main objects' from the surrounding circumstances.

[25] The point can be taken further by arguing that context is necessary to understand meaning: see Campbell and Collins, ch 2 in this volume and DV Snyder, 'Language and Formalities in Commercial Contracts: a Defense of Custom and Conduct' (2001) 54 *Southern Methodist University Law Review* 617. Also, even in some of the cases where literalism has been preferred the court has acknowledged that it was perfectly clear what was intended when viewed contextually; a notable example is *Hankey v Clavering* [1942] 2 KB 326.

Most of the examples of implicit understandings elaborated by Campbell and Collins are also cases of implicit understandings which are customary and which develop in contracting communities.[26] A contracting community can provide a relatively rich context which enables the court to draw on practices, customs and understandings which can inject meaning into open-ended standards.[27] Although many of these standards embody reasonableness in some guise, and reasonableness is readily mocked as an open licence to do anything a court wants, the shared practices of a contracting community can, in many cases, offer a way of clarifying meaning which enables it to remain a plausible search for objectivity.[28]

An emphasis on the context within which the parties contract, and on what they take for granted rather than what they have made express, is perhaps usually associated with relational contract theory. It is true that contracting communities may have strong expectations about high levels of co-operation, and may develop norms which inhibit opportunism and favour the harmonious settling of disputes without disrupting the commercial relationship, all of which are regarded as relational norms. However, this is not a necessary characteristic of a contracting community in the sense I am employing it; it is not intended to connote any necessary affiliation with communitarian or relational contract law,[29] and may equally display individualistic

[26] Clear examples include the mitigation and remoteness rule in damages law, and implied terms. Examples which are not covered seem to be the 'organisation rules' (Campbell and Collins, ch 2 in this volume) and possibly *Sagar v Ridehalgh* [1930] 2 Ch 117 (the case about defective piece work).

[27] There are also parts of the law where an exploration of customary understandings might have avoided doctrinal confusion. For example, in the battle of forms case *Butler Machine Tool Ex-Cell-O* [1979] 1 WLR 401 the issue was which form prevailed: the seller's form, which contained a price escalation clause, or the buyers form, which did not. The majority handled this using the orthodox offer/counter offer analysis. Arguably the key question should have been what, in the light of prevailing practice in the sector, the reasonable buyer would have expected: this would have provided a baseline or default position which required clear consent to adjust. *The Principles of European Contract Law* contain very clear contextual provisions, see especially eg Art 1.105 (on usage), Art 1.201 (good faith), and Art 5 101/102 (interpretation).

[28] I should make clear here that the argument is not coextensive with the conventionalist argument for default rules (for a very valuable discussion of the bases of default rules, see CA Riley, 'Designing Default Rules in Contract: Consent, Conventionalism and Efficiency' 20 *Oxford Journal of Legal Studies* 367.) The scope of what is understood as default rules varies (Riley equates them to implied terms), but they are less pervasive in doctrine than the implicit understandings I am addressing here.

[29] The term 'relational' is used in quite a few different senses; for example, it is sometimes used to mean norms which favour co-operation, and sometimes to mean norms which are derived form the parties context rather than from agreement. In contracting

norms. It is the idea of specialist, shared trading practices, embracing knowledge and expectations, which characterises the contracting community model, and this can exist in contracting contexts where co-operative norms are not well developed.[30] This neutrality regarding the content of contract norms at the level of contracting communities as a general category stems from the fact that the norms reflect actual practice, and the law will in turn reflect that reality: if the norms are individualistic, then contract law will often reflect those norms.

Contracting Communities and Neoformalism

An emphasis on the contextual interpretation of contracts has been seen as being at odds with a literal or formalistic approach. Macaulay's original article demonstrated that it may be a common practice in contracting communities to pay scant attention to the terms of the contract, and a central claim of Macaulay and many others has been that custom and conduct is vital when the terms of the contract are being construed in litigation, to the point that such custom may prevail over contradictory express terms in a standard form.[31] A neoformalist movement has now begun to reassert the case for literal interpretation, and this might be thought to undermine the claim that exchange relations in contracting communities are rich in implicit understandings.[32] Nevertheless, some aspects of neoformalist arguments valuably illuminate the role of implicit understandings in contracting communities.

Neoformalism has challenged the incorporationist approach of the UCC, which has for the last 50 years placed custom and conduct at the heart of the principles of commercial contract law.[33] After undertaking

communities, norms are always relational in the second sense and sometimes relational in the first sense.

[30] A clear example of this appears to be commodity sales of grain. Bridge argues that the practice of the five firms which dominate the world trade in grain includes adversarial activity: 'They sue each other regularly, but it is as if litigation is business carried on by other means. Opportunistic behaviour by one contracting party does not appear to sour continuing and prospective dealings between the same parties': Bridge, n 15 above, 151.

[31] See Macaulay's discussion of *Nanakuli Paving and Rock Co v Shell Oil Co* 664 F 2d 772 (1982) in 'Relational Contracts Floating on a Sea of Custom?', n 3 above, 791. A fairly close equivalent in UK law is *Schuler L (AG) v Wickman Machine Tool Sales Ltd* [1974] 235.

[32] Eg see D Charny 'The New Formalism in Contract' (1999) 66 *University of Chicago Law Review* 842.

[33] For discussion of reform of the UCC, see Snyder (n 25 above) and other articles in the *Southern Methodist University Law Review* Symposium (2001).

massive empirical work, Bernstein has argued that, even where customs or conduct can be established, it does not follow that courts should use them to depart from the plain meaning of written terms.[34] Her argument is based on a distinction between two kinds of norms: relationship preserving norms (RPN), and end game norms (EGN).[35] She sees the kind of norms contained in customs, for example where one party is prepared to make concessions by overlooking technical breaches, as typically relationship preserving. End game norms, on the other hand, are less concerned with co-operation, and are permissive of withdrawal. These norms are often found expressed in written terms relating to such things as the right to terminate for breach. Bernstein's point is that the custom and conduct enshrined in the UCC may embody RPN, which will be appropriate norms to apply where the parties are attempting to preserve the relationship. A contracting party may be happy to make concessions during the course of the relationship, but equally may not want to confer an entitlement to that concession when the relationship has broken down. Thus, given that the courts are only involved where one party (at least) has embarked on an end game, invoking RPN when the parties have reached the end game is an application of the wrong norms.

This argument recognises that custom and conduct may exist which are inconsistent with written terms, but argues that this is not sufficient reason to allow custom or conduct to prevail over written terms because that may not be what the party intended in the end game situation—in other words, the concession made in line with custom may not have been intended to be binding when things get rough and litigation results.

This argument has been subject to sustained criticism, some of it from writers otherwise sympathetic to Bernstein's position. However, what is of interest for present purposes is that even Bernstein's own position acknowledges an intricate relationship between custom and the operation of standard forms. Her argument is explicitly premised on a distribution between matters which the parties leave to the legal realm and matters which they withdraw from the legal realm, so that, although she found plenty examples of RPNs in her empirical work, she argues that these should be understood as confined by the parties to

[34] See 'Merchant Law in a Merchant Court', n 14 above.

[35] *Ibid*, 1796.

the non-legal rather than the legal realm. She claims that the distinction between RPNs and EGNs is in fact one of which contractors are aware:

> There is empirical evidence from a variety of contracting contexts that suggests that merchants behave in a way that reflects an implicit understanding of the distinction between end-game and relationship-preserving norms and that they do not necessarily want the RPNs they follow during the cooperative phase of their relationship to be used to resolve disputes when their relationship is at end-game stage.[36]

Interestingly, what Bernstein is doing here is adding a different kind of norm—not a substantive norm about preserving the relationship, or about the end game, but a meta-norm about the appropriate scope and context of those substantive norms. Paradoxically, by attributing to contractors in a commercial sector awareness not only of substantive customs, but also a meta-norm about when it is acceptable to switch between different kinds of norm, Bernstein is affirming that the implicit understandings of the contractors are even richer than may have been suggested by a focus on the substantive norms themselves.

An interesting upshot of Bernstein's analysis is that, although she provides support (in appropriate situations) for the formalist response of enforcing the written terms of the contract in the face of any contrary customary understandings, she does so by effectively inserting two additional steps in the reasoning. In orthodox terms, the justification for enforcing the terms is that this is what the parties have arrived at as their contract: legitimacy flows from their act of voluntary assent ('direct formalism'). Bernstein's analysis, however, does not derive the legitimacy of enforcing the terms solely from the act of consent in formation of the contract. Her first step is to recognise the RPNs which may be contained in the implicit understandings deriving from custom, which may displace the contract terms in actual performance. Step two is to reintroduce the express terms when the end game arrives, because at that point only the EGNs in the contract terms are appropriate. Now, if it was open to a contractor to trigger end game norms at any time, without reference to who was responsible for bringing about the end game, nor how they had done it, the extra two steps from direct formalism would be insignificant—anyone could throw the switch to end game at any time and wipe out the expectations derived from the RPNs based on custom. However, Bernstein does not appear to stake

[36] *Ibid*, 1798.

out this extreme ground, and this leaves in play the central question of when the switch can be thrown—in other words, the extent to which the RPNs of customary understandings play a role in defining when end game can be brought about.

I am not here concerned to pursue the issue of when the switch can be thrown. My point is that Bernstein provides copious support for the claim that the relationship between customary understandings and standard forms is a subtle and complex one in which not only is meaning conferred on the standard forms, but also understandings are established about when terms may be relied on and when they may not. In a nutshell, the role of implicit understandings derived from the contracting community of the parties can be seen as the means by which they come to know *not only what the usual written contract says, but when it can be taken to mean what it says*.

Moreover, the additional steps in the reasoning behind the enforcement of express terms can be seen as providing support for seeing express terms as nested in, or enclosed by, implicit understandings, in the sense that the meaning and significance of the express terms is drawn from the implicit understandings through which the parties understand and structure the transaction. And this point can be widened to apply not only to the approach to individual terms but to the whole process of dealing, so that the transition from negotiation to performance—which will sometimes involve a moment of conscious formation—can be understood as guided and given meaning by the parties' knowledge of how trading is conducted, and the usual expectations that arise. This perspective inverts the usual primacy of agreement, which to orthodox contract law comes first, and within which may appear implied obligations, or standards of reasonableness, which fill out gaps in the express agreement. If we start with implicit understandings, and see these as the essential precondition for the parties to engage in highly sophisticated commercial relations, these understandings frame the interaction and locate the role of express agreement as clarifying the details for a particular transaction, rather than as the primary source of obligations between the parties.

I have already suggested that the emphasis on the context within which the parties deal does not mean that the norms in contracting communities can only be those which are usually associated with relational contract law; the same neutrality applies to the present point about the nesting of express agreement within implicit understandings. Within a contracting community, it may be well understood that dealing is strictly at arm's length and that no obligations are undertaken until some recognised symbolic stage of contract formation has been passed. When the law declines to enforce anything short of this, it is indeed giving effect to the implicit understandings that the parties bring to the process of dealing. Formally, the law declares there is no contract, because there is no agreement with consideration. Yet this can equally well be construed as recognising that, in the sector in which the parties trade, it is understood that this is how commercial relations are formed—in other words, the holding of no contract is justifiable by reference to the parties implicit understandings.[37]

The Reach of the Contracting Community Model

Although the contracting community model covers many of the contexts dealt with by commercial contract law, the two are by no means coextensive. An important category of commercial contracts which are not covered are those where only one side is typically a repeat player. Thus, where a supplier is selling to businesses, the large majority of which are infrequent purchasers, not only will the purchasers not develop specialist knowledge, but the recurrent interaction between suppliers and buyers necessary for participation in the creation of recognised trading practices is much less likely to exist.[38] Contracts coming into this category are those for the purchase of large capital items like major machine tools, or premises. However, the size of the organisations concerned is a variable here too, as frequency is typically a function of scale, and so larger organisations will, through centralised purchasing or procurement departments, acquire experience which will not be available to smaller firms.

[37] On this view, the doctrine of intention to create legal relations may have more substance than it is usually granted. More generally, classical law doctrines can be seen as fitting with such implicit understandings whenever these understandings are grounded on individualistic norms.

[38] An illustration of this situation is *R and B Customs Brokers Co Ltd v United Dominion Trust Ltd* [1988] 1 WLR 321, where a firm of brokers sued the seller of a defective car, and the Court of Appeal held that they should be treated as a consumer, for the purposes of Unfair Contract Terms Act 1977 s 6, because this contract was not integral to their business, and nor was it made with any regularity. The decision has been roundly criticised (in my view correctly) for applying a concept of business which was developed in an entirely different context, especially when, even if the claimants had not dealt as consumer, the exclusion clause would have been subject to a reasonableness test. Nevertheless, it provides an example of business purchasing without a contracting community.

On the other hand, the contracting community model does cover those situations where there are background understandings of which regular contractors are normally aware, but in a particular case one party says they were in fact not aware of them. This is in line with the approach of the law, which is almost invariably objective: as Lord Hoffmann emphasised in his restatement of the contextual approach, it is the understanding of a reasonable person with the background knowledge of the parties that matters.[39]

The purpose in constructing the contracting community model is to assist in clarifying the circumstances in which contract law reflects implicit understandings, and also the kind of understandings that are typically represented. The model provides a coherent setting in which implicit understandings—typically customary—can emerge along with established practices and norms which confer meaning on often complex exchange relations. In legal terms, these implicit understandings can be seen as serving two related functions: they give content to legal obligation, through both framing contextual interpretation of the meaning of express contract terms, and providing the basis for implied terms, and by conferring meaning on standards of reasonableness. And they confer a degree of legitimacy on those obligations which flow from the familiar practices of the contract community.[40]

Not all contracts are made in the context of a contracting community, and I turn below to examine the way in which implicit understandings may arise in contracting contexts which are quite different from the contracting community model, principally in the personal consumption model.

3. THE PERSONAL CONSUMPTION MODEL OF CONTRACTUAL RELATIONS

The personal consumption model is intended to identify a pervasive type of contract which provides unfavourable circumstances for the emergence of the implicit understandings associated with the contracting community model. This should foster the drawing out of the features which inhibit such understandings, and so enable the two models

[39] *Mannai Investment Co Ltd v Eagle Star Life Assurance*, n 21 above, 775.

[40] In this respect the implicit understandings mirror the classical function of express agreement.

to be used to elucidate the scope and nature of implicit understandings in situations which are not entirely covered by either model.

The Features of the Personal Consumption Model

The personal consumption model refers to contractual relations which are characterised by three principal features which typically arise in many higher value consumer transactions. First, the contracts concern complex products which require specialist knowledge to appraise. This knowledge covers a spectrum from knowledge of the technical specification of the product, its features in use, the features which differentiate it from alternative products, to knowledge about its future performance. All this applies pretty clearly not only to purchases such as domestic appliances, vehicles, household services (plumbing, electrical, building), but also to financial services such as insurance, pensions, and mortgages, credit and banking, and to professional services such as legal services and medical services.

All of these transactions will involve either experience or credence goods.[41] Experience goods are those where attributes such as quality cannot be assessed until after they have been purchased, for example a restaurant meal. Credence goods are those where, even with experience of the good, the purchaser will not be able to assess its quality—either never, or not for a long time. Examples are many financial services, especially pensions, and many legal and medical services. These concepts can be used not just to designate a whole good, but also particular attributes, so that (for example) a new car has some search characteristics (it can be test driven), some experience characteristics

[41] Experience and credence goods are concepts developed in economic theory about information, and are contrasted with search goods, where the quality and nature of the good can be assessed before purchase. For a non-technical discussion see Director of Fair Trading's report *Competition in the Professions* OFT328 (2001) para 35. See also R Ekelund *et al*, 'Advertising and Information: An Empirical Study of Search, Experience and Credence Goods' (1995) 22 *Journal of Economic Studies* 33; R Smith and A Bush, 'Towards Developing a Measure of Search, Experience, and Credence Qualities for Products and Services', available at http://www.sbaer.uca.edu/Research/2000/swma/00swma194.htm. Although I am using this classification of goods, I am not directly interested in the overall issue it is used by economists to analyse, which is market failure. I argue below that the features associated with these different goods are of use in making sense of the incidence of the social processes which generate implicit understandings.

(eg petrol consumption, reliability), and some credence characteristics (eg safety features such as crumple zones, durability of components).[42]

The feature of complexity does not itself distinguish personal consumption contracts from those within a contracting community—in many cases the products which are transacted will be the same. The feature of complexity is a necessary characteristic, which is given significance when combined with the other features of the model.

The second feature is that one party—normally the purchaser of the product—enters contracts of any single type infrequently, while the other is in business to supply the product. This is typically the case with most of the items in the list above. Although it is of course a commonplace to point out that consumers are often not repeat players when they enter transactions, the feature I want to emphasise here is that the consumer is buying in a market where all the buyers are in a similar position of not being repeat players. This has implications for the social organisation of such markets (especially for experience and credence goods), in relation to information flows, and resulting expectations, which I pursue below.

The third feature is that consumers' purchasing behaviour is typically driven by a more complex engine—individual preferences—than is the case with participants in the production and distribution system who do not actually consume the end product. Economic actors other than consumers are generally taken to be driven by an instrumental search for profit, and by virtue of being repeat players, learn what mix of products and supplies serves this goal. This contrast has a number of implications. Consumers facing a choice about a complex product which is purchased infrequently will often find that they need to discover more than information about the product—they have to discover what their preferences are. Although experience with previous purchases can form preferences in relation to frequently purchased or unchanging goods (eg food), this is less possible where the product is purchased infrequently and technical development is rapid. This is because the consumer is faced with the problem of not having had the experience of using the product which is often necessary in order for preferences to be formed. When I need a new hi-fi I can use a consumer magazine (eg *Hi-Fi*

[42] In fact it is possible to see many goods having at least some credence elements, notably where the consumer will be unable to tell whether statements about the circumstances of production are accurate, eg whether it contains genetically modified ingredients, whether food was produced organically, whether paper came from renewable forests, whether beef originated in the UK, whether clothing was made using child labour, etc.

Choice) to find out about all the features of the systems currently on sale. But such magazines cannot tell me which features I want, as many of them did not exist last time I bought a system, and it is usually wholly impractical to acquire the varied experience necessary to establish properly what my feature preferences would be.[43]

But at least with a hi-fi one may discover, quite soon after purchase, something about one's preferences; even this is not possible with many credence goods, where it may be many years after contracting before the understanding of alternatives enables preferences to be formed. The problem with pensions, for example, is not just that in many cases the nature of what the purchaser eventually gets is not known for many years (often decades), but that it may only be around the point of retirement that the purchaser will have informed preferences about the various elements which different pension packages may combine.

The combination of the three features of the personal consumption model means that the role of implicit understandings here is quite different from the contracting community model. Most centrally, it seems much less likely that customary implicit understandings will be able to emerge. A key reason for this is the quite different ways in which information is generated and dispersed.

In the personal consumption model, the market in the products concerned is characterised by the infrequent purchase of complex products. The fact that the goods will be experience or credence goods means that purchasers do not acquire and refine information about specification or performance of the goods by the experience of trading itself, but are dependent on other sources of information. In the contracting community model, individual purchasers (businesses) not only acquire information about the product from experience, but may also share knowledge with each other. This will help shape a market context in which some knowledge is taken for granted between contractors, so that many expectations which stem from implicit understandings are generalised. In contrast, in the personal consumption model, not only is the market composed of purchasers who cannot acquire the information in the same way, but the information which is in circulation will predominantly be that generated by the manufacturer or supplier.

[43] This point about the role of experience in forming preferences is distinct from the notion of experience goods. With experience goods, purchase is necessary to discover information about a characteristic of the product itself; the role of experience in preference formation is that through it the purchaser discovers whether they want that characteristic or not.

Some of this information will be detailed product specification, although this will often be of limited use for the reasons already outlined. More importantly, suppliers and manufactures rely on reputation and branding as means of transmitting information about the product, and it is recognised in marketing theory that branding is a powerful means of communicating qualities such as reliability to consumers. However, whether it is branding, reputation, or detailed product information, the fact remains that expectations are shaped by information which emanates from one side (ie supplier or manufacturer). This contrasts sharply with the contracting community model, where information about complex products is generated not only by suppliers and manufacturers, but by contractors' own experience in trading in the products in question.

The information asymmetry between suppliers and consumers in relation to complex products is well recognised, but it is not this alone which results in the absence of the customary implicit understandings which are characteristic of commercial contracting communities. Implicit understandings also concern expectations about the typical behaviour of the contracting parties in relation to how contracts are negotiated, after-sales service, how hitches in performance are treated, and how disputes may be handled. Where there are customary understandings about such matters, this means that any contractor knows not only how the supplier they are going to deal with will generally behave, but also how others are likely to behave too. Moreover, if these expectations are generalised, suppliers may well know that those with whom they deal will have these expectations about behaviour where performance issues arise. We have seen how, in contracts covered by the contracting community model, implicit understandings may include not just knowledge about the product, but also norms about how problems will be sorted out. It seems less likely that these shared normative expectations will be present in contracts covered by the personal consumption model, for the infrequency of dealing, coupled with the absence of understanding of the dimensions of complex products (especially credence goods), mean that consumers in general do not get in the position to establish such implicit understandings.[44]

[44] An example of uncertainty about trade practices is that many consumers appear uncertain about when it is expected practice to attempt to negotiate a discount, and when it is not. Uncertainty about this, which of course is typically known to a supplier, leads to a form of price discrimination, where suppliers publish prices allowing a margin for discount, but only reduce the price when necessary. The absence of any shared understandings about negotiation may also make more possible discrimination on grounds of

It is possible to identify some clear contrasts between the two models by closing in on two aspects: under the next two headings I contrast the models in relation to the role of trust and the role of standard form contracts.

Consumers, Implicit Understandings and Trust

A clear contrast between the personal consumption model and the contracting community model can be seen in the role of trust.[45] In one sense, given the emphasis that many firms place on cultivating a reputation as a reliable provider of goods and services, one might expect to find that trust figures prominently in this contractual model. However, although trust does exist, it is in a significantly different form from that encountered in the contracting community model.

Although it is plausible to suppose trust flourishes most readily where the parties are known to each other, trust may arise between strangers, and it is normal in many consumer contexts. Thus large retailers will, through their customer service policies, typically wish to maintain consumer confidence in the quality of the products they sell. Similarly, manufacturers of brand named goods will go to great lengths to maintain brand integrity.[46]

However, although consumer contexts may exhibit trust in this way, it is nevertheless very different to that encountered in commercial contracting communities. The trust tends to be very much one sided, in that consumers are trusted hardly at all—for example, credit is normally only available when the risk can be transferred to a credit card company or other source of consumer credit. But the role of implicit understandings in permitting trust in commercial contexts helps to focus on what element is missing in many consumer contexts.

race and gender; see I Ayres, 'Fair Driving: Race and Gender Discrimination in the Retail Car Market' (1991) 104 *Harvard Law Review* 817, where the discrimination in the face of identical negotiation strategies deployed by customers in the retail car market is clearly demonstrated.

[45] By trust here I refer to the situation where one party voluntarily exposes themselves to the risk of opportunistic behaviour by the other.

[46] The classic instance of the prompt withdrawal of Perrier Water from shops across the world following the discovery of contamination by benzene has found its place in textbooks on marketing: eg S Dibb *et al*, *Marketing: Concepts and Strategies* (Boston, Houghton, Mifflin, 2001) 519.

It is possible to distinguish two different dimensions where one party trusts another to do (or not do) something. One is the factor already noted, ie the willingness to be exposed to the risk of the other behaving opportunistically by not performing. The other dimension is the content of the trust, ie the thing which the person trusted is trusted to do, and it is in relation to this that implicit understandings play a significant role. Some of the content of the trust will be spelt out by the main terms of contract—the price, the basic nature of the product or service being supplied. Much will not be spelt out, especially the incidentals of performing certain contracts, or what happens if the performance miscarries in some way. These are precisely the matters that are, in many commercial contracts, settled by implicit understandings—the parties know how the goods are packaged, how payment is typically made, what happens when a subcontractors' work is slightly substandard, and so forth.[47] Sometimes, these matters can be settled by general implicit understandings, and owe nothing to any customary knowledge of the trade. But equally, sometimes more specialist knowledge is necessary to give content to these expectations, which, where a contracting community exists, can be supplied by customary implicit understandings. Where no such contracting community exists, trust becomes problematic: one party may in principle trust the other, but trust them to do *what*?

Ignorance about the content of trust is clearest in relation to credence goods, for example legal or medical services, where the client or patient typically cannot assess the quality of what has been done. In these contexts, there are professionally defined obligations—the doctor's obligation to act in the patient's best interests, or the solicitor's fiduciary duty to act in the client's interests, not his or her own. These obligations place clear limits on the pursuit of self interest by such service providers, although they do not take the form of norms which are shaped by the practices of contracting community involving the recipients of the services, but stem instead from professional organisation or public regulation. In these contexts, the fact that the recipient of the service does not understand or know the content of the thing the provider is undertaking to do is dealt with by imposing an obligation to act in the recipient's interests. But, beyond these fiduciary-type cases,

[47] Indeed, the cost reducing function of trust, in avoiding the need to spell out all the obligations at the outset, depends upon the parties trusting each other that reasonable expectations will be met.

the content of trust, where this has not been spelt out, may be non-existent, because it will not have been formed by the emergence of implicit understandings. In this sense, the trust is open ended, and open to abuse. Thus, a bank may wish to be trusted by its ordinary private customers; this may unproblematically include the expectation that the bank will deal honestly (eg will produce statements which are not deliberately falsified), or will do those things the bank undertakes to do. But, beyond this, what is the content of trust that a consumer should expect? Does it, for example, include an expectation that the bank will inform customers when it introduces more favourable accounts than the ones they currently use?[48]

Where a service is bespoke—in that it is tailored to the circumstances of each customer—and it also has credence good characteristics, trust is even more problematic; the building trades provide a good example. From a private householder's point of view, plumbing or electrical services have large credence elements, and they will not be in any position to tell whether standard practices and specifications have been observed, nor how contingencies such as a change in materials, delay, or defective materials would usually be handled. In contrast, where the same trades are being employed on a construction project by a main contractor, it is plausible to suppose that, not only will monitoring of the plumber or electrician be more apparent (and thus less necessary), but there will be some understandings regarding the handling of contingencies.

The reach of trust thus depends upon the contractor having an expectation of the content of the trust (ie what the other will do), and on them being able to assess whether that thing has been done. Where the contractor being trusted knows that the other has such expectations, and can assess the outcome, they will be inclined, for reputational reasons, to justify the trust and do what is expected: trust places normative boundaries on the opportunistic pursuit of self interest.[49] In the contracts covered by the personal consumption model, it is much less likely that consumers will form these expectations and be able to assess whether they have been met, and so the ultimate policing of trust—the concern with reputation—is weaker as an influence on behaviour.

[48] This can arise whether the customer is a borrower or a lender; for examples, see the references to the Banking Code at n 72 below.

[49] For discussion of loss of reputation as a sanction in relation to contracts, see D Charny, 'Non-Legal Sanctions in Commercial Relationships' (1990) 104 *Harvard Law Review* 373.

The Taming of Standard Forms

It has long been recognised that standard forms pose particularly severe problems in consumer contracts. Many suppliers produce one-sided sets of terms, which aim to protect the interests of the supplier, and which are provided on a take it or leave it basis.[50] Although there is widespread recognition that these terms can often be oppressive, there is much less agreement about what the precise basis of the objection is. A recurrent theme in the critique of standard forms is that they have not really been agreed by the party who is confronted with them.[51] I will argue that it is useful to understand the problem with standard forms in terms of the absence of the customary implicit understandings which prevail in many commercial contexts. To establish this, I will identify the ways in which a standard form contract may be 'tamed': that is, the way in which a standard form may be rendered less objectionable by the circumstances in which it is used.

First, the terms may be the subject of express negotiation by the parties to the contract in question. Strictly, such negotiation would mean the terms are no longer standard terms, and so the objection of absence of agreement could not apply.

Secondly, the terms in question may have been the subject of term-shopping. This is a mechanism that can, in theory, result in terms being treated as the product of consent of the parties even where they are presented by any individual supplier on a take it or leave it basis. The argument is that, where different suppliers offer different standard forms, customers can, if the terms are visible to them, 'shop' for the more favourable terms by not contracting with the suppliers offering the less favourable terms.[52] As long as there is a sufficient margin of term shoppers, then the less favourable terms should be driven out; this happens without any need for negotiation, in the same way that price competition can take place without any haggling over prices. Term

[50] Various explanations for this phenomenon are possible, including the exploitation of monopoly power. See T Rakoff, 'Contracts of Adhesion—an Essay in Reconstruction' (1983) 96 *Harvard Law Review* 1174 for analysis of this position, and the argument that contracts of adhesion are explicable as the attempt of an organisation to exercise control over its internal processes.

[51] For a discussion of economic rationales for intervention, see MJ Trebilcock, 'An Economic Approach to the Doctrine of Unconscionability' in BJ Reiter and J Swan (eds) *Studies in Contract Law* (Toronto, Butterworths, 1980) 379; also H Beale, 'Unfair Contracts in Britain and Europe' [1989] *Current Legal Problems* 197, 199–201.

[52] See papers by Trebilcock (n 51 above) and Rakoff (n 50 above).

shopping can only occur where the terms are visible, and a sufficient margin of customers shop for them.

The 'taming' effect of negotiation and term shopping principally lies in the ability of customers to influence, by withholding consent to trade, the content of the terms. Taken at face value, neither negotiation nor term shopping would appear to require implicit understandings shared by the parties—at least as far as the term in question (negotiated or shopped) is concerned.[53]

Thirdly, a standard form may not be the one sided production of a supplier, but rather be the product of negotiation by the trade association or other bodies representing the various interests in a commercial sector. A clear example of this is the JCT family of standard forms used in the construction industry. These forms are drafted by the Joint Contracts Tribunal, on which is represented main contractors, surveyors, clients, architects and the like. These contracts are not designed to protect the interests of one side against another, but aim to achieve a balance of the interests concerned.[54] This kind of form will require the existence of a developed contracting community with established institutions which can undertake the work. The standard form is 'tamed' here not by the agreement of individual contractors who use it, but by a process of representative negotiation which means that drafting reflects the balance of interests, and so one sided terms are more likely to be eradicated.

The fourth way in which standard forms may be tamed is where the standard form—possibly one framed by the process just described—may be widely used across a market sector, and thus become well known through usage.[55] In this process, knowledge of what the terms

[53] However, even if a contractor has adequate knowledge of the term in issue, negotiation or term shopping can only be rationally conducted where there is some knowledge of the other terms which are not being negotiated or term shopped. As Rakoff points out, the risk is that, as visible terms are negotiated or term shopped, a contractor may be making non-maximising decisions in relation to the less visible terms which are also being affected: Rakoff, n 50 above, 1226.

[54] Other examples are the bills of lading, standard conditions for the sale for land, and commodities contracts. Note that one reason why the clause in *Mitchell (George) (Chesterhall) Ltd v Finney Lock Seeds* [1983] 2 AC 803, which limited the liability of a seller of seed, did not pass the statutory test of reasonableness was that it was promulgated by the seller's trade association without any consultation with representatives of farmers.

[55] For clear examples where forms were not incorporated by signature or notice but became part of the contract on this basis see *Henry Kendall & Sons v William Lillico & Sons Ltd* [1969] AC 31 and *British Crane Hire Corporation Ltd v Ipswich Plant Hire Ltd* [1975] QB 303.

mean—or more accurately are treated as meaning—will be disseminated by participation in the practices of a contracting community, a clear example of which is that of shipping. The knowledge which is diffused is not so much knowledge of the bare content of terms, but knowledge also of the circumstances with which they deal, and how and when they are usually invoked. Here, informally acquired knowledge will become embedded as customary implicit understandings, and, if the law gets out of line with such understandings, it may on occasion be made to swerve to reflect them.[56]

The fifth way is closely related to the fourth. Not only may a practical understanding of what the terms means become diffused as a recognised practice, but those practices may include the expectation that a party who is favoured by a particular term does not insist on it being enforced. In other words, a gap opens up between the formal meaning of the term and the actual practice of the parties.[57] Again, where the terms are used widely in a sector, it is possible for knowledge of the gap to be effectively part of the knowledge of what the terms mean. Bernstein's work makes clear the often subtle way in which informal understandings interact with the letter of the contract.[58]

Of the five ways in which standard forms can be tamed, three require the existence of a contracting community, in which customary understandings can be established. The two methods which may (at least in theory) work without implicit understandings—negotiation and term shopping—are in any case of debatable significance in relation to the content of standard forms.[59] Moreover, not only do the other three methods provide a way of removing one sided terms (or policing their use), they also provide an additional legitimacy for the terms which are

[56] The classic instance of this is the decision in *New Zealand Shipping v Satterthwaite* [1975] AC 154 where the commercial expectation that a third party (stevedores) was covered by a limitation clause in a bill of lading was vindicated by inventing a collateral contract to which they were party.

[57] For discussion of this gap see Macaulay, 'Relational Contracts on A Sea of Custom', n 3 above; see also the chapter by Campbell and Collins in this volume, which points out that in *Mitchell (George) (Chesterhall) Ltd v Finney Lock Seeds* [1983] 2 AC 803, when the House of Lords held that the limitation was unreasonable because it departed from usual practice, it was applying an implicit understanding of the trade. Where a gap is established between a practice and what a term provides, it does of course make term shopping more difficult: term shopping can only be rational, in the presence of a gap, where the contractor actually becomes acquainted with the practice.

[58] See articles by Bernstein, n 14 above.

[59] Even its advocates recognise that term shopping is only possible under relatively limited circumstances; for a rejection of the approach see VP Goldberg, 'Institutional Change and the Quasi-Invisible Hand (1974) 17 *J Law and Economics* 461.

regarded as part of the contract. Thus, if we defend the legitimacy of the terms in standard forms *solely* on the basis of some technical act of consent like signature, then not only is it difficult to justify the one-sided terms, but there is no more reason, *stemming from the mere act of signing*, for regarding the less objectionable terms as legitimate: standard forms are not read, still less understood. However, where terms are used in contexts where there are customary implicit understandings, not only are the inappropriately onerous terms likely to be removed or not relied upon, but those that are left are more likely to be seen as the product of a more legitimate process of consent.

If we now turn to the consumer context, we can see that the typical absence of customary implicit understandings lies behind some of the recognised problems with standard forms in consumer contracts. Most obviously, the third method—negotiation between representatives of interests—does not occur in consumer contracts, and this means that consumer contracts are typically drafted to protect the interests of the drafting party.

But it is the absence of the final two methods which arguably makes the enforcement of standard forms in consumer contracts especially unsatisfactory. Both methods involve the acquisition of knowledge of what the terms are usually taken to mean, which may or may not reflect their plain meaning. When this is coupled with knowledge about the circumstances with which the terms are intended to deal, and how performance problems will be handled, the parties will share understandings about what the terms mean in practice. But in contracts covered by the personal consumption model, it is much less likely that these processes can emerge, with the result that consumers do not learn of the terms, nor their usual meanings, and nor do they acquire practical knowledge of the circumstances which they are invoked. Moreover, it is also much less likely that recognised understandings will have developed around how the eventualities with which the standard forms terms deals will actually be handled in practice.[60]

It is also plausible to suppose that the gap method will be unusual in the consumer context, because there will not typically have been the frequency of contracting to establish diffused understandings about the practice in relation to the terms. This is not to say that suppliers invariably enforce terms against consumers when entitled to do so—indeed

[60] One way of investigating this claim would be to select a sector where firms routinely supply both business and private customers—possible examples may be found in the construction trades.

there is clear empirical evidence to the contrary.[61] Where the consumer context arguably differs is that there may be no generally known *practice* of not invoking the strict terms which the contractors will know or anticipate, because consumers will not typically form a contracting community within which such an expectation can be formed. This means the supplier can choose when to make a concession—in other words, they can 'concession discriminate', and allow the granting of concessions to be purely guided by their own self interest.

In summary, I am suggesting that the significance of implicit understandings in relation to standard forms is twofold. First, it is plausible to suppose that these understandings within a contracting community play an important role in 'taming' standard forms—by eliminating inappropriately onerous terms, by communicating the practical consequences of particular terms through the establishment of trade practices, and by fostering a contracting culture in which the practice not to enforce terms may become embedded. And the accumulation of experience and the sharing of background understandings about how contracts typically function in a sector may thus amount to a more powerful legitimating reason for holding the parties bound to terms which reflect practice than any act of express consent at the technical moment of formation.

Second, the absence of customary implicit understandings in the personal consumption model means that they cannot operate to tame or justify standard forms. Thus, it is not so much the lack of express agreement to the terms that renders them objectionable, but rather the fact that they are used in a context which, because there is no contracting community, is deprived of the social processes which may disseminate the knowledge, practices and norms which may make the resulting standard form a workable piece of self-regulation.

The Reach of the Personal Consumption Model

The two models are intended to capture the basic situations which are probably the most and least favourable to the formation of implicit understandings. Although many familiar contracting situations fall within them, some are not covered at all, or display some features of

[61] See W Whitford 'Strict Products Liability and the Automdobile Industry: Much Ado About Nothing' 1968 *Wisconsin Law Review* 83, 143–53.

both. Thus the models are not intended to divide neatly all commercial contracts from all consumer ones. For example, many contracts made by individuals in a private capacity are not covered by the personal consumption model. Purchases of simple products for cash—typically search goods—are not covered, and this exclusion makes sense as there is much less scope or need for the generation of shared understandings to provide a context in which transactions are carried out.

The situation where a product is purchased frequently also falls outside the model. Here, the fact that the market is adjusted to frequent purchase means that information will be gained by experience and so leave the consumer less dependent on suppliers. Where there is also recurrent experience of performance which miscarries, it is also possible for practices to develop about how these situations are typically handled.[62]

There are also some kinds of commercial contracts which display features of the personal consumption model. One is the situation already mentioned where the small or medium sized organisation purchases a large value item which, for it and most others typically buying in that market, is an infrequent transaction.[63] The same problem about the lack of customary implicit understandings built up in a contracting community can arise here too, although, the third feature of the personal consumption model, the pursuit of utility rather than profit, does not apply.[64]

A further use of the models is that they can be used to assess the prospects of customary implicit understandings in contract types that do not involve the same element of supply which is assumed in both of the models. For example, residential tenancy contracts differ from the personal consumption model in that there is no good or service supplied, and there seems to be a greater opportunity for the tenant to

[62] However, even here, there may be elements of a product about which it is difficult for the consumer to acquire knowledge; food is a notable example. Although food is a very highly differentiated product, with massive choice being communicated through branding, marketing and labelling, most foods still have some credence good charactistics, eg the amount of pesticide residues.

[63] This absence of contracting community can be combatted by small firms pursuing their interests through a trade association, so enabling them to obtain some of the benefits of being repeat players which may accrue to large organisations.

[64] One use of the analysis in terms of ideal type models is that it can identify hybrid or mixed contexts, which exhibit features of more than one model. An example is where there is a contracting community in the sense I have described, but a subset of the participants are infrequent contractors who, as a result, do not in fact share the knowledge of its practices, which will have been shaped by regular participants.

etablish understandings with a landlord over the period of a tenancy. Nevertheless, there will still typically be no contracting community, because individual tenants will tend not to contract with different landlords with any frequency, and so generalised customary understandings may well not develop. Without this background, the law may still find it difficult to give content to matters which were not rendered explicit.[65]

Another example is those contracts by which a person becomes a member of an institution, for example a trade union. These too are not readily characterised as 'supply', and will also typically sustain a long term relationship that may last many years. Yet, despite the thicker nature of the relationship between a member and an organisation, the 'market' in membership does not consist of frequent changes of allegiance, with the result that members are also not repeat players who establish with a number of 'suppliers' the background understandings which are typical of the contracting community model. Thus, when the courts have imposed an obligation on the organisation to treat the member according to the principles of natural justice, this is difficult to explain as deriving from the implicit understandings of a contracting community in which such shared expectations have been developed.[66]

In yet another category of contracts, the background understandings which the parties carry though a relationship are shared but not customary. This is the case with intimate relations (eg cohabitation) where the parties have not adopted an explicit cohabitation contract, but have reached tacit understandings about such things as the disposition of property or financial support. The law (especially in the UK) has been resistant to finding anything contractual in these relationships, and part of the reason for this may be that there will rarely be any contracting community available as a source of customary norms to be applied. However (as I have argued elsewhere) it is possible to see in some of these relations definite shared understandings which are implicit rather than express, and which deserve legal recognition.[67]

[65] See *Liverpool City Council v Irwin* [1977] AC 239, discussion at n 76 below.

[66] *Lee v Showmen's Guild* [1952] 1 KB 189; see also D Oliver, *Common Values and the Public Private Divide* (London, Butterworths, 1999) 177–86. The position is similar in the relationship between a student and a university: see J Wightman *Contract: A Critical Commentary* (London, Pluto Press, 1996) 122–36.

[67] See J Wightman, 'Intimate Relationships, Relational Contract Theory, and the Reach of Contract' (2000) 8 *Feminist Legal Studies* 93, 105–13.

Overall, the significance of the personal consumption model is that it identifies a widely found set of conditions which appear unpropitious for the development of the customary implicit understandings which are typically recognised in traditional contract law. Where all these characteristics are found together, a situation will fall entirely within the model, but equally it is possible to identify situations where only some of the characteristics will be found. In some of these (such as membership contracts), the credence characteristics will still be found, despite a long-term relationship between the parties. However, the absence of customary understandings does not mean that in situations displaying some or all of the features comprising the model there are no expectations nor understandings at all; there typically are, and the question thus arises of what, if anything, should be made of them. I now turn to examine that general issue.

4. BEYOND CUSTOMARY UNDERSTANDINGS

Given that the law relies on customary implicit understandings, what should happen when, because of the contracting context, these are thin or non-existent? I explore this below, but first turn to consider why the absence of such understandings should matter.

The Absence of Customary Understandings

It might be argued that, when contracting takes place in a context which is not rich in customary understandings, this is because the type of contracting in question has no need for them. This is partly true, but goes too far. Contracts covered by the contracting community model tend to be more relational, and hence less discrete, than contracts covered by the personal consumption model. However, this does not mean that all contracts covered by the personal consumption model are discrete in this sense.

It is possible to identify contracts which are of a discrete, or one shot kind which lack the relational dimension which is arguably necessary for customary implicit understandings (in addition to general understandings) to develop. An instance of this is Macneil's original stock example of the discrete contract—'the cash purchase of gasoline at a station on the New Jersey turn pike by someone who rarely travels the road'.[68] Here, customary implicit understandings do not exist. Conventions about payment are general, and the goods are identical to goods elsewhere (partly through regulation). There seems no need for customary implicit understandings because of the uniform expectations about what is received, its delivery and payment, and the apparent extreme rarity of any failure by the goods to correspond with the expectations formed about them; general implicit understandings are enough.

However, the position is different in relation to the infrequently purchased complex products which figure in the personal consumption model. Although these contracts may not be seen as particularly relational, in that the parties only come together for these sales, and there is typically no longer term relation between the parties,[69] these one shot sales nevertheless differ from the petrol example because they can be said to be *potentially relational*. By this I mean that in their nature, exchanges of this kind may lead to further contact and relations between the parties, usually arising out of problems in performance. In contracts covered by the contracting community model, implicit understandings may develop about how these issues will be dealt with—they may or may not embrace norms requiring high degrees of co-operation, but shared expectations about what will occur are possible. Where such problems arise in contracts covered by the personal consumption model, there is a gap in the parties understandings: although the supplier is likely to have encountered the situation before, for each consumer it will normally be the first time, and they will not have any expectation which derives from generalised practices in the sector that, in the case of the contracting community model, derive from previous shared handling. The upshot of this is that, in contracts covered by the personal consumption model, the functions that are performed elsewhere by implicit understandings remain unperformed.[70]

[68] 'Contracts Adjustments of Long-term Economic Relations Under Classical, Neoclassical, and Relational Contract Law' (1978) 72 *Northwestern University Law Review* 854, 857.

[69] Even where the consumer buys a succession of electrical goods from the same store, the transactions are typically treated wholly separately, and it would seem rare, after the retailing revolution, for face-to-face relationships to be established or endure between individual shoppers and staff in (for example) a large out-of- town electrical goods store.

[70] Perversely, this can also be true of contracts which may look very relational. Some contracts that consumers enter into may be very long term indeed, like a mortgage, yet there may be no actual contact between the parties, beyond the sending of statements and adjustment of standing orders for years (not even this with direct debit). It may only be when (say) an endowment mortgage fails to generate the expected returns 25 years later that parties have cause to speak. In terms of face-to-face relations, this is a discrete contract where the performance happens to be very spread out.

And the result of this is that the behaviour of the supplier is not disciplined by norms which encapsulate the reasonable expectations of the consumer, with the further consequence that, when legal determination is needed, it cannot draw on such expectations in framing obligations. We can thus identify a category of 'gap' situations where performance issues may arise which, in a mainstream commercial context, would be resolved by reference to customary understandings, but because of the context, lack this resource for the resolution or avoidance of disputes.[71]

Although there may be gaps in the customary implicit understandings in contracts for infrequently purchased complex products, it does not follow that there are no implicit understandings about the matters at all. It is here where shared understandings run out and we encounter the possibility of divergent or unilateral understandings, ie where the parties do not expect the same thing. One response is for the law to use these unilateral understandings in dealing with the gap.

Unilateral Expectations

The basic feature of unilateral expectations is that the assumptions which the parties bring to contractual relationships are different, and these are not aligned in the process of negotiation and performance. But a discrepancy in the subjective expectations is not enough, for this can happen in many commercial contexts. In addition, there must be no background of customary understandings which enables one to say that one party's set of assumptions are reasonable and the other's are not. For example, a mortgagor may have assumed that he or she would be able to redeem without penalty the mortgage which they have taken out to purchase their home, while it may be the practice of the bank or building society—expressed in a standard form which has been signed—to require a substantial release payment.[72] Each side may have formed an expectation about what happens which, as far as they

[71] The debate about 'default rules' addresses how gaps in the contract should be filled. One way of filling the gap is through custom and usage; my point is that this will be a less productive method in contracts covered by the personal consumption model than in contracts covered by the contracting community model (see Riley, n 28 above).

[72] This is somewhat analogous to the more complicated facts of the first case to be referred to the courts under the Unfair Terms in Consumer Contracts Regulations: *Director General of Fair Trading v First National Bank plc* [2002] 1 AC 481. These kind of unilateral expectations have posed serious problems in relation to financial products, and in 1992 the banks produced the Code of Good Banking Practice (now the Banking

are concerned, appears reasonable, and there is in this situation no customary understanding, shaped by the practices of a contracting community, which can provide the answer. As a result, it will often be more difficult to apply standards of reasonableness, since the court cannot give content to that standard by asking what the established understandings in that contracting sector are.

In at least some of the situations covered by the personal consumption model, there are cogent reasons why these expectations should be taken seriously. First, the nature of the informational asymmetry means that the supplier will have typically played a major role in establishing the information base on which the consumer relies. This applies not just to the hard information supplied in leaflets about (say) a financial product, but also more general output in the form of advertising and other marketing activity. This information conveys not only data about different products, but also, perhaps of more importance, impressions about reliability, trustworthiness, economy, as well as more diffuse social meanings and images which are attached to goods. In traditional legal terms, the further the supplier strays from hard information, the less likely it will be that they are held responsible for the content. Yet, where goods with credence chararacteristics are concerned, it may well be precisely the more diffuse communication about reputation, reliability etc which is influential, and which is targeted by suppliers in their marketing activity. Arguably, where suppliers are predominantly responsible for virtually the whole informational context in which a consumer acts, they should comply with the reasonable expectations which this engenders, even where these expectations are at odds with the express terms of the contract.

This argument is fortified by the fact that, as discussed in the context of trust, suppliers are not, despite the potentially massive informational asymmetry, acting in a fiduciary-type capacity. The problem that was posed in giving content to open-ended trust is an example of a wider phenomenon which exists wherever an organisation is simultaneously boasting of its customer service focus, and attempting to maximise its returns. Inevitably, profit-seeking firms do not pursue customers' interests in a fiduciary sense—this might involve recommending a cheaper or better competitor. They may well wish sincerely to meet customers expressed desires, while at the same time attempting

Code). The Banking Ombudsman (now the Financial Services Ombudsman) has also been critical of a variety of practices. See http://www.financial-ombudsman.org.uk/publications/ombudsman-news/banking/about-september.htm

to extract profit from other aspects of the deal. For example, an OFT report concluded that the selling of extended warranties on domestic appliance by electrical retailers was operating contrary to the consumers' interests.[73] The focus on customer care in marketing and reputation building may well mean that a supplier will go to great lengths to keep consumers content. However, the underside may be that, in activities invisible to the public, strategies are hatched to maximise returns by taking advantages of informational asymmetries and the absence of customary understandings which can, in a contracting community, set boundaries to the pursuit of self interest.[74]

Thus, in the kind of contracts covered by the personal consumption model, there may well be good reason for holding a supplier to the unilateral expectations which a consumer may have acquired as part of the transacting process—even when these do not reflect actual practice.[75] We now turn to see how far this kind of expectation is recognised in the law.

[73] It was found that the practice of 'bundling' the extended warranty with the sale, so that the warranty could only be bought with the appliance, coupled with the absence of alternative prices, or the incidence of the breakdowns which the warranties covered, meant that overcharging was taking place. (OFT 1994). Another strategy which belies the appearance of customer care is 'informational noise' where firms, by artificial over-differentiation of models and deals (eg cookers, mobile phones, pensions) make comparison impossible or too time consuming, which in turn will lead to differential pricing. Credence goods are especially susceptible to this: see generally *Consumer Detriment Under Conditions of Imperfect Information*, Office of Fair Trading Research Paper 11 (1997).

[74] An example of price discrimination can be seen in the practice of some banks and building societies in relation to certain new accounts. In the fight for more investors, one strategy is to advertise a new savings account with a very competitive rate. Some time later, a new marketing campaign will announce another new account, paying a similar rate. Meanwhile, the interest rate on the first account is edged back, and no new investors are offered it. Some investors will transfer to the new account, but those that stay in the old account will suffer price discrimination ie, will be paid less for the use of their money. The result is that the institution can maximise the number of new investors by offering rates of interest which do not have to be paid to all existing investors. The neatness of this (as with most price discrimination) is that the ones who lose out do not generally realise they have lost. This formerly prevalent practice is now being tackled by the Financial Services Ombudsman: see URL at n 72 above.

[75] Much more difficult are instances that concern more incidental aspects of a transaction, where the purchaser has no expectation at all, because the issue which crops up had never crossed their mind until it arises. It is much more difficult for expectations to provide content for any obligation here. Even so, the purchaser may well, retrospectively, take the view that what is now being offered or expected of them is not what they would have expected, had they known and understood the possibility. Although this is in one sense an expectation with the benefit of hindsight, which in traditional legal terms comes too late to shape obligation, the purchaser may be seen as crystallising an expectation that is atemporal, in that, had they understood and experienced this outcome before entering the contract, they would have formed the same expectation as they in fact formed when the performance issue arose.

Legal Recognition of Unilateral Expectations

Overall, the ordinary rules of contract law do not appear to be well adapted to recognising implicit understandings which are not customary. The usual tests for implied terms will not normally reflect expectations which are unilateral in this sense, because these tests arguably work best when there is a contracting community to provide a set of practices and meanings on which the courts can draw. For example, in *Liverpool City Council Irwin*,[76] the Council provided a 'tenancy agreement' to residential tenants of their flats which only contained the tenant's obligations and not the Council's. It was eventually held by the House of Lords that, under the test of necessity for the implication if terms, that the Council owed duties relating to the upkeep of common areas such as the lift and rubbish chute. However, difficulty was experienced in framing the duties, and this was arguably due to the fact that the court did not see the case as an instance of a general category of case in which the purposes and background understandings are well known. The House of Lords did not, for example, refer to other arrangements on blocks of flats, and instead attempted to derive the obligations on the basis of what was necessary. This, however, seemingly places no weight on the expectations of the tenants, which, had there been an operative contracting community, may well have shaped the background understandings on which the court would otherwise have drawn.[77] As it was, the enquiry into what was necessary muffled any explicit analysis of what the council tenants' reasonable expectations may have been regarding the maintenance of lifts etc.

[76] n 65 above.

[77] Another case where absence of a contracting community can be seen as posing problems for implication is *Reid v Rush Tompkins* [1990] 1 WLR 212. The claimant was an employee of the defendant working in Ethiopia, and was badly injured in a road accident which was not the defendant's fault. The claimant argued that there was an implied term in the contract of employment, either requiring the employer to provide insurance cover for accidental injury, or requiring the employer to inform the employee that insurance cover was essential given the conditions which prevailed in Ethiopia. This was rejected by the Court of Appeal on the basis of the test of necessity in *Liverpool City Council v Irwin*. Although not developed here, it is arguable that this case goes against a trend in employment law which has seen the courts prepared to develop terms that vindicate unilateral expectations; see in particular *Scally v Southern Health and Social Services Board* [1991] IRLR 522, *Spring v Guardian Assurance* [1994] 3 WLR 354, and *Malik v BCCI* [1998] AC 20.

Perhaps the main obstacle to the recognition of unilateral expectations has been the objective principle of agreement. Where there may be doubt about what the parties have agreed to, then what matters is how the offer or agreement would appear to a reasonable contractor. This has tended to involve applying a standard of objectivity drawn from the practice of the contracting community in question, and so results in those contracting in such situations being treated as having the usual background knowledge. It is more difficult to apply the objective principle where there is no contracting community to define the standard on which the courts may draw, yet this has not resulted in the courts using the principle to deprive terms (eg in standard forms) of effect where they have been incorporated into the contract.[78] Most of the situations covered by the personal consumption model involve standard forms, and these have caused serious problems for the law.

Once such terms have been incorporated into the contract by signature, there is little that can be done to reflect unilateral expectations other than through construction techniques.[79] Part of the problem here is the legacy left by the foundering of the English common law's attempt to deal with the standard form in non-commercial situations. The doctrine of fundamental breach was developed around the middle of the twentieth century as a means of dealing with onerous clauses (mainly exception or exemption clauses) in signed contracts. It developed out of a number of doctrines established in a commercial cases, notably deviation, which had been used as an aid in the construction of onerous terms. In the precursors of fundamental breach, attempts were made to construe the offending express term with reference to the main object or purpose of the contract.[80] This was plainly a contextual construction of the term, which looked beyond the term itself to the background knowledge and understandings the parties brought to the

[78] See JR Spencer, 'Signature, Consent, and the Rule in *L'Estrange v Graucob*' [1973] CLJ 104, where it is argued that it was open to the court in *L'Estrange v Graucob* [1934] KB 394 to hold, on the basis of the objective theory, that the terms were not part of the contract.

[79] The exception is a case like *Schroeder Music Publishing Co Ltd v Macaulay* [1974] 1 WLR 1308, where a standard form contract confining musicians' ability to record and compose for others was held invalid under the restraint of trade doctrine and so contrary to public policy. The public policy doctrine has not otherwise been used to handle standard forms, although there are cases which suggest this would not have been unarguable; see eg *Johnson v Moreton* [1980] AC 37, where the doctrine was used to render invalid a clause depriving an agricultural tenant of security of tenure conferred by statute.

[80] See eg *Glynn v Margetson*, n 23 above; Coote, n 24 above, 94–98.

contract. Virtually all the cases in which construction techniques were used concerned contracting communities, mainly concerned with the carriage of goods.

The construction approach was put under pressure in consumer cases where a clause was duly incorporated into the contract, and was not ambiguous, yet it apparently entitled a seller (for example) to deliver a heap of scrap instead of a car. It was of course obvious that such a clause defeated the reasonable expectation of the buyer, and in the 1950s and early 1960s doctrine emerged—mainly in consumer cases—which went beyond being a rule of construction, and became effectively a rule of law that some obligations could not be excluded. Considerable confusion reigned even after the rule of law approach was rejected by the House of Lords in 1966, and legislation was eventually introduced to handle the problem.

Although the legislation provided a much clearer and more satisfactory approach to exclusion clause cases, the effective abandonment of the common law doctrine meant that no principles were developed which directly addressed the problem of the unilateral expectation. The 'rule of law' cases like *Karsales (Harrow) Ltd v Wallis*,[81] or *Levison v Patent Steam Carpet Cleaning Co Ltd*[82] can be seen as an attempt to recognise that there was a problem in treating a clause as part of the contract when it was so plainly contrary to the reasonable expectation of the consumer, but no principled recognition of this was adopted in the general law of contract.[83]

Legislation since the 1970s can be seen to address clearly the problem of these unilateral expectations. Especially notable is the provision in the Unfair Contract Terms Act 1977 which imposes a reasonableness test on a clause by which one person claims to be entitled to render another a contractual performance substantially different from what was reasonably expected.[84] Similarly, the regulations implementing the directive on unfair terms in consumer contracts can be seen as a response to the problems of unilateral expectations, although expecta-

[81] [1956] 1 WLR 936.

[82] [1978] QB 69.

[83] It is possible that a contributory factor may have been that a construction approach, informed by context, was more adapted to dealing with commercial contracts because these tended to display customary implicit understandings which shaped the process.

[84] See s 3, which is however confined in its scope by Sch 1: the Act does not apply to contracts of insurance, contracts relating to an interest in land, and contracts creating or transferring securities, thus excluding contracts for most financial products.

tion is not used as a test of validity in either the general principle of good faith, or in the 'grey list' terms in the Unfair Terms in Consumer Contracts Directive.[85]

These provisions appear to deal with many of the substantive problems, but it is striking that they do so without disturbing the underlying basis of common law principle. Although a wider scope is granted to unilateral expectations where the issue is the incorporation of written terms by reasonable notice,[86] the common law approach to written terms which are signed remains inhospitable to the recognition of unilateral expectations.[87] The Directive on Unfair Terms in Consumer Contracts is less restricted than the Unfair Contract Terms Act 1977, but its capacity to recognise the unilateral expectation in relation to standard forms is limited in two ways. As it is confined to consumer contracts, it cannot apply to commercial or other kinds of contracts which display features of the personal consumption model. And it does not apply to contracts made before 1995, which means that many long term contracts relating to mortgages, pensions and life insurance are beyond its scope. In a recent consultation paper, the Law Commission has proposed a rationalisation of the law now contained in the Unfair Contract Terms Act 1977 and the Unfair Terms in Consumer Contracts Regulations 1999, and, although the proposals relating to consumer contracts mainly simplify the two regimes, in relation to commercial contract more striking changes are provisionally proposed.[88] Currently, the provisions of UCTA relating to business to business contracts only affect contract terms which attempt to exclude or limit a liability, or which entitle the defendant to render a performance substantially different from that which was reasonably expected.[89] They do not catch terms which seek to impose or modify the other party's obligations, for

[85] For other piecemeal reforms which can be seen in the same way, see the cooling off and cancellation rights contained in the Consumer Credit Act 1974, Timeshare Act 1992, Consumer Contracts (Distance Selling) Regulations 2000.

[86] The emphasis in the leading case of *Parker v South Eastern Rlwy* on what the party on the receiving end of the ticket or notice would reasonably expect it to contain has meant that this doctrine can work well where there is a contracting community *and* where there is not. Thus, in *Interfoto Picture Library Ltd v Stilletto Visual Programmes* [1989] QB 433 the court could refer to reasonable expectations about the usual rate for overdue slides (against which the plaintiff's rate was very high), while in consumer cases (like *Thornton v Shoe Lane Parking* [1971] 2 QB 163) unilateral expectations of consumers—which may diverge from corporate practice—could be reflected equally well.

[87] *The Principles of European Contract Law* contain provisions which could be the basis of a challenge to terms which defeat a unilateral expectation; see n 27 above.

[88] *Unfair Terms in Contracts*, Law Commission Consultation Paper 166 (2002).

[89] s 3(2)(b)(i).

example by entitling a seller to impose extra charges. The consultation paper tentatively proposes bringing such terms in business to business contracts within the scope of legislative control, and so it is possible that the problem of unilateral expectations will be addressed in a commercial as well as a consumer context.

Although these legal provisons can give expression to unilateral expectations, they do not generally embody the reasonable expectation standard in their formulations. If these provisions are seen in some ways as responding to the deficit or gap in governing norms which results when contracting for complex products takes place without a background of implicit understandings, then there is a case for an explicit focus on unilateral expectations as a resource for filling the gap.[90]

Conclusion

Taking it as established that implicit understandings play an important role in the formulation and application of contract law, I have explored how the incidence and nature of those understandings may vary across different kinds of contracting contexts. By constructing two models of contracting relations—the contracting community model, and the personal consumption model—I have attempted to identify features which favour the development of such understandings, and also features which are less hospitable to them. This analysis suggests that the implicit understandings which the law reflects most readily tend to be those reached between contractors dealing within a contractual community, and that these understandings are typically customary understandings.

Where the context is less hospitable to such understandings, this does not mean that there are no issues of the kind that, in other contexts, are dealt with by implicit understandings. Where the elements of the personal consumption model are present—complex products with

[90] This can be seen as the effect of applying the good faith standard in the US in situations where contracting communities are absent. For argument to this effect in the context of contracts between nursing homes and their residents see Maureen Armour, 'A Nursing Home's Good Faith Duty "To" Care: Redefining a Fragile Relationship Using the Law of Contract' (1994) 39 *St Louis University Law Journal* 217; and in contracts between students and universities see Timothy Davis, 'An Absence of Good Faith: Defining a University's Educational Obligation to Student-Athletes' (1991 28 *Houston Law Rev* 743.

experience or credence characteristics, bought infrequently—there can be a gap or deficit in the operation of the law: when performance issues arise, the legal doctrines normally applied do not have the raw material in implicit understandings that, in the contracting community model, provide the basis of the law's response.

However, the absence of these customary understandings does not mean that there are no implicit understandings at all. In contracts displaying features of the personal consumption model, there may often be understandings which are not shared and which thus give rise to unilateral expectations. I argue that, where there is no contracting community to foster shared understandings, these unilateral expectations may deserve to shape an obligation to fill the gap, in part because it is precisely in situations covered by the personal consumption model that the supplier provides the informational context and so significantly shapes the expectations which the purchaser brings to the transaction. And, where credence goods such as financial products are in issue, the massive assymetry of information, coupled with the supplier's pursuit of their own interest, suggests that the supplier should be expected to act in an almost semi-fiduciary capacity. Many detailed reforms, as well as sector-wide standards of self regulation (such as the Banking Code) can be seen as responding to unilateral expectations in contexts where there is no contracting community to generate and disseminate the background assumptions which confer meaning on most commercial contracting.

A further reason for granting weight to unilateral expectations in legal determination stems from the different view of the social processes of contracting which is revealed by an emphasis on implicit understandings. Once the formal act of signature to a written contract is placed in the context of the shared understandings of parties in a contracting community, it can be argued that it is on these understandings, in which the express terms are nested, that the contractual relationship substantially stands. The law's traditional emphasis on the usual outward manifestation of agreement—written terms—can carry the assumption that the act of consent is to be found in an isolated act of 'agreeing' the terms at the moment of formation. Certainly, it is when seen in this way that the argument for the literal enforcement of terms seems most persuasive. But an emphasis on the layers of implicit understandings makes clear that the ways in which contractors come to understand what complex transactions in contracting communities mean is by participating in these transactions and acquiring the implicit understandings. In purely cognitive terms, implicit understandings are arguably a necessary part in many contexts of making sense of the contracting process, and hence of consenting to one's participation in it.

Where a context of this kind exists, the law should—and generally does—reflect the social meanings context confers on the contracting process. But where there is no such context, and so no shared customary understandings, the contracting process will still often be given meaning by unilateral assumptions the parties make. These meanings are still part of the social processes of contracting, and the law should not ignore them on the basis that they do not appear in the form typical of commercial contracts.

6

A Comparison of British and American Attitudes Towards the Exercise of Judicial Discretion in Contract Law

WILLIAM C WHITFORD[1]

THIS PAPER HAS evolved from my comments on Mr J Wightman's conference paper which now forms chapter 5 of this book. That paper does an excellent job defining the customary understandings that can arise in a contracting community, and making the case for inclusion of those understandings in the judicial definition of the terms of the contract. The paper then turns to consumer transactions and again makes an excellent case for why understandings not incorporated in the written contract are likely to arise and should be included in the contract, but those implicit understandings are likely to be unilateral expectations on the consumer's side.

While I fully support Wightman's analysis and recommendations, at the conference I commented that implicit understandings in contract, both mutually shared ones and unilateral expectations, are often not precise. The understanding is commonly that contracting behaviour will fall within certain parameters. Certain actions related to contractual performance would clearly fall outside those parameters, but there are likely to be a number of possible actions that would fall within

[1] I am grateful for helpful comments on an earlier draft from Professors D Campbell, H Collins, S Macaulay, and I Ramsay. I wish to thank Jason Keener, JD, 2002, University of Wisconsin, for excellent research assistance in the preparation of these remarks.

those parameters. My point is not original, and has been developed extensively by many authors, most recently by Collins.[2]

An implication of this observation is that judicial recognition of implicit understandings does not leave courts simply with the complex fact-finding task of ascertaining the implicit understandings. Disposition of a case often requires determination of a precise term to govern the parties' relationship—for example, when expectation remedies are sought, it is necessary to define the particular performance that the court will use in calculating what benefits proper performance of the contract would have yielded for the party deemed not in breach. Consider a contract for the sale of a good or service in which an agreed index to adjust the price to reflect inflation fails, for unanticipated reasons, to provide a price consistent with customary understandings. If the court is to order specific performance, or award the buyer damages because it has negotiated a substitute purchase in the face of the seller's refusal to perform, the court will have to provide some substitute for the failed index.[3]

There are essentially four distinct approaches a court can take when confronted with a gap in implicit understandings. The court could resort to a precise (ie unambiguous) statement in the written contract, in order to avoid the exercise of judicial discretion that would be required to complete the parties' implicit understandings. If one assumes that the court would have enforced a precise implicit understanding even though inconsistent with express written terms, by definition enforcement of the precise terms of the written contract would be inconsistent with the parties' intentions. Alternatively, the gap in the implicit understandings could be filled with some kind of default (or 'off the rack') term—by which I mean a term that statutory or decisional law stipulates will be implied in all contracts of a particular type where the parties have not explicitly agreed to an alternative. These default terms may or may not fall within the range of acceptable terms established by the parties' implicit understandings, and if they do not, then enforcement of the default term once again ensures a result inconsistent with the parties' intentions at the time of contract. Still another possibility is for the court to declare the contract invalid because of the uncertainty in the parties' agreement. Both American and British

[2] H Collins, *Regulating Contracts* (Oxford, Oxford University Press, 1999) ch 7 149–73.

[3] Eg *Alcoa v Essex Group*, 499 F Supp 53 (WD Pa 1980), discussed extensively by my colleague, Stewart Macaulay, in his chapter in this volume.

contract law continue to recognise a doctrine decreeing that a contract intended by the parties to be enforceable can nonetheless be invalid for indefiniteness, but application of the doctrine is increasingly uncommon in both countries. And it seems particularly ironic for a court to declare unenforceable for indefiniteness a contract that contains a written term with the required specificity, but which term is deemed inconsistent with a vaguer implicit understanding.[4] The final option is for the court to invent a term to fill the gap. The court will be 'making a contract for the parties', something that centuries of decisions in both countries state that courts should not do. To be sure, the implicit understandings will set parameters on the range of terms that will be deemed consistent with the implicit understandings, and this will limit the extent of the court's discretion. The court will have to turn to other considerations in setting a precise term within these limits, however, and unless it is simply adopts a formulaic solution—like splitting the difference between the parameters established by the implicit understandings—normative judgements about fairness or efficiency of differing alternative solutions are likely to be made.

During the discussion at the conference, I came to appreciate that the academics in the room differed in how comfortable they were with the fourth alternative listed above—having judges make discretionary, policy-based decisions that in effect 'make a contract' for the parties. Almost everybody in the room purported in principle to favour judicial recognition of implicit contract terms, but many were uncomfortable with displacing a written contract term capable of easy and predictable application with an implicit term that required judicial discretion in specifying its application to the facts.[5] Generalisations are difficult and risky, but on the whole it seemed to me that the academics from the UK (the vast majority at the conference) were less comfortable with such displacement of a specific written term than were the Americans (only a few of us). It has often been observed that there is a difference in the opinion writing style of British and American judges, with the former more enamoured of detailed analysis of precedents and the latter much

[4] For a recent summary of American law on need for definiteness, see Allan Farnsworth, *Contracts*, 3d edn (New York, Aspen Law and Business, 1999) 207–22.

[5] Such would be the concern with the results reached in the American cases discussed at the end of my colleague Stewart Macaulay's chapter, for example. It is also a basic concern raised in Professor Lisa Bernstein's recent work. Eg Lisa Bernstein, 'Merchant Law in a Merchant Court: Rethinking the Code's Search for Immanent Business Norms', (1996) 144 *University of Pennsylvania Law Review* 1765.

more prone to appeal of policy justifications for a judgement.[6] Judges were not present at the conference, however; this was a room full of academics, most of whom I believe identified themselves as left of centre. Since the conference I have been speculating about what might account for these differences between academics of similar political outlook in countries whose legal systems claim common origins, and where knowledge of each other's precedents and leading academic works is commonplace. This comment summarises my speculations to date.

This comment is being written in response to discussions at a conference on implicit understandings in contract, but the issues respecting the exercise of judicial discretion are quite similar to other issues in contract law. The most obvious connection is with the problem of completing gaps in the explicit terms of written contracts. Many academics favour resort to predetermined default rules in such circumstances rather than a completion of the contract by a judge after a contextualised inquiry about what provision makes the most sense in the circumstances. Their reasons for this position are very similar to the reasons these same academics oppose judicial completion of gaps in implicit contracts, focusing on the disadvantages of judicial discretion.[7]

Another set of issues in contract law that concern the exercise of judicial discretion involve the use of very general regulatory standards like good faith or unconscionability in determining the validity of contracts that some would consider too one-sided or unfair. These general standards require discretionary specification by courts in their application. There are important differences between this category of issues and the gap-filling issues I am primarily addressing. Most importantly, application of a general regulatory standard in a particular case can specify that standard in a way in which the decision will have precedential force in other cases involving similar contract terms.[8] For the most part when courts fill in a contractual gap after a contextualised

[6] Karl Llewellyn was well known for such observations. See William Twining, *Karl Llewellyn and the Realist Movement* (London, Weidenfeld and Nicolson, 1973) 210–15.

[7] See Ian Ayres and Robert Gertner, 'Filling Gaps in Incomplete Contracts: An Economic Theory of Default Rules' (1989) 99 *Yale Law Journal* 87.

[8] See *Armendariz v Foundation Health Psychcare Services*, 24 Cal 4th 83, 6 P 3d 669 (CA S Ct, 2000) (setting standards for application of the unconscionability doctrine to arbitration provisions in employment and consumer form contracts). Courts do not always set precedents in applying general regulatory standards, however; sometimes they limit their decision to the circumstances of the case under consideration.

inquiry into the circumstances, the decision establishes that courts will complete contractual gaps in this way, but it has little other precedential effect. The precise term used to fill the gap is dependent on the particular facts of the case. Nonetheless there are important similarities between gap filling issues and the use of general regulatory standards. Both raise the issue of the appropriateness of the exercise of judicial discretion in contract law. Persons who oppose the completion of contractual gaps through contextualised inquiry by a court are likely also to oppose the use of very general regulatory standards, preferring instead legal tests for validity that provide judges with more specific guidance about what contracts should be ruled invalid. Furthermore, similar values are likely to guide the exercise of judicial discretion in the two circumstances. In applying general regulatory standards courts are likely to balance concerns of efficiency and fairness in deciding whether to override the apparent intent of the parties. And in completing contractual gaps, courts can rely on the intent of the parties to setting parameters on the exercise of discretion, but are likely to draw on some balance of efficiency and fairness concerns in deciding upon a particular term within those parameters.

Before speculating about what might account for differences between centre-left UK and American academics on these issues, I should mention briefly the general reasons why people are likely to be uneasy about the exercise of judicial discretion in contract law. One set of reasons is associated generally with what I will call 'rule of law' ideals. One key idea associated with the phrase 'rule of law' is the idea of equal justice before the law, meaning that all persons should be treated the same before the court. It is the facts of the case, not a litigant's relation to the judge, that should determine the outcome. That ideal is much easier to achieve if judicial outcomes are determined by analytic logic and not by discretionary, policy-influenced judgments by the judge, for it is difficult to ensure consistency in policy preferences across a large judiciary. A second set of ideas associated with the rule of law phrase concerns the appropriate role of the judiciary in a democracy. Grounded in democratic theory and the separation of powers, these ideas emphasise that the judiciary is not accountable democratically, and hence should not be in a position to make decisions about the substantive content of government policy.

Another set of ideas commonly employed to oppose the exercise of judicial discretion is generally associated with centre-right political thought in the United States and is grounded in concerns about economic efficiency. Predictability of judicial decisions—assumed to be inconsistent with the exercise of judicial discretion—is desirable, it is argued, because it lessens the amount of contingency planning in a well-run contractual transaction. Equally important, US advocates of formalism believe judicial predictability reduces the costs of dispute settlement when disputes do occur. If both parties share similar beliefs about the likely outcome of litigation, they are more likely to settle their case, saving unnecessary litigation expenses.[9] The centre-left in the US may agree that there are efficiency costs associated with judicial discretion, but tends to emphasise what it sees as the benefits of judicial discretion. It associates judicial discretion with redistributive ideas, and fears that an emphasis on predictability of result will inevitably favour enforcement of the literal or most evident interpretation of the actual wording of a written contract. It is the most powerful party in a transaction that normally exerts the greatest influence on that wording. If the contract is to be interpreted according to its plain or dictionary meaning, it will be to the advantage of the parties primarily responsible for that language. So the centre-left seeks to establish checks on superior bargaining power manifested in the language of written contracts by appealing to what it deems to be the real intent of the parties, exhibited in implicit understandings.

LEGAL CULTURE

There is one self-evident explanation for the American-British differences that I speculate exist and seek to explain. Legal realism happened in America. American academics of centre-left persuasion are taught to admire the legal realists, who for the most part shared the redistributive goals of the centre-left. Neil Duxbury, a contemporary British commentator on American juridical thought, has commented as follows on the influence of legal realism on American legal academics: '[A]n American legal academic without a perspective on legal realism is as improbable as an American legal academic without a word

[9] Two recent articles advancing these arguments are Robert Scott, 'The Case for Formalism in Relational Contract' (2000) 94 *Northwestern University Law Review* 847 and Eric Posner, 'A Theory of Contract Law Under Conditions of Radical Judicial Error' (2000) 94 *Northwestern University Law Review* 749. See also Alan Schwartz, 'Relational Contracts in the Courts: An Analysis of Incomplete Agreements and Judicial Strategies' (1992) 21 *Journal of Legal Studies* 271.

processor.'[10] In my judgement the statement is more true for the centre-left than for the centre-right in America. For the centre-right, law and economics has dislodged legal realism as a foundation for analysis.

The most famous of the legal realists in contract law was Karl Llewellyn, and his work is well known and respected by most centre-left contracts scholars in America today. Llewellyn shared the scepticism of most realists about the ability of legal doctrine to truly limit judicial discretion. Like most realists he found judicial discretion in ascertaining and applying legal rules inevitable; in the area of contracts in particular, he went further and positively championed the benefits of judicial discretion. He had great confidence in the ability of the judge to discern not only the parties' implicit understandings but also the practical implications of his/her decisions in the commercial world—what he called judges' 'situation sense'. The costs associated with unpredictability which are commonly cited as a reason to avoid judicial discretion did not bother Llewellyn greatly, for he had confidence that the courts would factor these potential costs into their thinking. They would exercise their discretion wisely and in a way that persons familiar with the case would regard as reasonable and not unexpected. By granting judges discretion we could achieve an ideal balance between predictability and change.[11]

Although legal realism certainly crossed the Atlantic and had influence in Great Britain, neither realism nor Llewellyn ever became so central to contracts scholarship in Britain as they did in America. Furthermore in Britain more attention than in America has been paid to HLA Hart and his emphasis on the rule-boundedness of judicial decisions. The differences between HLA Hart and the legal realists are often exaggerated. Hart did not claim that rules controlled all legal decisions beyond the finding of facts, hence he accepted the existence of judicial discretion in considerable degree. And most legal realists, certainly including Llewellyn, did not deny the influence of rules on judicial outcomes.[12] But the emphasis was different. Llewellyn emphasised

[10] Neil Duxbury, 'A Century of Legal Studies', in P Cane and M Tushnet (eds), *The Oxford Handbook of Legal Studies* (Oxford, Oxford University Press, forthcoming).

[11] The best and most comprehensive account of Llewellyn and his work is Twining, n 6 above. Twining discusses Llewellyn's sometimes mysterious concept of 'situation sense' at 216–29.

[12] For the best account of Llewellyn's sophisticated and nuanced view of the role of rules, see Twining, n 6 above, Appendix B, 488–96 (entitled 'A Restatement of Llewellyn's Theory of Rules').

the limits on rules, and stressed the influence and desirability of other factors on judicial outcomes. Hart made his name demonstrating that rules made a difference, and the very serious problems for rule of law concerns that would result if they did not.

MATERIAL CONDITIONS

In this section I suggest that differing attitudes towards the exercise of judicial discretion in enforcing incomplete agreements result in part from the different circumstances in which the discretion is exercised. My essential intuition is that the costs and benefits of judicial discretion in the administration of contract law differ between the two countries. This is because the countries' two principal law-making institutions, the judiciary and the legislature, differ significantly. As a result, persons with similar political values might sensibly favour greater exercise of judicial discretion in the US than in Britain.

I must initially make one important disclaimer. In the following discussion I will be discussing and contrasting the judiciary and the legislature in the two countries. My knowledge about American institutions is much greater than it is of British institutions, and hence it is likely my intuitions and assumptions about the capacities and limitations of these institutions are sounder for the former than the latter.

The Legislature

One of the important differences between the two countries is the nature of their legislatures. Britain's legislative system ensures that the same political party controls both the executive and the legislature, and that there is party discipline in the legislature. As a result, when there is legislative inaction in the face of perceived injustice, there is at least some possibility that the electorate will hold the party in power accountable for perpetuating an injustice. This is less likely in the United States. The lack of party discipline in the legislature, and the inability of the legislature to displace the executive by a vote of non-confidence, makes it very difficult for the electorate to hold accountable any political actor when a legislature simply fails to act. The person responsible for legislative inaction is often the chair of some legislative committee, and he or she is likely to come from what

Americans call a 'safe' district—one in which the possibility of electoral defeat for his/her political party is remote. The lack of party discipline is at least partly responsible for the tendency of American voters not to hold accountable, for inaction, the political party to which the legislative committee chair belongs. And the net effect is to make inaction by far the most desirable course of action for many legislators. Recorded votes can get an individual legislator in trouble in a forthcoming election; inaction gets nobody in trouble.

This bias towards inaction does not prevent the enactment of all legislation in America concerning contract law. When legislatures do act, however, the legislation is likely to concern some very particular matter where important campaign contributors have an interest. Alternatively, a particular legislator may be able to get a Bill passed on a specific matter in the interest of a particular constituent. For example, Wisconsin passed legislation concerning the consequences to an employer of including a overly broad restrictive covenant in an employment contract. The Wisconsin Supreme Court, in a decision explicitly changing established precedent, adopted a position favouring severability, allowing the employer to enforce as extensive a covenant as the court deemed reasonable.[13] Shortly thereafter the Wisconsin legislature adopted a statute altering this result (prospectively only) and providing that the employer was entitled to no protection from employee competition if the written contract contained an overly broad covenant.[14] The legislation was drafted and pushed through the Wisconsin legislature by the state legislator in whose district resided the losing party (Torborg) in the Supreme Court decision.[15]

My position is that in the United States there is far less legislation about contract law than is desirable, including about important issues of consumer protection. The prominence of the Uniform Commercial Code [UCC] over the past 50 years might seem inconsistent with this emphasis on the unimportance of legislation, but in fact the story of how the UCC was drafted and enacted largely supports my analysis. The UCC is unique legislation. The first drafts were crafted almost solely by a group of elite academics, led by Karl Llewellyn.[16] The effort

[13] *Fullerton Lumber Co v Torborg*, 270 Wis 133, 70 NW 2d. 585 (1955).

[14] Wis Stats §103.465.

[15] The full story of this litigation and its legislative aftermath is told in Richard Danzig, *The Capability Problem in Contract Law* (Mineola Foundation Press, 1978) 44–67.

[16] Allen R Kemp, 'Uptown Act: A History of the Uniform Commercial Code: 1940–49', (1998) 51 *Southern Methodist University Law Review* 275.

was sponsored and paid for by two private organisations who were autonomous from and independent of any legislative process. Ultimately, of course, the Code was introduced in and enacted by state legislatures, but rarely with significant legislative debate.[17] In between the original drafts and later introduction in state legislatures, the Code came under scrutiny by affected business interests, which led to significant changes. In Article 2—the part of the UCC having greatest relevance to contract law—these changes tended to replace specific provisions with sections phrased in general language and subject to varying interpretations when applied to particular facts. The tendency towards very general language is partly reflective of the preferences of its principal draftsperson, Karl Llewellyn, but it is also the product of lobbying by business interests seeking to blunt the desires of some academics for a contract law that would more closely regulate the exercise of superior bargaining power.[18] These business interests believed, correctly as it has turned out, that very general language would limit the influence of the Code on the course of contract law.[19] It is often not clear today that the result reached in a case under the UCC is different from what the judge would have decided if the Code had never been enacted. There has recently been an attempt to draft a revised Article 2, using more specific provisions that would very likely influence outcomes in future contract cases. It has been impossible for the elite academic organisations that continue to sponsor the UCC and changes in it to obtain a consensus on these changes, however, and the effort to make significant changes in Article 2 has been abandoned. This experience confirms my conviction that little significant concerning contract law ever happens in the United States.

Contracts scholars today would have difficulty determining whether the UCC or the two Restatements of Contracts have had greater influence on the course of contract law. I doubt that any section of Article 2 of the UCC has had as much influence on the content of contract law

17 Robert Braucher, 'Legislative History of the Uniform Commercial Code' (1958) 58 *Columbia University Law Review* 798. There was significant legislative activity in New York, where the legislature directed the New York Law Reform Commission, a state agency, to review the then current draft in detail. Significant amendments to the Code resulted. No other state repeated this process, however.

18 See Allen R Kamp, 'Downtown Code: A History of the Uniform Commercial Code 1949–1954' (2001) 49 *Buffalo Law Review* 359.

19 I have written frequently about the desirability of more and better legislation, especially in the consumer protection area. See eg William C Whitford, 'Contract Law and the Control of Standardized Terms in Consumer Contracts: An American Report' (1995) 3 *European Review of Private Law* 193.

as has Section 90—the promissory estoppel provision—of the original Restatement of Contracts. The Supreme Court of virtually every state has adopted promissory estoppel as part of the common law of that jurisdiction. The concept was virtually invented by the first Restatement of Contracts.[20] The Restatements are drafted and published by the American Law Institute, a private organisation consisting of elite academics and practitioners, and have no formal legal status.[21] Nonetheless, it can be seriously contended that they have had more influence than the UCC over the development of contract law, illustrating the limited influence of legislation.

The principal relevance of the lack of significant American legislation in contract law is to justify a tradition of judicial activism in formulating rules of law. I am not the first observer of differing American and British judicial traditions to have pointed to legislative inadequacies in the United States as an explanation for greater judicial activism in the United States.[22] Usually the discussion is in the context of justifying constitutional and administrative judicial review of an activist nature. I believe that legislative inactivity and irresponsibility in the United States is particularly marked with respect to contract law, and hence that the case for judicial activism in contract law is especially strong. If courts did not innovate in contract law, the law in most respects would be frozen.

In Britain the calculus regarding the desirability of judicial activism is different. While the legislative institution is surely not perfect, I am assuming that between Parliament and administrative rule-making agencies, more action can be expected than I find in the United States. And there are real deficiencies in relying on the judiciary as a change agent for contract law. In the first place, there are real limits on the capacity of a judiciary to change the law in any reasonably sensible way. Judges lack the means to carefully research issues for themselves, being largely dependent on information that the parties bring them. While

[20] For an interesting history of the drafting of Section 90, see Grant Gilmore, *The Death of Contract*, 2nd edn (Columbus, Ohio State University Press, 1995) 73–81.

[21] For background on the ALI, which also sponsors the Uniform Commercial Code, see NEH Hull, 'Restatement and Reform: A New Perspective on the Origins of the American Law Institute' (1990) 8 *Law and History Review* 55.

[22] See the wonderful little book by Louis Jaffe, *English and American Judges As Lawmakers* 69 (Oxford, Oxford University Press, 1969) 69: 'It would seem that the English Parliament is potentially capable of dealing with more of the country's law needs than our legislatures. If so, the demand for judicial lawmaking in England may be to that extent less'.

legislatures frequently act simply on the basis of information provided by lobbyists representing well endowed interests, they at least have greater capacity than courts to research issues thoroughly. Furthermore, courts can act only when they happen to get a case raising an issue with respect to which there is a need for change in the governing law. Legislatures have the capacity to act independently of the happenstance that some aggrieved party has litigated a case to the appellate level.[23] Finally, in Britain concern has been expressed about the homogeneity of backgrounds of judges in the higher appellate courts.[24] Perhaps there a system which depended on judicial activism as an agent of change would be more tilted towards the interests of established classes than a system more dependent on the legislature for legal change.

This comment is primarily about the exercise of judicial discretion to complete gaps in contractual understandings. Nonetheless, I think the United States' tradition of judicial activism in formulating the basic rules of contract law, which I attribute importantly to legislative inadequacy, bears on the topic under discussion in the following two ways. First, and most importantly, a tradition of judicial activism at least requires acceptance of the legitimacy of the exercise of judicial discretion in a legal system that professes allegiance to the rule of law. From the perspective of rule of law values, there is no real difference between judicial formulation of rules of law and judicial formulation of contractual terms—both kinds of decisions are discretionary. Second, the alternatives to the exercise of judicial discretion in the enforcement of incomplete contracts are less attractive in a jurisdiction where legislatures cannot be relied upon to cure inadequacies in contract law. Those alternatives are principally either (1) where it is the implicit understandings that are incomplete, to enforce unambiguous terms in the written contract even though the court believes they do not express the parties' intentions, or (2) to fill the gap with a default term established by judicial precedent or statutory provision to complete all gaps of a particular type. The former alternative is likely to empower the stronger party in the contractual relationship, who is likely to have greater influence on the content of the written contract. It can be seen as less attractive in legal systems in which it is more difficult to rely on

[23] My colleague, Neil Komesar, has written frequently and convincingly about the limitations of the judiciary as a policy-maker. Eg Neil Komesar, *Imperfect Alternatives* (Chicago, University of Chicago Press, 1994) 123–50.

[24] See John Griffith, *The Politics of the Judiciary* 5th edn (London, Fontana, 1997) 295, 338.

legislation to check excessive exercise of this bargaining power. The latter alternative is similarly unattractive because legislation is less available to alter default rules that were poorly designed or have become antiquated. To be sure, judicial activism is always a possible cure for these legislative inadequacies, and often resorted to in the United States, but if judicial activism—requiring the exercise of judicial discretion—must ultimately be relied upon, the reasons for avoiding exercise of judicial discretion in the completion of incomplete contract terms are less compelling.

The Judiciary

Though the United States and Britain are both common law jurisdictions, there are great differences in the institutional structure of their judiciaries. One of the biggest differences relates to America's federalism. Britain has only two jurisdictions for purposes of contract law, and there is but a single system of courts in each jurisdiction. America has 51 separate jurisdictions for purposes of contract law, where virtually all the law is state and not federal. In each of those jurisdictions there are two systems of courts, state and federal. Either party to a contract may bring a case into federal court if the amount in dispute exceeds $75,000 and the parties are citizens of different states. Because corporations are considered citizens of the state of their incorporation, regardless of where they do business, in practice federal courts hear many of the most important contracts cases. When federal courts hear a case involving contract law, with rare exceptions they are supposed to apply the substantive contract law of the state whose law is applicable under conflict of law rules. In practice, however, federal courts often invent their own views of what the state law is, failing to faithfully follow relevant state court precedents.[25] As a result, for purposes of contract law there is effectively somewhere between 51 and 102 separate jurisdictions in the United States.

[25] There is no single authoritative study establishing this proposition, but examples are easy to come by. I document one such divergence between federal and state law with respect to the parole evidence rule. The Seventh Circuit rather clearly fails to follow applicable Illinois state court precedent when deciding cases governed by Illinois law. See William C Whitford, 'The Role of the Jury (and the Fact/law distinction) in the Interpretation of Written Contracts' [2001] *Wisconsin Law Review* 931, 959–62.

The second important institutional difference concerns methods of judicial selection. In England and Wales, the larger of the two British jurisdictions, most important contracts cases are heard initially by the High Court. This court's jurisdiction is carefully limited, so the number of judges is not large. In 1996 in all of England and Wales there were less than 100 High Court judges, and only 35 judges in the Court of Appeal.[26] Recruitment to the High Court is for the most part limited to barristers with substantial experience (say 20 years). Experienced barristers represent a very small part of the total legal profession in the United Kingdom. Many of these experienced barristers will have had a substantial background in commercial law matters before appointment. Judicial appointments are made by the Lord Chancellor, a member of the Cabinet, and are therefore technically political. By tradition, however, the Lord Chancellor pays close attention to the views of existing judges and leaders of the Bar. Appointment of actively political persons is very rare.[27]

Judicial selection is quite different in the United States. Contract cases in federal courts tend to be important ones, and most federal judges have substantial legal experience before appointment. However, the selection process is much more politicised than in Britain. Political parties, or important people within them, are likely to be the most influential persons in judicial selection. Increasingly federal court appointees have held the position of prosecutor or some other semi-political position before appointment. Potential appointees come from a much wider section of the Bar than is the case with respect to England's High Court. Appointments of leading practitioners from the private Bar—persons who are more likely than most lawyers to have had substantial experience with sophisticated questions of contract law—are increasingly uncommon in the United States.[28] Judicial selection in state courts is different, and so diverse as to make difficult easy summary here. A majority of states have some type of election process.[29] In some juris-

[26] Griffith, n 24 above, 22.

[27] See Robert Stevens, 'The Independence of the Judiciary: The Case of England' (1999) 72 *Southern California Law Review* 597, 613–14; Griffith, n 24 above, 8–22.

[28] See Sheldon Goldman *et al*, 'Clinton's Judges: Summing Up the Legacy' (2001) 84 *Judicature* 228.

[29] There has been recent concern expressed about the potentially corrupting influence of campaign contributions on judicial performance in states where elections are used to select judges, but there is not yet an analysis on how this effect might influence the development of contract law. See David Barnhizer, '"On the Make": Campaign Funding and the Corrupting Of the American Judiciary' (2001) 50 *Catholic University Law Review* 361.

dictions those elections are partisan, with political parties playing an explicit role in selecting candidates. In many jurisdictions the elections are non-partisan, and usually in those jurisdictions an incumbent judge is re-elected. When vacancies arise between elections, commonly the Governor of the State is the appointing authority, making initial selection of judges not that different from the federal system (where the President is the appointing authority). Virtually all members of the Bar are deemed qualified for appointment or election to a trial court, but as with federal courts former prosecutors are over-represented. Members of State Supreme Courts, the court with the most important law-making responsibility with respect to contracts, commonly have substantial experience before selection, but once again selection from the experienced practising Bar is not common. Promotion of a lower court judge to the State Supreme Court is much more common.

A goal of limiting judicial discretion in contract law requires a legal system in which judges can be expected to follow pre-established rules for ascertaining an outcome whenever there is a gap in the parties understandings. As discussed above, the most likely alternatives to exercise of judicial discretion to complete the contract are (1) where the gap is with respect to implicit understandings, enforcement of an unambiguous term in the written contract, or (2) completion of the contract with some pre-established default rule for contracts of this type. In the United States, predictability in outcome of contract cases is hard to find. In the first place, there are 50 to 100 different jurisdictions. Academics nonetheless tend to write about contract law in general, as if there are not many separate jurisdictions. From this perspective academics are bound to find inconsistency in decisions. As the realists were fond of pointing out, and more recently participants in the critical legal studies movement as well,[30] consistency in decisions is not a characteristic of American contract law. Courts may be more faithful than academics to the idea that each jurisdiction is entitled to its own version of contract law, so that all that matters is consistency within a jurisdiction, not between jurisdictions. Nonetheless, it is frequent for a state court to cite a decision in another state as 'persuasive' precedent, and the American tradition of relative ease in overruling controlling precedent leads to an unpredictability about whether a court will be persuaded or instead follow a different precedent in its own jurisdiction. Furthermore contract

[30] See Claire Dalton, 'An Essay in the Deconstruction of Contract Doctrine' (1985) 94 *Yale Law Journal* 997.

cases in a particular jurisdiction are filed in both state and federal courts, and as I have mentioned previously, federal courts are not always faithful to their obligation to apply the law laid down by the state courts. What all this means is that in America, when a court refuses to 'make a contract for the parties'in order to fill a contractual gap, there is still a reasonable likelihood that the court will exercise discretion with respect to whether to enforce an unambiguous written term or apply a default rule, and if the latter with respect to what default rule to apply. If discretion is likely to be exercised anyhow, why not have the court simply fill in the gap based on what seems efficient and fair in all the circumstances of the particular case?

Predictability in judicial decisions requires that judges sometimes exercise self-restraint and set aside their personal preferences for how a case should be decided in order to maintain a line of precedent. Llewellyn often pointed out that a set of precedents at variance with strongly held views of a group of judges was not likely to be stable because those judges would look for some way to rationalise a distinction and reach the desired outcome. This is all the more the case in a system in which there is no consistency of precedent. Judges asked to set aside their personal preferences in order to uphold the predictability yielded by a stable set of precedents will find it easier to do if they can assume that other judges holding different personal preferences will do the same when those views clash with established precedent. If judges of only one political perspective exercise restraint, the inevitable long run effect will be to 'tilt' the law away from that perspective.

I believe that precisely this concern has influenced many American judges not to follow existing precedent when they disagree with its import. A good example in contract law is two recent decisions by the Seventh Circuit, in which the court invented a new doctrine allowing sellers of pre-packaged goods in stores or of mail order goods to have included in the contract boilerplate disclaimers that the consumer did not have a chance to inspect until well after the purchase transaction.[31] Both opinions were written by a well known, right-of-centre judge who has long championed judicial restraint and emphasised the importance of predictability in contract law. Yet in these cases the judge wrote very activist decisions that were wholly without previous authority, either in the applicable state or in federal courts, and that were inconsistent

[31] *ProCD Inc v Zeidenberg* 86 F 3d 1447 (1996) and *Hill v Gateway 2000 Inc* 105 F 3d 1147 (1997).

with what had been generally accepted principles of contract formation. The newly established doctrines were championed by the affected industries, who had made unsuccessful efforts to have them established by legislation. The Seventh Circuit delivered these business interests a victory by judicial decree.

I have argued that the English judiciary assigned important contract cases are, on average, better quality than their American counterparts. If true, one might expect that academics would be more supportive of having English judges exercise discretion in filling contractual gaps. After all, English judges should be better able than American judges to do a good job drawing on efficiency and fairness concerns to complete the contracts. One argument that centre-right American academics give for encouraging judges to enforce unambiguous meanings of written contracts, or in their absence to apply pre-established default terms, is precisely that American judges are sufficiently ignorant of the commercial settings in which important contracts are made that they are not likely to do a very good job in exercising discretion to complete contractual gaps.

I suspect, however, that the superior quality of the British judiciary in fact influences even centre-left academics to favour a more formalist approach to incomplete contracts. Clearly there are benefits to predictability of decision. Such predictability is difficult to achieve in the United States by reason of its chaotic court structure. But the quality of the judiciary also plays a role. Better quality judges are more likely to know existing precedent and apply it in a logical and consistent way. So ironically, while a higher quality judiciary implies that English judges would do a better job in completing incomplete contracts, it also implies that they will do a better job in administering a precedent system in a consistent manner. In such a system predictability may be easier to achieve if courts deal with contractual gaps by adopting the alternatives to the exercise of discretion to invent the missing terms after a contextualised inquiry into the circumstances of the parties and the transaction.

SUMMARY AND CONCLUSIONS

I began by hypothesising that British and American centre-left contracts scholars have differing attitudes towards how to fill gaps in the understandings of parties to contracts. American scholars, I have postulated, are more willing to have courts use their discretion to fill in the missing term, after conducting a contextualised inquiry into the bargain and subsequent contractual performance seeking to learn what term would best serve the parties' concerns about efficiency and fairness. British scholars, I suggested, are more reluctant to have courts make such wide-ranging inquiries because principle seems incapable of limiting the court's discretion in setting the appropriate term. The arguments on this issue closely parallel the arguments that can be made in favour of and against the use of very general regulatory standards, like good faith or unconscionability, to limit one-sided or unfair contracts. I hypothesise a similar difference in attitudes about such standards as well, with American centre-left contracts scholars more welcoming of such standards, which require extensive judicial discretion in their specification of particular fact situations.

Accepting this hypothesis as valid, though unproven, I have ventured explanations for the differences in attitudes. One set of explanations rests in what I have called legal culture—by which I mean the legal culture of the centre-left contracts scholar. On the average, American scholars are much more under the influence of Karl Llewellyn and his faith in the wisdom of the judge than are British scholars. But I have also suggested that differences in what I have called material conditions could contribute to the differences in opinion. The material conditions that I have identified relate not to differences in business conditions but in the nature of the American and British legislative and judicial institutions. I have suggested that the American legislative process is so unresponsive to contract law issues that Americans are forced to promote judicial activism with respect to doctrine, as well as the exercise of judicial discretion in the filling of contractual gaps, as a way of avoiding legal paralysis. I have further argued that there are qualities in the American judiciary—primarily related to America's federal structure and also its methods of judicial selection—that make it difficult to achieve predictability in judicial decision, even when it is precedent and not judicial discretion that is supposed to guide judicial decision. As a consequence, the most important benefit sought to be achieved by limiting the exercise of judicial discretion, which is predictability in decision, is hard to achieve in America.

What this analysis suggests is that the ideal approach to filling contractual gaps in one country may not be the ideal approach in the other. There are no doubt advantages to what I have identified as the approach favoured by American centre-left academics. When a court exercises discretion to fill a contractual gap, it is likely to try to guess what terms the parties would have negotiated if they had put their minds to it, informed themselves adequately, and bargained in a situation in which each is free of serious economic compulsion. The result is likely to be more respectful of the parties' autonomy or freedom of contract than the alternatives to the exercise of judicial discretion. One principal alternative to the exercise of discretion is application of a pre-established default term, which at best represents what typical contractual parties might have negotiated. Hopefully a court can do better in estimating what the particular parties would have negotiated through making a contextualised inquiry. The other principal alternative to the exercise of discretion, available where the contractual gap is in implicit understandings, is enforcement of unambiguous language in the written contract. In a legal regime that recognises implicit understandings in the belief that the written language of a contract frequently fails to state the parties' real understandings—and this is a regime favoured by centre-left contracts scholars of both countries where the implicit understandings are determinate—enforcement of the written contract where there are inconsistent though indeterminate implicit understandings is almost certain to reach a result contrary to at least one party's expectations.

Freedom of contract is a cherished value, and need not be defended solely or even primarily on efficiency grounds. But predictability in the law is also an important value. Centre-right academics in America are particularly fond of predictability, since they believe it contributes to the overall efficiency of contracts, and to the economy in general, even if at a cost to party autonomy in a particular case. I suspect my political soulmates, the centre-left British contracts scholars, are more attracted to predictability because of what I have called rule of law values. There is something to be said for having important policy decisions made by electorally responsible legislatures, where that is possible. There is even more to be said for judicial decisions not seeming to be determined by which judges happen to be assigned to the case, yet the latter appearance is hard to avoid where judges are given too much unbounded discretion. Where these rule of law values are practically achievable in a meaningful way, foregoing the advantages of the exercise of judicial discretion is an understandable choice. Where these rule of law values are not practically achievable, as I have suggested is the case in America, it seems wiser to favour the widespread exercise of judicial discretion.

7

Reflections on Relational Contract Theory after a Neo-classical Seminar

IAN R MACNEIL

INTRODUCTION

A WIDESPREAD PERCEPTION has long existed that relational contract theory is an analytical tool biased in favour of state-intervention in contractual relations; of co-operation rather than conflict; of communitarian, liberal, and/or radical values; of the continuance rather than break-up of relations; and many other 'soft and cuddly' values often associated with humanitarianism. In other words, relational contract theory is conceived as a political manifesto of a naive and dangerous humanitarianism, rather than as a relatively neutral tool of social, economic, political and legal (hereafter social) analysis.

This misconceived perception has been utilised repeatedly to discredit relational approaches to contracts in general, and my own—essential contract theory—in particular.[1] The purpose of this paper is to dispel this smokescreen by showing the following:

1. the core of relational contract theory is little more than a belief that analysis of transactions must always start with their context. This is a neutral analytical principle;

[1] In the 1970s I developed a description of contract behaviour and norms which came to be called relational contract theory, although it is but one of countless possible relational contract theories: IR Macneil, *The Relational Theory of Contract* (London, Sweet & Maxwell, 2001). To avoid confusion, I belatedly renamed my own work *essential contract theory*: IR Macneil, 'Relational Contract Theory: Challenges and Queries' (2000) 94 *Northwestern University Law Review* 877.

2. it is discrete analyses such as rational choice theory and classical contract law, rather than relational contract theory, that omit and distort, and hence are prone to social biases; and
3. essential contract theory, one of countless possible relational theories of contract, is a neutral analytical tool, not one oriented towards particular social views.

STARTING WITH CONTEXT: A SCOTCH EGG INSIDE A HAGGIS

Four core propositions inform *any* relational approach to contracts:[2]

1. *every transaction is embedded in complex relations.* Thus transactions may be treated as-if-discrete, but never in fact are discrete. So far as I can tell, almost everyone these days agrees with this, albeit often enough kicking and screaming and backtracking all the way;
2. *understanding any transaction requires understanding all elements of its enveloping relations that might affect the transaction significantly.* Once again few, if forced to the wall, will disagree with this;
3. *effective analysis of any transaction requires recognition and consideration of all significant relational elements.* No longer will we find unanimity of opinion, but judging from the papers and discussions at the seminar which has led to this book, few dissenters were present; and
4. *combined contextual analysis of relations and transactions is more efficient and produces a more complete and sure final analytical product than does commencing with non-contextual analysis of transactions.* This is the most controversial proposition of the relational approach to contracts.

Under the relational approach, express terms in contracts are no more than an extremely important part of a dense web of relations. Like the junk DNA making up most of our genes, much of that web will have little or nothing to do with whatever concerns us. Other parts of the relation will be more significant to those issues. Likely to be significant are various party-understandings lying outside the express terms (including those they imply factually), the implicit understandings referred to in several papers at the seminar. Among these are what

[2] 'Relational Contract Theory: Challenges and Queries' (2000) 94 *Northwestern University Law Review* 877, 881–92.

Stewart Macaulay calls the 'real deal', a much more appealing term for the widely scorned subjective will of the parties, yet meaning the same thing. As John Wightman argues, these and other implicit understandings should be the starting point to help us understand what the express terms mean and how they should be used.

Yet other aspects of the relations may have little or nothing to do with the understandings of the parties, express or subjective, but much to do with the relational frameworks in which they operate and which govern them. Try, for example, to pick up a phone and convince a broker to purchase shares for you on the exchange—one of those transactions so often used by discretists as prime examples of discrete transactions! Forty years ago that was the easiest thing in the world to do as long as the broker thought you were good for the purchase price and brokerage fees. Now it is absolutely impossible unless a relationship has previously been established in writing and in accordance with manifold semi-governmental and governmental regulations.

To dramatise a relational approach, let us consider the eating of a Scotch Egg embedded in the middle of a haggis. The thick coating that makes an egg a Scotch Egg[3] can be reached only through the haggis and the egg can be reached only through the Scotch Egg coating. With *any* relational approach to transactions, we reach the Scotch Egg of express terms only through the haggis of more remote relations and then through the thick coating of the relations closest to the express terms. It may be noted that unlike the discrete-egg of rational choice theory and classical contract law, a Scotch Egg has no hard shell to pierce.

Anyone who has ever eaten a Scotch Egg will know that the egg itself tastes different from a plain hard boiled egg, just as express terms of a contract take on different meanings when approached through relations. And undoubtedly a Scotch Egg embedded in haggis would taste different again. Needless to say, it is entirely unnecessary to consume *all* the haggis or *all* the thick coating to get at a Scotch Egg. Similarly, it is unnecessary to examine all the remote or often all the close relations in which an as-if-discrete transaction is embedded. Only things significantly relating to the question(s) at issue require examination. And finally, nothing in any relational contract theory requires repeating relational investigations respecting as-if-discrete transactions identical to preceding transactions which have already been thoroughly subjected to such investigations.

[3] D Smith, *Complete Cookery Course* (London, BBC, 1992) 465.

It is difficult to see how an approach of this kind can properly be accused of being biased either in favour of or against humanitarian concerns.

STARTING WITH EXPRESS TERMS: CONTRACT AS A DISCRETE EGG

The name of the seminar was *Implicit Dimensions of Contracts*. Most of the papers and comments seemed to take as their starting point: Dimensions of Contracts Implicit *in express terms*. (Stewart Macaulay's paper was the clearest and most complete exception; John Wightman's went almost, but not quite, as far, if I understand his paper correctly). Thus, even in such an enlightened group there was a strong tendency to start thinking about any contract with its express terms.

Starting with the express terms of a contract seems a natural and sensible thing to do, really the only sensible thing to do. But is it? Starting with express terms does make perfectly good sense—indeed is absolutely essential—in the countless situations where someone wants simply to ascertain the express terms of an undisputed agreement. To what address is a cheque to be sent? Does the insurance policy cover damage from freezing? What day of the month does the lease require the rent to be paid? Which wage category covers lathe operators? *Ad infinitum*.

But does starting with the express terms make sense when thinking about the kinds of contractual issues concerning the participants in the seminar? I think not. No longer is the concern with normal untroubled performance. Rather the issues concern trouble, disputes, regulation—actual or potential, possible litigation, etc etc. Whenever the focus shifts from normal performance to such questions there are virtually always *key issues lying outside the express terms* of the contracts in question. In these circumstances we almost invariably know that, whatever the end result may be, *the express terms cannot be the beginning and end of our analysis*. The express terms can at best therefore be no more than an *entry* point to consideration of all the pertinent issues.

If we start with the express terms in thinking about these kinds of issues, we have in essence started from the position of classical contract law. Classical contract law—the law of the discrete contract, the law of 100 per cent on/off consent—is a *complete and closed intellectual structure*. So too is its counterpart in economic analysis, rational choice theory. *Such closed structures provide no exit to other worlds*. In particular, the closed structure of classical contract analysis stands completely mute in face of the key question: *How much, if at all, should we erode that closed structure itself in the circumstances in which it occurs,* whatever these circumstances may be? Only *these circumstances*—those lying outside the express terms—can provide the factual bases for a decision whether the closed structure of classical contract must give way and if so, how and how much.

In light of this, the express terms are, from both practical and intellectual perspectives, a singularly inappropriate starting place for analysis when dealing with most contract cases and issues. But there is worse to come. Starting with the express terms and the classical contract approach almost invariably skews the analysis of the circumstances in which they are embedded. Instead of approaching those circumstances neutrally to permit assessing the express terms sensibly—as does John Wightman in his paper—a burden is imposed on the other circumstances to overcome literal application of the express terms. This is true no matter how strong the circumstances may be. Sometimes this burden is heavy, sometimes it is overwhelming. A vivid illustration is the patent but oft-repeated nonsense that consumers generally read or should read form contracts, simply because they are cast in specific words.

The result of such approaches may be analogised to a large, heavy and inverted pyramid teetering with one point on top of a small egg, inside of which we are trapped. The yolk of the egg is the express terms, the white is the terms they imply factually, and the hard shell is the boundary created by rational choice theory or classical contract law. The pyramid is all the other circumstances relating to the situation. Starting from either of the discrete models, our entry into the point of the pyramid is blocked by the egg shell. When we poke a hole through the shell by brute force and enter the bottom point of the pyramid, what we find there is subject to corruption by leakage of express and implicit terms from the egg. If we are sufficiently persistent we can, of course, push our way up the pyramid into areas less and less influenced by the contents of the egg. This pyramid is, however, in a very unstable position and any imbalance in our penetration may topple it off the egg altogether. Or we may cause the pyramid to spew a biased selection of its own contents into the egg itself in random or other destructive ways.

At best, starting with the express terms seriously handicaps achieving sound analyses of contract issues of the kind that concerned the seminar. Moreover, starting with express terms often means stopping with express terms. The dangers of such approaches appear in the following part of this discussion.

ESSENTIAL CONTRACT THEORY, HUMANITARIAN CONSIDERATIONS AND DISCRETIST MODELS

It is incumbent upon anyone claiming social neutrality for their analytical tools to demonstrate that neutrality. I have done this in respect of the core of relational approaches in the first part of this discussion. That does not, however, mean that any particular relational theory is free of such biases. Few would claim, for example, that Marxist, feminist, critical, or neofascist analyses of contractual relations are relatively neutral. Discretists regularly assume that their tools—rational choice theory and classical contract law—are socially neutral, but it is rare indeed that they make any effort to demonstrate their position. All is lost in *ceteris paribus* and the pure neutrality of consent-out-of-context.

What then about essential contract theory? As I shall show, essential contract theory itself is like a microscope—it does not determine the substance of what is being examined; it is nothing but a series of lenses for looking at that substance. The same cannot, of course, be said of particular applications of the theory, mine or anyone else's. Those who have asserted that the theory is biased in particular social directions including my own have confused it with applications of the theory. They have done so in disregard of my repeatedly stressing the distinction.[4] When extremely intelligent people ignore such a distinction one can only believe that they have done so deliberately in order to further their own particular social agenda.[5] At the seminar, David Campbell once again stressed this point, noting that essential contract theory can

[4] IR Macneil, *The New Social Contract* (New Haven, Yale University Press, 1980) and IR Macneil, 'Bureaucracy, Liberalism and Community—American Style' (1985) 79 *Northwestern University Law Review* 900.

[5] See eg IR Macneil, 'Contracting Worlds and Essential Contract Theory' (2000) 9 *Social and Legal Studies* 431, rebutting Professor Teubner's descriptions of essential contract theory as 'express[ing] indeed the romantic yearning for a mediaeval unity of the *buon governo*' and 'as the warm, human, co-operative interpersonal relation that overcomes . . . cold economic instrumentalism with a communitarian orientation': G Teubner, 'Contracting Worlds: The Many Autonomies of Private Law' (2000) 9 *Social and Legal Studies* 399, 405. Richard Posner has been particularly blatant in his distortions, see Macneil, 'Relational Contract Theory', above n 1, 900 fn 82, criticising R Posner, 'The New Institutional Economics Meets Law and Economics' (1993) 149 *J Institutional and Theoretical Econ* 73, 84.

lead to hard and tough conclusions just as well as to soft and cuddly, ie humanitarian, ones.

There is course, no such thing as truly neutral analysis of social or economic life. No tool of analysis can ever show social 'facts' with the 'neutrality' or precision of a microscope or anything remotely close to it. And, unquestionably, essential contract theory reflects my own life-assumptions, biases, etc. There is not, for example, much room in it for unqualifiedly non-reciprocal altruism. How much this matters I am not sure, as I have never seen nor heard of an act of apparent altruism that cannot quite sensibly be viewed in terms of reciprocity. And those who believe in unqualifiedly non-reciprocal altruism can import that concept into the model as an element of the social matrix as they perceive it.

In sum, the neutrality of essential contract theory is necessarily relative, although it is intended to be as socially neutral as is humanly possible. Were it not for the widespread perceptions of non-neutrality, misconceived though they are, it might suffice to stop here. After all, in all the years that essential contract theory has been around, to the best of my knowledge no attack has ever been made on its neutrality without first totally distorting its content. And the attacks made have then focused entirely on the distortions, not on the theory itself. Nonetheless, because of the prevalence of perceptions of non-neutrality, something more requires to be said.

The essence of essential contract theory is that 10 common contract behavioural patterns and norms constitute the core of *all* exchange behaviour. These are (1) role integrity (requiring consistency, involving internal conflict and being inherently complex); (2) reciprocity (simply stated as the principle of getting something back for something given); (3) implementation of planning; (4) effectuation of consent; (5) flexibility; (6) contractual solidarity; (7), the restitution, reliance, and expectation interests (the 'linking norms'); (8) creation and restraint of power (the 'power norm'); (9) propriety of means; and (10) harmonisation with the particular social matrix (supracontract behavioural patterns and norms).

Now, a theory may depart from relative social neutrality by both commission and omission. Thus two pertinent questions arise respecting alleged favouring of particular social desiderata by essential contract theory:

1. are its elements biased individually or collectively? and
2. does omission of important elements of human behaviour bias the theory?

I shall have to leave to each reader whether any of the 10 core elements of essential contract theory or their combination display biases in favour of particular social desiderata. The more complex question of bias lies, I believe, in omissions rather than in inclusions. As I pointed out in 1983,[6] essential contract theory neither is nor is intended to be a complete social theory. Several elements required for such a comprehensive theory are missing. The requirement of harmonising the relation with its social matrix—supracontract behaviour and norms—deprives essential contract theory of any claim to comprehensiveness in two ways. A virtually undefined social matrix is a vital element of essential contract theory. And that element can range, for example, from the social matrix of the Taliban to that of international capitalism. Moreover, the particular social matrix always introduces into *any* contractual relation an historical element. Since essential contract theory contains no theory or system of history, much less a comprehensive one, this leaves the theory a less than complete analytical system.

The theory is further incomplete because it offers no 'all inclusive' theory of personality. Indeed it goes little beyond insisting that human personalities are in major measure social phenomena. (It does not even postulate my own view, independent of the theory, that *all* human social relations are exchange relations, and hence that the human personality is fundamentally a reciprocal one with Others). Among many omissions relating to human personality is the following: is there a basic human need to be treated as a whole person in relations with others? Essential contract theory does not deal with that issue. Yet application of my theory may call for an answer. For example, such a need would affect the very possibility of as-if-discreteness being successful in particular circumstances, to say nothing of suggesting limits on the viability of the bureaucratic approach to life.

Again I shall have to leave to each reader whether these or other omissions from essential contract theory display biases in favour of particular social desiderata. So too, each reader must decide the further question whether, if they do, those biases will be genuine problems in particular significant applications of the theory.

Obviously, I believe that essential contract theory is as neutral as a social theory can be respecting both commissions and omissions. But is there any sense at all in which essential contract theory can be said *to*

[6] IR Macneil, 'Values in Contract: Internal and External' (1978) *Northwestern University Law Review* 340, 343 fn 5.

appear to have a bias towards humanitarian conclusions? The answer to this question lies not in essential contract theory itself, but in gross omissions in discretist models such as those of rational choice theory and classical contract law. These gross omissions result in the exclusion of highly relevant humanitarian factors in the application of such models. (It is, of course, true that rational choice theory *can* incorporate a humanitarian 'asset' as something to be optimised. That is, however, something rarely found. Moreover, there is no practical way the rational choice model can be used to cope with multiple and often conflicting humanitarian considerations where all are present in a single relationship).

In contrast, essential contract theory forces the analyst to consider such matters as creation and restraint of power, propriety of means, role integrity, balances of reciprocity, contractual solidarity and harmonisation with the social matrix (the supracontract norms). Any of these may render humanitarian factors existing in a contractual relation visible to the eye. Essential contract theory itself goes no further than rendering visible what is largely invisible in discretist models. It compels no particular conclusions about how to deal with what is revealed. Imagine, for example, Stalin locking at his slave labour camps through the lens of essential contract theory. He would have seen massive imbalances of power, the cruelest of means, widespread unhealthy shiftiness in roles, phenomenally imbalanced reciprocity, the weakest possible contractual solidarity, all tightly integrated with the Soviet social matrix and its dominating supracontract norm of terror. He would then have rejoiced that all was well with the world and told the NKVD to tighten the screws just a touch, all the while doodling more wolves on his notepad. A humanitarian using essential contract theory would have come to similar intermediate conclusions, but distinctly different final conclusions.

In typical applications of rational choice theory, there is simply no room for the elements made visible by essential contract theory. In particular, power, with its effect on all the other elements, is completely swept under the table. This occurs in one of two ways. One is through the usually unstated assumption that existing patterns of property ownership and rights of liberty are of no significance to the analysis. The other is through assumptions of *ceteris paribus*, quite commonly unarticulated.

In similar manner, the 100 per cent on-off consent ideas of offer and acceptance in classical contract law also largely prevent consideration of the elements of essential contract theory. Classical contract law is, however, distinguishable from rational choice theory. It is not an entirely theoretical structure, however abstractly its principles may be stated. Thus, people dealing with real-life contract law, in whatever capacity, do not enjoy the same freedom as economists dealing with the theoretical model of rational choice theory. As a consequence dancing about the edges of the consent model of real-life classical contract law are many issues, raised in a wide varieties of ways that can, and often do, introduce humanitarian considerations of many kinds. The more this occurs, the more we think of on-off contract law as being neo-classical contract law rather than classical.[7] Many doctrines of this order were raised one way and another in the papers of the seminar. Nonetheless, neo-classical contract law brings into view only some of the key elements revealed by essential contract theory. Moreover, often its view is a hazy and incomplete one, particularly respecting patterns of power.

Thus essential contract theory offers a vision of factors that permits—not requires—humanitarian conclusions unavailable within either rational choice theory models or the central doctrines of even neo-classical, much less classical, contract law. This poses a problem for anyone wishing affirmatively to exclude humanitarian considerations from their conclusions, whether factual or normative. Once humanitarian factors heave into view it may be extremely difficult to ignore them. This may partially explain the vehemence with which some discretists have first distorted essential contract theory and then criticised it for its non-existent humanitarian biases.

There may be an even more basic reason why discretists seek to discredit essential contract theory by any means possible. Making humanitarian issues visible is far from the only thing tending to distress discretists. The basic elements of essential contract theory can and do often reveal serious defects in discretist analysis of particular subjects. What seems optimal when all relational elements are excluded by discretists often turns out to be anything but optimal when they are included. What seems sound legal policy when analysis is confined to the basic doctrine of classical contract law may seem unsound indeed when relational elements are examined.[8]

[7] IR Macneil, 'Contracts: Adjustment of Long-term Economic Relations Under Classical, Neo-classical and Relational Contract Law' (1978) 72 *Northwestern University Law Review* 854, 865–86.

[8] IR Macneil, 'Efficient Breach: Circles in the Sky' (1982) 68 *Virginia Law Review* 947 and IR Macneil, 'Contract Remedies: A Need for a better Efficiency Analysis' (1988) 144 *Journal of Institutional and Theoretical Economy* 6.

CONCLUSION

The core relational principle—analysis must always start with context—makes it possible to determine what circumstances should or should not be taken into account in dealing with transactions. In addition, a relational approach can yield a better understanding of the more discrete aspects of the transaction such as express terms. If so designed, a relational approach can do these things neutrally, without orientations towards particular social views.

In contrast, approaching any transaction as a discrete egg always runs high risks of distorting both the express terms of the transactions and the limited circumstances such an approach opens to examination. In addition such an approach is by its very nature an unsound starting point for determining what other circumstances should be considered. Such approaches are far from neutral tools of social analysis.

Essential contract theory, one of countless possible relational theories of contract, is a neutral analytical tool, not one oriented towards particular social views. That it *appears* to discretists to favour humanitarian views is entirely the product of the non-neutrality of their own tools of analysis: rational choice theory and classical contract law.

8

Discretionary Powers in Contracts

HUGH COLLINS

MANY CONTRACTS CONFER discretionary powers on the parties. Contrary to the conventional image of a contract that fixes by agreement a set of precise rights and obligations, the express terms of the contract may confer a discretion on one party to determine the content of some of the obligations in the contract.[1] The discretion may apply to power-holder's obligations or those of the other party subject to the power. The discretion may be conferred either throughout the life-time of the contract or at periodic intervals. The power may assume many different forms. As well as express statements of the kind that a decision such as withholding consent to an assignment of a lease is in 'the absolute discretion' of one party, the terms may confer a power of qualification or variation of obligations. A qualification amounts to a form of exclusion clause under which one party has the discretionary power to limit or substitute its own obligations under the contract. For instance, a retailer may reserve the right to substitute different goods from those specified in a sale to a consumer. A power to vary the contract involves a discretionary power to change the obligations or rights of the other party to the contract. Such a term is often found in credit agreements with a variable rate of interest. The creditor is given the power to vary the interest rate on a loan either up or down at periodic intervals that may be as short as a month.

At first sight such a term conferring a discretionary power looks odd in the context of a contract. One might expect parties to be unwilling to agree to an arrangement that confers such a broad discretion on one

[1] It is beyond the scope of this essay to consider the regulation of discretionary powers conferred on a third party such as an architect in a construction contract, a valuer in a long-term lease with provisions for rent increases, or a commercial arbitrator. Different principles such as impartiality and a fair procedure may apply in those contexts: *Paramena Europa Navigacion (Compania Limitada) v Frederick Leyland & Co Ltd (J Russell & Co)* [1947] AC 428; *Sutcliffe v Thackrah* [1974] AC 727.

party that in effect permits that party to rewrite the content of the contract at will. Normally contracts can only be varied in such radical ways by the agreement of both parties. Yet there is nothing in principle to preclude the parties from expressly agreeing that one or both should enjoy discretionary powers under the contract. As Lord Woolf has observed in the context of the contract of employment:

> The general position is that contracts of employment can only be varied by agreement. However, in the employment field an employer or for that matter an employee can reserve an ability to change a particular aspect of the contract unilaterally by notifying the other party as part of the contract that this is the situation. However, clear language is required to reserve to one party an unusual power of this sort. In addition, the court is unlikely to favour an interpretation which does more than enable a party to vary contractual provisions with which that party is required to comply.[2]

These observations can, I suggest, be generalised to all contracts. In principle, the parties can agree upon discretionary powers, though express provision is usually required. The language will have to be particularly explicit if it confers a power to vary the obligations of the party subject to the power.

The courts demonstrate a reluctance to concede that a contractual term confers an unfettered discretionary power. Close inspection of the terms of the contract, putting the discretionary power in the framework of the whole transaction, may enable the court to conclude that the power is limited in some respects. The parties may have specified the conditions under which the discretion may be exercised, or the criteria by which it should be exercised. In the event of a dispute, the problem for a court is to interpret the contract in order to ascertain whether the relevant conditions and criteria have been satisfied. For instance, a *force majeure* clause that permits termination of the contract by one party establishes a standard by reference to which the power to terminate must be exercised. Although the meaning of *force majeure* may prove controversial, or its application on the facts disputed, a court can determine whether the power was exercised legitimately according to this criterion. Similarly, the contract may specify the grounds that should guide the exercise of a discretionary power. In *Clark v Nomura International plc*,[3] following dismissal from a post as a trader in

[2] *Wandsworth London Borough Council v D'Silva* [1998] IRLR 193, CA.
[3] [2000] IRLR 766, HC.

equities in the City of London, the employee claimed damages of £1.3 million for compensation for failure to pay a discretionary bonus for his work during his last nine months of employment. The claim was successful because the court held that the contract limited the employer's discretion by connecting the amount of bonus to the level of 'individual performance'. The discretion was not unfettered, but had to be determined by reference to the employer's normal performance criteria.

These examples may involve difficult questions of construction of the contract and controversial issues of fact, but from the point of view of regulatory technique, they do not present a novel problem for the law. A court has to provide an intelligent construction of the contract and apply it to the circumstances of the case, a familiar, if complex, task for the courts in relation to contracts.[4] The particular difficulty that can sometimes be raised in such cases is whether a court will challenge a subjective, good faith, belief that the standard for exercise of the power has been satisfied. It seems that honesty may be insufficient. For example, in a dispute concerning the application of a flexibility clause in a contract of employment, an employer exercised its power to transfer the worker to different tasks when this move was 'determined by requirements of operational efficiency.' The Employment Appeal Tribunal held that the employers had correctly exercised their discretion, though if there were no reasonable or sufficient grounds for believing that the standard had been satisfied, the employer would have acted in breach of contract.[5] Similarly, in a franchise agreement for distribution of soft drinks, the franchisor had the power to terminate the contract if in its sole, exclusive, final, but good faith determination the franchisee was not conducting its operations in a systematic and business-like manner. The US Court of Appeals upheld the franchisor's termination of the contract, stating that this discretion might only be challenged if the franchisee could show that its performance of the contract was so perfect that no reasonable person could have reached a good faith decision to terminate.[6] The approach to interpretation in these cases suggests that the holder of the power must have reasonable grounds for believing that the conditions for the exercise of the power have been met, including

[4] For discussions of interpretation in this volume, see Brownsword , above ch 4, and Campbell and Collins, above p 33.

[5] *White v Reflecting Roadstuds Ltd* [1991] IRLR 331, EAT.

[6] *Ard Dr Pepper Bottling Co v Dr Pepper Co*. 202 F2d 372 (Fifth Circ, 1953).

those conditions that are expressed in subjective terms such as honesty, to one party's satisfaction,[7] and good faith.[8]

As well as express terms that limit a discretionary power, many long-term commercial transactions that confer a power on one party to determine the content of its own obligation can be classified as establishing a fiduciary relation. The power-holder's discretion is then constrained by good faith fiduciary obligations. These obligations are likely to arise in any kind of agency relation, where the purpose of granting a power is to award a discretionary power to an agent to determine what is in the best interests of the principal. The familiar example of the duty of directors of companies to act in the best interests of the company, usually meaning its shareholders, illustrates how the law imposes a mandatory duty of good faith and loyalty on agents. Again the courts may encounter a difficult task of determining whether or not a fiduciary duty has been broken, but the legal framework for such a review of the exercise of a discretionary power is well established. The common law is, however, reluctant to impose fiduciary duties on parties to contracts outside well-established categories such as agency.[9] This reluctance stems from the perception that parties to contracts should normally be permitted to act in their own best interests. We are concerned solely here with instances of discretionary powers that fall outside the ambit of fiduciary duties, and which are not constrained by objective criteria or conditions. The absence of such express controls raises the presumption that the parties should be free to exercise their powers under a contract in any way that they see fit.

This presumption arises from the background principle of freedom of contract or party autonomy. It remains a powerful presumption in English common law. In other legal systems, Codes or legal doctrines may provide a tool for controlling the exercise of discretionary powers. Often this tool is described as a duty to perform the contract in good

[7] In a contract for the hire of a private detective, the obligation to pay was contingent on the detective discovering whether or not a diamond had been stolen and who had stolen it 'to the satisfaction' of the client. The client refused to pay when the detective proved that the client's wife had stolen the diamond. The court upheld the detective's claim, stating that the professed dissatisfaction of the client was a 'mere subterfuge and pretext.' *McCartney v Badovinac*, 62 Colo 76, 160 P 190 (1916).

[8] Cf *McClory v The Post Office* [1993] IRLR 159, HC—a power to suspend from work must be exercised on reasonable grounds.

[9] An uncertainty as to whether good faith obligations apply to a principal in an agency relationship persists, but in many instances the Commercial Agents (Council Directive) Regulations 1993, Regulation 5, (implementing Directive 86/653/EEC) imposes a mandatory good faith standard.

faith. In the United States, for instance, both the Uniform Commercial Code[10] and the Restatement (2d) of Contracts[11] acknowledge the existence of a general obligation of good faith in performance.[12] This mandatory principle permits challenges to the exercise of an otherwise unfettered discretionary power under a contract. It has been applied, for instance, to a requirements contract, so that the purchaser must exercise its discretion to determine its requirements in good faith,[13] and also to the withholding of consent to an assignment.[14] In jurisdictions where a good faith standard is available, the courts still recognise a strong presumption in favour of enforcing the explicit terms of the contract, including an unfettered discretionary power. The good faith standard, however, enables a court to control discretionary decisions that are perceived to be based on improper purposes, that is where the power is used for a purpose not originally expected by the subject of the power. In other jurisdictions, a similar function can be achieved by the doctrine of abuse of rights, under which a legal right, not necessarily a contractual right, is in the view of the court used for an improper purpose. This doctrine has been used in France, for instance, to place constraints on an employer's power of dismissal.[15] An abuse of rights is understood to mean the exercise of power predominately for the purpose of damaging the other party's interests rather than serving the interests of the power-holder.[16] Once again, however, the doctrine of abuse of rights does not rule out the possibility of an unfettered discretionary power.[17]

[10] s 1–203.

[11] s 205.

[12] For detailed discussions of US decisions: EA Farnsworth, 'Good Faith Performance and Commercial Reasonableness Under the Uniform Commercial Code' (1963) 30 *University of Chicago Law Review* 666; RS Summers, 'Good Faith in General Contract Law and the Sales Provisions of the Uniform Commercial Code' (1968) 54 *Virginia Law Review* 195; SJ Burton, 'Breach of Contract and the Common Law Duty to Perform in Good Faith' (1980) 94 *Harvard Law Review* 369; EA Farnsworth, 'Good Faith in Contract Performance', in J Beatson and D Friedmann (eds), *Good Faith and Fault in Contract Law* (Oxford, Clarendon, 1995) 153.

[13] *Homestake Mining Co v Washington Public Power Supply System*, 476 F Supp 1162 (ND Cal 1979).

[14] *Cheney v Jennett*, 693 P2d 1031 (Idaho 1984).

[15] M Plascencia, 'Employment at Will: The French Experience as a Basis for Reform' (1988) 9 *Comparative Labor Law Journal* 294; dismissal in France is now regulated by statute.

[16] J Ghestin, *Traite de Droit Civil: Les Effets Du Contrat*, 2nd edn (Paris, LGDJ, 1994), 287.

[17] Cass civ 15.4.1872, DP 1872.1.176 (discretionary bonus).

There exists one field, however, where English law has developed principles for controlling discretionary powers established by contract. In unincorporated associations such as clubs, trade unions, and self-regulatory financial markets, the member forms a contract with the association and possibly the other members as well.[18] Under the terms of this contract, a committee of the association is typically vested with powers to alter the rules of the association and to expel members for breach of the rules. The courts have evolved doctrines for the review of the exercise of the power of these committees, such as fair procedures (or natural justice), and substantive standards that the power should not be exercised arbitrarily, capriciously, or irrationally. The standards have been applied both to associations with some statutory or public law framework, such as financial and professional self-regulatory bodies,[19] and to more private associations, such as sports clubs and trade unions.[20] It is unclear whether the private nature of the association affects the standards to be applied or merely the civil procedure to be followed.[21] In all these cases, however, the judicial review of discretionary powers concerns the powers of the association, as represented by the committee. In the absence of a company law framework, the courts have forged some rules to protect members against the potential misuse of the powers of the association. We can detect analogies here with the corporate idea that the powers should be exercised within the rules of the association, in the best interests of the members, and without minority oppression.

These controls over discretionary powers within unincorporated associations provide an interesting parallel and hint at how a good faith or abuse of rights standard might be developed in English law for bilateral commercial contracts containing discretionary powers. The precise scope of application of these controls that have evolved in connection with unincorporated associations also raises puzzling issues

[18] *The Satanita* [1895] P 248, affirmed *sub nom Clarke v Dunraven* [1897] AC 59.

[19] *Shearson Leaman Hutton Inc v Maclaine Watson & Co* Ltd [1989] 2 Lloyd's Rep 570 (London Metal Exchange); *R v Life Assurance and Unit Trust Regulatory Organisation Ltd, ex p Ross* [1993] QB 17; *Swain v The Law Society* [1983] 1 AC 598.

[20] *Enderby Town FC Ltd v Football Association Ltd* [1971] Ch 591*; R v Disciplinary Committee of the Jockey Club, ex p Aga Khan* [1993] 1 WLR 909, CA; *Roebuck v National Union of Mineworkers (Yorkshire Area) No2)* [1978] ICR 676, Ch D; *Esterman v NALGO* [1974] ICR 625, ChD; the relation between trade unions and their members is now largely governed by the Trade Union and Labour Relations Consolidation Act 1992 ss 64, 174.

[21] J Beatson, 'Public Law Influences in Contract Law', in Beatson and Friedmann (eds), n 12 above, 263, 269.

concerning the current boundaries of this category. In networks of contracts between businesses, as for example in a distribution network, there are many similar features to the bargain at the heart of unincorporated associations. In particular, the expectations of members of the network with respect to reciprocal obligations extending beyond formal contractual undertakings appear rather similar to those found in clubs and unincorporated associations. There may be an expectation, not founded on contract, that members of the network, such as the distributors of cars, will not act to harm the interests of other distributors, just as members of a club expect that its members will not bring the club into disrepute.[22] Similarly, third parties outside the network may expect that the network, like an unincorporated association, should accept collective responsibility for the actions of its members.[23] The question therefore arises whether the doctrines used by the courts to control perceived abuses of power in unincorporated associations could have some application to networks of commercial contracts. We cannot pursue that question further here, however, for our focus of attention lies on bilateral commercial contracts that provide for an unfettered discretionary power.

Although English common law has not evolved a general good faith clause or an abuse or rights doctrine to regulate discretionary powers in ordinary commercial contracts, the courts, assisted to some extent by legislation, have nevertheless rejected the notion that contracts can confer completely unfettered discretionary powers on one of the parties. The courts have developed implied terms and other techniques for controlling even apparently unfettered discretionary powers. We might describe this phenomenon as the use of implicit understandings in the contractual relation to control the explicit undertakings. The implicit understanding involves a norm that the holder of the discretionary power will not exercise the power in certain ways despite the literal right to do so under the contract. This formulation of the issue posed by the control of discretionary powers in contracts fails, of course, to explain the source or basis of the implicit norm or its content. My central question is what is the source and dimensions of this implicit norm that enables the courts to control party autonomy with respect to unfettered, unilateral, discretionary powers in contracts?

22 H Collins, *Regulating Contracts* (Oxford, Oxford University Press, 1999) 252.

23 G Teubner, 'Piercing the Contractual Veil? The Social Responsibility of Contractual Networks', in T Willhelmsson (ed), *Perspectives of Critical Contract Law* (Aldershot, Dartmouth, 1993) 211.

ECONOMIC RATIONALE FOR DISCRETIONARY POWERS

Before examining in greater detail the reasoning used by the courts, it is helpful to consider an economic analysis of discretionary powers in contracts. In some instances of contractual discretionary powers, it is conceivable that the superior bargaining power of one party has permitted it to insist upon a one-sided transaction. In return for a fixed undertaking, the stronger party has merely indicated what it might perform in return, whilst reserving sweeping powers to vary its own obligations. At the extreme end of the spectrum of such unbalanced agreements, there will be doubt whether the requirement of consideration has been satisfied, as in the case of some requirements contracts.[24] It seems likely that the parties to such unbalanced agreements do not expect to have to use the legal system to enforce their expectations, but rather they rely on long-term self-interest to promote conformity to expectations. Such agreements may not satisfy a Pareto efficiency standard, since it is unclear whether the weaker party has obtained any significant economic benefit at all. As well as strong bargaining power, however, economic analysis suggests several reasons why the parties may expressly agree to discretionary powers for reasons of efficiency.

One reason why the parties may agree to a discretionary power is to create an adequate response to future uncertainty. If the parties recognise that future events will require adaptations of the contract, they may either adopt a short-term contract or create a mechanism for adjustment of the contract to handle future contingencies. A discretionary power is a 'governance mechanism' that enables adjustment of obligations.[25] In effect, the parties have left the contract incomplete by design, and have devised a technique for subsequently determining the obligations in the light of subsequent events. They need to provide for adaptation, for otherwise the contract may become inefficient for one or both parties. In the case of variable interest rates, for instance, a long-term fixed interest rate plainly creates a risk for both parties that fluctuations in financial markets will render the loan inefficient. Either

[24] S Macaulay, 'The Standardized Contracts of United States Automobile Manufacturers' 7 *International Encyclopedia of Comparative Law* 3 (1973).

[25] This terminology and economic analysis relies heavily on OE Williamson, 'Transaction Cost Economics: The Governance of Contractual Relations' (1979) 22 *Journal of Law and Economics* 233; OE Williamson, *The Economic Institutions of Capitalism* (New York, Free Press, 1985).

the creditor may find that it is lending money at a lower rate of return than it costs to raise the money on the capital market, or the borrower may discover that it is trapped into a credit bargain in which it has to pay greatly in excess of the market interest rates. These risks are avoided by a variable interest rate. The conferral of a discretionary power on one of the parties is merely a crude governance structure for completing or adapting the contract in the light of future events. Yet although it is easy to understand why the parties might agree to incomplete contracts with a governance mechanism, the puzzle remains why they should both agree to the governance mechanism that confers an unlimited discretionary power to vary the contract on only one party.

A discretion conferred on one party, without constraining criteria and conditions, plainly creates the risk of opportunism. The power-holder will surely be tempted to exercise its discretion in its favour. In the case of variable interest rates, the creditor must be tempted to push up the rate of interest in order to maximise its profits. Similarly, an employer must be tempted to exercise its discretion in granting a bonus to employees to the least extent permitted by the contracts of employment. If there is no express provision in the contract to stop such opportunism, there is no apparent legal reason to refrain from self-interested profit-maximisation. Why would a borrower agree to a bargain that makes him vulnerable to such opportunism about the variable interest rate without legal recourse? Similarly, if a contract confers an unfettered power to withhold consent for assignments, it seems like a recipe for 'hold-ups', that is demands for additional payments in return for granting consent.

From an economic perspective, however, there may be strong reasons in practice for the power-holder to refrain from blatant opportunism. If the party subject to the discretion believes that the power has been used opportunistically, it may invoke express or implied terms to exit the contract. For example, if a variable interest rate noticeably exceeds comparable market rates, the borrower can repay the debt by seeking another lender. It is of course true that exit from long-term contracts is rarely, if ever, costless. The exiting party may have to forfeit sunk costs or irretrievable investments. In addition, there will normally be transaction costs in seeking an alternative contractor. Even so, taking these costs into account, at some point the level of opportunism may be sufficiently great that it will be beneficial for the victim to exit the contract.

Furthermore, economic interest requires the holder of a discretionary power to exercise it reasonably, since misuse may damage its reputation in the market.[26] If it became common knowledge that one bank used its power to vary interest rates in such a manner that lenders usually had to pay well above market rates of interest, the bank would quickly damage its reputation and customer base. Similarly, if an employer in practice rarely awarded a substantial bonus, the workforce would quickly become apprised of this strategy, and then either demand a higher fixed rate of pay or quit. Economic interest does not prevent the power-holder from acting opportunistically, but it places an outer limit on the extent to which the discretion may be abused.

Both of the above economic considerations explain why opportunism may not occur, but they do not really explain why the subject of the discretionary power might agree to this vulnerability to opportunism in the first place. We may discover, however, in some contracts an incentive for the party subject to the discretion to agree to accept the risk of opportunism. The party subject to the power may obtain a price reduction or other consideration as compensation for accepting the risk of opportunism. In the example of variable interest rates, the borrower expects to benefit from the slightly lower rates of interest charged by creditors in variable rate contracts compared to fixed rate deals. Of course, opportunism by the creditor may defeat that expectation, but the borrower accepts that risk in return for the chance of obtaining lower rates of interest. Similarly in the case of the assignment of a lease, the tenant may obtain a lower rent in return for relinquishing the power to assign the lease than could be achieved with an assignment clause. In contracts of employment, a discretionary power to terminate at will is often balanced by an agreed level of compensation—the golden parachute.[27] From an economic perspective, therefore, many contracts that confer a unilateral discretionary power on one of the parties are not as odd as they first appear. It can be in the rational economic interest of both parties to enter such a transaction under the conditions of uncertainty described above combined with certain perceptions and assumptions of risk. This kind of arrangement

[26] For analyses of the importance of reputation in controlling the exercise of discretionary powers: AW Dnes, 'A Case-Study Analysis of Franchise Contract' (1993) 22 *Journal of Legal Studies* 367; R Epstein, 'In Defence of the Contract at Will' (1984) 57 *University of Chicago Law Review* 947.

[27] In an employment context these agreed sums seem to be accepted, but in the context of agency there appears to be a question of whether such terms may, in some instances, be invalid as penalty clauses if the agreed sum is not a genuine pre-estimate of loss: *Duffen v FRABo Spa*, CA (1998) 17 Tr LR 460, criticised in R Bradgate, *Commercial Law*, 3rd edn (London, Butterworths, 2000) 214.

is common enough in the form of an option agreement, where one party buys the right to decide at a future date whether or not to enter a contract. In the case of discretionary powers, the contract is made at the outset, but the power to determine its content is reserved for a future time.

One last strand of economic analysis suggests a further reason for the acceptance of unilateral discretionary powers in contracts. Discretionary powers may be symmetrical in the sense that each party enjoys a corresponding power to vary the obligations under the contract. This symmetry serves two purposes. First, it provides a credible threat against opportunism. If one party exercises its discretionary power in what is regarded as an opportunistic manner, the other party can retaliate in a similar vein. But, secondly, neither party wishes this dynamic to occur, for their hope and expectation is that the extra flexibility achieved by discretionary powers will contribute to the maximisation of joint wealth. One way to understand how wealth maximisation can be achieved through such arrangements is to analyse the contract as containing a dual, cross-over agency structure. Both parties are acting simultaneously as a principal in their own interest and at the same time as an agent for the other. As a principal they require a discretionary power to direct the other's performance obligations, and as an agent they require discretion to act in the best interests of the principal. What holds this complex structure together is the combination of credible threats against opportunism with the incentive structure of enabling both parties to share in the rewards of a successful transaction. Under the label of symbiotic contracts, this analysis has been applied, for instance, to business format franchises.[28]

It is also possible to apply the symbiotic contract analysis to some contracts of employment.[29] The traditional contract of employment vested a discretionary power in employers to direct the workforce to its most profitable use. This power was constrained, however, by the express terms of the contract of employment, which set outer limits to the tasks that employees could be required to perform. This arrangement becomes inefficient, however, to the extent that the employer

[28] E Schanze, 'Symbiotic Contracts: Exploring Long-Term Agency Structures Between Contract and Corporation', in C Jorges (ed), *Franchising and the Law: Theoretical and Comparative Approaches in Europe and the United States* (Baden-Baden, Nomos Verlagsgesellschaft, 1991) 67.

[29] H Collins, 'Is There a Third Way in Labour Law?', in J Conaghan, RM Fischl and K Klare (eds), *Labour Law in an Era of Globalization* (Oxford, Oxford University Press, 2002) 449, 459.

seeks to draw upon the knowledge and expertise of the worker in order to improve the profitability of the business. In many sectors of the economy, the employer provides financial capital, but depends crucially on the knowledge and expertise of the workforce to use this capital successfully. Thus the employer must grant considerable discretion to the workforce to determine its own tasks, and has to provide an incentive to the workforce to co-operate in the maximisation of the profits of the business. We can detect this pattern, for instance, in the *Clark v Nomura* case discussed above concerning the discretionary bonus for a trader in the City. The bank supplies the capital for speculation, and determines a trading sector for investments, but leaves the employee to use his or her own skill to choose the best investments. As an incentive, the employee receives a substantial part of his or her remuneration by way of a performance-related bonus. Further investigation might reveal other symbiotic dimensions, such as a discretionary power held by the employee on how much capital to draw on, which in effect permits the employee a discretion to fix the amount of the employer's investment. To the extent that increasingly every business sector has to compete using the knowledge of its workforce, we can detect elements of symbiotic relations in many contracts of employment. The following statement is a clause in a collective agreement in a traditional manufacturing sector, a clause which is probably incorporated into the individual contracts of employment of the workforce.

> During your employment with the Company, you will be required to co-operate in the development of new working arrangements as necessary, including participating in training in order to improve both individual skills and the profitability of the Company. This will include being flexible in regard to the duties undertaken and mobile within the Company's establishment in which you are employed.[30]

This 'flexibility' clause assumes that the worker can be directed towards any kind of task, and will exercise his or her discretion to contribute to better productivity. At the same time the employer undertakes to provide training and improvements to human capital, both for the worker's and the employer's long-term benefit. No doubt this clause is linked to assertions of long-term employment security and

[30] S Dunn and M Wright, 'Maintaining the 'Status Quo'? An Analysis of the Contents of British Collective Agreements, 1979–1990' (1994) 32 *British Journal of Industrial Relations* 23.

opportunities for financial participation in the profits of the enterprise for the worker as an incentive to co-operate. The combination of these incentives with the credible threat of the workforce not to use their knowledge and skills in the best interests of the employer secures the stability of this complex structure of discretionary powers and obligations.

These strands of economic analysis of discretionary powers in contracts suggest a number of efficiency reasons why a party might be willing to make itself vulnerable to the misuse of that power and why the risk of opportunism is likely to be substantially discounted in some contexts. The implication of this analysis is that courts should not be surprised to discover unilateral discretionary powers in contracts, and, more crucially, that they should be wary of seeking to impose their own controls over these powers. The case for judicial abstention is strong given the possible economic logic behind the transaction. There must be reason to doubt that the power-holder has in fact acted opportunistically, at least to any great extent. In any case, it can be argued that the party subject to the power has agreed to take the risk of opportunism in return for consideration, so that it would be unfair for the court to rewrite the bargain at a later stage when the risks have become known. Alternatively, it might be argued that the symmetrical pattern of discretionary powers provides each party with adequate safeguards against opportunism, and that to seek to control discretionary powers would be to misunderstand the balance of power under the contract and in fact undermine the wealth-enhancing potential of symbiotic contracts.

English courts have not, however, accepted this logic of economic arguments in favour of complete abstention with respect to discretionary powers in contracts. With the assistance of the legislature, they have begun to evolve principles for the review of the exercise of unfettered discretionary powers. The courts have deployed such standards as 'good faith', 'reasonable expectations', and 'irrationality' in order to control the abuse of discretionary powers. These principles may be consistent with a sophisticated understanding of economic efficiency. It can be argued that in many long-term contractual relations, which depend upon adaptation and co-operation in order to maximise the wealth achieved through the transaction, an unfettered discretionary power may jeopardise the economic potential of the contract. The parties can be assisted by the courts' provision of default rules that discourage behaviour which may destabilise or undermine co-operative behaviour.[31] Since the possible types of opportunistic behaviour are indeterminate, the default rule that may assist the parties to keep their business relation on track will have to be a vague standard such as good faith. In the express terms of such contracts, or in the preliminaries that state the parties' objectives, we can often discover a similar affirmation of good faith or best endeavours. A legal rule of this kind might therefore serve to preserve and enhance the efficiency of such transactions.

We certainly need to be cautious in recommending the evolution of such standards to control unilateral discretionary powers. The economic arguments for abstention are powerful, and the non-legal sanctions against opportunism may often prove a sufficient deterrent against opportunism. In the United States, legislation has sought to control abuse of discretionary power, especially the power to terminate the contract, in the context of franchises and distributorships.[32] It is unclear, however, whether this legislation has afforded any significant protection to the subjects of discretionary powers,[33] and there is some evidence that the existence of the regulation may have diminished the level of economic activity that takes this form of symbiotic contracts.[34]

Against this cautious approach, however, it must be observed that the economic analysis tends to assume the efficiency of the contracts that parties reach in an unregulated environment. But it is far from clear that parties with superior bargaining power in the market will not be tempted to bargain for broader discretionary powers than may be required for the purpose of efficiency. Alternatively, the stronger party may prevent a weaker party from acquiring a discretion that would be conducive to efficient co-operation. There is evidence to support this hypothesis concerning the use of superior bargaining power to obtain or exclude discretionary powers despite their potential to enhance joint wealth maximisation in various types of long-term transactions rang-

[31] D Campbell and D Harris. ' Flexibility in Long-term Contractual Relationships' (1993) 20 *Journal of Law and Society* 166; H Collins, 'Regulating the Employment Relation for Competitiveness' (2001) 30 *Industrial Law Journal* 17.

[32] Automobile Dealers Day in Court Act (1988), 15 USC ss 1221–25; Petroleum Marketing Practices Act 15 USC 2801–06; and various State laws.

[33] S Macaulay, 'Long-Term Continuing Relations: The American Experience Regulating Dealerships and Franchises', in Joerges (ed), n 28 above, 197.

[34] JA Brickly *et al*, 'The Economic Effects of Franchise Termination Laws' (1991) 34 *Journal of Law and Economics* 101.

ing from venture partnerships to employment.[35] The courts must be right to eschew an irrebutable presumption that whatever contract terms are used in fact must comprise the most efficient form for the transaction. Oliver Williamson demonstrates, for instance, that the presence of hierarchies and employers' discretionary powers in contracts of employment may achieve superior efficiency than other sorts of contractual arrangements governing productive activities in the context of conveyor-belt factory production. But he is also careful to acknowledge that this model of employment, though widespread in all business sectors, may not be the most efficient arrangement in all sectors, particularly those where the employer needs to rely on the innovations of employees.[36] The continuing presence of hierarchy or asymmetrical discretionary power in such employment relations may not be explicable by reference solely to efficiency considerations. The courts may therefore be justified on efficiency grounds to consider intervention to control the exercise of unfettered discretionary power.

Taking our cue from Lord Woolf's observations quoted above, the following examination of the legal techniques for controlling discretionary powers is divided into two parts. First, we consider the regulation of powers that give the holder a discretionary power to alter its own performance obligations, and second we inspect the techniques for controlling powers that enable the holder to vary the obligations of the other party. A third part considers the particular problem of discretionary termination clauses that enable one party to bring the contract abruptly to an end. Following this survey of legal doctrine, we return to the question of what is the rationale for legal controls over unfettered discretionary powers in contracts.

THE POWER-HOLDER'S PERFORMANCE OBLIGATION

Any attempt to control a discretionary power granted by the express terms of the contract has to overcome not only the principle of respect for freedom of contract or party autonomy, but also has to tackle a

[35] P Gompers and J Lerner, 'The Use of Covenants: An Empirical Analysis of Venture Partnership Agreements' (1996) 39 *Journal of Law and Economics* 463; SA Maragalin, 'What Do Bosses Do? The Origins and Functions of Hierarchy in Capitalist Production' (1974) 6 *Review of Radical Political Economics* 33.

[36] Williamson, *The Economic Institutions of Capitalism*, n 25 above, ch 9.

conceptual conundrum. If a discretionary power is described in broad terms, the contract appears to establish an arrangement under which the power-holder may act as it likes whilst holding the other party to its obligations strictly. The validity of such an agreement might be challenged on the ground of the lack of consideration, yet the parties rarely try to extricate themselves from the deal. The issue before a court is usually whether the discretion has been abused and whether damages for breach of contract might be available. Owing to respect for party autonomy, the common law never evolved a general requirement of fairness that enabled the courts to challenge the validity of particular terms or the good faith of performance. Instead, the courts had to rely on techniques of the construction of contracts in order to control discretionary powers. Yet construction or interpretation proved an unsatisfactory technique for establishing controls over discretionary powers because an express discretionary power could not simply be ignored or construed out of the picture. How, therefore, could a court declare that it was merely interpreting the contract when it was obviously seeking to rewrite the terms in order to place controls over a discretionary power?

For this purpose, the courts seized upon the device named 'fundamental breach'. This technique of construction argued that certain obligations were fundamental to any given contract, so that terms which purported to eliminate those fundamental obligations would be ineffective. This method of construction could be used to control broad discretionary powers that limited the power-holder's obligations under the contract. It was used most commonly to protect consumers against retailers who had conferred broad discretionary powers on themselves through the small print of a standard form contract.[37] But the same technique of construction was also employed in commercial transactions. For example, in *Anglo-Continental Holidays Ltd v Typaldos Lines (London) Ltd*,[38] a shipowner tried to rely on a term in a contract for a Mediterranean cruise that stated that 'Steamers, Sailing Dates, Rates and Itineraries are subject to change without prior notice'. Accepting that arguably this statement had been incorporated into the contract by a course of dealing with a travel agent, the Court of Appeal nevertheless found the shipowner in breach of contract when it purported to alter the booking made by a travel agency to an inferior ship

[37] Examples are found in *Karsales v Wallis* [1956] 1 WLR 936, CA and *Levison v Patent Steam Carpet Cleaning Co* [1977] 3 WLR 90, CA.

[38] [1967] 2 Lloyd's Rep 61, CA.

with a different itinerary. Lord Denning MR, a champion of the doctrine of fundamental breach, stated the principle in these terms:

> No matter how wide the terms of the clause, the Courts will limit it and modify it to the extent necessary to enable effect to be given to the main object and intent of the contract.

This principle or technique of construction required the court to construct a conception of the main object of the contract, but without relying exclusively on the terms of the contract to establish that conception. The conceptual problem was how to declare that the contract had a particular 'main object' or 'fundamental term' when the contract expressly denied any such obligation. The artificiality of the reasoning involved caused the downfall of the doctrine. In a case such as the one above, how could the court assert that the main object of the contract was a cruise on a particular ship following a specific itinerary when the express terms of the contract clearly stated that at the very least the shipowner could substitute a different ship, an alternative route, or both? The logical difficulty with such an analysis is both to identify such core obligations and to insist that they exist despite the contrary wording of the exclusion clause or discretionary power.[39]

The elimination of the doctrine of fundamental breach, though reluctantly accepted on the grounds of its logical difficulties,[40] was perhaps only finally confirmed,[41] when the courts received new statutory powers to control exclusion clauses under the Unfair Contract Terms Act 1977. Section 3 of the Act can be used to challenge broad discretionary powers.

> (1) This section applies as between contracting parties where one of them deals as a consumer or on the other's written standard terms of business.
> (2) As against that party, the other cannot by reference to any contract term-. . .
>   (b) claim to be entitled:
>   i. to render a contractual performance substantially different from that which was reasonably expected of him, . . .
>   except in so far as . . . the contract term satisfies the requirement of reasonableness.

[39] The logical difficulty was exposed particularly in B Coote, *Exception Clauses* (London, Sweet & Maxwell, 1964).

[40] *Suisse Atlantique Societe d'Arement Maritime SA v Rotterdamsche Kolen Centrale NV* [1967] 1 AC 361, HL.

[41] *Photo Production Ltd v Securicor Transport Ltd* [1980] AC 827, HL.

The Act instructs the court to examine the terms of the contract at the time of formation in order to determine their fairness. The potential for abuse of the discretionary power is certainly relevant to the question of fairness or reasonableness, but the claim that it has in fact been abused by the power-holder is not determinative of the question whether the insertion of the power was unfair from the outset. This approach permits, as the earlier economic analysis suggests is necessary, a court to recognise that it may be reasonable for one party to accept the risk of opportunism in the exercise of a discretionary power, provided that there is a potential corresponding benefit.

The key phrase in section 3 of the Act is the test of reasonable expectation. A party's reasonable expectation with respect to how a discretionary power will be exercised places outer limits on the lawful exercise of the discretion, thereby ruling out grosser forms of opportunism. The operation of this test can be illustrated by *Timeload Ltd v British Telecommunications plc*.[42] In a contract for the supply of a telephone service, a term in the contract authorised the supplier to withdraw the service at its complete discretion on giving one month's notice. The Court of Appeal accepted that it was at least arguable that this clause could be challenged as unreasonable under section 3, because the other terms of the contract created the reasonable expectation that the service would be provided and that it would not be terminated without good reason. It was also suggested that even if section 3 did not apply, the common law might be able to restrict the misuse of discretion. In this case the reasonable expectation of the subject of the discretionary power was ascertained not only from the terms of the contract but also the regulatory framework that governs the supply of telephone services to the public.[43]

In the absence of a regulatory framework, it may prove harder to determine the reasonable expectation of the subject of the discretionary power. The reasonable expectation of a particular performance under the contract cannot be based on a close reading of the contract itself, for the discretionary power must negative any precise expectations. A court has to resort to implicit expectations about the main purpose of the contract. This is, of course, the same logical problem that confronted the doctrine of fundamental breach. For example, in a car

[42] [1995] EMLR 459, CA.

[43] C Scott, 'The Juridification of Regulatory Relations in the UK Utilities Sectors', in J Black, P Muchlinski and P Walker (eds), *Commercial Regulation and Judicial Review* (Oxford, Hart, 1998) 19, 42, which explains the regulatory context and other similar cases eg *Zuckoll Group Ltd v Mercury Communications Ltd* [1999] EMLR 385, CA.

rental agreement, the contract may state that the hirer can substitute at its discretion a different make or model of car from that which the contract specifies. Is the reasonable expectation of the customer confined to the provision of some car, whatever the make, or a car that is equivalent in size and quality to that specified in the contract, or does it extend, despite the terms of the contract, to the precise model specified in the contract? To choose between these different versions of the customer's reasonable expectation, a court has to construct the expectation. Furthermore, the court must ignore the presence of the discretionary power in the contract, which would tend to defeat any expectations whatsoever. The question becomes how might a court delineate reasonable expectations?

One possibility is that a court may construct a reasonable expectation from customs and conventions that normally operate in the particular trade sector. On the basis of these customs or conventions, a court may conclude in the above example that the reasonable expectation of the customer is to receive a car that is equivalent in size and quality. Yet if that is not the custom or convention in the trade, but if rather the discretion is regarded by car hire firms as unfettered, a court will have no basis for challenging the validity of the term on the basis of custom or convention. Furthermore, a court may encounter considerable difficulty in discovering the content of the custom or convention, assuming its existence at all. The effective operation of section 3 depends upon the discovery or construction of a set of reasonable expectations of the party subject to the power, which requires the court to interpret the implicit dimensions of the contractual relationship, which include not only trade custom if that exists but also tacit assumptions and unarticulated expectations.

Section 3 does not apply to all instances of discretionary powers that enable the power-holder to modify its own obligations. The statutory control is limited by section 3(1) to consumer contracts or commercial standard form contracts. Schedule 1 of the Act also excludes certain types of commercial contracts and contracts of insurance. Some discretionary powers that affect the power-holder's obligations may fall outside the wording of section 3. In practice, legal advisers also may not always appreciate that a discretionary power may be challenged under the Act, because in form a discretionary power is unlike an exclusion clause. In cases where section 3 has not been raised, the courts have developed common law principles for tackling opportunistic use of discretionary powers.

This scope and tenor of these principles perhaps find their clearest statement in *Mallone v BPB Industries plc.*[44] The claimant managing director of the defendant's Italian subsidiary was dismissed for the reason that the directors of the parent company believed that he was not turning around the fortunes of the subsidiary quickly enough. Whilst in his post, as part of his remuneration, the claimant had acquired various share options in the parent group. The parties reached an agreed financial settlement, except with respect to the share options. The parent company had purported to cancel all the share options, worth about £100,000, under a power conferred by the group share option scheme. The rule under the scheme provided that the parent company could, on termination of employment, grant the employee an 'appropriate proportion' of share options in view of the employee's length of service and any misconduct. However, this rule was qualified by a statement that the amount of share options awarded should depend ultimately on whatever grant 'the directors in their absolute discretion determine'. The Court of Appeal denied the employer's appeal against an award of damages for breach of the share option scheme, holding that the parent company's decision was one which no reasonable employer could have reached.

The court considered various tests for determining the validity of the exercise of the discretionary power. It asked whether the power was exercised honestly, and in that sense applied a test of good faith. The court also asked whether the exercise of the power was capricious or made for an improper motive. It was possible on the facts of this case that the directors' decision passed these tests, because the board had certainly acted in the best financial interests of the company as in law the directors are bound to do. In a similar case, however, where a chief executive claimed damages for wrongful dismissal to cover loss of salary during a contractual notice period of three years, the contract provided for annual salary increases 'by such amount if any as the board shall in its absolute discretion decide'. The High Court held that a decision to award nil increase would have been a capricious or bad faith exercise of its discretion, which itself would have amounted to a breach of contract.[45] To assume that if the contract of employment had been performed the employers would not have given annual increases in salary was 'unrealistic'. The measure of damages was calculated on the assumption of a regular increase in line with past exercises of the

[44] [2002] EWCA Civ 126, [2002] IRLR 452, CA.
[45] *Clark v BET plc* [1997] IRLR 348, HC.

discretion. Here the non-legal constraints on opportunism, such as damage to the employee's motivation, were relied upon to support a finding that an exercise of an unfettered discretion to award a nil increase in salary would have been capricious.

In *Mallone v BPB Industries plc,* however, the employee's challenge was successful on the different ground that the decision not to grant stock options was held to be irrational. The Court of Appeal thought that the reason given by the employer for the decision, namely that the claimant was going to receive a generous settlement, was unimpressive, since the settlement merely provided compensation for breach of other statutory and contractual rights of the employee. The decision was irrational because the option scheme implied that this deferred remuneration would be given for good performance and loyalty. By withdrawing the options, the employer had broken this implicit understanding of the arrangement, even though it had acted within the literal terms of the express power of the contract. The 'irrationality' of the decision seems to depend on the reasonable expectations generated by the share option scheme, which implied that work performance and loyalty were the criteria for the exercise of discretion.

To complete this picture of control over discretionary powers that enable the holder of the power to modify its own obligations, some significant measures of consumer protection should be mentioned. The Unfair Terms in Consumer Contracts Regulations 1999 regulate retailers of goods and services using standard form contracts.[46] The general test of fairness of terms may invalidate discretionary powers if 'contrary to the requirement of good faith' the term 'causes a significant imbalance in the parties' rights and obligations under the contract to the detriment of the consumer.'[47] The 'grey list' in Schedule 2 indicates that unilateral discretionary powers are likely to be unfair terms. Examples of unfair terms include:

> (j) enabling the seller or supplier to alter the terms of the contract unilaterally without a valid reason which is specified in the contract;[48]
> (k) enabling the seller or supplier to alter unilaterally without a valid reason any characteristic of the product or service to be provided;

Other consumer protection legislation uses the technique of compulsory terms, such as the requirement of satisfactory quality for

[46] SI 1999, No 2083.

[47] Reg 4(2).

[48] There is a specific exception for variable interests rates in consumer credit transactions in Sch 3, Part 2(b).

goods,[49] which in effect override any express discretionary power. Similarly, the Package Travel Directive gives the consumer a right to cancel without penalty if the 'organiser is constrained before the departure to alter significantly an essential term of the contract', and a right to suitable alternative arrangements or compensation if during the holiday the organiser is unable to provide a significant proportion of the services.[50]

Drawing together the threads of this discussion of terms that grant a discretionary power to vary the power-holder's obligations, we have observed in the first instance that courts cannot easily challenge the opportunistic use of such powers. If the contract clearly confers a discretion on the holder of power to do or to refrain from some particular action, owing to respect for party autonomy, it is difficult for a court to assert that the party subject to the power had any expectation or entitlement other than to be subject to the whim of the other. The working assumption of the common law is that it must be possible through freedom of contract for the parties to create a legally binding contract that confers a unilateral, unfettered discretionary power. Statutory controls place constraints on a power-holder's ability to qualify its own obligations with respect to some contracts and terms. In principle the statute examines the question of fairness and reasonableness at the point of formation of the contract, but no doubt answers to the question will be influenced by the subsequent use of the discretionary power. The standard suggested by the statute is that abuse occurs if the power is exercised to offer contractual performance that is substantially different from that which was reasonably expected. This provision does not resolve the conundrum of what might be a reasonable expectation in the face of an unfettered discretionary power. In addition to the statute, however, English courts have developed a jurisprudence that suggests that an uncontrolled discretionary power is more of a theoretical possibility rather than a practical reality. Courts strive to discover from the other terms of the contract explicit or implied standards by which the discretionary power should be exercised. Even if these criteria establish a subjective standard, such as stating that the power-holder must be satisfied that a criterion has been satisfied, the courts may be willing to test the honesty or good faith of the power-holder by examining whether there

[49] Unfair Contract Terms Act 1977, s 6(2).

[50] The Package Travel, Package Holidays and Package Tours Regulations 1992 SI 1992/3288, Regulations 12 and 14, implementing Directive 90/314/EEC, OJ L 158, 30.6.1990, p 59.

were reasonable grounds for the belief. In the absence of any criteria established implicitly by other terms of the contract, English courts have developed tests of good faith and irrationality. The good faith standard in this context asks whether the power was exercised capriciously or for an improper motive. The test of irrationality asks whether no reasonable power-holder would have reached the decision that it did. The effectiveness of these controls depends on whether or not the courts accept that reasonable power-holders will act opportunistically in their own self-interest. It seems from the cases that evidence that the power was exercised in the power-holder's rational self-interest is not sufficient to escape judicial control. In other words, some self-interested action is regarded as opportunistic, and is not a permitted exercise of the discretionary power.

THE PERFORMANCE OF THE SUBJECT OF A DISCRETIONARY POWER

We turn now to the second scenario, where the terms of the contract confer a power to vary the other party's performance, as in the case of variable interest rates. The Unfair Contract Terms Act 1977 does not apply to terms that confer power to alter the other party's obligations, because it is aimed at exclusions or limitations of the power-holder's or promisor's obligations. The Unfair Terms in Consumer Contracts Regulations 1999 can apply to such discretionary powers contained in consumer standard form contracts. The general test of fairness could be applied in order to invalidate an unconstrained discretionary power that might operate to the substantial disadvantage of the consumer. The examples from the 'grey list' of terms that are presumptively unfair recited above might apply equally in these circumstances. In addition, price variation clauses are explicitly mentioned in the grey list as presumptively unfair terms:

> (l) providing for the price of goods to be determined at the time of delivery or allowing a seller of goods or supplier of services to increase their price without in both cases giving the consumer the corresponding right to cancel the contract if the final price is too high in relation to the price agreed when the contract was concluded.[51]

[51] This special attention to unilateral price variation clauses in sales reflects the broader practice in other jurisdictions to determine that such contracts are invalid (France) or subject to a court's control to ensure that the price is reasonable (Germany). The latter standard is adopted in Art 2.102, O Lando and H Beale (eds), *Principles of European Contract Law, Part 1: Performance, Non-performance and Remedies* (Dordrecht, Nijhoff, 1995).

For contracts that fall outside the scope of the Regulations, however, as will be the case for commercial transactions, challenges to the exercise of a discretionary power have to rely upon the common law. Once again a court may infer from a construction of the express terms of the contract that an apparently unfettered discretionary power is in fact limited by the contractual agreement itself. In addition, however, the courts have developed several techniques for controlling the use of discretionary powers.

In the first place, it seems likely that a court will imply a notification requirement. If the discretion is exercised in order to alter the obligations of the other party, notification of such a change seems to be essential. For example, if a bank raises the interest rate payable by a customer on a loan, the bank should not be permitted to wait until the customer defaults on the loan by failing to meet the higher repayments before alerting the customer to the rate change. Such a notification term might be justified on a narrow ground of business efficacy. No doubt the required period of notice will be fixed by reference to a standard of reasonableness, which permits the court to adjust the period according to all the circumstances of the case.

Such an implied term of reasonable notice may be one aspect of a broader principle that can be inserted into contracts through the mechanism of implied terms. The principle is that one party to a contract should not exercise its discretion under the contract in such a way as to render it impossible for the party subject to the power to perform its obligation. Although this statement of the principle may prove too broad in some circumstances, this notion of impossibility has been acknowledged as a possible basis for control over the misuse of this type of discretionary power. The implied term of reasonable notice and the notion of impossibility were combined in *United Bank Ltd v Akhtar*.[52] A junior employee working in a branch of the bank was subject to an express mobility clause that enabled the employer to transfer employees to other branches. The bank purported to transfer the employee from Leeds to Birmingham on a few days' notice. In order to establish a statutory claim for unfair dismissal, the employee needed to prove that the bank's exercise of its discretionary power amounted to a fundamental breach of contract. The Employment Appeal Tribunal held that the employers had broken an implied term that they would give reasonable notice of transfers, and an implied term that the

[52] [1989] IRLR 507, EAT.

discretion would not be exercised in such a way as to render it impossible for the employee to comply with the contractual obligation to move. Here the notion of impossibility was used to fix the period of reasonable notice. The employee needed time to find new accommodation for his family and possibly to take advantage of the bank's scheme for helping with relocations.

This test of impossibility may be related to the notion of repudiatory breach. Some exercises of a discretionary power that vary the obligations of the party subject to the discretion may in effect make it impossible to perform the contract. If this consequence is the intended result of the power-holder, it may be possible to argue that in effect this exercise of the power amounts to a repudiation of the contract. In which case, the subject of the power can accept the repudiation and bring the contract to an end. But this argument may be defeated where the exercise of the discretionary power is perceived to have served a legitimate purpose of the power-holder. Where a hospital introduced a 'no smoking' rule, the court concluded that this was a proper exercise of a discretionary power, because it was for a legitimate purpose and had been exercised only after due notice.[53] The fact that the new instruction rendered it impossible for a particular nurse, who was addicted to smoking, to continue working in the hospital was not sufficient reason for the employers to be regarded as having repudiated the contract of employment.

In the context of the contract of employment, the employer's discretionary power to direct performance of work and to set rules for the workplace has traditionally been subject to several controls, such as the requirement that the orders be lawful and that the instructions should not endanger the health and safety of the workforce.[54] In recent years a further strand of control has emerged in the implied term that an employer shall not, without reasonable and proper cause, conduct itself in a manner calculated and likely to destroy or seriously damage the relationship of confidence and trust between employer and employee.[55] An employer's exercise of discretionary power under the contract of employment can in some instances amount to a breach of this implied term of trust and confidence. In *French v Barclay's Bank plc*,[56] the employer required a manager to relocate. The bank provided

[53] *Dryden v Greater Glasgow Health Board* [1992] IRLR 469, EAT.
[54] *Johnstone v Bloomsbury Health Authority* [1992] QB 333, CA.
[55] *Mahmoud v Bank of Credit and Commerce International SA* [1998] AC 20, HL.
[56] [1998] IRLR 646, CA.

a scheme for a discretionary interest-free bridging loan to permit the employee to purchase a new home without having sold his present house. The manager took advantage of this scheme, but owing to its cost in a difficult housing market, the bank withdrew the scheme and replaced it with one much less favourable to the employee. The employee resigned from his position and claimed damages for breach of contract. The claim was successful, because the court concluded that the untimely replacement of the scheme that imposed considerable financial hardship on the employee was conduct that was likely to destroy trust and confidence. Although the bank's scheme was entirely discretionary, the manner of its revocation amounted to a breach of the implied term of trust and confidence. So far the implied term of trust and confidence has been confined in its application to contracts of employment,[57] but it seems possible that it might be extended to analogous contracts for the long-term provision of services.

Besides these techniques of implied terms, the courts have also demonstrated a willingness to control discretionary powers in contracts by reference to the standards of good faith and irrationality. Once again the courts permit a challenge to the exercise of a discretionary power, if no reasonable person having the relevant discretion could have reached such a decision. This standard of irrationality, which is often perceived as no more than an elaboration of a good faith requirement, has been applied to many types of contractual discretionary powers. In *Paragon Finance plc v Nash*,[58] the Court of Appeal confirmed this development in a case concerning the power of a mortgagee to vary interest rates. It approved the earlier application of the standard in two earlier decisions of the court in commercial cases. In *Abu Dhabi National Tanker Co v Product Star Shipping Ltd (No 2)*,[59] the owners of a ship under charter exercised a contractual discretion to determine whether any port to which the charterer ordered the ship was dangerous. The Court agreed with the first instance decision that the owner had misused the discretion in breach of contract, because there was no material on which a reasonable owner could reasonably have exercised the discretion in the way that it did. The irrationality or

[57] With the possible exception of its application to the employer's discretionary power to withhold consent to a proposal by trustees to increase the benefits conferred by an occupational pension scheme: *Imperial Group Pension Trust Ltd v Imperial Tobacco Ltd* [1991] IRLR 66, 71, HC.

[58] [2001] EWCA Civ 1466; [2002] 1 WLR 685.

[59] [1993] 1 Lloyd's Rep 397, CA.

perversity standard has also been applied to a discretionary power to withhold a consent in *Gan Insurance Co Ltd v Tai Ping Insurance Co Ltd (No 2)*,[60] where a reinsurance contract provided that no settlement or compromise of a claim could be made by the insured without the prior approval of the reinsurers.

It is important to notice that in applying the standard of 'irrationality', the courts are deliberately rejecting a standard of reasonableness or fairness. The courts want to position themselves so that they are reviewing the exercise of the power rather than substituting their own view of how the power should have been exercised. Although the courts sometimes say that a power must not be used 'unreasonably', it is clear that in this context the meaning of 'unreasonably' is intended in the sense of irrationality in the public law doctrine founded in *Associated Provincial Picture Houses Ltd v Wednesbury Corpn*.[61] The decision has to be perverse, arbitrary, or capricious, not simply unreasonable or unfair. Furthermore, these decisions do not always invoke the technique of an implied term, but rather appear to assume that a discretionary power has to be exercised in conformity with the good faith or irrationality principle. This technique of control may be significant, for it suggests that no matter how clearly the express terms confer an unfettered discretion, a court will exercise these controlling standards. Finally, we should observe that the irrationality principle has itself been based on a reasonable expectation test. In *Paragon Finance plc v Nash*,[62] Dyson LJ justified the application of the irrationality test on the ground that it was 'necessary in order to give effect to the reasonable expectations of the parties'. Thus, what is regarded as irrational or perverse is an exercise of discretion that falls outside the reasonable expectations of the subject of the power, a test which imitates the standard of section 3 of the Unfair Contract Terms Act 1977.[63]

TERMINATION CLAUSES

Termination or cancellation clauses in contracts do not fit easily into the above discussion. Under such express terms, one or both parties,

60 [2001] 2 All ER (Comm) 299, CA.

61 [1948] 1 KB 223.

62 [2001] EWCA Civ 1446; [2002] 1 WLR 685, 703.

63 The phrase 'reasonable expectations' has acquired considerable currency as a result of Lord Steyn, 'Contract Law and the Reasonable Expectations of Honest Men' (1997) 113 *Law Quarterly Review* 433.

obtain the right to bring a long-term contract to an abrupt conclusion. Although the contract may specify conditions for the exercise of this power, including a notice provision, it is possible that an express term confers an unfettered right to terminate the contract at will. The exercise of such a discretionary power affects the obligations of both parties, since once the power has been validly exercised neither is bound to perform any further obligations under the contract.

Termination clauses have to be examined separately because they may rest on the economic rationale of a protection from opportunism in the exercise of a discretionary power. In a contract where one party has considerable discretion to set its own performance obligations, a termination at will clause provides the party who is subject to the power a strong protection against opportunism. This is the familiar arrangement in contracts of employment, where both employer and employee have considerable discretion in their performance obligations, but they also enjoy the protection at common law that either can terminate the contract on reasonable notice for any reason. Given this possible economic rationale for termination at will clauses, we should expect the courts to be reluctant to control this particular form of discretionary power in contracts.

Nevertheless, it is certainly possible to find instances where termination under an express clause appears to deserve censure. The problem arises where the termination clause is invoked not to punish actual or suspected opportunism, but to obtain some additional or collateral benefit. In the United States, the courts have wrestled with this issue under the standard of good faith. In the context of employment, it has been recognised that an employer may breach the obligation to perform in good faith even when invoking an express or implied term of termination at will. In *Fortune v National Cash Register Co*,[64] the employer terminated the contract in order to avoid having to pay a substantial commission to a sales representative. Despite the presence of a termination at will clause, the employer was held to have breached the obligation to perform in good faith. The good faith standard, (together sometimes with the general provision on unconscionability in the Uniform Commercial Code,[65]) has been invoked to protect distributors and franchisees against the exercise of termination at will clauses.[66] In these relations, distributors and franchisees risk losing irretrievable

[64] 373 Mass 96, 364 NE 2d 1251 (1977).

[65] UCC s 2–302; Restatement of Contracts 2d s 208.

[66] *Shell Oil Co v Marinello*, 63 NJ 402, 307 A 2d 598 (1978).

investments as a result of the exercise of termination clauses, though the termination clauses are necessary for the other party to protect its interest in the quality of performance.[67] Provided that the franchisor exercises its powers under the contract for a 'rational business' purpose, a court is unlikely to permit a challenge to its exercise of discretion.[68] But a franchisee will be protected under a good faith standard against decisions that are 'arbitrary' or based on 'improper motives'.[69] For example, the termination of a franchise for the purpose of giving it to another franchisee better placed to maximise sales was regarded as an improper motive.[70] A similar jurisprudence applying a good faith standard to the exercise of the power to terminate franchises and distributorships has also emerged in France.[71] We can explain such decisions as confining the termination clause to its expected purpose, namely to protect the franchisor against poor performance or opportunism by the franchisee.

With respect to termination at will clauses in long-term contracts under English law, the legal position is far from clear. It is possible that the 'reasonableness' standard of section 3 of the Unfair Contract Terms Act 1977 might apply to termination clauses. The question is whether a cancellation clause in a standard form contract falls under the phrase in section 3(b)(ii), in that the term permits the power-holder to 'claim to be entitled . . . in respect of the whole or any part of his contractual obligation, to render no performance at all'.[72] As a matter of statutory construction, section 3 appears to be focussed on terms that exculpate the power-holder from its own obligations, thus rendering those obligations illusory. In contrast, cancellation clauses both limit the power-holder's obligation to perform, but also terminate the rights and obligations of the other party. Assuming that this statutory test of reasonableness is unavailable, the question becomes whether the courts will imply terms that confine the exercise of a power to terminate at will.

67 G Hadfield, 'Problematic Relations: Franchising and the Law of Incomplete Contracts' (1990) 42 *Stanford Law Review* 927.

68 *David R McGeorge Car Co v Leyland Motor Sales*, 504 F2d 52 (4th Cir. 1974), *cert. denied* 420 US 992 (1975).

69 *Moody v Amoco Oil Co*, 734 F2d 1200 (7th Cir. 1984). *American Mart Corp v Joseph E Seagram & Sons*, 824 F2d 733 (9th Ci. 1987).

70 *Universal Computers Ltd v Daramedia Corp*, 653 F Supp 518 (DNJ 1987), aff'd 838 F2d 1208 (3d Cir 1988).

71 Cass com 5 avril 1994, *JCP* 1994, ed GIV, 1529.

72 The question is left open in *Timeload Ltd v British Telecommunications plc*, n 42 above, 468.

In the context of employment, English courts seem to have turned against the possibility of regulating the power to terminate contracts at will. Although the common law inserts an implied term that reasonable notice of termination must be given unless the employee has committed a repudiatory breach of contract, the traditional view is that an employer's power of termination by notice can be exercised 'unreasonably or capriciously'.[73] The recent decision in *Johnson v Unisys Ltd*[74] firmly rejects the notion of another implied term that controls the 'manner of dismissal'. But the principal reason given for this rejection was that an employee usually has an alternative statutory right under the law of unfair dismissal, so that a development of an alternative common law claim for misuse of the power to terminate a contract of employment without cause was unnecessary and undesirable. Nevertheless, in a subsequent case before the Privy Council, where no statutory claim for dismissal was available, it was confirmed that an express term that conferred the power to dismiss summarily 'without cause' could not be fettered by any implied term. In particular, the Privy Council rejected the contention that the power could only be exercised for a proper purpose and insisted that the express term ruled out any implied term that placed constraints on the reasons for dismissal.[75] It should be noted, however, that the House of Lords in *Johnson v Unisys Ltd* carefully did not reject the wider possibility that in long-term contracts containing termination clauses, apart from contracts of employment, the courts might in some cases insert a good faith standard to control the exercise of the power.

There are certainly some indications that courts are prepared to investigate the good faith of the exercise of a power to terminate the contract in commercial transactions. If a power to terminate the contract is exercised improperly and in bad faith, the exercise of the power will be regarded as a repudiation of the contract rather than an exercise of the power.[76] Similarly, the courts strive to interpret the contractual power to terminate in ways that prevent opportunistic use of the power. In *Schuler AG v Wickman Machine Tool Sales Ltd*,[77] for instance, although the contract for marketing a product specified that

[73] Lord Reid, *Malloch v Aberdeen Corp* [1971] 1 WLR 1578, 1581.

[74] [2001] ICR 480, HL. For a similar conclusion in the Supreme Court of Canada: *Wallace v United Grain Growers Ltd* (1977) 152 DLR (4th) 1.

[75] *Reda v Flag Ltd* [2002] UKPC 38 [2002] IRLR 747, 753, PC.

[76] *Woodar Investment Development Ltd v Wimpey Construction (UK) Ltd* [1980] 1 WLR 277, HL.

[77] [1974] AC 235, HL.

an obligation for sales representatives to visit on a weekly basis all major customers was a 'condition' of the contract, the House of Lords declined to interpret the word 'condition' in its technical sense of a term, breach of which entitles the injured party to terminate the contract. Such an interpretation would have permitted opportunism, for if only one visit out of the intended 1,400 had been missed, the producer would have been able to cancel this marketing contract. Yet few disputes about termination clauses in long-term franchise and distributorship have reached the courts.[78] The termination clauses in these contracts usually provide for a notice period such as six months, a provision that might be inserted by a court in any case as an implied term to protect sunk investments. The notice period weakens the threat of termination, and places a procedural obstacle in the way of its opportunistic use.

Although there are these hints of the application of a good faith standard with respect to termination clauses, it is clear that the courts are for the most part reluctant to constrain the exercise of a discretionary power to terminate at will. In particular, there is no sign of the development of a test of irrationality or reasonable expectation in order to assess whether an unfettered contractual power to terminate has been exercised properly.

IMPLICIT DIMENSIONS

Our brief survey of the techniques used to control unfettered discretionary powers has revealed a willingness on the part of the courts, sometimes assisted by the legislature, to assert the existence of limits to such powers even in the teeth of the express terms. The different standards that we have observed, such as good faith, irrationality, and substantially contrary to a reasonable expectation, share the feature that they rely upon a source for the standard other than the express terms of the contract. How can we explain the source of this regulation of discretionary powers in contracts? What justifies legal regulation of unfettered discretionary powers?

We commenced by observing that it seemed odd that a person might agree to a contract that in effect gave the other party a discretionary to

[78] H Beale, D Harris and T Sharpe, 'The Distribution of Cars: A Complex Contractual Technique' in D Harris and D Tallon (eds), *Contract Law Today* (Clarendon, Oxford, 1989) 301, 330.

alter obligations at will. In some instances, such power relations may be created as a result of some kind of market failure with respect to information about contract terms, such as those caused by the insertion of a discretionary power in the small print of a standard form contract with a consumer. Yet many of our examples have been drawn from commercial contracts and contracts of employment, where the parties were probably fully aware of the potential implications of the discretionary power. We observed in these cases that an economic explanation of the presence of a discretionary power might assert that it is a governance mechanism for dealing with problems of adaptation, the convenience of which is paid for by some corresponding consideration such as a price reduction or incentive payments. Furthermore, the risk of opportunism is often countered by the possibility of unilateral, discretionary termination, together with other non-legal sanctions. These economic arguments explained the presence of discretionary powers, but also tended to discourage the courts from seeking to control their exercise, because interference might upset the balance of advantage struck under the contract. Nevertheless the courts and the legislature have felt impelled to introduce controls over discretionary powers. Can these controls be justified?

In thinking about such a justification for legal regulation, it is helpful, I suggest, to recognise that business transactions typically operate on three levels or involve three kinds of social relation.[79] The written contract between the parties establishes an explicit self-regulation of rights, powers, and obligations. It provides a frame of reference for dealings between the parties, in which they can point to the discrete terms of the agreement as justification for their demands and excuses. Behind the contract, however, lies an economic relation, which both parties have entered for wealth-enhancing reasons. This framework for the relation between the parties concentrates on whether or not the deal is working for both parties in the sense that they will either in the short-term or the long-term improve their economic positions. The behaviour of the parties in this dimension of the relationship is guided by rational self-interest, without paying close attention to the terms of the contract. Beyond this economic relationship, however, lies a third dimension that concerns trust between the parties.[80] This relationship

[79] This analysis is developed at greater length in Collins, n 22 above, ch 6.

[80] For a helpful discussion of a different sense of 'trust' in a contractual context: S Deakin and F Wilkinson, 'Contract Law and the Economics of Interorganizational Trust', in C Lane and R Bachmann, *Trust Within and Between Orgnaizations* (Oxford, Oxford University Press, 1998) 146.

involves all the social interactions surrounding the trade including personal contacts and the history of the connection between the parties. Within this framework of their relationship, the parties strive to preserve or enhance trust between themselves, and avoid being regarded as having acted in bad faith or opportunistically. Trustworthiness certainly has an economic value in the sense of business reputation, but more importantly it has the potential to sustain a long-term business relation (whether or not consolidated in a long-term contract) even when the economic deal is working badly.

We can describe both the economic deal and the trust dimension of a contractual relation as comprising its implicit dimensions. These aspects of the business relation, though not formally recorded in the contract, are vital to sustain its existence and to support proper performance. Economic interest may induce adaptation to changing circumstances, co-operation, and a willingness to sacrifice short-term disappointments under the contract for the sake of long-term economic interests. The need to preserve trust between the parties can induce not only a willingness to forgo contractual rights, but also sacrifices of economic interests under the deal for the sake of preserving the business relationship.

Using this analysis we can explain the presence of unfettered discretionary powers in contracts not only as a technique for adaptation, but also as a device to establish trust between the parties. A willingness to accept subjection to a discretionary power provides a signal rather like an expenditure on irretrievable investments that there is a willingness to trust the good faith of the other party. This trust is certainly not blind to the risks involved in subjection to a discretionary power. There is an element of calculation that the non-legal sanctions such as damage to reputation and harm to long-term economic interests will deter opportunism.[81] Furthermore, the subject of the discretionary power is likely to bargain for the possibility of rapid exit from the contract through a termination clause if the trust is betrayed. Such a cancellation clause is likely to be readily conceded, since the power-holder can appreciate that once trust is lost, the effectiveness of the discretionary power as a governance mechanism is likely to be undermined by passive resistance and retaliatory opportunism.

Viewed in this light of the three dimensions of contractual relations, including the two implicit dimensions of the economic deal and the

[81] OE Williamson, 'Calculativeness, Trust, and Economic Organization', (1993) 36 *Journal of Law and Economics* 453.

business relation based on trust, we can understand the practice of the courts in seeking to control the exercise of unfettered discretionary powers as legal responses to the presence of the implicit dimensions of the contract. These responses take two forms, one examining the economic logic of the deal in order to protect the interests of both parties, and the other to protect the trust signalled by willingness to be subject to a discretionary power.

For the purpose of protecting the economic interests of the parties, the court seeks to understand the purposes for which the discretionary power was created. It picks up many clues about the aim of establishing a discretionary power and its potential to enhance the wealth of the parties from the general framework of the contract. Beyond the terms of the contract, however, a court appreciates the economic logic of the transaction and how it can serve the interests of both parties in the long-term when it functions as expected. In the example of discretionary payments to employees, for instance, the economic logic of tying payments to performance criteria is explained as an incentive structure for the employee to exercise discretion in the best interests of the business. No matter how sweeping the discretionary power described in the contract, the court insists that the power should be exercised within the framework of this economic logic for the transaction. Any other use of the power is labelled perverse, irrational, contrary to reasonable expectations, or bad faith.

For the purpose of protecting trust in the relation, a court is not usually in a position to restore trust once there is a perception of misuse of a discretionary power. The question is rather whether the abuse of power should entitle the party subject to the power to exercise a right to exit the relation and recover compensation. In answering this question, the courts emphasise the dimension of good faith in the exercise of the power. Is the power-holder's decision one that, though falling within the express terms of the contract, nevertheless demonstrates an unwillingness to continue the business relation. In the legal terminology, the question is whether the exercise of the power amounts in effect to a repudiation of the contract, a signal of an unwillingness to try to keep the business relation alive. In the contract of employment, this question is formalised in the implied term of trust and confidence: has the employer acted in a way that is calculated to destroy the necessary trust and confidence that sustains this long-term co-operative economic relation?

With respect to discretionary termination clauses, the courts are rightly more wary of intervention. A termination clause protects a party against an economic deal that is going bad, and in particular provides a means of exit when a discretionary power is used opportunistically. The courts should therefore in general defer to the business judgement of the holder of the power to terminate in order to protect the economic logic of the deal. Nevertheless, the exercise of a termination clause might be reviewed where it is exercised not for the protection of economic interests but some collateral purpose. Such an exercise of the power to terminate the contract represents a betrayal of trust that the business relation would be preserved and enhanced. In legal terminology, a good faith standard can be employed to ascertain whether or not the power was exercised honestly, that is on the basis of evidence that the power-holders' economic interests were at stake.

This suggested rationale for judicial control over unfettered discretionary powers in contracts may not fit exactly the details of legal practice in English common law. Our courts have perhaps been less willing than courts in other jurisdictions to embark on reviews of discretionary powers based upon vague standards such as good faith, reasonable expectations and irrationality. The courts have frequently affirmed their fidelity to the principle of freedom of contract, which they believe entails 'the general principle that an express and unrestricted power cannot in the ordinary way be circumscribed by an implied qualification'.[82] Courts have preferred wherever possible to present their controls as somehow derived from the express terms of the contract, using rather elaborate techniques of construction. The recent cases described above, however, reveal a greater willingness to acknowledge that the courts are exercising an independent power of control. The borrowing or transplanting of terminology from public law in the test of irrationality is particularly striking in this respect, for it abandons any pretence that the courts are merely enforcing terms that the parties agreed explicitly or by necessary implication. But also the use of good faith, with its equitable connotations of loyalty within a relation, suggests the presence of an independent source of control.

Although this borrowing of terminology across traditional divisions in the law is fascinating as a matter of legal technique, my view is that it does not tell us much about the nature of the implicit dimensions of a contractual relation that a court is bringing to the fore. The general standards of irrationality, good faith, and reasonable expectation, serve as a legal method for broadening the enquiry beyond the

[82] Lord Millet, *Reda v Flag Ltd*, n 73 above.

contractual frame of reference, but they do not determine where that enquiry should seek the implicit dimensions of the contract. In this context of unfettered discretionary powers, the implicit dimensions of the contractual relation on which the court draws may be explained in part by reference to customs of the trade and other established practices. But the implicit dimensions that seem to me to be most important are those that form essential, though unwritten, elements of the parties' understanding of the nature and objective of the transaction. The strand that runs through the legal control over discretionary powers is the reasonable expectations of the parties, that is their expectations that go beyond the written terms of the contract. The general standards permit the courts to respond both to the economic logic of the transaction, in the sense of how it is intended to improve the wealth of both parties in the long run, and also to the use of unilateral unfettered discretionary powers as a signal of trustworthiness that can sometimes prove false.

9

Recontractualising the Corporation: Implicit Contract as Ideology

PADDY IRELAND

IN RECENT YEARS, under the influence of law-and-economics, it has become increasingly common in academic circles for companies, including the large, public, joint stock corporations[1] which dominate modern capitalism, to be depicted as nexus-of-contracts. The resulting accounts of company law and the corporation have proved highly controversial, not only for their empirical claims but for their very particular normative implications and policy prescriptions. According to these theories, corporations are the products of voluntary, consensual exchanges between a range of different commodity owners and, as such, are fundamentally private, market-contractual affairs which from a neo-classical economic perspective are a priori 'efficient'. It follows that there is a strong presumption not only against state intervention in and regulation of corporate affairs but in favour of the out-and-out shareholder primacy which characterises Anglo-American corporate/company law.

Despite its growing influence, however, it is far from clear how far corporate contractualism[2] has genuinely furthered our understanding of either company law or the modern joint stock corporation. Certainly, the attempts to depict corporations as nexus-of-contracts have proved problematic. In order to try to sustain their analyses

[1] In this chapter, the term 'company' is generally used as an abridgement of 'limited liability company' to refer to any firm which has incorporated and acquired corporate status, while the term 'corporation' is reserved for the large, incorporated, public, *joint stock* companies which dominate contemporary economic life.

[2] I use the term 'corporate contractualism' to refer to all theories which broadly subscribe to the view of corporations as nexus-of-contracts.

contractual theorists have been compelled to dissolve corporations as entities of substance, dismissing their separate legal 'personhood' 'as a matter of convenience rather than reality'.[3] They have also been forced to deem some of the alleged contracts constituting the corporation to be radically 'incomplete'. It is in this latter context that the idea of implicit contract has been shoved on to the corporate stage, cast in the role of theoretical saviour: the problem of incompleteness, contractualists argue, is resolved by implicit contracts. But is this a proper and appropriate use of the concept? This paper seeks critically to evaluate the contractual depiction and analysis of corporations and, more specifically, the use of the idea of implicit contract within corporate contractual theory. It argues that while the contractual account has considerable analytical value when applied to small, closely-held, private companies—indeed, it can be used to explain (and to legitimate) some of the modifications which have been made in this context to the traditional principles of company law—it does not when applied to the large joint stock corporation. On the contrary, here contract has been pushed beyond its proper limits: the contractual account of the corporation does not stand up to empirical scrutiny, confusing and distorting rather than clarifying. In making these arguments, the paper seeks to identify the ideological use to which the concept of implicit contract has been put in the corporate context and some of the more general problems associated with using it to try to grasp obligations.

INTO THE NEXUS-OF-CONTRACTS TIME-WARP

One of the most curious things about corporate contractualism is that it runs directly against the grain of history, in that the processes whereby company law crystallised out from the law of partnership in the nineteenth century were processes of what one might aptly, if inelegantly, call *de*contractualisation.[4] Modern company law has its roots in the development and growth in the nineteenth century of the joint stock company as an organisational form and in its gradual divergence from the partnership form which dominated early industrialisation.

[3] Frank H Easterbrook and Daniel R Fischel, *The Economic Structure of Corporate Law* (Cambridge, Mass, Harvard University Press, 1991) 12. In this paper I have used the influential work of Easterbrook and Fischel as my principle exemplar of contractualism.

[4] The arguments outlined in this section of the chapter are elaborated in Paddy Ireland, 'Property and Contract in Contemporary Corporate Theory' (2003) 23 *Legal Studies*, forthcoming.

Until the middle of the nineteenth century, all joint stock companies, incorporated or unincorporated, were treated and regarded as 'public' partnerships and were distinguished from 'ordinary' or 'private' partnerships on a quantitative rather than a qualitative basis. As such, they were considered to be subject to the established principles of the law of partnership, except where the operation of the latter had been modified by the granting to companies of corporate status or privileges.[5] However, as the century progressed, and particularly after the rise of the railways and the emergence in their wake of a developed and sophisticated market for company securities, joint stock companies, with their increasingly large, *rentier* memberships and their unencumbered,[6] freely transferable shares, were increasingly distinguished from 'ordinary' partnerships on a qualitative rather than on a quantitative basis. As part of this process, the courts and legislature gradually developed a discrete body of rules for specific application to joint stock companies, a body of rules which increasingly departed from the contract and agency based rules and principles of the law of partnership. 'The law relating to joint stock companies', as it was first called, having originally been subsumed within the law of partnership, had by the century's end emerged as a quite distinctive and autonomous legal category.[7] Crucially, this was in many ways precisely a product of the gradual *de*contractualisation of the law of partnership as it applied to joint stock companies.

During the first half of the nineteenth century, when joint stock companies were considered to be large, 'public' partnerships, both incorporated and unincorporated companies were identified with their members and conceptualised as aggregates of people, albeit in the case of incorporated concerns people merged for certain purposes into a single, separate legal entity. Correspondingly, shareholders were conceptualised as the owners in equity of the company's assets and as having

[5] See, for example, Charles FF Wordsworth, *The Law Relating to Railway, Banking, Insurance, Mining and other Joint Stock Companies* (London, Henry Butterworth, 1836; enlarged 2nd edn, 1837).

[6] It was not until the rise of the fully paid-up share and the resulting elimination of residual shareholder liabilities that joint stock company shares became completely unencumbered rights to revenue to which no responsibilities or obligations attached.

[7] This development was marked in 1888–89 when Nathaniel Lindley, author of the leading English treatise on the law of partnership, finally devoted a completely separate text to 'company law', having hitherto subsumed his coverage of 'joint stock company law' within his treatise on partnership. See Ireland, above n 4.

a share, directly or indirectly, in the company's contracts.[8] As a result, at this time there really were important senses in which companies resembled nexus-of-contracts in the manner described by contemporary corporate contractualists. Joint stock company shareholders stood in an essentially contractual relation *inter se*—as reflected in the bespoke nature of deeds of settlement and instruments of incorporation. They also had contractual connections to outside third parties, for even after general limited liability was introduced, residual shareholder liabilities and therefore contractual links between shareholders and those dealing with the company remained until the triumph of the fully paid-up share. However, the emergence of a developed share market and the gradual recognition of the overwhelmingly *rentier* nature of joint stock company shareholders saw not only the disconnection of the share from any direct link to the company's assets but the gradual abandonment of the notion of shareholders as 'partners', with its connotations of activity and function, and a range of legal changes that swept aside the old notions of both (joint stock) companies and shareholders. Some of these changes, such as the shift of power from shareholders and General Meetings to Boards of Directors, simply reflected the changing economic realities of passive shareholding and the share. Other changes, such as the introduction of standard statutory articles and limited liability, recognised the inability of most shareholders to protect themselves, contractually or otherwise, and sought actively to protect the share as a new intangible form of property.[9] Gradually, the share was reconstituted as a restricted but freely circulating bundle of rights—most importantly, of course, a right to revenue—largely external to and detached from the company as a productive entity. Together with the elimination of residual liabilities which freed shares of any remaining liabilities or responsibilities, these changes served to erode the contractual links not only between shareholders *inter se* but between shareholders and outside third parties. Indeed, with them companies ceased conceptually to be as closely identified with their shareholders, and the old partnership notions of the company were eroded, replaced by the reified conception of the company which

[8] See Paddy Ireland, 'Capitalism Without the Capitalist: The Joint Stock Company Share and the Emergence of the Modern Doctrine of Separate Corporate Personality', (1996) 17 *Journal of Legal History* 41; see also the comments of Best CJ in *Duvergier v Fellows* (1828) 5 Bing 248, discussed in Ireland, above n 4.

[9] See, for example, the comments of Lord Langdale in *Colman v Eastern Counties Railway* (1846) 10 Beav 1, discussed in Ireland above n 4.

precipitated the development of the modern doctrine of separate corporate personality, one of the cornerstones of company law. In short, then, what distinguished the newly emerging body of 'company law' from the law of partnership from which it grew was precisely that unlike the former it was not rooted in agency and contract. It was, rather, a body of law which, above all else, constituted and protected a peculiar new property form. 'A complete exposition of the law of stock and stockholders', wrote William Cook, author of one of the leading American corporate treatises, was 'a complete exposition of the law of corporations'.[10]

Against this historical backdrop, it is hardly surprising that many commentators are critical of the current academic vogue for treating the contemporary public, joint stock, corporation as nothing more than a nexus-of-contracts. Indeed, given their many non-contractual, non-market dimensions, one is bound to ask *how* contractualists manage to depict such corporations as fundamentally contractual and *why* they are so determined so to do. The answer to the first of these questions is largely to be found in historical erasure. Nexus-of-contracts theorists try, in effect, to turn the corporate-theoretical clock back to the early nineteenth century and to expunge many of the crucial qualitative changes which have taken place since that time in the nature of the joint stock company. They (try to) ignore the effects and significance of the gradual relegation of the shareholder to the status of a *rentier* external to the company, of the emergence of the share as an autonomous form of property, and of the legal constitution of the company as a property-owning person. They endeavour instead to treat the modern joint stock corporation as though it is still a type of partnership whose constitutive relations can comprehensively be analysed through the old partnership prisms of agency and contract. Central to these processes of what we might call corporate *re*contractualisation is a nostalgic recharacterisation of the corporate shareholder.

In reality, of course, the great majority of corporate shareholders have long been nothing more than buyers and sellers of titles to revenue, *rentier* traders in shares issued and fully paid-up long ago, radically detached from the companies in which they hold shares.[11] Indeed, as the great majority of share-owners now own shares through

[10] William W Cook, *A Treatise on Stock and Stockholders, Bonds and Mortgages* (Chicago, Callaghan and Co, 1894) vol 1, viii.

[11] See, for example, Adolf Berle, 'Modern Functions of the Corporate System' (1962) 62 *Columbia Law Review* 433.

intermediaries, they are usually unaware of the identities of the companies in which they have holdings, let alone knowledgeable of their business activities and practices. With the rise of portfolio investment and, more recently, of capital assets pricing models (CAPM), the impersonality of corporate investment has reached new heights and the already vast gulf between companies and shareholders widenened still further.[12] Rather than recognising this, however, and addressing the difficult conceptual, practical and ethical problems that the social character of corporate activity and the nature of modern corporate shareholding throws up for the allocation of corporate rights and for corporate governance, nexus-of-contracts theorists attempt instead to reinstate corporate shareholders to their earlier role as owners and providers of capital. This anachronistic and outmoded view is reflected in the kinds of questions that contractualists pose, suggesting as they do that shareholders actually give something to corporations rather than simply place bets on their future profitability. We thus find Jensen and Meckling asking, in a seemingly puzzled tone, 'how does it happen that millions of individuals are willing to *turn over* a significant fraction of their wealth *to organisations* run by managers who have so little interest in their welfare?'[13] And Kenneth Scott pondering in an equally bewildered manner why it is that shareholders—who '*furnish inputs into the business*'—are 'willing *turn* large sums of money *over to* other people (managers) on very ill-defined terms?'.[14] The simple answers, of course, at least so far as public, joint stock corporations are concerned, are that in the great majority of cases it doesn't ('happen that . . .'.) and they don't ('furnish inputs into . . .'). But the very posing of such questions serves subtly to reinvigorate corporate shareholders, discretely returning them to former glories. Treated not as redundant traders in titles to revenue, but re-elevated to their earlier,

[12] Whereas portfolio investment theory generally takes account of what companies produce, seeking to spread risk by stipulating investment in different productive sectors, CAPM takes little interest in what companies are producing, focusing instead on share price movements and on what is called the company's *beta*, a measure of the way that the company's stock price has moved in relation to the market as a whole. For a brief account, see Lawrence E Mitchell, *Corporate Irresponsibility* (New Haven, Yale University Press, 2001) 140–45.

[13] Michael Jensen and William Meckling, 'Theory of the Firm: Managerial Behaviour, Agency Costs and Ownership Structure', (1976) 3 *Journal of Financial Economics* 305, extracted in Louis Putterman and Randall S Kroszner (eds), *The Economic Nature of the Firm*, 2nd edn, (Cambridge, Cambridge University Press, 1996) 315.

[14] Kenneth Scott, 'Agency Costs and Corporate Governance' in Peter Newman (ed), *The New Palgrave Dictionary of Economics and the Law* (London, Macmillan, 1998) 26.

more exalted status as 'real' investors, they are undeservingly restored to an entrepreneurial function as risk-taking 'providers of capital'. The reality—that the contemporary stock market 'counts for little or nothing as a source of finance'—is studiously ignored.[15]

It is not, therefore, insignificant that these theorists commonly start their analyses with newly formed enterprises[16] or with small firms,[17] contexts in which, because of the closer relationship of shareholders both *inter se* and with the company, the contractual account more accurately captures key aspects of the relations which constitute these organisations. However, they then move on to apply these analyses with little or no modification to large, established joint stock corporations, where they don't.[18] Brian Cheffins, for example, recognises that 'the fact' that a firm is a nexus-of-contracts 'is more obvious with sole proprietorships', and admits that companies 'seem different from other firms' because of their existence as distinctive legal entities. This, he concedes, creates 'the impression . . . that the corporate entity is the appropriate focal point for analysis and not the underlying bargaining relationships', an impression which is 'accentuated when the role which companies legislation plays is taken into account . . . [for] it 'seems [companies] could not exist in their present form without legislation'. The 'inference which one might draw from this—that companies are a creation of statute rather than contract'—is, he admits, reinforced by the 'great privilege' of limited liability. He nevertheless insists that 'companies . . . resemble other types of firms in important ways', that 'companies legislation has had in and of itself only a modest impact on the bargaining dynamics which account for the nature

[15] See Doug Henwood, *Wall Street* (London, Verso, 1997) 292.

[16] See, for example, Easterbrook and Fischel, above, n 3, 5–7.

[17] See, for example, Armen Alchian and Harold Demsetz, 'Production, Information Costs, and Economic Organization' (1972) 62 *American Economic Review* 777; Oliver Hart, *Firms, Contracts and Financial Structure* (Oxford, Clarendon, 1995); Christopher A Riley, 'Contracting out of Company Law: Section 459 of the Companies Act 1985 and the Role of the Courts' (1992) 55 *Modern Law Review* 782.

[18] Oliver Hart, for example, by initially developing his so-called 'property rights' theory in the context of closely-held or owner-managed firms, feels able to assert that the owners of a company's assets are its shareholders, because it is they who exercise residual control rights over them. In economic reality, if not in law, this is a defensible assertion in relation to firms of this sort. However, although Hart recognises that it is to closely-held firms that his theory 'applies most directly', he proceeds to extend it, virtually unmodified, to large corporations, blithely arguing that 'even though there are important differences between the owner-managed and large company cases, the main insights of the property rights approach continue to be relevant'. See Hart, above n 17, 62.

and form of business enterprises', and that, analytically, an incorporated company is, like other types of firms, fundamentally a nexus of contracts'. 'From a practical perspective', he concludes, 'incorporation of a commercial enterprise often changes little', a point he illustrates by reference to a 'video rental business operated as a partnership by three equal partners' which later incorporates.[19] Cheffins is, of course, right that when a partnership of this sort incorporates to form a (quasi-partnership) company, little changes. But this rather misses the point. The key contrast is not that between a partnership and an *incorporated* company, but that between a partnership and a *joint stock* company. What is at issue is not the impact of the act of incorporation, of adoption of the *legal* form of an *incorporated company*, but the consequences of adoption of the *economic* form of the *joint stock company*. What changes matters—and changes them more than a little—is when a partnership becomes a joint stock company, for the underlying relations and nature of shareholding in a joint stock company are qualitatively quite different from those in a partnership, incorporated or not.[20] Indeed, as noted earlier, it was precisely the growing distinctiveness of the joint stock company as an organisational form which generated the emergence of a specific body of 'joint stock company law' and the eventual establishment of 'company law' as a separate legal category quite autonomous from the law of partnership.

One of the things that contractual theory tries to do, then, is to recharacterise—or 'misdescribe', as Adolf Berle rather more bluntly put it—corporate (joint stock company) shareholders, treating them as little different from shareholders in small, closely-held companies. In similar vein, it recharacterises or misdescribes corporations, treating them as little more than large partnerships with a few valuable legal privileges.[21] In this process, the crucial distinction between corporate assets and corporate shares is elided. The two distinctive and autonomous property forms which emerged with the development of the modern joint stock corporation—reflecting the reduction of shareholders to the status of *rentiers* external to production and the judicial and legislative desire to protect them—are conflated under the rubric

[19] Brian Cheffins, *Company Law: Theory, Structure and Operation* (Oxford, Clarendon Press, 1997) 31–41.

[20] Cheffins uses the term 'company' as an abridgement of 'incorporated company', focusing on a firm's legal status rather than on its economic nature.

[21] Contractualists would, of course, object to use of the word 'privilege', believing (erroneously) that corporate privileges are capable of being achieved in a purely private, contractual manner.

'capital', discretely re-uniting the shareholder with the corporate assets and eliminating the corporate entity as an owner of property other than in a purely formal sense. With corporate shareholders recharacterised as the 'providers of capital', and with assets and shares conflated, 'the corporation' is stripped of substance and more or less conceptualised out of existence, reduced to a mere cipher through which the owners of different factors of production are brought contractually together. The corporation, Jensen and Meckling inform us, is merely 'a legal fiction which serves as a nexus for contracting relationships', 'a legal fiction which serves as a focus for the complex process in which the conflicting objectives of individuals . . . are brought in equilibrium within a framework of contractual relationships'.[22] Eugene Fama concurs, arguing that the corporation (or 'firm') is:

> a set of contracts among factors of production . . . just the set of contracts covering the way inputs are joined to create outputs and the way receipts from outputs are shared among inputs.[23]

This conceptual elimination of the corporation not only once again places shareholders in direct touch with the corporate assets (the 'capital'), it also once again places them, in theory at least, in direct touch with corporate managers, for with no corporate entity of substance to come between them, the relationship between shareholders and managers is characterised as 'fit[ting] the definition of a pure agency relationship'.[24] Nexus-of-contracts theory thus takes us back in time to the early nineteenth century when, in the days before general limited liability, fully paid-up shares and developed share markets, the corporation was conceptualised as an essentially artifical, fictional entity—a large partnership composed of shareholders merged into one

[22] Jensen and Meckling, above n 13, 312. See also Daniel R Fischel, 'The Corporate Governance Movement' (1982) 35 *Vanderbilt Law Review* 1259, 1273, arguing that the corporation is 'a legal fiction that serves as a nexus for a mass of contracts which various individuals have voluntarily entered into for mutual benefit'.

[23] Eugene Fama, 'Agency Problems and the Theory of the Firm' (1980) 88 *Journal of Political Economy* 288. See also Frank H Easterbrook and Daniel R Fischel, 'Voting in Corporate Law' (1983) 26 *Journal of Law and Economics*, 395, 396. For Fama the terms 'firm' and 'corporation' are more or less interchangeable, reflecting his view, common among contractualists, that there is no essential difference between the small owner-managed firm and the large public corporation other than that the management and risk-bearing functions are separated.

[24] An agency relationship is 'a contract under which one or more persons (the principle(s)) engage another person (the agent) to perform some service on their behalf which involves delegating some decision making authority to the agent'. Jensen and Meckling, above n 13, 318–19.

body—and when shareholders were conceptualised as performing managerial or monitoring functions and directors conceptualised, partnership-style, as their agents. Unfortunately, while the company it portrays bears some resemblance to the joint stock companies of an earlier era, it bears little resemblance to their contemporary counterparts.

FIDUCIARY DUTIES AS IMPLICIT CONTRACTS

This becomes apparent when contractualists attempt to elaborate the contracts which they claim constitute the modern joint stock corporation. In this respect, even the corporation's relationships with third parties, many of which are clearly contractual in nature, are not entirely problem-free because the rights possessed by third parties are, of course, held against the corporation rather than against the shareholders, and necessarily so for *rentier* shareholders wanting the benefits of unencumbered, no-liability, no-responsibility, freely transferable shares. As a result, in this context at least, contractualists require the 'fictional' corporate entity that their theory tries so hard to dissolve to spring briefly to life. Thus, in their book *The Economic Structure of Corporate Law*, the leading contractual theorists, Frank Easterbrook and Daniel Fischel, begin by dismissing the 'personhood' of the corporation as 'a matter of convenience rather than reality', only to find themselves forced to resuscitate it a few pages later when defending limited liability—'perhaps *the* distinguishing feature . . . of corporate law'. 'Not so fast', they briskly instruct those who might misguidedly be thinking of suggesting that limited liability is 'the antithesis of contract' and 'a privilege bestowed on investors'.[25] Limited liability can 'be depicted as anticontractual only if it is inaccurately described', for '*corporations* (their emphasis) do not have limited liability; they must pay all of their debts, just as anyone else must'.[26] In other words, limited liability can be treated as anticontractual only if the 'personhood' of the corporation is not taken sufficiently seriously. If this looks sus-

[25] Easterbrook and Fischel, above n 3 40–41. Paradoxically, they make this comment shortly before elaborating in impressive and loving detail precisely the benefits that the privilege of limited liability bestows on investors.

[26] Elsewhere, Easterbrook and Fischel claim that the 'the liability of "the corporation" is limited by the fact that the corporation is not real', a view which might act as a temptation to over-literal, unscrupulous corporate debtors, see 'Limited Liability and the Corporation' (1985) 52 *University of Chicago Law Review* 89.

piciously like a case of having one's corporate cake on page 12 and eating it on page 40, it does at least convincingly demonstrate that for contractualists the reality of the 'personhood' of the corporation, or lack of it, is indeed a matter of convenience. It comes as no surprise, therefore, to find that when (on page 91) Easterbrook and Fischel turn their attention to other matters, the corporate entity—the legal person brought to life to 'pay all of its debts just as anyone else must'—is made to vanish into thin air once again. When considering the relationship between shareholders and directors, which they wish to characterise in pure agency terms and in which context the presence of the corporate entity is decidedly *in*convenient, they simply look through it, unblinkingly telling us that the 'corporate contract makes managers the agents of equity investors'.[27] Now you see it, now you don't.

The problems continue when Easterbrook and Fischel attempt to identify and elaborate the content of the alleged contract between directors and shareholders. Firstly, as many have pointed out, 'many of the most significant rights attached to shares are conferred by the Companies Acts . . . and cannot be abridged by agreement', something which gives them a less-than-contractual hew.[28] Secondly, even those rights within the share-bundle that are formally for shareholders to determine—most importantly, those contained in the company's articles—are, in the case of joint stock corporations, rarely the products of anything resembling contractual negotiation or agreement. Although described by the Companies Act as having the effect of a contract between the company and its members[29], the rights conferred by the articles are the products of what has been called a 'peculiar', '*statutory*' contract[30], 'a "contract" which', as Sealy observes, '. . . departs radically in a number of respects from the contract of classical tradition'[31],

[27] Easterbrook and Fischel, above n 3, 91.

[28] Robert Pennington, *Company Law*, 7th edn (London, Butterworths, 1995) 70–71.

[29] Companies Act 1985, s 14.

[30] See, for example, Sarah Worthington, 'Shares and Shareholders: Property, Power and Entitlement: Part I' (2001) 22 *Company Lawyer* 258, 264; and Pennington, above n 28, 70. Sealy observes that 'section 14 was enacted to cover a gap which was thought to have been created when the memorandum and articles replaced the deed of settlement in 1856, and in particular to ensure that a company could enforce a member's liability to pay calls'. He goes on to argue that 'its relevance in today's conditions may be regarded as questionable, for it perpetuates the notion that the only "constituents" of a company are its shareholders (ignoring the claims of employees, management and other "stakeholders" whose interests in the company are arguably quite as significant) . . .', LS Sealy, *Cases and Materials in Company Law*, 7th edn (London, Butterworths, 2001) 116.

[31] The inverted commas are Sealy's. See Sealy, above n 30, 116.

not least in that it is not always enforceable by those supposed to be parties to it. For those who might have thought 'that the law would provide that the members would be able to enforce the articles', writes Ben Pettet, 'UK case law has prepared a disappointment'.[32] Nor, in reality, are corporate articles capable of amendment by shareholders, notwithstanding their allegedly consensual, contractual status: even Easterbrook and Fischel concede that it is 'almost impossible' for investors in public companies to amend their rights, there being 'no practical way' for them to do so.[33] It is hardly surprising that John Parkinson concludes that 'a substantial proportion' of the rules of company law are, in fact, 'determined by law' and that 'contract . . . accounts for only a very limited proportion of the[m]'.[34]

Contractualists attempt to deal with some of these awkward realities by arguing that the seemingly non-contractual, statutory and common law rules in fact represent a set of ready-made, standardised contractual terms, whose function is to reduce transaction costs. Thus Easterbrook and Fischel would have us believe that corporate law simply provides 'a set of [contractual] terms available off-the-rack' which prevail 'unless varied by contract', enabling 'participants in corporate ventures' to save on the costs of contracting.[35] In this context, it is not insignificant that their starting point is not established corporations but imaginary, newly-created enterprises in which hypothetical founders muse about whether to organise as a corporation or something else, about what kinds of claims to issue, about to whom to allow voting rights, and about how to organise the firm. Easterbrook and Fischel admit that corporate law contains some mandatory rules, but insist that it is and should be essentially 'enabling', maximising choice and volition. Different American states are thus seen as 'offering different menus of devices (from voting by shareholders to fiduciary rules to derivative litigation) for the protection of investors'. And even though it is acknowledged that in reality passive investors do not con-

[32] Ben Pettet, *Company Law* (Harlow, Longmans, Pearson Education, 2001) 95. Under the rule in *Foss v Harbottle*, for example, some breaches of the statutory 'contract' cannot be litigated and the courts have on occasions used this principle to prevent members from insisting that the management of the company be conducted in accordance with the memorandum and articles, see *McDougall v Gardiner (No 2)* (1875) 1 Ch D 13 (CA).

[33] Easterbrook and Fischel, above n 3, 93.

[34] John Parkinson, *Corporate Power and Responsibility* (Oxford, Clarendon, 1993) 181.

[35] Easterbrook and Fischel, above n 3, 34.

sciously choose one corporate contract (menu) over another, it is argued that choices about governance structures are nevertheless effectively made by investors or their expert representatives through their buying and selling of shares in the stock market. The price of a company's share, Easterbrook and Fischel tell us, thus 'reflects the effects, good or bad, of corporate law and contracts . . . [it] reflects the value of the firm's governance and related rules. . .'.[36] Through thick and thin, whatever the odds, they cling on to the claim that corporate law is about shareholder choice, agreement and market selection. The less credulous might be tempted to call for a helicopter and rope-ladder.

Even after their contorted depiction of corporate articles, however, contractualists still face problems with the 'corporate contract' between shareholder and directors, for it turns out that it fails adequately to spell out the obligations of directors: it suffers from a radical lack of 'specification'.[37] According to contractualists, this is a result of the difficulties faced by shareholders trying to draft sufficiently detailed, prescient and binding agency contracts to control their potentially disloyal managerial agents.[38] Shareholders could, they argue, try to 'combin[e] ever more elaborate contractual strictures with full-time monitors to look over the shoulders of managers'[39], but this is 'an implausible solution' because of the difficulty in 'anticipating all problems [and] contracting about them'. To the open-minded agnostic this might suggest that the firm is a realm *beyond* contract and the market, as Ronald Coase intimated when he famously argued that it was a non-market mechanism for co-ordinating economic activity in which the price mechanism—and, by implication, the market and contract—had been supplanted by administrative planning.[40] But not to the fundamentalist imbued with the belief that markets and contract are capable of encompassing all economic activity (and that they should), and that it therefore 'makes little or no sense to try to distinguish those

[36] Easterbrook and Fischel, above n 3, 19.

[37] Easterbrook and Fischel, above n 3, 91.

[38] The presumption throughout is that shareholders have the capacity, power and wherewithal to do so.

[39] Or try to rely on so-called *ex post* democracy, meaning majority rule in the GM, see Riley, above n 17, 786–7.

[40] Ronald Coase, 'The Nature of the Firm' (1937) 4 *Economica* 386. Coase's ideas about the firm have, of course, been advanced and developed not so much by nexus-of-contracts theorists as by the new institutional economists led by Oliver Williamson, whose work draws on a wide range of material—from management studies, industrial sociology and organisational theory—in order to try to provide an empirically more accurate (and believable) description of the firm.

things which are "inside" the firm from those things that are "outside" of it'.[41] For contractualists, the fact that it is impossible to foresee and plan for future contingencies, and, correspondingly, practically impossible to write a contract which comprehensively specifies rights in the many varied situations which might arise[42] is merely evidence that the contracts constituting the corporation, and especially those involving shareholders, are an example, albeit an extreme one, of contractual 'incompleteness'.

It is here that the idea of implicit contract is thrust into the breach, for contractualists claim that the corporation is made up of *implicit* as well as explicit contracts[43] and that the solution to the problem of incompleteness is found in an implicit contract between shareholders and managers—an implicit contract contained in the fiduciary duties of directors. Fiduciary principles may, Easterbrook and Fischel concede, be 'uncommon in contractual relations', but, we are told, they 'sneak into' (sic) corporate contracts.[44] Like 'many of the rules in corporate and securities law, even the seemingly rigid ones', fiduciary duties, the argument runs, are 'best understood as implicit contractual terms', as 'obligations [on the part of directors] to act in shareholders' interests when explicit contracts are silent'.[45] In contractual theory, then, fiduciary duties become rules 'for completing incomplete bargains in a contractual structure'; rules which provide shareholders with 'an alternative to elaborate promises and extra monitoring' in which 'the duty of loyalty replaces detailed contractual terms'. The fiduciary relation is thus depicted as 'a contractual one characterised by unusually high costs of specification and monitoring', in such a way that contract and fiduciary duty come to 'lie on a contiuum best understood as using a single, although singularly complex, algorithm'.[46] It follows that fiduciary duties 'have no moral footing' but are binding only by contract: 'they are the same sort of obligations, derived and enforced in the same way, as other contractual undertakings'.[47]

[41] Jensen and Meckling, above n 13, 321.

[42] Even if plans could be made for every contingency, it would extremely difficult for the parties to capture these plans in a comprehensive written manner amenable to later adjudication, see Hart, above n 17, 23.

[43] Easterbrook and Fischel, above n 3, 12.

[44] *Ibid*, 90.

[45] Frank H Easterbrook and Daniel R Fischel, 'Contract and Fiduciary Duty' (1993) 36 *Journal of Law and Economics* 425 at 429; Easterbrook and Fischel, above n 3, 110.

[46] Easterbrook and Fischel, above n 45, 427, 446.

[47] *Ibid*, 427.

Indeed, with the bit now firmly between their teeth, Easterbrook and Fischel not only assert the private, contractual nature of fiduciary duties but claim that 'socially optimal fiduciary rules approximate the bargain that investors and managers would have reached if they could have bargained (and enforced their agreements) at no cost', and that the courts should, therefore, 'routinely conduct wide-ranging enquiries to determine the bargain that managers and investors would have reached if transaction costs were zero'.[48] Quite apart from the retrospective telepathy that such 'hypothetical bargaining models'[49] would seem to demand, their suppositional nature suggests that they differ somewhat from the implicit contractual dimensions arising out of real relations and understandings that contract lawyers have sought to identify. Easterbrook and Fischel's 'socially optimal fiduciary rules' also, of course, require that any ideas about the separate existence or social nature of the corporation be firmly suppressed, for fear that directors might not give exclusive priority to the financial interests of *rentier* shareholders, something which, we are meant to believe, would be to the detriment of society as a whole.

PROPER AND IMPROPER USES OF IMPLICIT CONTRACT

Although the invocation of the idea of the implicit contract enables them to dress up corporate shareholder rights in contractual clothing, however, contractualists are acutely aware that they have unleashed a potentially unruly horse, capable of being used not only by shareholders but by other corporate participants in support of their claims in and over corporations. While, therefore, to sustain their analysis contractualists are bound to uphold the view that the 'specification of [corporate] rights is generally effected through contracting, *implicit as well as explicit*'[50], they are also very anxious to impress upon their readers that the rights of 'any employee or investor other than the residual claimant'—meaning, of course, the rights of everyone but the shareholders—are *all* to be found in 'explicit negotiated contracts'. Thus the rights of 'suppliers, laborers, and debt investors', they claim, can all 'be specified' and 'written in enough detail' in advance. These groups must, therefore, 'look to their contractual rights rather than invoke

48 Easterbrook and Fischel, above n 3, 90–94.

49 For a discussion of such models, see Cheffins, above n 19, 264–307.

50 Jensen and Meckling, above n 13, 318.

fiduciary claims'.[51] No supplementary rights derived from implicit contracts for them.

The problem, as a number of writers have pointed out, is that it can forcefully be argued that it is no more possible to write in advance 'complete contracts' which protect the interests of employees and other corporate participants, particularly those who have made so-called 'firm specific investments', than it is to write them in advance for shareholders.[52] And that the provision of rights derived from implicit contracts for these stakeholders would also, therefore, serve merely to complete or perfect the terms of incomplete contracts, giving them the rights 'due to [them] . . . because the firm imposes upon them costs or risks which cannot be effectively contracted for'.[53] From this perspective, one of the roles of corporate managers might be to 'mediate, ex post, between the different implicit contractual claims of the various groups whose input is needed to make the corporate enterprise possible.' Indeed, it has been argued that should corporate managers prioritise the financial interests of shareholders, leaving the 'implicit contract interests' of non-shareholder stakeholders unprotected, the latter will be deterred from making 'firm-specific investments ex ante' to the detriment of the companies concerned.[54] More importantly, perhaps, there are good reasons for believing that unlike the relationships involving *rentier* corporate shareholders—which evince scant signs of Ian Macneil's long-term processes of commitment and co-operation around which relational understandings evolve—the relationships of many corporations with their employees and suppliers not only often involve genuine contractual negotiation and agreement, but are commonly embedded in genuine, long-term relationships of trust with the 'relational' characteristics thought capable of generating implicit obligations.[55] Because one is often dealing in these contexts with active

[51] Easterbrook and Fischel, above n 3, 37, 90–91. As we have seen, in another context Easterbrook and Fischel claim that the fiduciary claims of shareholders constitute *contractual* rights.

[52] See Gavin Kelly and John Parkinson, 'The Conceptual Foundations of the Company: A Pluralist Approach', in John Parkinson, Andrew Gamble and Gavin Kelly (eds), *The Political Economy of the Company* (Oxford, Hart, 2000) 125–32. See also the work of Katherine Stone, for example, 'The New Psychological Contract' (2000) 48 *UCLA Law Review* 560.

[53] See Simon Deakin, Richard Hobbs and Giles Slinger, ch 10 in this book.

[54] *Ibid.*

[55] See, for example, Ian Macneil, 'The Many Futures of Contract' (1974) 47 *University of Southern California Law Review* 691. There are parallels here with Oliver Williamson's intermediate modes between arms-length exchange and internal organisation.

relationships involving real interactions and negotiations, the idea of the implict contract has more analytical purchase here than it does in those involving *rentier* corporate shareholders. It seems that contractualists might be invoking the idea of implicit contract in the wrong corporate contexts.

It is, indeed, precisely because long-term, personal relationships of trust involving real (if informal) agreements and understandings entailing contractual and other obligations lie at the heart of many small or quasi-partnership companies—companies not organised on a joint stock basis—that such companies provide a context in which ideas of implicit contract are descriptively and analytically valuable.[56] 'In such cases', writes Parkinson, 'as well as having the legal status of a contract, the articles' *content* (his emphasis) can also be meaningfully described as having been determined by a contractual process'.[57] Robert Goddard reiterates this, arguing that 'contractual incompleteness is of greater significance to the minority shareholder in a close or quasi-partnership type of company' because even though such a company's articles are more likely to have been modified, they might still fail to capture important aspects of the actual agreements and understandings of the parties. As he observes, shareholder expectations in such companies 'are likely to be more complex and intricate', in part because shareholders are likely to have a management role and in part because 'intra-corporate relations are likely to be personal in nature . . . and will often be founded upon mutual confidence and trust'.[58] Indeed, using section 459 of the Companies Act 1985 and the idea of 'unfair prejudice', the courts have given effect to the oral agreements and implicit understandings of the shareholders in many small, quasi-partnership companies, de facto introducing in various ways notions of informal and implicit contract into their analyses and decision-making.[59]

Put slightly differently, the shares in smaller, closely-held companies are more *personam* than *rem* in character. They are not usually freely transferable and 'have or significantly involve personality, such as people, their actions, and their ongoing, dynamic relations with other

[56] See, for example, Sealy's discussion of the idea of relational contract in this context, above n 30, 116.

[57] Parkinson, above n 34, 183.

[58] In other words, the shareholder's rights are more *in personam* than *in rem*. See Robert Goddard, 'Enforcing the Hypothetical Bargain: Sections 459–461 of the Companies Act 1985' (1999) 20 *Company Lawyer* 66, 69–70.

[59] See CA Riley, ch 12 of this book.

people', unlike the shares in large public (joint stock) corporations, which are freely transferable 'things' lacking personality.[60] In other words, shareholding in small, closely-held companies is, to use James Penner's phrase, 'personality-rich' while shareholding in large corporations is 'personality-poor'; shares in small, closely-held companies have the (personality-rich) *personam* character of contractual rights rather than the personality-poor, propertied character of corporate shares. It is for this reason that when one explores the mechanisms whereby the rights of corporate shareholders are protected one quickly sees that they do not take a predominantly private, contractual form. On the contrary, in addition to the protections incorporated into company law itself, in the last century or so the desire to protect corporate shareholders has seen the growth of a new legal discipline—variously called securities regulation or capital markets law—whose 'central fact', as Ben Pettet recently observed, 'is the pervasive presence of the state, in the form of the regulator who seeks to achieve the requisite degree of investor protection', often through minute regulatory detail. The non-contractual, regulatory, public nature of this area of law is only too apparent.[61]

CONTRACTUALISM AND THE DEFENCE OF THE *RENTIER*

Given all this, it is hardly surprising that nexus-of-contracts theory has come under attack, seeking as it does to build a comprehensive contractual edifice on the rather threadbare contractual remnants still to be found within contemporary joint stock corporations and company law. Paradoxically, this is to some extent recognised—implicitly, of course—by some of those sympathetic to agency theory. Chris Riley, for example, concedes that 'ordinary contractual analysis . . . applies uneasily [to corporations]' because of the 'specific and peculiar' nature

[60] JE Penner, 'The Bundle of Rights Picture of Property' (1996) 43 *UCLA Law Review* 711, 801. The personality-rich (contractual) nature of the shares (and therefore of shareholder rights) in many small companies is further enhanced by shareholder agreements and the frequent insistence on personal guarantees for company debts.

[61] Traditionally, securities regulation has not been treated as part of company law on the grounds that it examines what happens in markets rather than in companies. However, as Ben Pettet points out, as corporate shareholders are 'in' the market rather than 'in' the company (in any meaningful sense), this exclusion is inappropriate. See Pettet, above n 32, 6–9, 333 *et seq*.

of the inter-shareholder relationship. The corporate contract, he argues, 'is characterised by a process of active judicial construction rather than mere passive judicial discovery, a constructive process in which contractual freedom becomes, of necessity, limited'.[62] His summary of the 'corporate contract' is correspondingly revealing. '[W]hilst the relationship between shareholders might be described as contractual', he writes, 'that label needs adapting to the peculiarities of the corporate context in a number of ways'. Thus, 'much of the contract will be informal and confused, and . . . constructed in an unusually active way by the courts', entailing 'an unusually high degree of legislative and judicial intervention [which] inevitably limits the contractual sovereignty enjoyed by shareholders . . . Beyond mere gap filling, the informational problems inherent in the long-term corporate relationship demand and justify mandatory terms and the judicial control of the parties' express bargain'.[63] One might be forgiven for thinking that this amounts to more than a few encroachments on and supplements to the corporate 'contract'.[64] And for wondering why he persists in insisting that agency theory 'provides the most appropriate theoretical framework for characterising the inter-shareholder relationship'[65], for he seems to be confirming David Campbell's assertion that the roots of the 'empirical implausibility' of contractual theory's description of the corporation are to be found in the simple fact that it 'carries [contract] beyond its proper bounds'.[66] In the context of the joint stock corporation, contractualists use the idea of implicit contract not so much to add supplementary detail and nuance to express agreements, but to try to dress up as (exclusively) 'contractual' relationships which are seriously lacking in both contractual form and content. They use it, in other words, to try to contractualise something which is, fundamentally, other than contractual. The reason why fiduciary duties are transformed by contractualists into implicit contracts is less to respond to a problem of contractual incompleteness but to address a problem of contractual near-absence.

[62] Riley, above, n 17, 785.

[63] *Ibid*, 790.

[64] On the role of the exclusion of such 'supplements' and exceptions on the constitution of the idea of 'contract' and the 'law of contract', see Alan Thomson, 'The Law of Contract', in Ian Grigg-Spall and Paddy Ireland (eds), *The Critical Lawyers Handbook* (London, Pluto, 1992) 69.

[65] Riley, above, n 17, 785.

[66] David Campbell, 'The Role of Monitoring and Morality in Company Law' (1997) 7 *Australian Journal of Corporate Law* 343, 345, 357.

In this context, it is not difficult to see why so many have suggested that contractual theories of the corporation actually comprise nexus of metaphors rather than nexus of contracts. As Campbell observes, for example, the binding quality of fiduciary duties can hardly lie in real contractual negotiation for, at least in large corporations, there are no such negotiations.[67] This point has been amplified by the social and political theorist Alan Wolfe. 'Large corporations', he explains, 'are composed of people who speak many different languages, have never met each other, work in positions defined by different degrees of power and responsibility, and have wildly different motives, loyalties, and talents. Can contracts exist between people who never meet, have nothing in common, and are unavailable to pass judgment on the behaviour of the other parties to the contract?'. It might be possible, Wolfe concedes, to see these relationships as contractual 'in a metaphorical sense, in roughly the same way that early social contract theorists understood the body politic to operate', though even as a metaphor, he suggests, this conception is problematic. More to the point, 'no one ever claimed that the social contract was an *empirical* description of actual real world events'.[68] As a matter of theoretical necessity real contracts have to be placed on the same ontological plane as 'unreal' contracts, 'contracts that, in empirical reality, simply do not exist'. As a result, despite its claims to tough, hard-nosed realism, contractual theory is actually strikingly *un*realistic and empirically *in*accurate. Carried as it is 'by metaphor and assertion based on that metaphor', it is 'not an empirically based theory at all' and is not therefore open to rational debate.[69]

Given this lack of empirical restraint, it is hardly surprising that there are many different accounts within agency theory of the 'contracts' that constitute the corporation. In one crucial respect, however, the theories are indistinguishable: they all conclude that the retention by shareholders of their residual income and control rights is legitimate and justifiable. The very predictability of this normative outcome lets the ideological cat out of the bag. No matter how carefully neutralised their tones or algorithmic their theoretical garb, contractualists are at root apologists. Indeed, paradoxically, although contractual theories

[67] Campbell, above n 66.

[68] Alan Wolfe, 'The Modern Corporation: Private Agent or Public Actor?' (1993) 50 *Washington and Lee Law Review* 1673, 1680.

[69] Campbell, above n 66, 360.

of the corporation rest in many ways on a denial of the historical changes which have taken place in the nature of shareholding and shareholder rights, it is, in fact, precisely to the impact of these changes on the perceived legitimacy of shareholder rights to which they are a response.[70] No longer managers or monitors of managers, no longer major sources of new capital, the great majority of corporate shareholders ceased long ago to perform any discernable function. Relegated by the early twentieth century to the status of *rentiers*, the legitimacy of their rights began in some quarters to be questioned. With the rise of the company as a separate, property-owning person and the transformation of the share into an autonomous property form external to the company, it could no longer be claimed that shareholders were the owners of the corporate assets, and although the alternative view emerged that shareholders were 'owners' of the company itself, on close analysis this view also proved hard to sustain, lacking legal grounding.[71] The empirical work of Berle and Means (and others) further suggested that shareholders had lost control of the companies in which they held shares. Although this was not something which seemed greatly to concern them, corporate shareholders increasingly found themselves being described as 'absentee owners', owners of claims to 'unearned or free income', and likened to corporate bondholders. With this, their 'ownership' status inevitably came under question, as did their exclusive claim to the corporate surplus. There was also a growing perception of productive activity as an increasingly social affair and of corporations as public institutions rather than private associations, and this led many to query the traditional belief that corporations should be run solely in the interests of shareholders. In his famous debate with Adolf Berle, Merrick Dodd advanced a radical version of entity theory in support of this proposition, contesting the close identification of corporations with their shareholders and offering a view of the corporation as an essentially social institution with wider social obligations. Indeed, although Berle and Means couched their arguments in terms of a 'separation of ownership and control', their frequent and pointed insertion of inverted commas around the word

[70] For an elaboration of the arguments in this section, see Paddy Ireland, 'Defending the Rentier: Corporate Theory and the Reprivatisation of the Public Company', in Parkinson *et al* (eds), above n 52, 141.

[71] See, for example, E Merrick Dodd, 'The Modern Corporation, Private Property and Recent Federal Legislation' (1941) 54 *Harvard Law Review* 917.

'owner' when describing the relationship of shareholder to corporation suggested that they suspected the problem might be even more fundamental. Eventually they too began to question whether the 'traditional logic of property' applied to corporate shares, wondering aloud whether it was not appropriate for various groups to be assigned a portion of the corporate income stream 'on the basis of public policy rather than private cupidity'.[72] Although these arguments waned somewhat during the war years, they re-emerged in the 1950s, particularly in the debates about industrial democracy and worker participation. 'With the equity holder joining the bond holder as a functionless *rentier*' and having only 'the vaguest idea where "his property" is or of what it entails', wrote Edward Mason in 1959, the 'traditional justifications' of private property had 'gone forever'.[73] In a different context, Coase's observation that intrafirm organisation was a quite distinctive, non-market form of economic co-ordination, with its suggestion that planning was already endemic in the capitalist economy, clearly had the potential to add fuel to this particular political fire, which is probably why it was largely overlooked by economists until the 1960s.[74]

THE RISE OF CORPORATE DARWINISM

Contractual theories first emerged as a response to these shareholder-threatening views and are best seen not as honest endeavours to grasp empirical reality but as attempts to provide a defence of the rights of *rentier* shareholders and, more recently, to resist growing calls for corporate 'regulation'. As such, their immediate intellectual origins are to be found in the 1950's and the work of Henry Manne, one of the founding fathers of law-and-economics. During this period, Manne, fearing that the rise of managerialism and of the corporate social responsibility movement posed a threat not only to shareholder primacy but to the capitalist market economy as a whole, began to construct a novel defence of shareholder rights which was markedly less dependent on

[72] Adolf Berle and Gardiner Means, *The Modern Corporation and Private Property* (New York, Macmillan, 1932; revised edn, New York, Harcourt Brace, 1967).

[73] Edward Mason, 'Introduction', in Edward Mason (ed), *The Corporation in Modern Society* (Harvard University Press, 1959; reprinted, New York, Athenaeum, 1966) 1, 2–6, 14–15.

[74] See Louis Putterman and Randall S Kroszner, 'The Economic Nature of the Firm: a New Introduction', in Putterman and Kroszner (eds), above n 13, 1, 16–17.

the moral claims associated with traditional notions of ownership. In short, Manne sought to transform the detached and *rentier* nature of modern corporate shareholding from a vice which undermined the moral basis of shareholder rights into a virtue which provided the basis for new instrumental legitimations of them. The *rentier* nature, lack of loyalty and financial orientation of corporate shareholders, Manne famously argued, had created a market for corporate control, a market which operated in such a way as to compel corporate executives to pursue shareholder-oriented policies of profit maximisation, guaranteeing productive 'efficiency' for the benefit of all.

It is far from clear even now, 30 years after Manne first posited its existence, whether the market for corporate control operates to weed out inefficiency in anything like the way claimed. On the contrary, there is much empirical evidence suggesting the contrary. The empirical validity (or otherwise) of the theories, however, is less important than their ideological value. Thus, despite the many legitimate doubts about the way in which the stock market actually operates, the claims made for the contribution of the market for corporate control to economic efficiency have become 'among the least restrained to be found in agency theory'.[75] Whatever the reality, the alleged existence and efficacy of this market and of a close correlation between corporate managerial efficiency and the market price of the corporation's shares have become one of the theory's bedrocks. As Campbell explains, the significance of Manne's 'discovery' of the market for corporate control thus lay above all else in its suggestion that corporate managers were subject to market disciplines and that it was, therefore, possible to construct a market-based theory of the firm to rival the non-market based theories spawned by managerialism. The idea of the properly functioning market for corporate control became 'the fundamental concept of agency theory' precisely because, theoretically at least, it placed the managerially controlled company 'back under the market'.[76] Accordingly, from the late 1960s, beginning with Alchian and Demsetz, followed a little later by Jensen and Meckling, there started to emerge a growing body of literature which explored and expanded upon Manne's basic themes. As we have seen, this work, of which nexus-of-contracts theory is a manifestation, purports to show not only that corporations are subject to market disciplines but that they are themselves, in essence, market institutions. Indeed, in the most

[75] Campbell, above n 66, 362.
[76] *Ibid*, 359.

extreme, market-fundamentalist versions it is suggested that firms lack any hierarchical elements or in-built structures of authority. Thus Alchian and Demsetz argue that while it is 'common to see the firm as characterised by the power to settle issues by fiat, by authority, or by disciplinary action superior to that available in the conventional market', this is in fact a 'delusion'. The firm is merely 'a highly specialized surrogate market', with 'no power of fiat, no authority, no disciplinary action any different in the slightest degree from ordinary market contracting'. To speak of the management or direction of workers is merely 'a deceptive way of noting that the employer continually is involved in renegotiation of contracts on terms that must be acceptable to both parties'.[77] This is a view echoed by Easterbrook and Fischel when they argue that 'the contractual approach does not draw a sharp line between employees and contributors of capital'.[78] As William Lazonick wryly observes, the firm thus depicted, with its denial of disciplinary power, appears not to be a *capitalist* firm at all.[79]

Irrespective of its empirical accuracy, however, the 'marketisation' of the corporation is theoretically crucial because, as John Parkinson has pointed out, once it is 'established' (or presumed) that a particular set of corporate arrangements are the product of consensual (free market) contracting, it follows that they are, by definition, not only just but 'efficient'. It has, therefore, enabled contractualists to offer a defence of shareholder corporate rights which is ostensibly less reliant on the moral claims associated with troublesome ideas of shareholder corporate 'ownership'—though ownership issues are, as they have discovered, difficult to avoid[80]—and which focuses more on the alleged

[77] Alchian and Demsetz, above n 17. In this respect, the work of Williamson is markedly different, as from his perspective, hierarchy and authority within the firm remain very important.

[78] Easterbrook and Fischel, above n 3, 37. In Easterbrook and Fischel's work, all participants are seen, formally at least, as equal. The question is 'not whether employees and other "constituencies" of the firm have entitlements or expectations—they do—but what those entitlements are'. And this is a matter for contractual negotiation. The big difference lies in the specification of the contractual rights of the different participants: it is, the argument runs, easier to specify the contractual rights of these 'other groups' in advance and to specify them with greater precision: enforcing the contracts of 'any employee or investor other than the residual claimant' thus usually involves enforcing 'the explicit negotiated contract'.

[79] William Lazonick, *Business Organisation and the Myth of the Market Economy* (Cambridge, Cambridge University Press, 1991) 181–88.

[80] Having a habit of re-entering through the theoretical back door. See Ireland, above n 70, especially 152–68.

contribution of these rights to productive efficiency. From this perspective, the recent attempt to depict (joint stock) corporations as nexus of contracts—the retro attempt to *re*contractualise them—emerges as part of a more general, ideological project aimed at *reprivatising* them in order to justify the private appropriation of corporate surpluses which are the products of an increasingly *social* production process. The essential claim being made by contractualists is that, however things might appear, corporations are *not* public institutions and *not* publicly constituted entities, but are, rather, the products of voluntary, private, contractual exchanges. It is for this reason that contractualists are so insistent that the benefits (for investors) of incorporation, including limited liability, could have been achieved entirely 'privately' through contract without any assistance or interventions from the state, claims which, quite apart from their historical inaccuracy and practical implausibility,[81] overlook the constitutive 'public' dimension to all 'private' rights, powers, privileges and immunities. The contractualists make a further claim, however: that public 'regulation' of these contractual, market-created, market-regulated arrangements would damagingly interfere with the natural process of market selection. There is, therefore, more than a whiff of Herbert Spencer's pro-laissez-faire Social Darwinism in contractualism, for Spencer's rules of nature were, of course, essentially those of the market. In his view, the market would ensure that only the fittest survived, breeding out of existence unfit and inefficient institutional forms. Likewise for corporate contractualists: as long as the state doesn't spoil things by seeking to 'regulate', the market-contractual nature of corporations will ensure that the processes of natural selection operate so as to purify the corporate species. Indeed, these processes are regarded by many contractualists as generating global convergence on a superior, shareholder-oriented, Anglo-American model of company law and corporate governance, justifying the pressure that they are exerting for its adoption worldwide, something which happens to have the happy consequence of opening up new markets for the institutional representatives of western *rentier* investors seeking the best possible returns.[82]

[81] 'It is clear that without the legislative intervention, limited liability could not have been attained in a satisfactory and clear-cut fashion . . .', see LCB Gower, *Principles of Modern Company Law* 6th ed by Paul L Davies (London, Sweet & Maxwell, 1997) 46.

[82] See Richard Minns, *The Cold War in Welfare* (London, Verso, 2001).

IMPLICIT CONTRACT AS IDEOLOGY

The utilisation by corporate scholars of the idea of implicit contract thus demonstrates not only its analytical value in certain contexts but also its ability, when misapplied, to hinder understanding in others. In the context of many small, closely-held companies, where shareholding has a genuinely contractual, *personam* character grounded in specific relations, it has considerable analytical worth, helping to capture aspects of those relations suppressed and distorted by the generalities of company law and standard-form articles of association. In the context of joint stock corporations, however, with their 'personality-poor' shareholding and shares more *rem* than *personam* in character, use of the metaphor of implicit contract obfuscates rather than clarifies. Here it has been invoked not as an analytical aid but as a tool of ideology.

Contractualists seeks to portray corporate shareholders as the possessors of uncontroversial, pre-political property rights over a factor of production, 'capital' (defined variously as money or the tangible assets of 'the firm'), who, using these pre-existing rights, are able to negotiate (with a little legislative help) further contractual rights with fellow shareholders, directors and (in the fictional guise of the corporation) outside third parties such as employees.[83] The image conjured up is thus one in which property creates discrete, vertical relationships between individuals and the things they own, while contract creates voluntary, horizontal relationships between individual property-owners. Both sets of relationships are said to be 'private' in the sense that neither involve domination or coercion, the state acting only to enforce and protect pre-political property rights and any contractual rights individuals have bargained for. Depicted as nothing more than nexus of such contracts, corporations are themselves deemed 'private' affairs, the non-coercive products of agreements voluntarily and consensually entered into by a range of private property owners.[84] Company (corporate) law simply provides a set of contractual terms available 'off-the-rack', 'supplement[ing] but never displac[ing] actual bargains' struck by holders of pre-existing property rights.[85] In this

[83] With (modest) assistance from courts and legislatures, either directly or indirectly through the provision of standard, off-the-peg, contractual terms which can be adopted and/or adapted.

[84] By implication, the distribution of wealth resulting from market arrangements is not only justifiable but in some sense 'natural'.

[85] Easterbrook and Fischel, above n 3, 34.

way, contractual theory offers two related legitimations of the shareholder-centred, Anglo-American corporate status quo. The first is based upon a separation of processes and outcomes, of law and politics, and seeks to avoid political scrutiny of consequences. Corporations, it is claimed, are contractual expressions of exercises by individual property owners of their freedom, and any state intervention in or regulation of internal corporate affairs would constitute an unwarranted intrusion into individual liberty, a politically non-neutral interference into the natural operations of a market. The second is more overtly consequentialist: as the products of freedom of contract and market selection, prevailing corporate governance arrangements, are, it is argued, a priori 'efficient'. The claims are, of course, linked in that what allegedly makes the arrangements arising out of market exchange 'efficient' is precisely that they are supposedly the expressions of individual choice and volition: contractualists tell us that even if we don't want to protect the property rights of shareholders and a private sphere of liberty and autonomy (the market, freedom of contract) from state incursions for their their own sakes, we should do so for reasons of efficiency and competitiveness.

But history brings the inaccuracies of this account into sharp relief, showing that in certain important respects company law emerged from a retreat from contract; from a complex and fundamentally political and *public* process whereby an unusual, new, intangible *rentier* property form, the joint stock company share—a responsibility-free, liability-free, transferable right to an indeterminate income derived from the corporate surplus—was constituted and protected. Indeed, as we have seen, it was in many ways precisely the gradual transformation of the share from *personam* to *rem* that underlay the divergence of (joint stock) company law from the partnership principles of agency and contract, and its emergence as an autonomous and separate category of law. As a result, corporations and company law, at least as it applies to those corporations, are both best understood not through the prism of contract but through the prism of property. And, indeed, through the prism of a property form whose establishment and development was highly controversial precisely because of its violation of the traditional contractual principles of individual responsibility, as evidenced by the nineteenth-century debates about the transferability of shares and limited liability. These controversies persisted into the twentieth century as perceptions of the increasingly social character of corporations and the redundancy of 'absentee', *rentier* shareholders led commentators as diverse as Thorstein Veblen, E Merrick Dodd, Adolf Berle, and, later, LCB Gower, George Goyder and Lord Wedderburn to question the scope of shareholder rights and the legitimacy of the exclusively-shareholder-oriented corporation.[86] The most recent manifestation of such views has, of course, come in the form of arguments for a less shareholder-oriented, 'stakeholding' conception of the corporation. At root, corporate contractualism is a response to these controversies, an attempt to (re)contractualise and (re)privatise company law and the corporation in order to evade the difficult questions surrounding the disposition of corporate rights. It seeks to shield existing shareholder rights from public scrutiny and to delegitimate the claims of other corporate participants and of society at large to rights in and over corporate activities. Hence Easterbrook and Fischel's claim that the essentially market-contractual nature of corporations 'removes from the field' some of the 'interesting questions' which have hitherto occupied many corporate legal scholars, such as 'what is the goal of the corporation? Is it profit, and for whom? Social welfare more broadly defined?' Such questions, they tell us, can be dismissed with a simple 'who cares?'[87]

One of the clearest examples of this attempted privatisation of the corporation is provided by the contractualist recasting of directors' fiduciary duties as implicit agency contracts with shareholders, for traditionally fiduciary obligations have been seen as possessing important public dimensions. Fiduciary duty, observes Lord Wedderburn, 'is imposed in private law' but is done 'with a *public* function. It is a vehicle of social purpose'.[88] Historically, fiduciary duties have been imposed to control self-serving and unconscionable behaviour, even within what many see as fundamentally private relationships, creating obligations over and above any expressly bargained for by the parties themselves. This has long been seen as perfectly legitimate, particularly where 'the relevant relationships, while private in intent, are seen as

[86] See Ireland, above n 70; and also Paddy Ireland, 'Company Law and The Myth of Shareholder Ownership' (1999) 62 *Modern Law Review* 32.

[87] Easterbrook and Fischel, above n 3, 35–6. See also Jensen and Meckling, who, having likened the firm to a market, argue that questions such as 'does the firm have a social responsibility?' are 'seriously misleading'. From this perspective, corporate governance revolves not around complex questions of productive organisation, social welfare and social justice, but simply around the difficulties facing shareholder-principals trying to negotiate sufficiently binding contracts with agent-managers, above n 13, 311.

[88] Lord Wedderburn, 'The Social Responsibility of Companies' (1985) 15 *Melbourne University Law Review* 4, 24. Emphasis in original.

existing for public purposes and sustained on that basis'.[89] Thus the application of strict fiduciary principles to corporate managers has been described as 'a necessary supplement, in the public interest, of statutory regulation and accountability', and as an 'acknowledgement of the importance of the corporation in the life of the community and of the need to compel obedience by it and its promoters, directors and managers to norms of exemplary behaviour'.[90]

In some situations the maintenance of standards of proper conduct is seen as a value in its own right, and the public imposition of fiduciary obligations as one mechanism of enforcing them. This is reflected in the fact that in English law there are important restrictions on the freedom of shareholders to modify the fiduciary duties of directors, something which clearly runs counter to the interpretation of them as contractual. The recharacterisation of fiduciary duties as implicit contracts represents an attempt to suppress their moral, social and public dimensions.

It also requires the deployment of a capacious, bordering on all-embracing, notion of 'contract'. It is not insignificant that Brian Cheffins, for example, tells us that he uses 'some terms', among them contract, in a 'special or distinct fashion' which bears little relation to their commonly understood legal meaning. He defines contract 'broadly' to encompass 'any economic arrangement entered into voluntarily which involves mutual expectations and understandings.'[91] From this perspective, for which the term 'broad' is perhaps rather too narrow, more or less all voluntary interactions and exchanges with a material dimension are defined not only as specifically 'economic' but as 'contractual'. Notwithstanding the reference to 'mutual expectations and understandings', therefore, the actual subjective meanings which the parties ascribe to their interactions and exchanges—meanings which, as Max Weber observed, constitute 'the essence of what happens' and which will regulate the course of the parties' future conduct—are irrelevant to contractualists, for they substitute the 'meanings of their own economic actors for the real ones of persons in complex social relationships'.[92] In short, they assume that all such 'voluntary' interactions are, by definition, 'economic' and 'contractual'

[89] Parkinson, above n 34 201–2.

[90] The words of Bora Laskin J in *Canadian Aero Service Ltd v O'Malley* (1974) 40 DLTR (3rd) 371, 384.

[91] Cheffins, above n 19, xlviii.

[92] Campbell, above n 66, 356.

in nature, effectively rendering contract and market exchange (not to mention rational economic men from Chicago) historically, culturally and institutionally ubiquitous, potentially encompassing everything from the material practices of the Trobriand islanders to domestic divisions of labour. The contractualists notion of 'contract' thus betrays the tell-tale imprint of the conceptual and linguistic limitations of law-and-economics, vividly illustrating what Karl Polanyi called a 'market mentality', in which all activity is translated, forcibly if necessary, into 'economic', market-contractual terms and all obligation grounded in individual consent and agreement.[93]

CONTRACT AND THE MORALS OF THE MARKETPLACE

The use made by contractualists of the idea of implicit contract thus highlights not only the ideological uses to which it can be put but also some of its conceptual shortcomings. For many scholars, the attraction of ideas such as implicit contract and relational contract lies in their ability to heighten awareness of dimensions of obligation not always apparent in express agreements, foregrounding the tacit incorporation of expectations, understandings and unspoken assumptions into contracts which were not explicitly agreed and which may, indeed, even precede exchange relationships. The obligations arising out of these informal, latent, implicit agreements and understandings, it is argued, supplement and sometimes modify those contained in express agreements. Crucially, many of these expectations and understandings not only involve notions of trust, good faith and relationality but are context-specific, arising out of particular customs, practices and market conventions. As such, they can only be identified by reference to the particular contexts in which they arise and the specific 'contracting communities' involved. The concept of implicit contract, drawn from economic analyses, is thus seen as one of a number of useful analytical tools which can help to overcome the deficiencies of the classical model of contract, with its individualistic, abstract disinterest in context and its emphasis on the explicit and objective manifestations of agreement. It directs attention to the often unacknowledged contextuality and 'embeddedness' of obligations, underlining their reliance on good faith and co-operation, their complexity and subtlety, and their fundamen-

[93] Karl Polanyi, 'Our Obsolete Market Mentality' (1947) 3 *Commentary* 109.

tally social nature. As a result, as David Campbell and Hugh Collins point out, implicit contract is a potentially dangerous supplement to classical contract. This is in part because, as they suggest, it undermines the idea of contract as 'an instrument of explicit, rational choices'.[94] But it is also in part because although notions such as implicit contract intimate that these implicit dimensions are rooted in choice, agreement and consent (in *contract*), in directing attention to the social context and complexity of interactions and relationships they highlight elements and sources of obligation which are, at best, only partially consensual and, at worst, markedly less-than-consensual.

In some contexts, for example, expectations and understandings may be divergent rather than shared. In others, where shared expectations and understandings have emerged, they might be the products of power rather than consent, as in situations where there is an imbalance in the bargaining strength of the parties or serious informational assymetry. In some of these situations—consumer contracts provide an obvious example—law takes account of the context and nature of the relationships involved and steps in to impose obligations on the stronger party in order to try to realise what it considers to be the 'reasonable' or 'legitimate' expectations of the weaker party. Sometimes this is done through such means as implied terms, sometimes through more detailed (public) regulation about the ways in which certain goods and services are made or traded, regulations of which the benefitting party may have little or no awareness. As John Wightman observes, therefore, the language of reasonable expectation 'tends to be used to mean more than merely saying that one party's expectations are a mirror image of whatever the contract terms provide'.[95] It has a normative (and social) dimension: it refers to law's view of what the party is entitled to expect regardless of whether the other party agrees. In this way law sometimes gives contractual effect to 'unilateral expectations', prompting Wightman to argue that in certain situations suppliers of goods and services should perhaps be conceptualised as acting an almost 'semi-fiduciary capacity'.[96] Indeed, some economists have gone as far to suggest that 'non-market controls, whether internalised as moral principles or externally imposed, are to some extent

[94] David Campbell and Hugh Collins, ch 2 of this book.
[95] John Wightman, ch 5 of this book.
[96] *Ibid*.

essential for efficiency'.[97] As this suggests, over time some of these legally-imposed obligations become part of what is implicitly understood by both parties, crystallising into the customs and expectations of the 'contracting community', further underlining that implicit understandings and expectations are shaped not only by agreement but by wider, social and normative considerations. Despite its apparently consensual basis, therefore, the idea of implicit contract, in emphasising such things as the specific social contexts and 'embeddedness' of interactions, and their frequent dependence upon trust and co-operation, tends to bring to the surface the public, normative dimensions of obligation, and the fuzziness of the line separating the consensual and the non-consensual. In short, it has the potential to be a rather *un*contractual supplement.

Paradoxically, however, what we see in the corporate context is assertion of the specifically *contractual* nature of these aspects of obligation. In this context, the idea of implicit contract is used to stress the private, contractual nature of directors' duties and of corporations as a whole; and to downplay and, if possible, expel the social, less-than-consensual dimensions that elsewhere it is being used to foreground. Through recourse to the concept of contract, corporate contractualists seek to *dis*embed corporations, to reduce them to mere sets of market relations. The aim, as the attempt to divest fiduciary duties of their public and normative dimensions shows, is precisely to strip corporations of their social and public elements, for fear that recognition of them would open up those 'interesting (normative) questions' about corporate goals and the disposition of corporate rights. Contractualists wish to characterise all corporate obligations as specifically contractual, as purely 'economic', to suppress the deeply social character of the modern corporation. And given their desire to protect and legitimate shareholder rights, this fear is well founded. What would happen if we began to reflect upon the 'legitimate expectations' of *rentier* shareholders, or to examine with an open mind the 'reasonable expectations' of corporate employees and of society at large?

This use of implicit contract may have wider implications. It suggests, perhaps, that the idea of 'contract', with its emphasis on agreement, consent and the 'private' origins of obligations, may be ill-equipped adequately to capture the normative, moral, 'public' quality

[97] Kenneth Arrow, 'The Economics of Moral Hazard: A Further Comment', in *Collected Papers*, vol 4 (Cambridge, Mass, Belknap Press, 1984) 103, 104–5.

of many obligations; ill-equipped adequately to capture their 'embeddedness' and their less-than-consensual dimensions. Rather, therefore, than trying to sustain through ideas of informal or implicit contract the myth that all obligations are rooted in consent, it might be better to try, as some have,[98] to shed Polanyi's 'market mentality' and recognise that there are other, equally legitimate and important sources of obligation, even in market relations, and that these have been, and are, in various ways socially and publicly shaped and determined. In short, there may be a need to expand the language of obligation, even if this means confronting head-on the difficult normative questions that this would bring to the fore. Indeed, it is arguable that corporate contractualism reveals only too clearly the dangers of attempting to contractualise and marketise all relations and obligations, for there are certain senses in which, despite its unyielding shareholder-orientation, the contractualist approach to corporations can be self-undermining. As we have seen, the attempt to recharacterise fiduciary duties not only represents an attempt to privatise and disembed them but also an attempt to demoralise them: fiduciary duties have 'no moral footing' Easterbrook and Fischel insist, as they try to divest the corporation of its public elements.[99] David Campbell suggests that this creates an 'amoral framework' for company law, but it might be more accurate to describe the moral framework proposed as that of the market. Not that this is necessarily much better. As Benjamin Cardozo once observed, those in positions of trust have to be held to 'something stricter than the morals of the marketplace'.[100] For the morals of the marketplace are, of course, those of impersonal self-interest and competitive individualism, in which other people are simply means to your ends. One of the purposes of introducing ideas of trust, co-operation, good faith and fiduciary duty into obligations is precisely to place 'normative boundaries on the opportunistic pursuit of self-interest'.[101] Perhaps the shareholders of Enron and WorldCom should not be surprised that the directors of those corporations, encour-

[98] See, for example, David Campbell's discussion of the work of Kenneth Arrow in 'The Relational Constitution of Contract and the Limits of "Economics": Kenneth Arrow on the Social Background of Markets' in Simon Deakin and Jonathon Michie (eds), *Contracts, Co-Operation, and Competition* (Oxford, CUP, 1997) 307.

[99] Should this demoralisation be extended to the employment contract, with the eradication of the implied duties of employees to loyalty, fidelity and co-operation?

[100] *Meinhard v Salmon*, 249 NY 458 (1928). 'Forms of conduct permissible in a workaday world for those acting at arms length', Cardozo explained, 'are forbidden to those bound by fiduciary ties'.

[101] Wightman, above, n 95.

aged by their share options and the demand for increased share prices, seem to have treated everyone, including the shareholders themselves, as tools in pursuit of their own self-interest.[102] Whatever one's view of the answers to Easterbrook and Fischel's 'interesting questions', contract and the morals of the marketplace are simply not adequate bases upon which to ground the obligations of public corporations and their directors.

[102] See Daniel JH Greenwood, 'Fictional Shareholders and Enronitis', paper delivered to the Feminism and Legal Theory Project (Cornell Law School) workshop on *Corporate Citizens in Corporate Cultures: Restructuring and Reform*, at Osgoode Hall Law School, Toronto, Canada, September 2002.

10

Implicit Contracts, Takeovers and Corporate Governance: In the Shadow of the City Code

SIMON DEAKIN, RICHARD HOBBS, DAVID NASH AND GILES SLINGER

1. INTRODUCTION

CORPORATIONS CREATE ECONOMIC value through the mutual specialisation of human, physical and intangible assets. The mechanisms of corporate governance are the means by which this value is realised. The issue to consider here is how long-term economic relations involving complex commodities, repeat trades, and an uncertain contractual environment are governed, under circumstances where the invisible hand of the market functions less than perfectly to bring about efficient outcomes.[1] The presence of multiple stakeholder groups whose inputs are required for production gives rise to overlapping and competing claims to share in the income stream which the firm generates. In the (inevitable) presence of transaction costs, there are limits to how far incentives can be perfectly aligned in advance through express contracting. As a result there is scope for the mutual adjustment of claims at every stage of the economic relation. The mechanisms of governance will be more or less successful depending on how well they resolve these distributional conflicts and thereby establish a basis for inter-stakeholder co-operation.

[1] L Zingales, 'Corporate Governance', in P Newman (ed), *The New Palgrave Dictionary of Economics and the Law*, vol 1 (London, Macmillan, 1998) and S Deakin and A Hughes, 'Economic Efficiency and the Proceduralisation of Company Law' (1999) 3 *Company, Financial and Insolvency Law Review* 169.

In the modern Anglo-American corporation, the predominant solution to this problem is to assign residual rights of ownership and control to the shareholders. Of all the different corporate constituencies, shareholders, it is argued, have most at stake in the economic success or failure of the enterprise, and so they are most likely to act in a way which enhances the value of the productive venture as a whole, thereby benefiting all concerned.[2] In addition, internal governance costs within the group of shareholders are low, precisely because they share the common goal of maximising their financial return; there is less scope for costly divergences of interest of the kind which arise between different employee or supplier groups. The prevalence of the shareholder model in the USA and Britain is therefore said to represent the 'survival' of an efficient form of governance, at the expense of less efficient alternatives.[3] In this vein it is further argued that, as a result of globalisation, corporate governance systems are converging on the Anglo-American 'shareholder primacy' norm.[4]

A contrary view is that the dominance of the shareholder primacy norm has potentially negative distributional implications for other stakeholder groups, which in turn call into question the norm's wider effects on corporate performance and national competitiveness. If prioritising returns to shareholders means that other stakeholders are less willing to risk firm-specific investments in human and physical capital than they would otherwise be, the negative effects on corporate performance will be felt more widely. In the long run, shareholders would lose out too.[5] This can be read as implying that the shareholder primacy norm enjoys its elevated status in the Anglo-American systems to factors other than efficiency, such as institutional lock-in and other consequences of path dependence. It also suggests that systems which do not observe the shareholder primacy norm are not necessarily, for that reason, suffering a competitive disadvantage.

[2] E Fama and M Jensen, 'Separation of Ownership and Control' (1983) 26 *Journal of Law and Economics* 301.

[3] H Hansmann, *The Ownership of Enterprise* (Cambridge, Mass, Belknap Press, 1996).

[4] H Hansmann and R Kraakman, 'The End of History in Corporate Law' (2001) 89 *Georgetown Law Journal* 439.

[5] M Blair, *Ownership and Control: Rethinking Corporate Governance for the Twenty-First Century* (Washington, DC, Brookings Institution, 1995); S Deakin and G Slinger, 'Hostile Takeovers, Corporate Law and the Theory of the Firm' (1997) 24 *Journal of Law and Society* 124 and M Blair and L Stout, 'A Team Production Theory of Corporate Law' (2001) 85 *Virginia Law Review* 247.

These issues are crystallised at the time of a hostile takeover bid. Supporters of an active market for corporate control claim that it serves to shift assets to more efficient uses while also enhancing the accountability of managers to shareholders. However, it has been suggested that the source of gains in takeovers derives not from the more efficient use of corporate assets post-merger, but from the ability of managers to breach with impunity the 'implicit contracts' of non-shareholder constituencies. Because the expectations of employees and other constituencies with asset-specific investments are not adequately protected by law, they are vulnerable to a 'breach of trust' which serves to transfer wealth to shareholders at the expense of the long-term performance of the enterprise.[6]

This paper offers a qualitative, empirical perspective on the operation of implicit contracts within takeover bids. The evidence is drawn from case studies of hostile takeover bids mounted in the UK in the mid-1990s under the regime established under the City Code on Takeovers and Mergers. On the basis of interviews carried out following takeover bids, we report the perceptions of the bid process of market professionals and others involved, including company directors and employee representatives. We thereby provide evidence of the relative weight placed on particular regulatory factors by those involved in the takeover process, and of the perceived degree of influence of the different stakeholder groups. We then look at the outcomes of the bids five years on. We find that, almost without exception, successfully-completed takeovers led to large-scale job losses and asset disposals. However, almost none of the bids were considered by financial analysts, at this point, to have generated shareholder value for investors in the merged company.

The argument is developed as follows: Section 2 outlines the theoretical positions which have been taken within the law and economics literature on the role of implicit contracts and related mechanisms of corporate governance in the takeover context. Section 3 then outlines the contents of the City Code and evaluates its provisions from the point of view of the rival theoretical positions on implicit contracts and takeovers. The Code's provisions on equal treatment of shareholders, takeover defences and the position of non-shareholder constituencies are for this purpose compared to the equivalent measures in the US and

[6] A Shleifer and L Summers, 'Breach of Trust in Hostile Takeovers', in A Auerbach (ed), *Corporate Takeovers: Causes and Consequences* (Chicago, University of Chicago Press, 1988) 33–67.

Germany, and reference is also made to the contents of the draft EC Directive on takeover bids (the 'Thirteenth Directive'). Section 4 then reports the empirical findings of the empirical study of the operation of the Code and section 5 traces the subsequent history of mergers arising from the bids. In the concluding section we consider the significance of the findings for the theory of implicit contracts within corporate governance.

2. IMPLICIT CONTRACTS IN HOSTILE TAKEOVERS: THE 'BREACH OF TRUST' HYPOTHESIS

For its supporters, the hostile takeover mechanism serves to align the interests of managers and shareholders, thereby minimising the agency costs associated with the separation of ownership and control in large, publicly-held corporations. The appropriate response of management to a hostile bid is to adopt a position of 'passivity' or 'neutrality', ruling out takeover defences and leaving the shareholders free to decide the fate of the company in the event of a bid.[7] In so far as the target board is required to take any positive steps in response to the bid, its duties are confined to instigating an 'auction' based on competing offers, thereby ensuring that shareholder returns are maximised. Some combination of these two positions—the 'passivity' and 'auction' views of the role of target management—represents the broad consensus within corporate finance and corporate governance scholarship and also among policy circles in Britain and America.

A bidder is normally required to offer a market premium to the existing shareholders, in the form of an offer price well in excess of the current market value of the shares, if it is to be successful. The technical form in which this is done is called in the USA a 'tender offer'—this means an offer made directly to the shareholders, over the head of the board (by contrast, a 'proxy fight' involves the use of votes in a general meeting to replace the existing board with a new one). The equivalent of a tender offer is also the normal way of proceeding with a bid in the UK, under the rules of the City Code on Takeovers and Mergers. The premium paid by the bidder as part of a tender offer may be justified by its confidence that it can run the company more efficiently after the merger has been completed. The logic of the bid is that, at the time of

[7] F Easterbrook and D Fischel, *The Economic Structure of Corporate Law* (Cambridge, Mass, Harvard University Press, 1991).

the bid, the target's share price has fallen below its potential value, thanks to mismanagement by the incumbent team. This, at least, is the theory which lies behind the 'passivity' and 'auction' views. Empirical evidence, however, has not provided clear confirmation of the theory's predictions.

Since the late 1970s, the economic effects of takeovers have been the focus of intensive study. Econometric analyses have shown that it is not necessarily the worst performing companies which are targeted for takeover; in particular in the UK (and to a lesser extent in the United States), size is a more relevant factor.[8] Nor do mergers following hostile bids consistently lead to improved performance. While hostile bids do better than agreed mergers, on average there is only a small positive effect on share prices from hostile takeovers,[9] and the range of outcomes is wide.[10] Thus, while target shareholders undoubtedly do well from hostile takeover bids, shareholders in bidder companies, on average, make only slight gains, if that. Such evidence puts in doubt the theoretical claim that hostile takeovers enhance the efficiency and competitiveness of organisations.

An alternative explanation for the high takeover premiums paid to target shareholders was provided by the 'breach of trust' hypothesis developed by André Shleifer and Lawrence Summers in a much discussed paper published in 1988. The paper was developed against the backdrop of the activities of corporate 'raiders' such as T Boone Pickens and Carl Icahn, who were active in US takeover markets in the mid-1980s. Several hostile bids mounted at this time led to large-scale job losses in organisations where employment security had previously been a stated priority of management.

The key to the 'breach of trust' hypothesis was the analysis of implicit contracts. According to the theory, employees are willing to make firm-specific investments in human capital in return for an implicit promise of job security which amounts to a return on their 'investment'. Firm-specific human capital in this context means:

[8] J Franks and C Mayer, 'Governance as a Source of Managerial Discipline', paper prepared for the DTI Company Law Review (2000), available at <http://www.dti.gov.uk/cld/franksreport.pdf>

[9] A Cosh and P Guest, 'The Long-run Performance of Hostile Takeovers: UK Evidence', Centre for Business Research Working Paper No. 215, University of Cambridge (2001).

[10] D Mueller and M Sirower, 'The Causes of Mergers: Tests Based on the Gains to Acquiring Firms' Shareholders and the Size of Premia', Centre for Business Research Working Paper no 109, University of Cambridge (1998).

> skills or knowledge or networks of personal relationships that are specialized to a given enterprise and that are more valuable in that enterprise than they would be in alternative uses.[11]

Because of such specialisation, employees become 'locked in' to a particular enterprise. They thereby become vulnerable to ex post renegotiation of implicit contract terms by management. In the context of a hostile takeover, downsizing enables management to capture the future 'rents' or income streams which would otherwise have accrued to employees, and to convert them into takeover premiums for the shareholders' benefit.

Because this practice directly benefits shareholders at the employees' expense, it is a simple wealth transfer. Its impact on productive efficiency is at best neutral, but more likely negative. As Margaret Blair puts it:

> Firms that focus solely on share value will have an incentive to shut down operations that are not generating profits for shareholders even though these operations may still be generating substantial real economic rents. From the point of view of society at large, this is, obviously, inefficient. Moreover, over time such policies are likely to discourage further investments by employees in firm-specific human capital.[12]

The Shleifer and Summers paper identified the hostile takeover as the principal mechanism by which the redistribution of wealth from employees to shareholders takes place. As long as the incumbent management remains in place, implicit contracts with employees are enforced through reputational effects. Companies which renege on expectations of continuing employment will be unable to motivate existing employees or attract new ones. However, following a successful bid, a new management team comes in and finds itself in a different position. The new team aims to realise short-term gains to meet the costs of the takeover through asset disposals which, in themselves, reduce the need to attract and retain employees. In effect, the post-bid restructuring places the parties in an endgame in which implicit contracts have ceased to be self-enforcing. The effect was summed up as follows:

[11] M Blair, *Wealth Creation and Wealth Sharing. A Colloquium on Corporate Governance and Investments in Human Capital* (Washington, DC, Brookings Institution, 1996) 8.

[12] *Ibid*, 12.

> Hostile takeovers are external means of removing managers who uphold stakeholder claims. Takeovers then allow shareholders to appropriate stakeholders' ex post rents in the implicit contracts. The gains are split between the shareholders of the acquired and the acquiring firms. At least in part, therefore, the gains are wealth redistributing and not wealth creating.[13]

Yet a similar argument could equally well have been made in the case of shareholders. The 'nexus of contracts' view of the corporation sees managers as the agents of the shareholders, running the enterprise on their behalf with the aim of achieving a return on their investment. This 'contract' (which in legal terms can be thought of as consisting of the terms of the memorandum and articles of association or, in the US context, the corporation's by-laws), like the employment contract, is potentially open-ended, and similarly subject to unforeseen contingencies. However, in each of the cases considered by Shleifer and Summers, there was a fundamental difference in treatment (not referred to in their paper) between shareholders and employees which arose from the prevailing institutional framework. Shareholder expectations were just as 'implicit' as those of employees, but shareholder's claims were protected by corporate and (in particular) securities law in a way which had no equivalent for employees.

Enforcement of implicit contracts through reputational effects is very far from being the whole story. Understandings which are implicit ex ante may become explicit ex post through the device of a *property rule* which grants residual decision-making power to one party. Thus, at the point of deciding the fate of the company in response to an outside bid for control, in Britain and the USA residual control rights are asserted in such a way as to ensure that shareholders, *and only shareholders*, get to decide. In order to explain the differential treatment of shareholders and employees, it is necessary to examine these institutional origins of shareholder primacy in the Anglo-American systems in more detail.

3. INSTITUTIONAL SUPPORT FOR SHAREHOLDER PRIMACY: DIRECTORS' DUTIES, TAKEOVER CODES AND EMPLOYEE VOICE

There is only limited legal support for the shareholder primacy norm within the core of corporate law. In UK company law, directors, when

[13] Shleifer and Summers, above n 6, 44.

taking commercial decisions, are said to owe a duty to act in good faith in the interests of the *company*. In the USA, Delaware corporate law (the choice of legal regime for most large US companies) has an essentially similar rule, although it is sometimes phrased more explicitly as a duty owed to the *members*, that is, the shareholders. Both UK law and Delaware law allow directors leeway to take into account the interests of non-shareholder constituencies, to the extent that this is done with the aim of enhancing shareholder value. The DTI Company Law Review, which was completed in 2002, referred to this as the idea that directors are entitled to pursue 'enlightened shareholder value'; its proposed restatement of directors' duties 'requires directors to act in the collective best interests of shareholders, but recognises that this can only be achieved by taking due account of wider interests'.[14]

Section 309 of the Companies Act 1985 already requires directors to consider the interests of employees along with those of the shareholders when exercising their fiduciary duties. In the US, a large number of states passed so-called 'stakeholder statutes' in the 1980s which shielded boards from potential liability to shareholders in respect of decisions including responses to takeover bids. Although Delaware was not among these states, its judges have, from time to time, stressed that boards have scope to balance the interests of different stakeholders in the overall interests of the company as a productive entity.[15] Procedural rules and protections for directors against suit also confer considerable discretion on boards. Shareholder litigation is very rare in the UK thanks to procedural bars including the rule in *Foss v Harbottle*.[16] Under Delaware law, a generously wide 'business judgement rule' protects directors from personal litigation in most cases where they are shown to have acted in good faith.

Looking purely at the general principles of corporate law, target boards have considerable leeway to resist hostile takeover bids, almost to the extent of adopting a 'just say no' policy. Indeed, until comparatively recently, boards in both the US and the UK did precisely this. During the 1930s, UK boards routinely dismissed outsiders' attempts to prise away control, often not even informing shareholders that a bid

[14] Company Law Review Steering Committee, *Modern Company Law for a Competitive Economy: Developing the Framework* (London, DTI, 2000) 14–5.

[15] In particular in *Unocal Corp v Mesa Petroleum Co* 493 A2d 946 (1985), discussed further below.

[16] (1843) 2 Hare 461.

was on the table. Directors of listed companies insisted that negotiations with bidders had to be conducted on a confidential basis.[17]

The position began to change as the consequence of the revolution in securities law and accounting practice which began in the US with the passage of federal securities legislation in the 1930s (the Securities Act 1933 and Securities and Exchange Act 1934) and in the UK with the Companies Act 1948. These measures, together with the gradual development of stock exchange rules, required companies to disclose a wider range of information in their published accounts and to inform the regulatory authorities of an increasingly large category of material changes in commercial circumstances. Hostile takeovers were a response to this new regulatory regime which began to gather momentum in the late 1950s and increased in significance in the course of the 1960s. From an early stage, there was concerted pressure from shareholder groups for regulatory intervention to protect their interests. In the UK this led to the issuing in 1959 of the Notes on Amalgamations of British Businesses, a code of conduct drawn up with the encouragement of the Bank of England. This laid down the principle that the decision to sell or retain shares was a matter for the shareholder, who was entitled, in making that decision, to receive all relevant information from the board of the company.[18] In 1968, the Notes gave way to the City Code on Takeovers and Mergers, which was drawn up and administered by a self-regulatory body, the City Panel on Takeovers and Mergers. Also in 1968 the US adopted federal legislation, the Williams Act, which amended the Securities and Exchange Act of 1934. In common with the trend in the UK, the Williams Act introduced disclosure requirements in connection with takeover bids, with the aim of protecting shareholder interests.

Since the late 1960s the City Code has evolved to encompass a substantial body of principles and rules relating to the conduct of takeover bids. Formally, the Code is 'soft law' which depends for its enforcement on the threat that an individual found to be in breach of its provision may lose the necessary license to practise in the area of investment business in the UK. This is a sufficiently powerful threat to ensure near-complete compliance with rulings of the Panel. The power

[17] L Hannah, 'Takeover Bids in Britain Before 1950: An Exercise in Business Prehistory' (1974) 16 *Business History* 65 and W Njoya, 'Ownership and Property Rights in the Company: A Law and Economics Analysis of Employee and Shareholder Interests', PhD thesis, University of Cambridge (2002) 144–5.

[18] *Ibid*, 146 and A Johnston, *The City Takeover Code* (Oxford, OUP, 1980).

is currently exercised by the Financial Services Authority (FSA), which has endorsed the City Code as a relevant instrument of self-regulation under the terms of section 143 of the Financial Services and Markets Act 2000. The involvement of the FSA, a statutory body, does not diminish the essentially self-regulatory character of the Panel, which consists of representatives from a number of financial organisations and professional associations in the City of London.

The Code is founded on a principle of equal treatment of shareholders: 'all shareholders of the same class of an offeree company must be treated similarly by the offeror'.[19] This means that 'partial bids' which discriminate between classes of shareholders are forbidden. The Code's 'mandatory bid rule' requires the bidder, once it has acquired 30 per cent or more of the voting rights of the company, to grant all shareholders the chance to sell for the highest price it has paid for shares of the relevant kind within the offer period and the 12 months preceding it.[20] Likewise, the Code stipulates that information given out by either the bidder or target directors must be made 'equally available to all shareholders as nearly as possible at the same time and in the same manner'.[21] The Code also imposes on target directors a series of specific obligations. They must obtain competent, independent financial advice on the merits of the offer,[22] which they must then circulate to the shareholders with their own recommendation.[23] Any document issued by the board of either the bidder or the target must be accompanied by a statement that the directors accept responsibility for the information contained in it. The effect of this is to create a legal duty of care, owed by the directors to the *shareholders* to whom the information is issued, and not to the *company* as is the case with their general fiduciary duties.[24] In effect, then, the directors of the target are required to give disinterested advice on the merits of the offer.

The Takeover Code is not silent on the interests of other stakeholders. General Principle 9 states that:

[19] City Code on Takeovers and Mergers (London, Panel on Takeovers and Mergers, 2000ff) General Principle 1.

[20] *Ibid*, rule 9. Also relevant here are the Companies Act 1985, s 430A, providing a statutory right to sell where the bidder and its associates control 90% in value of the relevant shares, and the Companies Act 1985, s 428, on the bidder's right of compulsory purchase of the last 10% of shares.

[21] City Code on Takeovers and Mergers, above n 19, rule 20.1.

[22] *Ibid*, rule 3.1.

[23] *Ibid*, rule 25.1.

[24] *Ibid*, rule 19.2.

> it is the shareholders' interests, taken as a whole, together with those of employees and creditors, which should be considered when the directors are giving advice to shareholders.[25]

In addition rule 24.1 requires the bidder to signify, in its offer document:

> its intentions regarding the continuation of the business of the offeree company; its intentions regarding any major changes to be introduced in the business, including any redeployment of the fixed assets of the offeree company; the long-term commercial justification for the proposed offer; and its intentions with regard to the continued employment of the employees of the offeree company and its subsidiaries.[26]

However, these provisions do little to counter-balance the specific duties of disclosure owed to shareholders under the Code. General Principle 9 is no more enforceable by employees than is section 309 of the Companies Act.[27] Employees have no standing to make representations before the City Panel. Moreover, the statement of future intentions which rule 24.1 requires of the bidder is unlikely, in itself, to give rise to any legal commitments. In practice, it is easily satisfied by a boilerplate formula inserted into offer documents by which the bidder simply undertakes to observe the employees' pre-existing legal rights, something which is little more than a statement of the obvious in this particular context.

The Code, together with other aspects of securities law, also hampers potential anti-takeover defences in various ways. Once an offer is made or if the target board has reason to believe that it is about to be made, the target board cannot issue new shares; issue or grant options in respect of any unissued shares; create securities carrying rights of conversion into shares; sell, dispose or acquire assets of a material amount,

25 *Ibid*, General Principle 9.

26 *Ibid*, rule 24.1.

27 s 309 has given rise to a rather patchy and inconclusive case law, which mainly turns on whether this provision can be used by directors to deflect possible claims for breach of fiduciary duty brought by disgruntled shareholders: see J Parkinson, *Corporate Power and Responsibility: Issues in the Theory of Company Law* (Oxford, Clarendon Press, 1993). Because employees have no standing to enforce the obligation apparently imposed for their benefit by s 309, it is not surprising that its only practical use to date has been to protect managers against shareholder-led litigation, thereby lending weight to the charge that s 309 and the US stakeholder statutes are merely manager-entrenchment devices (see M Robilotti, 'Codetermination, Stakeholder Rights and Hostile Takeovers: A Reevaluation of the Evidence from Abroad' (1997) 38 *Harvard International Law Journal* 536.

or contract to do so; or 'enter into contracts otherwise than in the ordinary course of business'.[28] The 'proper purposes' doctrine of company law likewise prevents the board issuing shares for the purpose of forestalling a hostile takeover, even well in advance of any bid being made.[29] The issuing of non-voting stock, which a board might do in an attempt to entrench its control, is permissible as a matter of company law, but has been vigorously opposed by organised shareholder interests, as expressed through the Institutional Shareholders' Committee's Code of Practice.[30] Under both company legislation and the rules of the UK Listing Authority, companies must take active steps to contract out of protection for pre-emption rights, that is the rights of existing shareholders to be granted preference when new stock is issued.[31]

The overall effect of the Code is that the open-ended duty of directors to act in good faith in the interests of the company is, for the duration of the takeover bid, transmuted into a specific duty to have regard to the immediate financial interests of the shareholders. The board is required to be neutral during the bid, and may only, with difficulty, erect takeover defences in advance; hence management 'passivity' is, by and large, the order of the day. Management's obligation to provide an objective assessment of any bid implies a limited duty to hold the ring during an auction, but it is not required to take active steps to solicit additional bids.

US law on takeovers is broadly similar to that in the UK, although it is tilted more clearly in the direction of an auction rule rather than a rule of neutrality or passivity, and there are significant institutional differences which have implications for the way in which takeover bids are conducted. The Williams Act is a less extensive regulatory instrument than the Takeover Code. It does not impose a bid timetable as the Code does, and its impact on takeover defences is less far-reaching. The main effect of the Act is to require information disclosure and to impose (from 1995 onwards) a version of the equal treatment principle, under which the tender offers must be made available to all shareholders of the relevant class.

[28] City Code on Takeovers and Mergers, above n 19, rule 21.

[29] *Howard Smith Ltd v Ampol Petroleum Ltd* [1974] AC 821 and Parkinson, above n 27, at 143.

[30] Institutional Shareholders Committee, *The Responsibility of Institutional Shareholders in the UK* (London, Institutional Shareholders Committee, 1991) s 6 and P Davies, 'Institutional Investors in the United Kingdom', in D Prentice and P Holland (eds), *Contemporary Issues in Corporate Governance* (Oxford, Clarendon Press, 1993).

[31] Companies Act 1985, ss 85–89.

The closest equivalents to the Code's provisions on defences and treatment of stakeholders are to be found in the Delaware case law, the result of the more prominent role played by shareholder litigation in the US system. Contrary to the position in the UK, the Delaware courts allow target boards to put in place 'poison pills' or shareholder rights plans which require bidders to buy out existing interests at an enhanced premium or, with the same result, have the effect of diluting the bidder's own stock following the acquisition. Under *Unocal*[32] the Delaware Supreme Court effectively operates a proportionality test, by virtue of which a defensive measure will be protected by the business judgement rule if it is 'reasonable to the threat posed'. The directors are entitled to conduct an analysis of the impact of the bid on the corporate enterprise, taking into account factors which include:

> inadequacy of the price offered, nature and timing of the offer, questions of illegality, the impact on 'constituencies' other than shareholders (i.e., creditors, employees, and perhaps even the community generally), the risk of nonconsumption, and the quality of securities being offered in the exchange.

Notwithstanding this dictum, in *Revlon*[33] the Court ruled that a particular kind of takeover defence—a 'lock up' of assets, such as giving a friendly third party or 'white knight' the right to buy them at a discount should its own offer fail—was subject to a special test. This kind of device would be acceptable only if the effect was to elicit an auction between competing bidders, rather than deterring potential bids. The court came close to articulating an exclusive shareholder interest test by ruling that, once the sale of control to one bidder or another becomes inevitable, the board's only duty is to ensure that shareholder receive the highest value possible for their stakes. Later decisions[34] have demonstrated the Delaware courts' continuing ability to 'zig zag'

[32] Above n 15

[33] *Revlon Inc v McAndrews & Forbes Holding Inc* 506 A 2d 173 (1985). See also *Smith v Van Gorkom* 488 A2d 858 (1985) in which, exceptionally, the business judgment rule failed to protect a board which decided to favour one bid over another. The crucial factor here appears to have been the potential conflict of interest in the role of the company's own CEO in promoting the adopted bid.

[34] See in particular, *Paramount Communications Inc v Time Inc* 571 A.2d 1140 (1990); *Paramount Communications Inc v QVC Network Inc* 637 A2d 34 (1993); *Unitrin Inc v American General Corporation* 651 A2d 1361 (1995). For discussion see Blair, above n 5; B Black and R Kraakman, 'Delaware's Takeover Law: The Hidden Search for Corporate Value', 96 *Northwestern University Law Review* 521, M Kahan and E Rock, 'How I Learned to Stop Worrying and Love the Pill: Strategic Responses to Takeover Law' (2002) 69 *University of Chicago Law Review* 87.

between pro- and anti-defensive rulings,[35] a quality which helps to ensure that neither of the two core constituencies to which Delaware has to appeal—managers and institutional shareholders—is sufficiently alienated to consider pressing for reincorporation in a more 'friendly' jurisdiction.[36]

In the US context, then, it would seem that regulatory competition between the states, some of which are willing to adjust their corporate laws to attract reincorporations, has resulted in a particular configuration of takeover law, under which takeover defences in the form of poison pills are permissible. There are two schools of thought on the effects of this evolution. One maintains that as a result of the leeway allowed to poison pills, Delaware law is unduly pro-management, the consequence of the need to appeal to incumbent managers who have the all-important say in where the company is to be incorporated.[37] The other, by contrast, evaluates the process of regulatory arbitrage in a more positive light, by suggesting that the Delaware rule permits poison pills, by and large, only to the extent compatible with the goal of maximising shareholder choice in the event of a takeover; poison pills are in general legitimate only to the extent that they are redeemable, so that rather than posing an insurmountable barrier to an external bid, they merely increase the price which a bidder is required to pay.[38]

While it is difficult to resolve this debate in the absence of more compelling evidence of the efficiency effects of poison pills, the comparison with the UK position is instructive from a public choice point of view. The UK lacks a similar mechanism of regulatory competition to that which operates in the USA. The City Code, in articulating a strongly pro-shareholder position on the issue of management passivity, reflects the influence which institutional shareholders and City professionals have been able to bring to bear on the regulatory process. It is largely thanks to concerted shareholder pressure that poison pills and the more

[35] M Roe, 'Takeover Politics', in M Blair (ed), *The Deal Decade* (Washington, DC, Brookings Institution, 1993) 321–380.

[36] The potential role of state-level stakeholder statutes, and the constitutional jurisprudence surrounding them, should also be noted in this context (see Njoya, above n 17; E Orts, 'Beyond Shareholders: Interpreting Corporate Constituency Statutes' (1992) 60 *George Washington Law Review* 16 and L Mitchell, 'A Theoretical and Practical Framework for Enforcing Corporate Constituency Statutes' (1992) 70 *Texas Law Review* 579.

[37] L Bebchuk and A Ferrell, 'On Takeover Law and Regulatory Competition', Harvard John M Olin Center for Law, Economics and Business, Discussion Paper No 363 (2002).

[38] Kahan and Rock, above n 34.

obvious kinds of takeover defence, such as 'shark repellents' and 'flip overs', have not been adopted to any anything approaching the levels seen in the USA.

It is also clear that neither system has generated processes which would have the effect of protecting stakeholders against the threat of expropriation postulated by the 'breach of trust' hypothesis. The *Revlon* decision suggests that stakeholder considerations will tend to take second place once it is clear that the company will be auctioned off to the highest bidder. In the UK, the same effect arises from the absence of any standing for employee representatives in the City Panel's processes of adjudication and rule-making. Nor does employment law provide a substitute remedy in either system. In the context of US federal labour law, restructurings and reorganisations of the enterprise which result from commercial transactions such as takeovers are not covered by the employer's duty to bargain under the National Labor Relations Act[39] (and in any event mandatory collective bargaining covers less than 10 per cent of the US private sector workforce). The equivalent UK provisions are those parts of employment law which impose a duty on the employer to inform and consult employee representatives in situations of redundancy and business transfers.[40] Although the sale of a business or part of a business triggers a duty to consult, there is no such duty merely in the event of a hostile bid being mounted; neither the target nor the company is obliged to consult at this point. The rules of the UK Listing Authority, which mandate prompt disclosure of material information to shareholders, also make it difficult for companies to consult employee representatives over the substance of large-scale restructurings at an early stage in the decision-making process.

The approach taken by the German Takeover Law, in force from 1 January 2002, highlights, by comparison, the marginalisation of employee voice in the Anglo-American systems. Section 33 of the new law permits the target management to put in place anti-takeover defences if they are either supported by a 75 per cent vote of the shareholders, or authorised in advance by the supervisory board. This last

39 See *First National Maintenance Corp v NLRB* 452 US 666 (1981).

40 These are found in, respectively, the Trade Union and Labour Relations (Consolidation) Act 1992, s 188 *et seq* (implementing the EC Collective Redundancies Directive, 98/59/EC), and the Transfer of Undertakings (Protection of Employment) Regulations 1981 (implementing the EC Acquired Rights Directive, 2001/23/EC). See generally J Armour and S Deakin, 'Insolvency, Employment Protection and Corporate Restructuring: The Mixed Effects of the Acquired Rights Directive' (2003) 22 *International Review of Law and Economics* 443–463.

reference is highly significant as, in the case of companies subject to the codetermination laws, employees have equal representation with shareholders on the supervisory board, and in some cases the casting vote will be exercised by a non-shareholder chair. Section 33 had initially required shareholder approval for defensive measures in all cases, but was redrafted at a very late stage in the legislative process to incorporate the alternative of authorisation through the supervisory board. Richard Painter and Christian Kirchner comment that:

> [t]his change in section 33 was clearly motivated by protectionist forces, forged together by certain management interests and the lobbying of labor unions fearful of the impact of hostile takeovers on German codetermination.[41]

Whether or not the measure is any more 'protectionist' in favour of labour than the City Code is in favour of shareholders, it would seem that the feature of German corporate governance which most clearly distinguishes it from its British and American counterparts, namely the incorporation of employee voice directly into corporate decision making and lines of accountability, has here come to be reflected (at least thus far) in the takeover regulation regime.[42]

A further contrast is provided by the proposed EU Thirteenth Company Law Directive. This measures aims to put in place a harmonising set of rules for shareholder protection which are essentially inspired by the City Code. The Directive would outlaw bid-frustrating tactics by target boards, require the target board to obtain neutral financial advice on the merits of a bid, and impose various duties on bidders, including an obligation of equal treatment with regard to shareholders of the target, thereby ruling out 'coercive' bids. When a revised draft of the Directive was considered by the European Parliament in late 2000, the Parliament insisted that the implications of takeovers for employment should play a part in the assessment of bids. It also rejected the European Commission's view that the correct attitude for the target board to take during a bid was one of 'neutrality'. The Commission responded by insisting that employee consultation

[41] R Painter and C Kirchner, 'Takeover Defenses Under Delaware Law, the Proposed Thirteenth EU Directive and the New German Takeover Law: Comparison and Recommendations for Reform', Illinois Law and Economics Working Papers Series, Working Paper No 00–36 (2002) 15.

[42] M Höpner and G Jackson, 'An Emerging Market for Corporate Control? The Mannesman Takeover and German Corporate Governance', MpIfG Discussion paper 01/4 (2001).

was not an appropriate objective for the Directive, and (somewhat disingenuously)[43] claimed that adequate protection was already provided by the Acquired Rights Directive.[44] A Conciliation Committee was set up to mediate between the Commission and the Parliament on this and other matters. This led to agreement on a new set of amendments which (among other things) would have required the board of the target company to set out its

> views on the effects of the [bid] on all the interests of the company, including employment, and on the offeror's strategic planning for the offeree company and its likely impact on jobs and locations;

The board of the bidder would have been required to issue a similar statement, relating to its intentions. This fell short of a requirement on either company to enter into consultations with employee representatives. When the Directive was finally put to the vote in July 2001, the result was a tie (273 votes on each side), which meant that the proposal fell.[45]

Notwithstanding this failure, the Internal Market Directorate of the European Commission has made clear its intention to resurrect the draft Directive. In January 2002 the Commission published the report of a high level group of company law experts.[46] This report sidestepped the issue of employee consultation on the grounds that while:

> the interests of other stakeholders and in particular of employees may be at stake in the context of a takeover bid, [the group] believes that this in itself does not justify measures by the board which deny shareholders the opportunity to successfully tender their shares to a bidder who is willing to buy their shares.[47]

In this context, it would seem to be significant that the Thirteenth Directive is an internal market measure, over which the Directorate General for Employment and Social Affairs, which is responsible for employee consultation measures, has no say. Since the report of the high level group, a judgment of the European Court of Justice, ruling

[43] The correct reading of the Acquired Rights Directive is almost certainly that it has no application to mergers by share transfer, for the reasons examined in Armour and Deakin, above n 40.

[44] See COM (2001) 77 final.

[45] See the European Parliament Daily Notebook, 4 July 2001: <http://www.europarl.eu.int/press/index_recherche_en.htm>. For the recent history of the draft Directive, with references to relevant texts and official documents, see <http://europa.eu.int/prelex/detail_dossier_real.cfm?CL=en&DosId=11887#322077>

[46] European Commission, *Report of the High Level Group of Company Law Experts on Issues Related to Takeover Bids* (Luxembourg, OOPEC, 2002).

[47] *Ibid*, 16.

that the retention by governments of 'golden shares' in privatised corporations could contravene EC rules on freedom of establishment,[48] has put further pressure on the Parliament to reach agreement on the text of the Thirteenth Directive.

In short, the City Code embodies in a particularly clear way the principle that, during the course of a takeover bid, directors of the target company are meant to act as the agents of the shareholders. Appeals to 'enlightened shareholder value' are of little relevance in this context; the shareholders are entitled to the protection of their short-term financial interests. It would appear, then, the claims of non-shareholder constituencies to the protection of their implicit contractual interests in the corporate enterprise as a continuing productive entity count for little. The position appears to be starkly pro-shareholder not simply by reference to recent German practice, but also by comparison to the US position, which allows certain poison pill defences (although, it would seem, only to the extent that they lead to a higher immediate return to the shareholders). We now turn to an examination of how the City Code works in practice.

4. EMPIRICAL EVIDENCE: A QUALITATIVE STUDY OF TAKEOVER PROCESS

4.1 The Study: Aims, Methods, Scope

Although there are literally hundreds of econometric analyses of aspects of hostile takeover bids, the breach of trust hypothesis has been relatively little studied using this methodology. The quantitative methods which are used to measure the effects of bids upon shareholder wealth are not able to specify whether those gains came from increased productive efficiency or wealth transfers. One study, which found evidence that hostile takeovers in the UK between 1987 and 1996 were associated with significant falls in both employment and output, concluded that, after controlling for the change in output, the overall effect of such mergers was to enhance the efficiency with which labour was utilised at firm level. On this basis the paper claimed that 'the results are generally supportive of the view that merger activity, particularly related and hostile merger activity, promotes efficiency'. However, the authors also accepted that:

[48] *Commission v France*, Case C-483/99, judgment of 4 June 2002, and *Commission v Spain*, Case C-463/00, judgment of 3 May 2003.

> if the observed employment reductions constitute a reneging on the implicit terms of the labour contract, in the sense of Shleifer and Summers,[49] there may be associated costs generated through the subsequent reductions in firm-specific human capital investment by employees. These will be manifested in lower output levels but any such changes would be very hard to identify'.[50]

To make progress in understanding the effects of hostile takeovers and of takeover law, there is scope for alternative methods including qualitative analyses and case studies. These can provide richer information on the motivations and perceptions of those affected by bids and on the potential range of trajectories of companies following bids than is available from econometric studies which are, by definition, remote from these kinds of data. In this vein, the present paper reports the findings of a qualitative study of hostile takeovers and their aftermath. The first aim was to analyse how the takeover process and takeover regulation, including the City Code, structured the consideration by boards of different stakeholder interests. A non-random sample of 15 takeover bids was identified for close study. The objective was to construct a sample of bids which contained examples of both hostile and agreed bids, and cross-border bids by UK companies and for UK companies mounted during the period 1993–1996. Interviews were conducted with company directors, legal and financial advisers and trade union officials in the relevant companies. During 1993–96 over 40 interviews were conducted with institutional investors, company directors, employee representatives, lawyers, merchant bankers and representatives of various official market bodies (including the Association of British Insurers and the Takeover Panel). The purpose of this stage of the research was to assess how those directly involved in takeover bids perceived their effects, in particular their distributional implications for the different stakeholder groups. In 2001, a further sub-sample of companies was revisited for the purpose of assessing how, several years after the bid, the takeover was now viewed.[51]

By way of background to the study, it is useful to note some features of the takeover wave of the mid-1990s, of which our sample of bids formed a part. From a peak in 1989, the UK takeover market became

[49] Above n 6.

[50] M Conyon *et al*, 'The Impact of Mergers and Acquisitions on Company Employment in the United Kingdom' (2002) 46 *European Economic Review* 31–49, at 40.

[51] In a small number of cases, it was not feasible to conduct a study of the impact of the bid either because no merger resulted from it or because the subsequent history of the merged company made it impossible to trace the effects of the bid.

relatively quiet during the early 1990s. This slump ended dramatically with an explosive increase in takeover value—rather than numbers of bids—in 1995 and 1996. A few extremely large hostile takeover bids were seen, most notably Glaxo/Wellcome and Lloyds/TSB. In value terms, the market for corporate control became as important in the mid-1990s as it had been in the late 1980s. Features of the market in the mid-1990s included a huge jump in the value of continental European acquisitions in the UK, and a septupling in the value of UK public deals from £5 billion in 1994 to a then record £36 billion in 1995.

Table 1 charts hostile bids as a proportion of all bids for the period in question and indicates the overall incidence and success rates of bids. Table 2 lists details of the 15 bids which formed the sample. This indicates the pre-bid prices, the first and final offers, the bid timetables (relevant dates), the composition of offers (cash, shares and debt), the takeover premiums paid in successful bids and the outcomes of bids.

4.2 Perceptions of the Regulatory Process

We asked market participants for a description of a particular bid, and in connection with that particular instance, their opinions about the effects of the regulatory system, company law, the Takeover Code, European law, tax law and the MMC. Interviewees answered whether a particular factor had or had not affected the outcome of a bid. The Takeover Code and related Rules Governing Substantial Acquisitions of Shares were rated as an important factor by 90 per cent of respondents, the highest score of any single factor (see Figure 1). A quarter of all respondents considered that regulatory factors had affected the outcome of the bid.

We then asked interviewees whether consideration and priority had been given to shareholders, employees and creditors. All 33 responding interviewees thought that directors had 'considered' shareholders' interests. In the 31 of these cases where 'priority' was addressed, the result was again unanimous that shareholders had been given priority. At the other end of the scale, 'priority' was never given to creditors, and 'consideration' was only thought to have been given to this group in a few cases—merchant bankers discussing agreed bids were the most likely to report that consideration had been given to creditors. While 31 per cent of all respondents reported that employees had been given priority, this result depended on high ratings from trade union

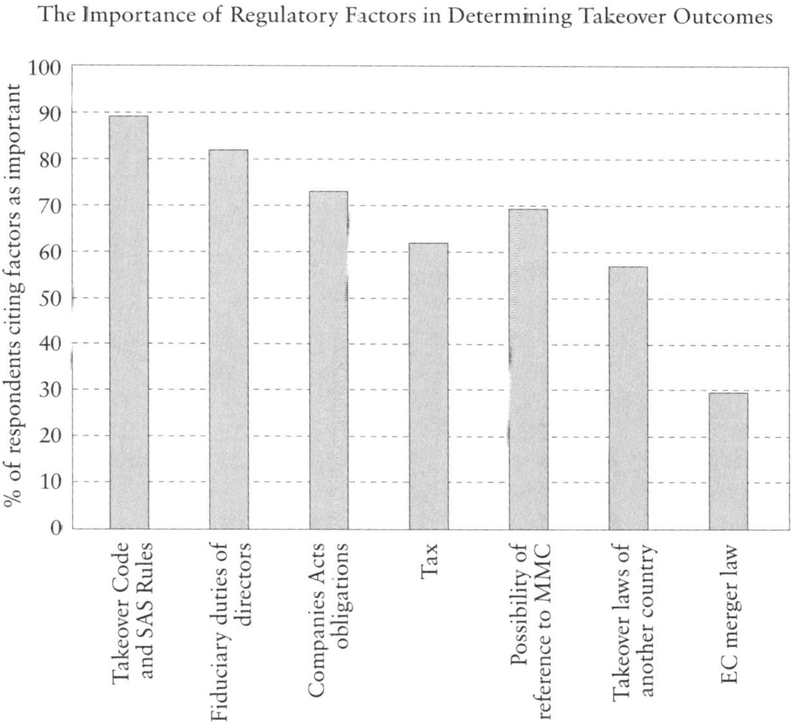

Figure 1

representatives (80 per cent) and directors (50 per cent) rather than lawyers (8 per cent), and on a large number reporting priority to employees in agreed bids (55 per cent) rather than hostile bids (13 per cent).

The effects of the bid were then analysed using questions which asked about net benefit or net loss to various groups on each side of the bid. Respondents had to assimilate gains and losses to individual groups and even to individuals—for example to employees or directors who might have lost their jobs, but who experienced capital gains from shareholding value rises and from redundancy pay-offs. While 100 per cent of respondents considered that target shareholders gained from bids, only around 40 per cent considered that target employees did so. Table 3 reports these results and Figure 2 represents the means of the perceived effects on different groups.

Table 1. Incidence and success rates of UK Public Takeover Bids, 1993–1996

UK Public Bids 1993–1996		**Contested Bids**			**Agreed Bids**			**% of Total Bids**		**All Bids**
		Contested	Late Agreement	Total Contested	Agreed	White Knight	Total Agreed	Contested	Agreed	Totals
1993:	Completed	2	3	5	51	2	53			58
	Failed	6	0	6	4	0	4			10
Success Rate (%):				*45.5%*			*93.0%*			85%
	Total:	8	3	11	55	2	57	16.2%	83.8%	68
1994:	Completed	6	2	8	55	0	55			63
	Failed	3	0	3	6	0	6			9
Success Rate (%):				*72.7%*			*90.2%*			88%
	Total:	9	2	11	61	0	61	15.3%	84.7%	72
1995:	Completed	6	4	10	75	2	77			87
	Failed	7*	1	8	5	0	5			13
Success Rate (%):				*55.6%*			*93.9%*			87%
	Total:	13	5	18	80	2	82	18.0%	82%	100

1996:	Completed	8	2	10	77	0	77			87
	Failed	5	0	5	5	1	6			11
Success Rate (%):				*66.7%*			*92.8%*			*88%*
	Total:	13	2	15	82	1	83	15.3%	84.7%	98
1993–96 Totals:										
	Completed	22	11	33	258	4	262			295
	Failed	21	1	22	20	1	21			43
Success Rate:				60%			92.6%			87.3%
	Totals:	43	12	55	278	5	283	16.2%	83.8%	338

Source: *Mergers and Acquisitions Monthly*, 1992–1997.

* Includes 3 bids in a new category: 'recommendation given then withdrawn,' which was not mentioned before the report on 1995.

Note: The category 'initially contested, then agreed,' was not used prior to the report on 1992. These bids have been counted as hostile bids.

Table 2. Dates, prices, takeover premiums and results in selected takeover bids 1993–1996

Bidder	Target	Bid type	Pre-bid price	Formal offer	Final offer (if different)	Premium	Result
Kingfisher	Darty	Agreed	3 Feb 1993 519FF	18 Feb 1993 520FF		0%	18 Feb 1993 Agreed
British Aerospace	VSEL	Agreed	28 Sept 1994 973p	12 Oct 1994 1260p (shares) 1140p (cash)	31 May 1995 1747p (shares) 1600p (cash)	64%	10 June 1995 Withdrawn
GEC	VSEL	Agreed	28 Sept 1994 973p	28 Oct 1994 1400p (cash)	8 June 1995 1081p (cash + shares) 1100p (cash)	121%	19 June 1995 Agreed
Trafalgar House	Northern Electric	Hostile	13 Dec 1994 910p	19 Dec 1994 1077p (cash + shares) 1048p (cash)	23 Feb 1995 1081p (cash + shares) 1100p (cash)	21%	4 Aug 1995 Withdrawn
Glaxo	Wellcome	Hostile	20 Jan 1995 688 p	20 Jan 1995 1025p (cash)		49%	8 Mar 1995 Agreed
Southern	SWEB	Hostile	7 July 1995 801p	13 July 1995 900p (cash)	25 Aug 1995 981 p (cash + debt)	22%	18 Sep 1995 Unconditional

Scottish Power	Manweb	Hostile	21 July 1995 730p	24 July 195 945p (cash + shares) 915p (cash)	18 Sep 1995 1025p (cash + shares) 990p (cash)	36%	6 Oct 1995 >50% acceptances
Hanson	Eastern	Agreed	28 July 1995 700p	31 July 1995 975p (cash)		39%	31 July 1995 Agreed
RPR	Fisons	Hostile	17 Aug 1995 193p	18 Aug 1995 240p (cash)	5 Oct 1995 265p (cash)	37%	11 Oct 1995 Agreed
Harnishfeger Industries	Dobson Park Industries	Hostile	1 Sep 1995 83p	8 Sep 1995 110p (cash)	26 Oct 1995 130p (cash)	57%	26 Oct 1995 Agreed
United Utilities	Norweb	Agreed	6 Sept 1995 917p	8 Sept 1995 975p (cash) 1015p (cash + shares)	11 Oct 1995 1170p (cash + shares + debt) 1150 p (cash + debt)	25%	7 Nov 1995 Unconditional
Texas Energy	Norweb	Agreed	6 Sept 1995 917p	28 Sept 1995 1050p (cash + debt)	3 Oct 1995 1085p (cash + debt)	18%	11 Oct 1995 Withdrawn

Table 2 (*cont.*)

Bidder	Target	Bid type	Pre-bid price	Formal offer	Final offer (if different)	Premium	Result
Lloyds Bank	TSB	Agreed	6 Oct 1995 274p	11 Oct 1995 335p (shares + debt)		22%	11 Oct 1995 Agreed
Granada	Forte	Hostile	21 Nov 1995 275 p	22 Nov 1995 338.6p (cash + shares) 321.7p (cash)	9 Jan 1996 373p (cash + shares) 362p (cash + debt)	32%	23 Jan 1996 >50% acceptances

Table 3. Effects of the merger on different groups

	Group	*Benefit %*	*No effect %*	*Lose out %*	*Cases*
Shareholders	Bidder	64.5	25.8	9.7	31
	Target	100.0	0.0	0.0	31
Employees	Bidder	19.0	66.7	14.3	21
	Target	23.1	38.5	38.5	26
Managers	Bidder	21.1	63.2	15.8	19
	Target	19.2	38.5	42.3	26
Directors	Bidder	50.0	44.4	5.6	18
	Target	30.8	23.1	46.2	26
Suppliers	Bidder	0.0	77.8	22.2	18
	Target	16.7	54.2	29.2	24
Customers	Bidder	43.5	56.5	0.0	23
	Target	63.0	33.3	3.7	27
Banks	Bidder	36.4	59.1	4.5	22
	Target	25.0	62.5	12.5	24
Bondholders	Bidder	0.0	100.0	0.0	18
	Target	10.5	84.2	5.3	19
Competitors	Bidder	4.8	38.1	57.1	21
	Target	4.2	41.7	54.2	24
Local community	Bidder	16.7	66.7	16.7	18
	Target	21.7	56 5	21.7	23
Advisers	Bidder	87.5	8.3	4.2	24
	Target	62.5	12.5	25.0	24

In interviews we put the same question to company directors, lawyers, merchant bankers, institutional shareholders and employee representatives:

> Did directors' duties to consider interests of creditors and employees as well as those of shareholders affect the preparations for, the conduct of and the aftermath of the bid?

On the central question of directors' duties, the response was almost invariably that while directors might consider employees' and creditors' interests, the outcome of a bid was determined by shareholder value. Shareholder value took precedence over all other considerations. The responses to the question are separated out below by group, with advisers first, followed by directors, employee representatives, and institutional investors.

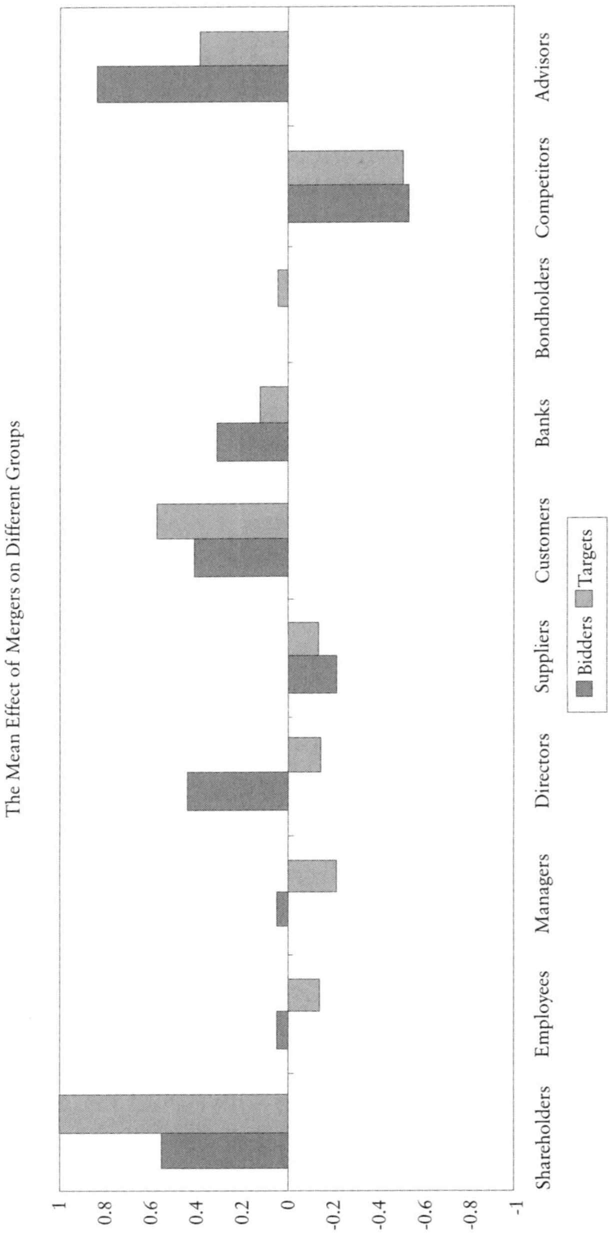
The Mean Effect of Mergers on Different Groups
1
0.8
0.6
0.4
0.2
0
-0.2
-0.4
-0.6
-0.8
-1
Shareholders
Employees
Managers
Directors
Suppliers
Customers
Banks
Bondholders
Competitors
Advisors
Bidders
Targets

Figure 2

Comments from advisers were as follows. Some of these acknowledged a need to communicate to employees, but without exception they indicate that employees' interests play little role in the deliberations of directors during a bid. According to one interviewee:

> in a takeover situation, the duty to act in the interests of the company effectively means a duty to act in the interests of the shareholders of the time: not present and future. Section 309 of the Companies Act and General Principle 9 of the Code are not so important.

Another commented:

> the effect of General Principle 9 is that you are given permission to temper your pursuit of your shareholders' interests with your employees' interests. It is used as an argument but never really has an influence on the outcome.

More generally, there was widespread agreement that it was the duty of directors to deliver advice to shareholders on the valuation or valuations which they were being offered. A typical comment was as follows:

> Directors *do* consider employees' interests, but no-one really knows what that means. At the margin the touchy-feely things matter, but the board of directors, faced with 2 people offering £1 and £1.10 must go for the higher. The decision, of course, is not usually put like that, but I don't know of any cases where employees' interests have come first.

Aside from cases of companies in financial distress, when the position of creditors and employees would come under consideration, employees were only mentioned out of lip service to the obligation in rule 24.1 to state intentions with regard to the treatment of pre-existing rights:

> Directors' duties to consider other interests are rarely an issue unless the company is near to insolvency. These clauses together are a bit of a sop. Rule 24 of the Code requires a statement of intentions towards employees, which always gets reduced to the standard phrase: 'the bidder will ensure that all rights of the target employees will be met in full.' Sometimes people do say more—sometimes a target will screw a stronger statement out of the bidder. And where companies intend not to make redundancies, they will tend to say it.

More pithily, 'much is spoken about directors' duties to employees, but it is rarely relevant'; in this context, 'the Takeover Code and Companies Acts just muddle these issues up: directors have to recommend "the deal" when they are really just recommending the price.'

Directors were also asked whether directors' duties to consider the interests of employees, creditors and the company as a whole had influenced the company's actions. Most expressed ignorance of this formulation of directors' duties ('[t]hese were not especially relevant in this case') or considered such duties irrelevant ('[w]e checked these, but there were none of any special relevance to this case'). In only a minority of cases was a role for consultation acknowledged: '[t]here was consultation with employee representatives as soon as the merger was announced (both with trade unions and with staff associations).' By contrast, several interviewees perceived a major role for directors' duties, with the focus, generally, on shareholder interests. Advisers played a particularly important role in focusing attention on the financial aspects of a bid:

> The one thing that [our merchant bankers] kept saying was that 'you have to be sure that when you say that a price is inadequate, you mean it and can back it up.' Were we advised that we could take into account the interests of the company as a whole? No—the primary advice was that 'there is a price at which you have to say yes.'

In addition, non-executive directors were identified as advocates for the shareholder interest, even where this meant dismembering the corporate enterprise:

> Were we advised of our legal obligations to our shareholders? Yes—there was lots of advice. One of the non-executive directors did push us hard to consider closure and selling up as an option to get maximum shareholder value (about 5 years before the bid).

Exceptionally, in one case where a utility company's future had been at stake, shareholders did not perceive their own financial interests to be the priority:

> [An American investment trust manager] arrived at the extraordinary general meeting at the City Hall and tried to explain why he was looking for shareholder value. He started by saying that he was a marine and that he had fought alongside the Royal Marines, or in Vietnam or some such, and that he invested funds on behalf of the widows and orphans of New York City. Well, he just got shouted down.

Institutional investors likewise thought that directors should be aware of their fiduciary and other duties during a bid. One was happy with the idea that directors owe duties to 'the company' but was of the view that 'during a bid, especially, the directors understand this as being a duty to shareholders.' Another considered that for directors to perform according to their fiduciary duties, 'they had to show that it was in the interests of shareholders to sell.' The pursuit of stakeholder interests was not seen as a viable alternative to shareholder value:

> It is hard to make a case that [the duty to further the interests of the company as a whole] affected the bid greatly. In principle a defending company might put employees' interests before those of shareholders but they are basically serving shareholders' interests first. If directors have a duty, it is to ensure that employees have marketable skills. I see directors' duties to employees as being more like pension rights protection than long-term employment safeguards.

Employee representatives were less clearly opposed to bids than might have been thought. Hostile bids were sometimes seen as shaking up incumbent managerial teams with which the employees had little by way of common interest. Hence employee representatives commented unfavourably on the tendency of target directors to be excessively well-rewarded even before bids, in pay and share options, and on the negative effect this had on the workforce:

> I was very concerned about the calibre of directors we had—most were engineers, or old civil servants and a few marketing boys parachuted in from outside. They were not always competent. One thing they all shared was great share packages. And when the bid came in, they were primarily motivated by the gains they would get. They were all close to retirement. In my view they allowed themselves to be bound, not to say various things. There were 2 weeks of phoney cold war, where the bid was hostile, followed by agreement after a raised offer.

A similar comment was as follows:

> Labour relations pre-bid were quite hierarchical, with the workforce quite isolated from the senior management. All the old electricity boards had a Chairman, Deputy Chairman, board, all way up there. When they were privatised, they appointed non-executive directors, who then set the salary levels for directors, who then reappointed the non-executive directors and in turn voted through their wages. Directors' salaries went up from £40,000 to £60,000 per year, to £140,000 to £215,000. That really upset the workforce, as did the share options for directors.

Particular criticism was reserved for the practice of linking managerial remuneration to the number of workers dismissed:

> The other thing that caused trouble was the directors' incentives schemes. They had a bonus system which had work completed according to certain

> targets divided by the number of staff that they employed to do it. So what they did was to sack a lot of staff, and employed outside contractors, to fulfil their conditions and increase their bonuses.

By contrast, relations with bidders were often good. There was evidence of informal consultation taking place. One employee representative reported getting tacit assurances about future plans from a future managing director in private meetings; another stated that he received non-specific but basically reliable undertakings about redundancy policies from the future management during the bid. The target management was more elusive. One union whose members worked for the target reported receiving repeated offers from an agency employed at several removes from the target for under-the-table funding for opinion polls about employees' and the public's view of a foreign bid. They turned this down. Meanwhile the union reported that the management of the target only once directly spoke to the union about the bid—whilst union members were picketing an EGM, one director quietly congratulated a union representative on the union's efforts to resist the bid. No formal consultation by target management with the union was carried out:

> Employees? They never came into it. I spoke to one [target] director once, on a picket line outside an extraordinary general meeting. He shook my hand and thanked me for all I was doing for shareholders. I told him I was doing it for employees. In general, as long as the new owner tells us that they intend to carry on as before, the directors feel that they've done their job. In reality, employees' interests (and differences in company practices) are not considered. [The target] directors never came to see us at all.

Strikingly, none of the employee representatives was convinced that a higher commitment from management to consultation would have materially affected the bids in which they were involved. In part this was out of a frank recognition that the decision was in the hands of shareholders and hence was 'purely a commercial thing.' The priority was to keep lines of communication open after the bid in an attempt to avoid compulsory redundancies and smooth the way of the new owners. This was a typical comment:

> We take the view now that we're not going to be able to prevent [the takeover]—so we try to get the best deal we can. Given the current industrial relations climate, I don't think that even a 'requirement to consult' would make much difference.

Several of the union respondents had been involved in bids for companies in the general utilities sector (water, gas and electricity). They were of the view that hostile takeovers had simply accelerated a wave of redundancies which had already been put in train within the industry. Several welcomed the new management team which had come in. In one case, the new team reintroduced union recognition arrangements which the target management had abandoned following privatisation a few years previously. Another respondent highlighted the issue of the share options for the workforce as a whole, and the way that these had muted employee, management and union opposition to takeovers in their industries:

> We had to recognise that the higher the share price went, the better it was for our members who had shares. Some of them even had to get advice on how to sell their shares in a way which would minimise their exposure to capital gains tax. Union officials as much as anyone else were caught by the attractiveness of the bid, through the big share value rise and the generous redundancy packages that were on offer.

Some tentative findings can be drawn. For target directors, the nature of the advice they received was of paramount importance. During bids they saw their duty in terms of maximising the potential value of the company as a financial asset of the shareholders. This obligation stood before any requirement to consult employees, to consider their interests, or to further the interests of the company as a whole. Even outside the bid period, the perceived 'duty' to focus on shareholder value could lead a non-executive director to see it as his role to force management to consider closing down the enterprise. Correspondingly, institutional investors applauded directors who saw their responsibilities in these terms.

The attitudes of employee representatives are best described as pragmatic. They expected little from target managers whose interests were seen to be tied up with share options and remuneration packages which would leave them better off whatever the outcome of the bid. There was no expectation of consultation with the target management, and no prospect of it making a difference to the outcome of the bid if it did take place. By contrast, the intervention of bidders could be seen in a positive light, particularly where there had already been a breakdown of trust with incumbent management. Informal links could be established with the bidder at an early stage, and a relationship constructed with a view to the future, even if it was recognised on both sides that the most immediate issue was likely to be the management of redundancies.

5. RETROSPECTIVE ASSESSMENTS OF THE OUTCOME OF MERGERS

The evidence we have so far reported concerns near-contemporaneous perceptions of the takeover process. The success or failure of takeovers must also be judged by the longer-term performance of merged firms. As we have seen, there is some evidence to suggest that hostile bids produce small but positive returns over time for shareholders, by comparison with negative returns in the case of agreed bids.[52] There is less evidence measuring the long-run effects of takeovers on employees and communities. There is US evidence to the effect that employees with firm-specific human capital who are displaced from employment by redundancy suffer long-term losses in earning capacity as a result.[53] However, this research does not separate out the effects of hostile bids from other causes of corporate restructuring.

Case studies, while not necessarily representative in the way that quantitative studies are, can nevertheless provide useful evidence on the dynamics of stakeholder relations post-takeover. Of the 15 bids in our original sample, 12 led to mergers which could be meaningfully studied in this sense. We analyse their effects in two parts. First, we examine how far the takeovers in this sample led to job losses and short-term disposals. Secondly, by reviewing the informed opinion of analysts and the financial media, we assess whether the takeovers have been perceived to be successful from the point of view of creating value for shareowners.

5.1 Job Losses and Disposals of Assets

The two key themes that emerge from a review of reports of events in our case study firms are, firstly, that in general takeovers are often followed by significant job losses, and secondly, that takeover activity is characterised by a short-term asset disposals.

Significant job losses followed several of the takeovers in our case studies. As a result of Glaxo's takeover of Wellcome 7,500 jobs

[52] Above n 9.

[53] C Schultze, 'Has Job Security Eroded for American Workers?', in M Blair and T Kochan (eds) *The New Relationship: Human Capital in the American Corporation* (Washington, DC, Brookings Institution, 2000) 28–65.

were shed, 5,000 being lost in the first year following the takeover.[54] Furthermore, in October 1999, Glaxo Wellcome announced it was to shed a further 3,400 jobs, 16 per cent of its manufacturing workforce, as part of plans to slash annual costs by £370 million by 2003. Half these job losses were in the UK. According to the unions involved, there had been no prior consultation and it was 'a unilateral decision by an arrogant management'. Analysts suggested that the restructuring was welcome, but overdue, given overcapacity in manufacturing following the takeover.[55]

Another example is the announcement by Rhone-Poulenc of plans to eliminate 2,900 jobs from the 28,000 strong payroll by the end of 1997. The job cuts were intended be the most important contribution to savings of $200 million a year following the $4 billion acquisition of Fisons.[56] BIFU, the Banking Insurance and Finance Union, warned that the Lloyds/TSB merger, with its promised £350 million annual cost savings, would eventually mean that the then workforce of 87,000 would be cut by 10,000. In April 1996 the bank announced 500 job losses at their head offices, and a further 3,000 job losses in February 2000 which were directly related to the takeover. Harnischfeger's announcement in 1998, that it was axing 3,100 jobs, or 20 per cent of the workforce, is yet a further example of significant job losses in our case study firms.[57]

As well as significant job losses, several of the case studies also demonstrate a strategy of short-term asset disposal rather than a strategy of growing the entire acquired business over the long term. Some takeovers were clearly aimed at producing disposals and hence value in the short term. A key element of Granada's strategy for the takeover of Forte was the proposed disposal within six months of Forte's Exclusive and Meridian hotel chains for £1.6 billion. More striking is the full demerger of Eastern Group from Hanson in February 1997, less than two years after the original takeover.

Southern's takeover of SWEB further illustrates this point. Less than 12 months after acquiring SWEB, Southern Company sold a 25 per cent interest to another US utility company, and this was later increased

[54] *Financial Times*, 8 September 1995.

[55] *Financial Times*, 6 October 1999.

[56] *Financial Times*, 30 January 1996.

[57] *Financial Times*, 27 August 1998. However, the Harnischfeger job losses may have been more directly related to the company's dire financial position, than to the takeover of Dobson Park.

to a 49 per cent interest. Southern said that this deal was beneficial to shareholders as it realised a small premium on its investment and in any case it was part of its normal strategy of finding minority partners for overseas acquisitions. However, in June 1999, Southern went a stage further and sold SWEB's power supply business.[58] Again, this was argued to be beneficial to Southern shareholders as EDF, the French utility company, paid a price above analysts' expectations. At the same time the sale was seen as a response to tough regulatory price controls and the government-imposed windfall tax, which were said to have cost almost two years of SWEB's earnings. Furthermore, in 1999 Southern's chairman acknowledged that SWEB was not the type of investment that they would make again as it did not fit into their overall strategy of developing the supply business in Continental Europe.

The Lloyds/TSB and Rhone-Poulenc/Fisons deals are further examples of takeovers characterised by asset disposals. They also suggest that so-called undertakings made during the course of a bid tend to be disregarded later. Within six months of giving written assurances of continuing employment to the staff of Hill Samuel merchant bank, Lloyds set about dismantling it, leaving 600 staff facing redundancy. Although Lloyds said this was a useful benefit to shareholders as they had preserved a substantial part of the revenues but removed a considerable proportion of the costs, the *Financial Times* considered that 'the crushing of Hill Samuel Bank has more significance than it represents for the dividends of Lloyds-TSB investors'. According to another commentator, Hill Samuel had been 'blown apart by people who do not know what they are doing.'[59] The Fisons deal left Rhone-Poulenc in a highly leveraged position. In the light of analysts' comments that the deal had set Rhone-Poulenc back two years in terms of getting its balance sheet sorted out, it was little surprise that in June 1996 Fisons' US businesses were sold for £263 million. However, the sale was regarded by analysts as a short-term response in the sense that these assets had been considered likely to be value enhancing for Rhone-Poulenc.

5.2 Variable Success in Creating Shareholder Value?

Notwithstanding attempts to raise value for shareholders from short-term disposals, there is evidence that, over the medium term which our

[58] SWEB's distribution business was retained.
[59] *Financial Times*, 5 September 1996.

study is able to take (five-six years from the merger), even hostile takeovers are in general not perceived as value enhancing for the shareholders of the acquiring companies. We will focus here on one particularly prominent case, Granada's £3.9 billion takeover of Forte. Lauded at the time of the takeover, five years on this deal was seen, generally if perhaps controversially, to have failed to enhance shareholder value. In 2001 a *Financial Times* analysis suggested that 'the returns for Granada have barely matched the group's cost of capital and that its shareholders might have been better off if the deal had never been done.'[60] Total disposal proceeds were estimated to amount to £5.059 billion, while Travelodge and Little Chef, which had not been sold, were generously estimated to be worth £1.5 billion. Entering these figures into a discounted cash flow model gave a present value of £5.327 billion, just £10 million more than the total acquisition cost including debt of £5.317 billion. Another way of looking at the figures suggested that the internal rate of return was 8 per cent, or roughly in line with estimates of Granada's weighted cost of capital, suggesting that the deal was at best neutral for Granada shareholders. However, investment analysts were also of the view that if a more realistic valuation of £1 billion was applied to Little Chef and Travelodge 'the takeover would appear to have destroyed value'.[61] The *Financial Times* analysis also argued that although the deal destroyed value for Granada shareholders, as a result of the takeover being so well defended '[u]nquestionably the Forte shareholders were the winners because of the massive upfront premium paid.' The *Financial Times* suggested that the advisers to the deal were also clear winners, as they received an estimated £250 million in fees.[62]

Similarly, the £9 billion acquisition of Wellcome by Glaxo came to be perceived as having done little to enhance shareholder value. By August 1997 the *Financial Times* was declaring that, 'Glaxo Wellcome is destroying shareholder value at the moment.'[63] The same article suggested that in five years' time the company would be creating more

[60] *Financial Times* 29 May 2001.

[61] *Ibid.*

[62] However, the *Financial Times* did point out that the issue of whether the deal created value for Granada was far from clear cut, because Granada made material improvements in the operation of the assets and pace of value realisation. It can also be argued that Granada needed a hospitality acquisition to build up that side of the business with the aim of splitting it off from its media business, as has now been achieved. Moreover, the deal can be seen as being driven by earnings considerations, achieving earnings enhancement of 10% in the first full year of ownership. This helped buoy Granada's share price, which performed in line with the FTSE 100 Index in the period 1996–2001.

[63] *Financial Times*, 1 August 1997.

value than any other European drug stock. This was because newly launched treatments for asthma, Aids and migraine would most likely replace the loss of sales resulting from the expiry of the US patents for its top selling Zantac and Zovirax products. However, this prediction proved to be excessively optimistic. In July 1999, Glaxo formally abandoned its double-digit growth target, and 11 per cent was knocked off the share value.[64] From the beginning of the year Glaxo underperformed the FTSE 100 Index by 24 per cent, making it the index's tenth worst performer.[65] By the end of 1999 analysts described Glaxo's performance as 'pedestrian'[66] and Glaxo's 1999 results showed underlying pre-tax profits up just 5 per cent, compared to 11 per cent earnings growth reported by SmithKline, with which Glaxo was then in the process of merging. Moreover, without disposals Glaxo's profits would have been virtually level with the previous year, while annual sales were up just 5 per cent compared to SmithKline's 10 per cent.[67] All of this meant that in comparison to SmithKline, Glaxo had looked 'rather sickly' over the previous couple of years.[68] The key problem for Glaxo was the withdrawal of three new drugs on safety grounds and the disappointing launch of a new flu drug. In answer to its own rhetorical question: 'What has gone wrong at Glaxo Wellcome?' the *Financial Times* concluded that the 'uncomfortable answer seems to be that the company became seduced by the glamour of innovation to the detriment of its core competence: commercial savvy.'[69]

Other takeovers in our sample, such as the Rhone-Poulenc/Fisons and Lloyds/TSB deals, by contrast were reasonably successful at creating value for owners of shares in the acquiring company, but only in the short to medium term. At the beginning of 1996 the *Financial Times* said that a profits warning from Rhone-Poulenc had become almost an annual event[70] and that it had long been 'the most unloved of pharmaceutical companies.'[71] However, during the year net income increased by 28 per cent, earnings per share increased 26 per cent, dividends increased by 17 per cent[72] and the share price increased by 50 per cent.

[64] *Financial Times*, 30 July 1999.
[65] *Financial Times*, 20 July 1999.
[66] *Financial Times*, 18 November 1999.
[67] *Financial Times*, 17 February 2000.
[68] *Financial Times*, 28 July 2000.
[69] *Financial Times*, 4 December 2000.
[70] *Financial Times*, 10 January 1996.
[71] *Financial Times*, 30 January 1996.
[72] *Financial Times*, 31 January 2001.

Analysts argued that as well as the re-rating of the whole pharmaceuticals sector and the benefit of a number of favourably received new products, the takeover of Fisons had been a key factor. Not only were costs savings starting to come through but the deal had also acted as a catalyst to develop a clearer focus so that 'the effect induced by Fisons was almost as important as Fisons itself.'[73] Nevertheless, despite the apparent success of the Fisons deal, growth was said to be lower than for other drugs companies and the company felt that its stock was undervalued. In June 1997, driven by the aim of increasing the stock market valuation and price/earnings ratio for the entire group, Rhone-Poulenc restructured by splitting itself into a life sciences company and a chemicals business. Even at the time of this announcement the company and its financial adviser were suggesting that the best way for it to achieve its targeted price/earnings ratio was to do a deal with another chemicals company, similar to the merger between Sandoz and Ciba to form Novartis.[74] In 1999, this came to fruition when Rhone-Poulenc agreed to merge with Hoechst, the German pharmaceuticals and chemicals company, to form a new company called Aventis, the world's biggest life sciences company. Although a full merger was originally planned over three years, the deal was brought forward and was completed by the end of 1999. This was due to the insistence of a 25 per cent shareholder in Hoechst that shareholder value should be boosted as quickly as possible.[75]

The financial media also rated the Lloyds TSB deal a success in creating shareholder value. In December 1996 analysts said that Lloyds TSB 'is and will remain by far the most profitable UK bank.'[76] The *Financial Times* put this down to two key advantages. First, the £400 million of annual cost savings from the TSB merger, most of which were still to flow through and which would eventually be achieved in 1999. Second, its heavy weighting towards high-margin retail lending.[77] Indeed the group was said to have set new standards of profitability, delivering to shareholders return on equity of 33 per cent in 1996, and 37 per cent in 1997.[78] However, even the Lloyds TSB story is not one of continual progress. By 2000 the *Financial Times* was reporting that

[73] *Financial Times*, 19 November 1996.
[74] *Financial Times*, 27 June 1997.
[75] *Financial Times*, 17 March 1999.
[76] *Financial Times*, 5 December 1996.
[77] *Financial Times*, 27 July 1996.
[78] *Financial Times*, 23 June 1999.

shares had underperformed the market by 35 per cent since their peak in the summer of 1998. Although it was still trading at 3.5 times book value, against a sector average of just 2.5 times, the premium was narrowing.[79] Lloyds had acquired a reputation for extracting costs and synergies from mergers, which had left it with one of the lowest cost-income ratios in the industry and a return on equity above 30 per cent. The problem, according to the *Financial Times*, was that fashions change and investors increasingly preferred banks with international growth strategies.[80] Lloyds needed to convince investors that it could grow revenue faster than its rivals. But, according to the *Financial Times*, Lloyds' record here had been less impressive. Lloyds' revenues had grown at about 6 per cent a year over the last decade, against 4–5 per cent for Barclays and National Westminster.[81] Lloyds' stock market rating had fallen below competitors able to offer the prospect of top-line growth, such as HSBC, which had been buying aggressively in Europe and America. The result of this was Lloyds' prolonged and very expensive bid for Abbey National, which ultimately failed on competition grounds in the course of 2001.

One conclusion to be drawn from the Rhone-Poulenc and Lloyds cases is that even where a takeover initially appears to have been successful in creating shareholder value, this is insufficient to satisfy investors over the medium to long term. As a result these companies have had to engage in further corporate activity in order to satisfy demand for even greater returns. However, it is also clear that corporate restructuring that is driven by a desire to enhance shareholder value can have an entirely opposed effect. This point is also illustrated by the case of GEC. It is particularly difficult to assess the impact of GEC's takeover of VSEL on shareholder value, given GEC's highly complex corporate structure. However, following the takeover VSEL seems to have made steady progress and won several shipbuilding contracts. At the time of the takeover the *Financial Times* commented that the takeover made little sense apart from GEC preventing VSEL falling into the hands of BAe and so leaving BAe vulnerable to a takeover by GEC. However, following the succession of a new managing director, and in pursuit of a new strategy of specialising in telecommunications and electronic systems, GEC sold the whole of its defence business to BAe in 1999. At the end of 1999 the *Financial Times* was lauding this

[79] *Financial Times*, 12 February 2000.
[80] *Financial Times*, 7 December 2000.
[81] *Financial Times*, 12 February 2000.

new strategy. It said the former GEC, now renamed Marconi, was beginning to look like the high technology and high margin growth story promised to shareholders and that it had outperformed the market by 40 per cent since the start of the year.[82] However, the result of this corporate restructuring, designed to enhance shareholder value, was ultimately the destruction of shareholder interests as financial disaster hit Marconi in 2001, in the wake of the severe slowdown in the high technology sector. In the summer of 2002 the company had to be rescued by a consortium of banks, leaving shareholder interests virtually valueless.

6. CONCLUSIONS

At first glance, company law recognises the multi-stakeholder nature of the firm and the co-operation problem which it engenders: in order for the firm to flourish as a productive enterprise, the open-ended commitment of the different stakeholders is required. This cannot be completely contracted for ex ante, so a space is created for implicit contracts and similar informal mechanisms of governance to come into play. The legal framework has a role to play in providing an environment in which sustained co-operation is feasible. Directors' fiduciary duties are phrased in such a way as to make it possible for management to take into account the interests of multiple constituencies; 'enlightened shareholder value' provides a focal point for multi-stakeholder co-ordination. In principle, then, the law allows management to mediate, ex post, between the different implicit contractual claims of the various groups whose input is needed to make the corporate enterprise possible.

The hostile takeover, by contrast, is a mechanism aimed at enhancing the accountability of corporate managers to just one constituency—shareholders (or, more precisely, shareholders in the target). This is particularly so in the UK context, where the self-regulatory norms governing takeover bids, mainly derived from the City Code, combined with certain well-established practices (such as pressure to maintain pre-emption rights), impose a particularly strong form of the managerial passivity rule. This is in contrast to the 'auction' orientation of US law and practice, which allows some leeway for takeover defences, and the more clearly pro-stakeholder approach of the recent German

[82] *Financial Times*, 26 November 1999.

takeover law. In the UK, there is no adequate mechanism for the expression of employee voice during the takeover process (in contrast to the position in respect of restructurings carried out through a business transfer).[83] Once a bid is launched, target management's concerns are focused on the short-term, financial interests of the shareholders. In effect, the open-ended fiduciary duty to act in the best interests of the company becomes a much more precise obligation to have regard to the interests of the shareholders in getting the best price for their shares. As a result, there is no firm basis on which implicit contracts with non-shareholder constituencies can be maintained.

The long shadow cast by the City Code in this process is crucial. The Code is the consequence of the mobilisation of a collective interest on the part of institutional shareholders and financial professionals. The empirical evidence reported here suggests that those involved most immediately in takeover bids—directors, advisers and institutional investors—view the Code as the most important regulatory factor influencing bid process. We also saw that almost all participants, including employee representatives, see target directors as acting in the short-term, financial interests of target shareholders, and that directors are also seen as being unable to take into consideration employees' interests in continuing job security.

The studies of post-bid performance demonstrate the range of possible trajectories for companies in the post-bid period. Since the sample is non-random, these studies are illustrative only. However, it is striking that in many cases, measured by the standard of investor opinion, merged companies were struggling to live up to the expectations of the investment community at end of the 1990s. This raises fundamental questions about the manner in which the market for corporate control currently operates in the UK. Target shareholders, who effectively decide the outcome of a bid, may cede control in return for a premium over the market price of their shares. Bidder shareholders, by contrast, have little or no opportunity to hold management to account. Disenchantment ex post with the outcome of bids is a sign of inadequate accountability ex ante between managers and shareholders in bidder companies. In addition, the prioritising of financial interests over production interests during bids prevents managers respecting implicit contracts with non-shareholder constituencies, exposing their interests to expropriation in the form of the asset disposals and redun-

[83] Armour and Deakin, above n 40.

dancies which almost routinely follow hostile takeovers. It would be surprising if this practice had no effect at all on the willingness of employees and suppliers to make firm-specific investments in human capital and the joint development of products and services. Further research along the lines indicated in this paper may be able to tell us more about the potentially negative influence of the Takeover Code on UK productivity and competitiveness, and about the possible repercussions of extending that model throughout the European Union via the Thirteenth Directive.

11

Expertise as Social Institution: Internalising Third Parties into the Contract

GUNTHER TEUBNER

EXPERT LIABILITY—AN IMPLICIT DIMENSION OF CONTRACTING?

A Landmark Case in German Law

A PROPERTY OWNER INTENDS to sell his house. He asks an architect, who is the official and registered expert at the local bank (*Sparkasse*), to write an expert valuation for the house and pays him the usual fee. Under the influence of the owner, the architect does not properly check the roof so that the factual statements in his valuation are inaccurate. On the basis of the valuation, the buyer pays a price which is disproportionally high. For factual reasons, the buyer cannot obtain relief from the seller, and sues the architect.

In a landmark decision of 1995, the German High Court (*Bundesgerichtshof*), whilst disregarding the principle of privity of contract, though following a long series of precedents in so doing, constructs an analogy with a third party beneficiary contract.[1] The contract for the expert valuation between the seller and architect is regarded as containing an implied term, according to which the architect owes a contractual duty of correct performance—in technical terms: not only an integrity interest but also a performance interest—to a third party, the buyer.[2] Moreover, disregarding its own

[1] BGHZ 127, 378—Dachstuhl. The earliest precedent was decided in 1902, RGZ 52, 365.

[2] To be precise, according to the implied terms construed by the court, the architect is not under an obligation of specific performance to the buyer, but once he performs, he owes a duty of care, including correct performance, not only to his contractual partner (the seller), but to a third person who is not a party to the contract (the buyer).

precedents, according to which a fiduciary relation between the mandator and beneficiary would have to exist, the court boldly extends the construction, which is already bold in itself, to competitive market situations, like the housing market, where the parties have antagonistic interests. Finally, disregarding the explicit wording of § 334 BGB (the German Civil Code), which permits the promisor to rely upon contractual defences against the third party, the court does not allow the architect to raise any defence stemming from his contract with the seller, who after all was to a considerable extent responsible for the flawed valuation. The result is that the architect has to pay full damages to the buyer.

This recent expansion of professional or expert liability to third parties with antagonistic interests on the other side of the market—a judge-made law *praeter legem*, if not *contra legem*[3]—entails high financial risks for a whole range of professionals, auditors, accountants, tax consultants, architects, accident insurance experts—and more recently analysts in the stock market. And there is a whole variety of concrete projects of considerable scale for which their expertise is purchased: complex acquisitions of property, large credit operations, construction projects, high risk financial transactions. Usually there is a triangular situation: the *expert*—in our example the architect—and two partners to a project, one of them the *mandator*—our seller—contracting with the expert who is supposed to give expert advice on the project, and the *beneficiary*—our buyer—the third party, who as a rule does not participate in the contract for professional services. Frequently, the situation extends into a multilateral relation, including fourth, fifth, sixth . . . umpteenth additional actors. They may directly co-operate in the project, they may be potential partners, they may finance the project via credit or support it with a guarantee, they may form part of a subsequent transaction chain, or they may be outsiders who suffer a damage from the project risks, and so on *ad infinitum*. The floodgates are open.

The threat of open floodgates is the main reason why in most legal orders expert or professional liability towards third parties is a highly

[3] Critics of the court use this strong language, eg H. Honsell, 'Die Haftung für Gutachten und Auskunft unter besonderer Berücksichtigung von Drittinteressen' *Festschrift für Dieter Medicus*, (Köln, Heymann, 1999), 211, 233; see also D Medicus, *Bürgerliches Recht* (Köln, Carl Heymanns, 1999) 258f.

contested subject.[4] Although there seems to be a broad consensus that expert liability should in principle go beyond the narrow boundaries of the bilateral expertise contract, the underlying principle is rather obscure, and the details of liability, particularly with respect to the scope of the protected persons, are hopelessly controversial.

Open questions

(1) *Underlying principle?* Why should expert liability toward third parties be an implicit dimension of contract? It is only Germany, Austria and Switzerland that construe a third party beneficiary contract, while many other legal orders in the civil and common law world treat it as a question of tort law. And there are voices that argue for quasi-contractual, quasi-tort constructions and, last but not least, for 'contort' solutions as a third way, independent of contract and tort. My point is: Whatever doctrinal construction is chosen, the substantive question remains the same: Is there in tort, contort or quasi-contract a 'special relation'—in the words of a British judge 'equivalent to contract'[5] (!)—that justifies the expert's duty of care particularly toward the third person? Under what conditions does a relation between strangers qualify for such a 'special relation', so that the expert becomes liable toward the third person, in a manner similar to the contractual liability between expert and

[4] Comparative law analysis of expert liability in English and German law, C von Bar, 'Liability for Information and Opinions Causing Pure Economic Loss to Third Parties: a Comparison of English and German Case Law', in BS Markesinis (ed), *The Gradual Convergence: Foreign Ideas, Foreign Influence and English Law on the Eve of the 21st Century* (Oxford, Oxford University Press, 1994). In general, H Kötz, 'The Doctrine of Privity of Contract in the Context of Contracts Protecting the Interests of Third Parties' (1990) 10 *Tel Aviv University Studies in Law* 195; H Kötz, *Europäisches Vertragsrecht* (Tübingen, Mohr and Siebeck, 1996); P Gottwald, *Haftung für Auskunft und Gutachten gegenüber Dritten: England, Deutschland, Schweiz* (Schriftenreihe deutscher Jura-Studenten in Genf, Heft 7, Genf, 1994); F Müller, *Auskunftshaftung nach deutschem und englischem Recht* (Berlin, Duncker and Humblot, 1995); WF Ebke, *Die zivilrechtliche Verantwortlichkeit der wirtschaftsprüfenden, steuer- und rechtsberatenden Berufe im internationalen Vergleich*, (Heidelberg, CF Müller, 1996) 493. B Schönenberger, *Haftung für Rat und Auskunft gegenüber Dritten. Eine rechtsvergleichende Studie* (Basel, Helbing & Lichtenhahn, 1999). For the floodgate problem in comparative perspective, EK Banakas (ed), *Civil Liability for Pure Economic Loss* (London, Kluwer Law International, 1996); J Spier, *The Limits of Liability: Keeping the Floodgates Shut* (London, Kluwer Law International, 1996).

[5] *Hedley Byrne & Co Ltd v Heller & Partners Ltd* [1964] AC 465, HL, 529 and 539 *per* Lord Devlin.

mandator? In substance, this is the same question which from a different vantage-point of contract law is asked again and again: Is there an implied term, a hidden clause, a latent obligation, a deep structure, a dangerous supplement, in the contract which requires that third parties be internalised into the contractual liability regime? For the discussion of implicit contracting, expert liability has the attraction of the extreme and the paradigmatic. While in the normal situation, implied terms do nothing but change somewhat the standards of duties within an existing contract between two parties, in expert liability the 'implicit' nature of the contract asserts that 'in reality' there exists a third party to the contract. Implicity of third parties means here complicity of a hidden parasite who is not only profiting from the valuable expertise itself, but who is also insured against its risks, without paying for it. Expert liability transforms—whatever its doctrinal construction—a voluntarily agreed bilateral liability risk into an judicially imposed trilateral or even multilateral one. Is it not a blatant fiction to call this expansion an implicit dimension?

(2) *Scope of protected persons?* This is the crucial question for the law in action, whatever doctrine the law in the books is using. Tort law starts with a rather broad scope and is at pains to identify criteria that limit the potentially infinite liability for pure economic loss. It looks for restrictions on an unlimited liability of the expert toward an infinite variety of persons that are causally influenced by the expert's wrong information. And vice versa, contract law starts with the narrow scope or range of liability set by the doctrine of privity and encounters problems in including additional beneficiaries. Both approaches aim at protecting persons who are affected by the expertise in a comparable way to the party to the contract. In practice, the courts differ dramatically. Using the criterion of foreseeability, some courts in the USA have drastically expanded the liability risk toward an almost indefinite range of third persons. French courts attempt to identify limits within the infinite chain of causation principle. German courts try to determine the 'objective' purpose of the expertise contract in order to limit the beneficiaries. British courts try to do the same by applying the 'particular transaction rule' on a case-by-case approach.[6] Is it realistic to say that

[6] *Caparo Industries Plc v Dickman* [1990] 2 AC 605, HL.

there is something latent in the expertise contract that determines the number of protected persons?

(3) *Conditions of liability?* Equally controversial are the standards of duty of care that are owed to the third party. Are they determined by the contract between the mandator and the expert, and then transferred to the beneficiary? Or do they result from standardisation processes in the market? Or are they derived from decisions of professional organisations?

(4) *Restrictions of expert liability?* What about defences that the expert can raise against the mandator. Are they available to the expert against the beneficiary? What about exclusions of liability? Is there a third party effect? Can the expert exclude liability against the beneficiary?

THE ORIGIN OF IMPLICIT DIMENSIONS: INSTITUTIONAL EMBEDDEDNESS OF CONTRACT

Does the concept of implicit dimensions of contract take us any further? Indeed, it does. However, one needs to abandon the narrow juridical concept of 'implied terms in fact/in law' and related concepts of purely contractual interpretation. In order to make explicit the implicit dimension of contracting, the law will have to look beyond the limits of the interpersonal relation and to inquire into those social institutions in which the contract participates, and into conflicts between them. Implicit aspects of contract have their origin in the 'embeddedness' of contract in a variety of social institutions, outside the text and outside the interpersonal relation of the contracting parties. In identifying the institutions in which the contract is embedded there is a certain but limited amount of assistance to be obtained from external disciplines. Recourse to the economic concept of 'complete contracting' is helpful, as are sociological theories of economic transactions, but only to a limited degree.[7] The main work has to be done by legal theory and contractual doctrine, namely to identify social institutions relevant to

[7] For incomplete contracting: GM Cohen, 'Implied Terms and Interpretation in Contract Law', in B Bouckaert and Gd Geest (eds), *Encyclopedia of Law and Economics, Volume III. The Regulation of Contracts* (Cheltenham, Elgar, 2000) 78; R Craswell, 'Contract Law: General Theories', in *ibid*, 1. For social embeddedness M Granovetter, 'Economic Action and Social Structure: The Problem of Embeddedness' (1985) 91 *American Journal of Sociology* 481.

contract and to reconstruct them within the boundaries of the legal discourse.[8]

Indeed, institutional economics and empirical sociology suggest that one should interpret implicit dimensions of contract as a matter of the context of economic transactions. What is needed, they propose, is a thorough empirical analysis of both the recursive patterns of interaction of the contracting parties, and the stable conventions of the market. The advantages of such a contextualist approach as compared to pure legal hermeneutics which unfolds the meaning of contractual texts are obvious.[9] Relying on the richness of empirical details, judicial decisions will become more realistic. They will profit from the 'tacit knowledge' of spontaneous orders, ie individual interaction patterns and collective customs of the trade.[10] Since legal decisions will be informed by social norms, their legitimacy will grow and the chances of compliance will increase.

However, there are serious limitations to a spontaneous order approach if it is used to inform legal decision-makers. Interactional patterns and social customs inform legal arguments only about the results of underlying social conflicts, not about the conflicts themselves. They may be a wise or an unwise compromise, they may result from balanced negotiations or from a unilateral imposition of power, a sophisticated response to conflicting demands or thoughtless compliance with outmoded traditions, rational discourse or blind evolution, but in themselves they do not reveal the collisions between social systems to which the contract is exposed. Thus, patterns and customs do not provide for what legal argument would need urgently: a critical reconstruction and reflection of the meaning of those social practices in which the contract is participating. Things get worse when in the concrete conflict—as in our case of expert liability—there exists no reliable interactional pattern or enduring custom of the market that could be identified. What is left is nothing but conflict between different social practices about which the law now is supposed to decide.

[8] An exemplary analysis that pursues such a division of labour between socio-economic analyses of contract and legal theory and doctrine is H Collins, *Regulating Contracts* (Oxford, Oxford University Press, 1999).

[9] For a systematic overview in terms of different contractual techniques, see, D Campbell and H Collins, ch 2 in this volume.

[10] On tacit knowledge M Polanyi, *Personal Knowledge: Toward a Post-Critical Philosophy* (Chicago, Chicago University Press, 1958) 69; on spontaneous orders vs constructivism FA Hayek, *Law, Legislation and Liberty. Volume 1: Rules and Order* (London, Routledge & Paul, 1973) 17ff, 85ff, 118ff; FA Hayek, *Law, Legislation and Liberty. Volume 2: The Mirage of Social Justice* (London, Routledge & Paul, 1976) 11ff, 54ff.

My suggestion is, thus, not to abandon the contextual approach but to push it further. Do not just look for existing patterns and customs in the structural coupling of colliding social systems, but analyse the collision itself and do so from the standpoint of legal argumentation. Reconstruct the internal rationalities and the internal normativities of those social institutions that seek to impose their contradictory demands on the contract. This will produce the surplus value needed for legal argument. Once the collision is understood, a critical evaluation of the colliding normative principles, a careful re-assessment of the compromise found in actual patterns and customs, and a reasoned rule of preference between conflicting social practices will inform the legal decision.

As I have argued at length elsewhere, for such an extended contextual approach, contract law needs to provide for an autonomous social reality construction which reformulates the contractual relation in terms of the polycontextural character of contemporary society.[11] To cut a long story short: the social embeddedness of contract today does not mean its integration into a comprehensive social framework symbolised by coherent behavioural patterns and social customs, rather it means the conflict-ridden exposure of contract to a multitude of highly developed social rationalities that collide with each other. This situation may be described as a difference of language games, but it entails more than to decide between two language games of contracting, the descriptive language of the historian and the normative language of the lawyer.[12] A concrete contract is written in terms of several language games which simultaneously impose their rules on the agreement.[13] In making explicit these implicit dimensions of contract, the law takes account of the conflicting requirements of three social practices in which the contract always already participates (1) the ongoing interactional relation of the parties, its history and its context, (2) the

[11] See G Teubner, 'Contracting Worlds: Invoking Discourse Rights in Private Governance Regimes' (2000) 9 *Social and Legal Studies* 399 and critical comments by Macneil, Gerstenberg, Campbell.

[12] Campbell and Collins, above n 9, 34.

[13] See the concept of 'internormativity' developed by J-G Belley, *Le contrat entre droit, économie et société* (Cowansville, Yvon Blais, 1998) 203ff; J-G Belley, 'Le pluralisme juridique comme doctrine de la science du droit,' in J Kellerhals, D Manai and R Roth (eds), *Pour un droit pluriel: Etudes offertes au professeur Jean-Francois Perrin* (Basel, Helbing and Lichtenhahn, 2002) 135, 142ff; from a systemic point of view HC von der Crone, *Rahmenverträge: Vertragsrecht—Systemtheorie—Ökonomie* (Zürich, Schulthess, 1993) 162ff; T Müller, *Verwaltungsverträge im Spannungsfeld von Recht, Politik und Wirtschaft* (Basel, Helbing and Lichtenhahn, 1997) 146ff.

economic institutions of financing the transaction, (3) most importantly in our context, the social institutions within the productive process in which the contract is embedded.

THREE IMPLICIT DIMENSIONS OF TRANSACTIONS

What insight is gained into the problem of expert liability if it is re-examined in the context of these three configurations and their conflicts? In the current debate on expert liability, it has become common practice to present exclusively one of them as the single basis for deciding on third party liability. Contextualist lawyers point to the contractual relation, legal economists point to markets and hierarchies, legal sociologists point to relations of trust. In our perspective all three appear as narrow and one-sided approaches. Instead, we shall identify as the basis of expert liability fundamental conflicts between these contracting worlds. In particular, the conflicts concern the boundaries of the obligation. An expertise transaction participates in different language games—in the contractual interaction of mandator and expert, in the economic context of monetary operations, in the social context of producing the expertise. Each of these contracting worlds imposes on the transaction a different 'privity', ie different boundaries, different rules of membership, different principles of exclusion and inclusion. The language games involved display variations of bilateral, trilateral and multilateral obligations. While in many types of contract, the implied configurations have more or less identical boundaries, it is the peculiarity of the expertise transaction that is exposed to a collision of different privities which contract law is asked to decide.

Interaction of the Parties to the Contract

Over and over again, attempts have been made to identify the foundations for expert liability toward third parties in the contractual relation itself. In Germany, courts started with constructions of a silent agreement between mandator and expert according to which the expert would be liable toward outsiders.[14] Since third party beneficiary contracts were solidly established and the general erosion of the privity

[14] Starting 1902, RGZ 52, 365.

principle had already begun, this seemed an elegant solution. But again and again this had been rejected as a blatant fiction. Thus the courts moved from fiction toward contextual interpretation, to terms implicit in the contract.[15] But the criteria they were using clearly had their origin outside of the contractual interaction. Basically, they inquired whether the transaction was creating considerable risks for third persons *(Leistungsnähe)*, a question which obviously could not be answered by either silent agreement between the parties or by norms and practices that had emerged in the history of their interaction.

Actually, all the dimensions of the bilateral interaction—whether explicit or implicit, whether classical, neo-classical or relational—militate against the inclusion of third parties into the liabilities of the expertise contract.[16] What is worse, the contract is not the solution; it is part of the problem. Contract itself is at the very root of the collision of privities. The contract between mandator and expert is actually building up a relation of co-operation, of trust and of responsiveness to mutual interest between them. And it is this mutual dependency relation between the mandator and the expert that creates or at least strengthens the conflict of interest involved. Thus, recourse to the actual negotiation of the parties, their agreement in its details, the history of their interaction, the co-operative relation between them, the norms that emerge over time—all this has never uncovered and will never uncover traces that might serve as a foundation for liability toward third parties. It is recourse to other social practices outside of the parties' interaction that may justify this liability which is only poorly covered by contractual rhetoric.

Economic Institutions

What about the embeddedness of the expert contract in economic processes? Does recourse to the context of monetary operations provide criteria for third party liability? Contracts are not simply interpersonal

[15] For a recent case analysis, H Zugehör, 'Berufliche 'Dritthaftung'—insbesondere der Rechtsanwälte, Steuerberater, Wirtschaftsprüfer und Notare—in der deutschen Rechtsprechung' (2000) 53 *Neue Juristische Wochenschrift* 1601.

[16] J Gernhuber, *Das Schuldverhältnis: Begründung und Änderung, Pflichten und Strukturen, Drittwirkungen* (Tübingen, Mohr and Siebeck, 1989) 518ff; E Picker, 'Gutachterhaftung: Außervertragliche Einstandspflichten als innergesetzliche Rechtsfortbildung' *Festschrift für Dieter Medicus* (Köln, Heymann, 1999) 400ff; J Esser and E Schmidt, *Schuldrecht: Allgemeiner Teil I 2* (Heidelberg, CF Müller, 2000) § 34 IV 2c.

relations of negotiation, consensus and performance; they participate in wider economic institutions, in markets, economic organisations, financial arrangements, transaction chains, co-operative networks. And indeed, economic concepts related to these institutions—avoidance of opportunistic behaviour and the idea of complete contracting—have been presented to justify expert liability toward third parties.

One economic argument for expert liability is to reduce the risks of opportunistic behaviour.[17] Monetary sanctions of liability will serve as a deterrent against deceptive expertise. Of course, this is a valid argument and economic calculation may indeed determine the optimal sanction which steers a middle course between deterrence of the expert's opportunism and the beneficiary's opportunism to use expert liability as a cheap insurance against speculative risks.[18] However, economic analysis in itself does not and cannot provide the standards for defining what counts and what does not count as opportunistic behaviour by the expert. What is the economic mechanism that could possibly determine whether the expert's behaviour was opportunistic? Rational action? No, rational choice may determine according to what cost/benefit calculations rational actors will respect social norms of professional expertise. However, these norms do not result from the action of self-interested actors, rather 'the rational pursuit of self-interest is constrained by social norms'.[19] Mandator and expert delineate their respective interests but they will never agree on liability for third parties. This is the reason why the concept of complete contracting does not help in this context.[20] Judges who mimic the behaviour of rational actors in contracting would never come up with the expert's liability toward third persons. Transaction costs mini-

[17] For implied terms in general see Cohen, above n 7.

[18] R Ewert, 'Auditor Liability and the Precision of Auditing Standards' (1999) 155 *Journal of Institutional and Theoretical Economics* 181, 200.

[19] This is of course hotly debated. For a reference in the rational choice camp that makes this point J Elster, 'Economic Order and Social Norms' (1988) 144 *Journal of Institutional and Theoretical Economics* 357; J Elster, 'Rationality and Social Norms' (1991) 32 *Archives Européennes de Sociologie* 109; J Elster, 'Rationality, Emotions, and Social Norms' (1994) 98 *Synthese* 21. Elster gives a classification of those social norms that cannot be derived from rational choice principles (consumption norms, norms against behaviour contrary to nature, norms regulating the use of money, work norms etc.).

[20] Convincing arguments are given by Picker, above n 16, 402ff. It is indicative that J Köndgen Köndgen, 'Die Einbeziehung Dritter in den Vertrag' [1999] *Karlsruher Forum 1998*, 3 attempts to utilise the economic concept of complete contracting for third party effects in general, but when it comes to expert liability (44ff), feels compelled to resort to sociological concepts (expectation, trust, role conflicts, profession).

misation? No, this is an approach that reckons openly with opportunism defined as seeking self-interest with guile.[21] Transaction cost considerations come into play when parties choose institutional arrangements to protect themselves against opportunism from the other side. Cost-benefit calculations? No, these are made once the social norm exists, and the intensity of the sanction and the probability of sanctioning is known. To be sure, there are social norms that are emerging within economic institutions (eg rules of co-operation, competition, hierarchy etc). But expertise responsibility involves social norms that are defined in the context of science, morality or politics, or in any case in non-economic contexts.

Social Relations

Thus, the implicit dimensions of contracting, where principles of expert responsibility toward third parties are established, are referring to non-economic social relations. In the current debate, three related social configurations are offered as the implicit source of expert liability: trust, profession, institution.

Trust is at present a concept that has been rediscovered by economists and sociologists.[22] It refers to a social situation in which risky actions are undertaken without sufficient security about future developments.[23] Lawyers also use the category of trust in this context and propose reliance liability as a complement to contractual liability.[24]

[21] OE Williamson, *The Economic Institutions of Capitalism: Firms, Markets, Relational Contracting* (New York, Free Press, 1985).

[22] For a detailed economic analysis of trust T Ripperger, *Ökonomik des Vertrauens: Analyse eines Organisationsprinzips* (Tübingen, Mohr and Siebeck, 1998); for its organisational analysis RM Kramer, 'Trust and Distrust in Organizations: Emerging Perspectives, Enduring Questions' (1999) 50 *Annual Review of Psychology* 569; for socio-legal studies on trust in contract C Lane and R Bachmann, 'The Social Construction of Trust: Supplier Relations in Britain and Germany' (1996) 17 *Organization Studies* 365; S Deakin, C Lane, and F Wilkinson 'Contract Law, Trust Relations, and Incentives for Co-operation: A Comparative Study,' in S Deakin and J Michie (eds), *Contracts, Co-operation, and Competition : Studies in Economics, Management, and Law* (Oxford, Oxford University Press, 1997) 105.

[23] For a sociological theory of trust N Luhmann, *Trust and Power* (New York, Wiley, 1979) (trans H Davis, J Raffan and K Rooney) ch 4

[24] The protagonist of a legal concept of trust in German law is C-W Canaris, *Die Vertrauenshaftung im deutschen Privatrecht* (München, Beck, 1971); C-W Canaris, 'Schutzwirkungen zugunsten Dritter bei "Gegenläufigkeit" der Interessen' (1995) 9 *Juristenzeitung* 441; C-W Canaris, 'Die Reichweite der Expertenhaftung gegenüber Dritten' (1999) 163 *Zeitschrift für das gesamte Handelsrecht und Wirtschaftsrecht* 206.

There is no doubt that trust is the right category to describe the social relation between the expert and the beneficiary, who, owing to his reliance on the expertise, takes a risky decision. Under certain circumstances this trust deserves to be legally protected. But trust is an ubiquitous social phenomenon and its juridification has produced very specific legal constructs against which it makes no sense to reinterpret them as an expression of trust. The crucial question, whether a social trust relation should be supported by legal sanctions or not, cannot be answered by the inner structure or by the intensity of the trust relation itself.[25] Unlike contract, which contains in itself the conditions under which a legal obligation is created, trust is in itself legally empty. For its promotion to legal status it needs external criteria. It is the object of trust, the social institution toward which trust is oriented, that decides about the legal relevance of trust.[26]

Profession is another social configuration which lawyers use as a basis for expert liability.[27] Referring back to mediaeval concepts of 'public calling' and 'common carrier', it revitalises old status obligations that are supposed to complement modern contractual obligations. Even in the absence of a binding contract, members of a profession carry specific obligations to other people as a consequence of their position in society. But there is a strange asymmetry in the concept of professional obligation. It is as asymmetric as would be the complementary concept of consumer protection. It derives rights and duties from the social status of only one person within a complex social relation, instead of taking into account all the different positions in a multilateral relation and their interdependence. Furthermore, it relies too much on self-regulation in professional associations, instead of looking to the requirements of the whole social relation of which the association is just one part. And it is much too static in stressing the established norms of a status role, instead of looking to the dynamic process of norm

[25] Luhmann, above n 23.

[26] Leenen comes very close to this position: D Leenen, 'Die Funktionsbedingungen von Verkehrssystemen in der Dogmatik des Privatrechts' in O Behrends, M Dießelhorst and R Dreier (eds), *Rechtsdogmatik und praktische Vernunft* (Göttingen, Vandenhoeck and Ruprecht, 1990) 108, 119ff.

[27] S Lammel, 'Zur Auskunftshaftung' (1979) 179 *Archiv für die civilistische Praxis* 337, 345ff; K Hopt, 'Nichtvertragliche Haftung außerhalb von Schadens- und Bereicherungsausgleich' (1983) 183 *Archiv für die civilistische Praxis* 608; K Hopt, 'Die Haftung des Wirtschaftsprüfers' (1986) 39 *Die Wirtschaftsprüfung* 461, 498; K Hopt, 'Dritthaftung für Testate' (1987) 40 *Neue Juristische Wochenschrift* 1745; K Hopt, 'Die Haftung des Wirtschaftsprüfers. Rechtsprobleme zu § 323 GB (§ 168 AktG aF) und zur Prospekt- und Auskunftshaftung', *Festschrift Pleyer* (Köln, Heymann, 1996) 341.

production in a social configuration that from the beginning involves other autonomous actors than just the professional person.

If our goal is to make visible the social configuration as a whole in which the transaction participates, one would have to leave aside asymmetric status concepts like professional responsibility (or consumer protection). One would have to identify the entire multilateral social context in which the productive aspects of the transaction takes place. One would need to look at the social dynamics and not only to a set of rules around the role of a professional. Mere roles are insufficient; instead, the dynamic interplay of operations, structures, boundaries and systems need to come into play. For this purpose, the concept of *institution* seems to be most adequate.[28] Against the concept of profession it has three advantages. Institutions reflect the whole social system involved and not only partial aspects. At the same time, as complexes of social norms, institutions bridge the focal social system to the legal system, in our case to the concrete contract, by their very normativity. Finally, institutions are more than just sets of norms or existing customs. They are coherent complexes of normative structures within fully fledged social systems, and are the result of a more or less explicit reflection of their social function and their contribution to other systems. Seen from the side of law, institutions and not social systems as such are the object of legal decisions to accept the social norm in question as legal or not.[29] Contract law decides on the legal positivisation of

[28] The concept of institution, which has been rather neglected after a promising start (S Romano, *L'ordinamento giuridico*, 2nd edn (Firenze, Sansoni, 1918); M Hauriou, *Die Theorie der Institution* (Berlin, Duncker and Humblot, 1965)) has experienced a remarkable revival. For sociology, R Friedland and R Alford, 'Bringing Society Back In: Symbols, Practices, and Institutional Contradictions' in WW Powell and PJ DiMaggio (eds), *The New Institutionalism* (Chicago, Chicago University Press, 1992) 232; P Selznick, *The Moral Commonwealth: Social Theory and the Promise of Community* (Berkeley, University of California Press, 1992); for organisational analysis, WW Powell and PJ Di Maggio (eds), *The New Institutionalism in Organizational Analysis* (Chicago, University of Chicago Press, 1991); WR Scott, *Institutions and Organizations* (Thousand Oaks, Sage, 1995); for economics Williamson, above n 21; E Furubutn and R Richter, *Institutions and Economic Theory: The Contribution of the New Institutional Economics* (Ann Arbor, University of Michigan Press, 1997); PG Klein, 'New Institutional Economics' in B Bouckaert and Gd Geest (eds), *Encyclopedia of Law and Economics, Volume I. The History and Methodology of Law and Economics* (2000) 456; for socio-legal analysis, N MacCormick and O Weinberger, *An Institutional Theory of Law* (Dordrecht, Kluwer, 1996); J Black, 'New Institutionalism and Naturalism in Socio-Legal Analysis: Institutionalist Approaches to Regulatory Decision Making' (1997) 19 *Law and Policy* 51.

[29] N Luhmann, *Grundrechte als Institution: Ein Beitrag zur politischen Soziologie* (Berlin, Duncker and Humblot, 1965)12f; N Luhmann, *A Sociological Theory of Law* (London, Routledge, 1985) ch II.4 and 6.

social institutions when it refers to the implicit dimensions of contract.[30] These may be economic institutions, as mentioned above, or wider social institutions.

EXPERTISE AS A SOCIAL INSTITUTION

The foundations of expert liability, as we said above, cannot be found if one looks to economic institutions (market, economic organisation, financing practices, networks). But what about 'expertise' as an autonomous social institution? Indeed, expertise bridges scholarship (natural sciences, social sciences, humanities) with other social practices. Of course, expertise is not to be identified with science as a social system in its own right. Professional expertise serves other social ends than the advancement of knowledge as such. But it necessarily brings the institutional logic of scientific inquiry into social fields that are governed by a different rationality.[31] Expertise cannot simply be equated with any production of information by professionals. Rather, people turn to independent expertise as a special institution once they experience the limits of negotiation, of economic exchange, of political power processes, of legal conflict resolution, or of family relations and friendship for resolving their problems. They separate the issue involved from its familiar context and subsume it under the rationality of expertise which differs sharply from their day-to-day practices.

As a consequence, scientific expertise in mundane projects suffers from orientation conflicts. It is a highly fragile social institution which is exposed to a paradoxical situation. Although it is introduced into other social fields in order to help to resolve some of their pressing problems, it depends at the same time on strict insulation against the interference of their competing rationalities.[32] While science itself as a social institution enjoys at least the protection of the ivory tower, an institutional separation from the exigencies of social life in universities and scholarly publications, expertise is systematically exposed to the temptations of influence, persuasion, power relation, family ties and profit. This inherent risk of expertise is the very reason why the above

[30] G Teubner, 'The Two Faces of Janus: Rethinking Legal Pluralism' (1992) 13 *Cardozo Law Review*1443, 1446ff.

[31] For this problematic relation N Luhmann, *Die Wissenschaft der Gesellschaft* (Frankfurt, Suhrkamp, 1990) 616ff.

[32] D Sciulli, *Theory of Societal Constitutionalism* (Cambridge, Cambridge University Press, 1992) 205ff.

mentioned social mechanism of trust in expertise cannot give sufficient protection, but needs to be supported by law.

There are many rules of public law that aim to protect the integrity of expertise. Public law regulation on education, on professionalisation, on academic degrees, on licensing and on monitoring and supervision of experts have played an important role forming expertise as a 'public service'.[33] The important point here is that expertise as a rule is not—cannot be and should not be—integrated into public administration.[34] Instead, public law utilises a type of regulation that is supposed to respect the autonomy of independent expertise also within the public sector and to shape its rules so as to insulate it against the pressing demands of power politics and bureaucratic administration. Thus, law seeks to guarantee the interplay of three crucial orientations—function, contribution and reflexion[35]—within the institution of expertise itself. The question of function is: What is the role of expertise in the social context involved? How can expertise combine its potential with ongoing social processes? The question of contribution is: What are the advantages that different actors gain from the knowledge production of expertise? The question of reflexion is: How can these two divergent perspectives be reconciled? Public law regulation does not answer one of these questions directly. Rather, it creates procedures and obligations that allow for an internal balancing of function, contribution, and reflexion within the dynamics of expertise itself. But it interferes directly in cases of blatant 'misuse' when the subtle mechanisms of self-regulation are perceived as not to work properly.

Once expertise is utilised in the private sector, the same problem comes up, but now in a different institutional context. Of course, buying and selling expertise is nothing new in the private sector, but under the auspices of ongoing privatisation processes, the production of knowledge for projects in the private sector is increasingly taking place as an economic transaction. If the institution of expertise is no longer under a public law regime but under a regime of private contracts, how will its institutional integrity survive?[36] Do the rules of private law have

[33] Lammel, above n 27, 362ff.

[34] For all the kinds of 'public services' that do not fall into public administration, G Teubner, 'After Privatisation? The Many Autonomies of Private Law' (1998) 51 *Current Legal Problems* 393, 402ff.

[35] N Luhmann, *Religious Dogmatics and the Evolution of Societies* (New York, Mellen, 1984): ch 2; N Luhmann, *Die Gesellschaft der Gesellschaft* (Frankfurt, Suhrkamp, 1997) 757ff.

[36] This is the general theme in Teubner, above n 28.

the capacity to guarantee—or at least to facilitate—an autonomous balancing of function, contribution and reflexion?

One solution in the private sector is collective action. Private standardisation associations are a case in point.[37] Private actors create non-profit associations that become independent of the short-term interests of their founders. Although these associations act in commercial contexts, their institutional design increases their chances to display sufficient autonomy to develop a firm normative orientation toward principles of independent inquiry. Their character as an autonomous formal organisation facilitates reflection processes—within the organisation and/or in the context of a larger public—that strike a precarious balance between their social function and their contribution to private projects. The sensitivity of public opinion against a 'politicisation' of these associations and against other forms of structural corruption testifies to a successful institutionalisation of expertise in the private sector.

But what about buying and selling expertise via a bilateral contract? If the provision of expertise—and here comes the crucial question—is to be delivered by contractual mechanisms, what conditions of implicit dimensions need to be established for this mechanism for delivery to operate as intended?[38] Here, a fundamental conflict, the direct collision between the principles of contractual loyalty and expertise impartiality, comes to the fore.[39]

Expertise, if it is to work properly, needs to be supported by (in)visible hand mechanisms which guide its orientation firmly toward principles of scientific inquiry. Application of rigorous methodical standards, orientation toward a comprehensive body of concepts and theories, reliance on inter-subjective consensus in the community of experts, strict insulation against interference of outside political or economic interests, neutrality and impartiality in relation to the interests of the clients involved, are primary among them.[40]

Bilateral contracting on the other side creates for the expert the legitimate obligation of co-operation, trust, interdependence and loyalty

[37] C Joerges, K-H Ladeur and E Vos, *The Integration of Scientific Expertise into Standard-Setting* (Baden-Baden, Nomos,1997).

[38] Campbell and Collins, above n. 9, 47.

[39] For theorising the larger historical and social background of these conflicts, see Sciulli, above n 32, 40ff.

[40] For a recent comprehensive reformulation of the fundamental social norms in the scientific community, J Ziman, *Real Science: What It Is, and What It Means* (Cambridge, Cambridge University Press, 2000) 28ff.

toward the economic interests of the mandator. The expert is under a contractual obligation to further the interests of his client, to use his scientific-methodical instruments to advance the position of his partner to the contract, who after all finances the expertise.[41] From the contractual perspective it would even appear disloyal if the experts took into account interests other than those of his partner, or worse, if he took into account interests antagonistic to the party on the other side of the market, or yet still worse, if he balanced these interests against each other independently.[42] The contract legitimately favours the orientation of the person supplying the expertise toward its contribution to the benefit of the mandator at the expense of its contribution to other social actors and at the expense of its social function.

Thus, private law faces a sharp collision between two legitimate self-regulatory institutions—contract and expertise. The situation can be compared with private arbitration where the ethos of dispute resolution by third parties clashes with the ethos of self-interest in contracting. In the case of the private expertise, the ethos of contract—privity, particularism, interest orientation, utility and loyalty—clash directly with the ethos of scientific inquiry—public knowledge, universalism, disinterestedness, originality and scepticism.

Judicial intervention or non-intervention—that is the question. It is frequently suggested that private law should leave this collision of self-regulating institutions to meta-self-regulation.[43] Economists tend especially to recommend this strategy as a 'penalty default'.[44] If the parties to a contract fail to include terms that refer to a third person, the incompleteness is presumed to be inefficient, whether unintended or strategic, and the court's approach should be to deter this behaviour and encourage complete contracting. The foreseeable result would be an evolutionary process, a 'drift' toward unmediated interest competition, in which over time private independent expertise will transform itself into partisan expertise.[45] The constant pressures of the institution of contract will gradually change the institution of expertise into a procedure which will become known (not necessarily as 'junk science' but) as partisan expertise. In the long run, people will get used to second-order

[41] G Philippsen, *Zur Dritthaftung des privat beauftragten Gutachters für fahrlässig verursachten Vermögensschäden* (Karlsruhe, Versicherungswirtschaft, 1999) 9.

[42] *Ibid*, 23.

[43] Honsell, above n 3, 233.

[44] Cohen, above n 7, 83.

[45] This is the central tenet of the theory of societal constitutionalism, Sciulli, above n 32, 40 ff.

observation: Who paid for the expertise? And they will act accordingly. As a consequence, independent private expertise via bilateral contracting will vanish from the market. In commercial situations where expert information becomes necessary, the other side of the market will be compelled to provide for its own partisan expertise. Then law's job will be more limited, to make sure that deceit and fraud are somewhat reduced in those frequent situations when partisan advice is sold on the market as 'independent' expertise. At this point it becomes clear why a mere orientation of law toward those contractual patterns and conventions of the market discussed above is problematic. They merely record the result of blind evolutionary processes—in our case the 'drift' of independent expertise to partisan expertise—without making it visible that two legitimate self-regulatory regimes are conflicting.

Judicial intervention is needed, however, if the integrity of independent expertise is to be maintained within the private sector. More abstractly, it is needed to facilitate an internal reflective balancing of institutional contributions to social actors (the mandator, beneficiary, and others) against its social function (advancement of knowledge in non-scientific sectors of society). This is the reason why it is an important matter of public policy to declare that expertise should comprise a legally 'protected sphere' within civil society. Thus,

> the state in essence buffers these enterprises 'artificially' from all other spheres' more 'natural' condition, that of immediate competition within economic and political market places.[46]

Once this is accepted, the options are either to exclude bilateral contracts generally from expertise matters, or to search for spaces of compatibility. Now, it is obvious that an outright prohibition of bilateral contracting is counter-productive. Contracting expertise serves here as a flexible and productive social mechanism that makes expertise responsive to projects in different areas of social life.[47] It is a healthy antidote to the old disease which is that expertise as an independent social institution has in itself a tendency to follow its self-interested path of inquiry and to lose contact with the social projects that are at its roots. In many situations there are good reasons for a tightly written contract to discipline the internal dynamics of expertise and to oblige the process of inquiry to concentrate on its contribution to a

[46] Sciulli, above n 32, 207.
[47] For a general account, Luhmann, above n 31, 616ff.

concrete project, provided that we can avoid the problem of the contract undercutting the principles of independent inquiry.

Thus, the task at hand is to search for spaces of compatibility between contract and expertise, to search for a legal regime that furthers an internal reflection on the balance between function and contributions. Third party liability comes in here. It appears as an adequate means to create a space of compatibility. It provides a solution for a typical collision of contracting worlds. It does so by redefining 'privities', ie the external boundaries of the interpersonal relations. While the concrete project, whether in the technological, social, scientific or medical sector, requires one comprehensive multilateral relation, which formalises the agreed-upon co-operation of several actors, the concrete contract and the economic market relation tends to fragment the multilateral complex into various strictly bilateral relations. The 'privity' of the relation is defined differently by the contract and by the project. Third party liability dissolves this conflict of different privities in favour of the multilateralism inherent in the expertise. Via liability law, the social institution of expertise forces the bilateral contract to transform itself into a multilateral obligation. The conflict between multilateral social networks and the bilateral economic transactions forces the law to account for third party effects of contracting, even if this contradicts the sacred privity of contract, reduces allocative efficiency and increases transaction costs.

If therefore, as a matter of law, responsibility for third parties is included in the contract, the one-sided contractual duty of loyalty is counter-balanced by a liability supplement towards the other participants in the project. Thus, despite its contractual loyalty, private expertise can regain its requisite neutral and impartial orientation. Independent expertise as an institution, as a complex of social expectations, thus represents one of the non-contractual elements of contract, which—as a matter of law—the private autonomy of the parties has to respect.[48] Whenever expertise is organised under a private law regime, the requirement that it is complemented by third party liability is a necessary implicit dimension of this regime.

[48] This refers of course to Durkheim's famous formulation of 'non-contractual elements of contract' which in our words represent the embeddedness of contract in various social institutions, E Durkheim, *The Division of Labor in Society* (London, Macmillan, 1984) 155. It is indicative that the German courts use the concept of 'purpose' to internalise the non-contractual elements into the contract. The courts define the 'purpose' of an expertise contract 'to create trust and to serve as an instrument of proof', BGHZ 127, 257, 261.

What happens here to the collision of language games? Once third party liability is introduced, the fundamental conflict between contractual loyalty and disinterestedness of expertise which seemed to be irreconcilable is not resolved by law in favour of the one or the other. Rather, it is transformed into something else. There are two major moves involved. (1) Seen from the perspective of social contribution, the third party liability rule changes the asymmetric contractual obligation to the interests of the mandator into a symmetrical obligation to the interests of both parties to the project. This is important enough, since it creates equidistance between the commercial interests involved, and allows the experts to balance their interests against each other. But this is a limited perspective, since it takes only individual interests into account. (2) Seen from the perspective of expertise's social function: the second move transforms the expert's obligation towards personal interests into his *obligation to the project*.[49] With this new project-orientation, liability begins to achieve the institutionalisation for which we were searching. Expectations of contractual loyalty with their potential for corrupting independent expertise will be 'translated' into the impersonal, disinterested and objective orientation of expertise. At the same time, expertise is no longer free to escape into the lofty space of a self-sufficient logic of discovery, but the legal bonds of contractual loyalty and the bonds of third party liability tie it firmly down and 'translate' abstract knowledge into the concrete expertise which is needed for the real world project.

To express our result in one quasi-magic formula: *third party liability symbolises the transformation of interest-bound expertise into project-bound expertise*. The existence of this liability is a highly visible threshold that separates two institutions. It draws a line between partisan expertise where knowledge is (legitimately) used for the pursuit of private interests, and independent expertise where knowledge is applied in an disinterested way with in-built controls of reliability and where it is independent from personal loyalty and reciprocity considerations. Expert liability towards a third party marks the boundary between the fields of economic and scientific rationality.

[49] From a different theoretical perspective, the trust relation, Canaris (1999), above n 24, 234ff stresses the project-orientation of expertise as the relevant legal criterion. Again from a different perspective, the special factual relation which shuts the floodgates of infinite expert liability, Picker, above n 16, 440ff, focuses on the project which binds expertise even without a contract.

It should be stressed again that it is not the abstract ideal of scientific inquiry as such, but the close entwinement of both, independent expertise and the concrete project, that lies at the roots of third party liability. 'Project-bound expertise'—this is the institutional *idée directrice*. This idea unfolds along two implicit dimensions of contracting. As such, expertise imports principles of the scientific community that need now to be respected in the contract: disinterestedness, impartiality, independence, orientation on methodical standards, and responsibility toward each participant in the realisation of the project. The details of third party liability—doctrinal construction, scope of beneficiaries, standards, defences and exclusion of liability—however, are to be determined in an institutional perspective, which is informed by the concrete project to which the expertise is under an obligation.

PROJECT-ORIENTED EXPERTISE: SELECTED LEGAL ISSUES

Adequate Doctrinal Construction

To find the adequate doctrinal construction for an institutional liability toward third parties is not an abstract exercise on the *tabula rasa* of sociological jurisprudence; rather it depends on the historical contingencies of how different national legal systems have drawn the fine line between contract and tort in general, which in its turn depends on how they developed the conceptual potential (and/or deficiencies) of several specific doctrines, like implied terms, consideration, contractual privity, *culpa in contrahendo*, third party beneficiary contracts, on the one hand, and special tort relations, duty of care, *respondeat superior*, compensation for pure economic loss, limits of causation, on the other hand.[50] In this context, it has often been mentioned that there is a striking similarity of the criteria for third party liability, whatever the doctrinal construction. These criteria are: the professional position of the expert; the relevance of the information for the third party; the concrete circumstances of the production and communication of the information; foreseeability of the usage of the information by third parties; and the amount of reliance on the information.[51] This is also

[50] See C von Bar, 'Diskussionsbeitrag' in Karlsruher Forum 1998 (ed), *Die Einbeziehung Dritter in den Vertrag* (Karlsruhe, Versicherungswirtschaft, 1999) 105.

[51] H Schneider, 'Reichweite der Expertenhaftung gegenüber Dritten: Die Sicht des Experten' (1999) 163 *Zeitschrift für das gesamte Handelsrecht und Wirtschaftsrecht* 246, 252.

true for the implicit dimension of 'project-bound expertise'. In the inner structures of this private institution we find the conditions of the special relation 'akin to contract' that tort and quasi-tort law is looking for, as well as the famous non-contractual element of contract law.[52]

In legal systems that have opted for a contractual solution, a fierce battle is raging between two camps of legal doctrine. One camp—among them the courts—favour a contract for the benefit of a third party and its doctrinal derivatives. They start with the contract between mandator and expert and extract from its implicit dimensions the liability of the expert toward the third party beneficiary.[53] The other camp—among them eminent scholars—fight for *culpa in contrahendo* liability towards non-contracting partners. They start with the second contract involved, the project contract between the mandator and the beneficiary, and extract from its implicit dimensions a quasi-contractual liability of the expert who is not participating in the contract but is as close to it 'as if' he were a partner.[54]

From our institutional perspective, both are right and both are wrong at the same time. It is right to find the origin of the liability in the 'implicit' dimensions of the expertise contract, although these dimensions are non-contractual. And it is equally right to see an 'implicit' dimension of the project contract, although these dimensions are also non-contractual. But both perspectives are also wrong, since they miss the crucial element of 'binding' the expertise tightly to the project. The key concept to the understanding of third party liability is the interdependence of the two contracts, in our terms, the legal obligation of expertise to the project and vice versa.[55] Thus, for legal systems that are gradually developing a doctrine of 'connected contracts', like *groupe de contrats* in the francophone world, network contract and

[52] I have a certain preference for a contractual solution for expert liability which, I hope, is not exclusively determined by national bias. The main reason is that expert liability is oriented to the performance interest and not to the integrity interest. The beneficiary does not suffer from the realisation of a risk that the expertise entailed for his belongings, rather he suffers from performance risks of a transaction of a valuable good, the information.

[53] The main protagonist is BGH 127, 378—Dachstuhl.

[54] The main protagonist is Canaris (1999), above n 24, 222ff. Cf also J Adolff, *Die zivilrechtliche Verantwortlichkeit deutscher Anwälte bei der Abgabe von Third Party Legal Opinions* (München, Beck, 1996) 118ff; J Neuner, 'Der Schutz und die Haftung Dritter nach vertraglichen Grundsätzen' (1999) 54 *Juristenzeitung* 126, 135.

[55] This is where Picker, above n 16, 432ff identifies the 'special relation' needed for liability for purely economic loss.

connected contract in the Anglo-Saxon world, *Vertragsverbund* in the German speaking countries, the doctrinal foundation that is most adequate to account for the institution of project-bound expertise should indeed lie here.[56] Project-oriented expertise relations would be just another case of a whole variety of contractual networks with more than two actors involved.[57] In these relations, the law regularly discovers implicit dimensions beyond the mere party consensus in bilateral contracts.[58] As a matter of course, in contractual networks quasi-contractual liabilities emerge between parties that have no explicit contractual ties.[59] Obviously, this is a promising perspective for the future. However, at present, only second-best solutions are available in legal doctrine, ie contractual or quasi-contractual constructs, each with their well-known deficiencies.

In my view, a contract for the benefit of a third party is in the end a more adequate analysis of the institutional dimension of project-expertise than is the idea of *culpa in contrahendo* towards third parties. The latter was originally created as a liability of third parties (*Sachwalter*) who are not formally participating in the contract, but who fulfil three conditions: (1) they act within the 'camp' of one of the

[56] For network contracts, JN Adams and R Brownsword, 'Privity and the Concept of a Network Contract' (1990) 10 *Legal Studies* 12; M Rohe, *Netzverträge: Rechtsprobleme komplexer Vertragsverbindungen* (Tübingen, Mohr and Siebeck, 1998). For a general concept of 'connected contracts' which would cut through contract law and company law: MG Gulati, WA Klein, and EM Zolt, 'Connected Contracts' (2000) 47 *University of California Los Angeles Law Review* 887.

[57] Picker, above n 16, 440ff, argues to qualify expertise relations as 'connected contracts' which would be the 'special relation' as basis of liability.

[58] For 'connected contracts' in general Gulati, Klein and Zolt, above n 56, 929f; for *Vertragsverbund* in German law Gernhuber, above n 16, 711; PW Heermann, *Drittfinanzierte Erwerbsgeschäfte: Entwicklung der Rechtsfigur des trilateralen Synallagmas auf der Grundlage deutscher und U.S.-amerikanischer Rechtsentwicklungen* (Tübingen, Mohr Siebeck, 1998): 93; 96ff; 106.

[59] For networks in general, G Teubner, 'Hybrid Laws: Constitutionalizing Private Governance Networks', in RA Kagan, M Krygier and K Winston (eds), *Legality and Community: On the Intellectual Legacy of Philip Selznick* (Berkeley, Public Policy Press, 2002) 311, 325ff. For heterarchical networks Rohe, above n 56, 195ff; for just-in-time networks: KW Lange, *Das Recht der Netzwerke: Moderne Formen der Zusammenarbeit in Produktion und Vertrieb* (Heidelberg, Recht und Wirtschaft, 1998) 195ff; for franchising networks G Teubner, 'Beyond Contract and Organization? The External Liability of Franchising Systems in German Law', in C Joerges (ed), *Franchising and the Law: Theoretical and Comparative Approaches in Europe and the United States* (Baden-Baden, Nomos, 1991) 105, 129ff; AK Baumgarten, *Das Franchising als Gesellschaftsverhältnis: Eine Studie zur spezifischen zivilrechtlichen Qualität des Rechtsverhältnisses zwischen Franchise-Geber und Franchise-Nehmer* (Göttingen, Universität Göttingen, 1993) 169ff.

contracting parties, (2) they themselves have a substantial economic interest in the transaction which makes them 'quasi-parties' to the contract, (3) however, they act in such a way that the other party to the contract has reasons to trust them.[60] Independent experts clearly fulfil the third condition, but they stand in diametrical opposition to the first and second one.[61] Disinterestedness in the economic stakes of either party to the project contract is a necessary precondition of project-bound expertise. Thus, independent experts should not be treated within the same legal category as partisan experts, who are acting in the same camp as the party who furnishes information to the other party. To put both into the same category, as *culpa in contrahendo* suggests, would blur the fundamental legal distinction between partisan expertise and independent expertise. The liability standards of independent experts should not be downgraded to the standards of partisan advice.

There is another reason to prefer the analysis of a contract for the benefit of a third party. If the problem at hand is to reconstruct in law a comprehensive multilateral institution-like project-bound expertise, *culpa in contrahendo* would only arrive at three (or more) bilateral relations that are isolated from each other. Conversely, contracts for the benefit of third parties explicitly open the conceptual space for one overarching legal relation, in which the interdependencies between the project, the expertise and the interests of several actors can be reconstructed, and the rights and duties of all the parties involved can be fine-tuned in relation to each other.[62] Although remaining still a second-best solution, a contract for the benefit of a third party comes closest to the institutional core, the unitary network of three closely interconnected transactions.

[60] Emmerich in K Rebmann, FJ Säcker and R Rixecker (eds), *Münchener Kommentar zum Bürgerlichen Gesetzbuch* (München, Beck, 2001) vor § 275, 172ff. The leading monographs on *Sachwalterhaftung* are A Wiegand, *Die 'Sachwalterhaftung' als richterliche Rechtsfortbildung* (Berlin, Duncker and Humblot, 1991) 30ff; A Henke, *Sachwalterhaftun* (Frankfurt am Main, Lang, 1997) 16ff, 53, 132f.

[61] Canaris (1999), above n 24, 226 downplays the importance of this difference.

[62] Of course, it needs to be stressed that the reduction to consensus of two parties which the term 'third party beneficiary contract' suggests is misleading. It should be replaced by 'third party beneficiary obligation' in order to stress the non-contractual institutional character of the underlying expertise relation which is internalised into the contract via judge-made law.

Scope of Protected Persons

The most difficult concrete problem is to determine which among the persons that are exposed to the risk of the expertise and rely on it for relevant decisions will be entitled to claim as a third party. What are legitimate criteria to determine the scope of protected persons? Several court decisions have applied the criterion of foreseeability of the informational contact between expert and beneficiary-victim.[63] As a consequence, the financial liability of auditors and accountants has expanded to an almost infinite number of investors. Other courts have looked to the degree of exposure to risk, and some have manipulated the doctrine of causation in order to limit the number of protected persons. From our institutional perspective, all three criteria are misplaced. The relevant legal question is not to identify the integrity interest of all those persons who while relying on certain information take risks and suffer loss. Rather, the task is to take account of the specific institutional integrity of expertise. If project-bound expertise is the social institution in which the contract participates, then it is the obligation to the project that defines the limits of responsibility to third persons.[64] Here again, the intertwining of expertise and projecting decides who is entitled to claim. The limits of the project determine the limits of special responsibility for other persons, and not foreseeability of damage, exposure to risk, nor principles of causation. Accordingly, the expert is responsible for the performance of his information transaction exclusively to the participants to the concrete project. Liability to third parties—an implicit dimension of project-bound expertise—is not a general responsibility for the integrity interest of outsiders. As we said above, it is a countervailing device to rectify the asymmetry of contracting. It serves to protect the complex expertise relation against its bilateralisation through contract, but it does not serve as a general insurance against risky transactions that rely on expert information.

[63] For a careful comparative analysis, WF Ebke, 'Abschlussprüferhaftung im internationalen Vergleich' *Festschrift für Reinhold Trinkner* (Heidelberg, Recht und Wirtschaft, 1995) 498ff.

[64] Picker, above n 16, 440ff arrives at the same result from a different starting point. Canaris (1999), above n 24, 234ff who favours a liability based on trust, stresses this point, but admits at the same time that trust as such provides for no criteria and needs to be supplemented by additional criteria. Here is exactly the point where the institution of 'project-bound expertise' comes into play and provides criteria.

Equally misplaced are typical contractual criteria. In order to determine the scope of protected persons, courts again and again search for indicators that refer to the intentions of the parties, subjective knowledge of the destination of the expertise, concrete contacts between expert and beneficiary. These are misleading criteria, insofar as they are supposed to identify the will of the parties to *create an obligation* to the third party. In our institutional perspective, third party liability arises independently of such an explicit or implicit agreements. It emerges even against the will of the parties. The central criterion is: Who participates in the project? One should hasten to add that the concrete circumstances of the three transactions involved do play a role in the determination of who is protected and who not. But there is a fine line to be drawn. These circumstances serve as indicators for the delimitation of the concrete project, but not as indicators for a bilateral agreement with respect to the range of the expert's liability. It is in the hands of the contracting parties to define the scope of information needed for the project-bound expertise, but it is no longer in their hands to determine the subsequent liability to third parties.

Participation in the project as a criterion for the range of liability is easy to apply in the core area when there is a full-fledged project contract for which the expertise is required. Independent expertise for sales, credit arrangements and investment projects are cases in point. Here the scope of protected persons is determined by contractual participation in the project. More difficult to define is a project that does not rely exclusively on contract. An example: after a car accident, the victim pays an independent expert for an assessment of the damage; the person responsible for the accident and her insurance company pay compensation, relying on the correctness of the assessment. In our view it is decisive that the expertise is bound to the concrete project of compensation for the concrete car accident, thus, the expert is liable to three actors: the victim, the person responsible for the accident and to the insurance company.[65] It is not the legal contract, but the economic project, or more generally the social project, that determines the range of protected persons.[66] Project-orientation provides guidance also for auxiliary activities. When a sale of a house is supported partially by a

[65] E Steffen, 'Diskussionsbeitrag' in Karlsruher Forum 1998 (ed), above n 50, 95, 96.

[66] For the generalisation from legal contract to economic project, Canaris (1999), above n 24, 236; Picker, above n 16, 440ff; for the inclusion of projects from different 'contracting worlds' Teubner, above n 11, 402ff.

bank credit and backed up by the guarantee of another actor, all the actors involved, buyer, seller, bank, and guarantor have a claim against the expert in terms of an umpteenth-party beneficiary contract.[67] The project orientation would also include refinancing and insurance activities as covered by the 'real finality' of the expertise.[68]

Difficulties arise when the project changes its character over time. Again an example: the expertise is in the end utilised for a credit transaction instead of a sale of the object.[69] Indeed, here we enter the grey area of a social system's identity. Again, one should not look only to the project as such, but to its interrelation with the expertise and define the limits accordingly. In the change from sale to credit, one would have to draw distinctions. If the requirements for expertise in connection with a sale are different from those required for a credit transaction, then there should be no liability toward the creditor; if they are the same, then the expert should be held liable.

Similar difficulties arise when the group of project participants becomes more or less indeterminate. If there is a clearly defined small group of participants to the project then liability to third parties will cover each of them. The more, however, the group of potential participants moves into the direction of the public at large, the less justified is liability to third parties.[70] Given the public character of disinterested expertise, this may sound somewhat counter-intuitive. But here we reach the institutional limits of private law liability. There are many legal rules that support the neutrality of public expertise, private law liability being one among them. Liability to third parties is adequate for situations where expertise is committed to a project with calculable risks. Thus, it protects the integrity of expertise. But it loses its adequacy when it is employed to support the general production of public knowledge. An incalculable risk of liability would no longer protect but stifle the integrity of expertise. This type of liability to third parties makes sense only in the context of project-bound expertise. For example, a private consumer testing institution cannot be made liable to all

[67] For the extension of expert liability toward the bank who gives a credit for the sale BGH NJW 1987, 1758; for the extension toward a guarantor of the transaction BGH JZ 1998, 627.

[68] Picker, above n 16, 443.

[69] This was the situation in the case BGH NJW 1987, 1758. The court held the expert liable despite the change of project from sale to credit.

[70] Here, the limitation of an indefinite scope of beneficiaries comes in as a legitimate concern of law. For the argument see BGH NJW 1987, 1758, 1760 and particularly Picker, above n 16, 438ff.

potential buyers of the product on the basis of expert liability.[71] In the case of auditors, one should distinguish between two types of liability. If they fulfil their statutory duties of writing the yearly report, their statutory liability towards the enterprise and its affiliates is applicable and should not be expanded via judicial interpretation. If, however, the auditors write a special report at the request of the enterprise in relation to a particular project of investment, credit, or sale, then liability towards a third party may legitimately arise.[72]

Chains of transactions require the use of a similar distinction. If the risk involved in the subsequent transactions is identical, then expert liability applies. If the risk is increased, then the expert is not liable to the subsequent buyers.[73] In all three cases, it is the idea of compensating for contractual bilateralisation that limits the scope of protected persons. The aspects of calculation of risk and its insurability enter legitimately in shaping concretely the institution of project-bound expertise. If the primary aspect of expert liability is to stabilise this private institution, then professional insurance is reinforcing this aim and the limits of insurability are of relevance to the limits of expert liability.

What should be the position with respect to the protection of third parties with antagonistic interests on the other side of a competitive market? Is the architect in our original example to be held responsible to protect the expectations of the buyer and his financial satellites, or should the range of his liability be limited to those persons for whom the seller bears certain responsibilities? This has been a long controversy, particularly for the doctrinal construction of a contract for the benefit of a third party. However, for project-bound expertise, the antagonism of economic interests is as irrelevant as is the existence of a fiduciary relation between mandator and third persons.[74] It is their participation in the project at hand that determines whether the expert should be liable to them, whatever may be their legal relations with the mandator. The existence of cut-throat competition in the market and non-co-operative relations, antagonistic interests, or the absence of any fiduciary element between the parties to the project do not militate

[71] Canaris (1999), above n 24, 238. The monograph by Boecken demonstrates, against its own intentions, the paralysing effects of a liability toward an infinite number of creditors. TH Boecken, *Die Haftung der Stiftung Warentest für Schäden der Verbraucher aufgrund irreführender Testinformationen* (Berlin, Duncker and Humblot, 1998) 120ff.

[72] For this distinction BGH JZ 1998, 101; Canaris (1999), above n 24, 233f.

[73] Hopt (1987), above n 27, 1746; Canaris (1999), above n 24, 211.

[74] BGHZ 127, 378; BGHZ 138, 257. See also P Zumbansen, 'Drittschützende Wirkung eines Anwaltsvertrages und verdeckte Sacheinlage' (2000) 55 *Juristenzeitung* 442, 443.

against expert liability; on the contrary, the very antagonism of interests strengthens the requirement of strictly independent advice and supportive third party liability.

What about the distinction between partisan counsel vs. independent expertise? It should be stressed that partisan counsel in itself is a time-honoured social institution. And it needs a careful 'institutional analysis'[75] in order to determine which set of expectations is required in a concrete social situation.[76] Tax counsels, lawyers and accountants are cases in point. As a rule their advice is partisan advocacy; they exploit professional knowledge legitimately for furthering the interest of their mandator. If their expertise is utilised by the other party, there is no requirement for liability to the third party.[77] However, there exist some exceptional situations where these typically partisan professions take over the role of a neutral expert.[78] A case in point is the recent practice of 'third party legal opinions', where the second partner to the project explicitly asks for a (binding) legal opinion of the first partner's lawyer.[79] There are other situations, eg the so-called 'tax opinions' or 'comfort letters', in which the interrelation of project contract and expertise contract make clear that independent advice of a lawyer, accountant, tax counsel or another partisan expert is required.[80]

Another fascinating situation is the case of politically biased research institutions when they are asked to provide expertise on concrete projects. Again, the contract between expert and mandator does not furnish criteria for responsibility. Rather the criteria should be determined by the broader institutional context of function/contribution/reflection. At first glance, this seems to be a classical case for project-bound liability

[75] For the concept of institutional analysis and its methods, P Selznick, *Law, Society and Industrial Justice* (New York, Russell Sage, 1969) 35ff; Selznick, above n 28, 229ff.

[76] Cf the criterion of the expertise's function in the concrete situation, Canaris (1999), above n 24, 233.

[77] This was the situation in a case where the third party was influenced by partisan expertise for the mandator in settlement negotiations, BGH WM 1962, 933. The courts are also reluctant to create the fiction of a 'silent' agreement between a lawyer and third persons to whom he gives information, BGH WM 1978, 576; BGH NJW 1991, 32.

[78] This is especially true when they give advice in investment projects, BGHZ 74, 103; BGHZ 100, 117; BGHZ 116, 209; BGHZ 123, 126. Then expert liability towards third parties becomes the rule.

[79] See M Gruson, S Hutter, and M Kutschera, *Legal Opinions in International Transactions* (London, Kluwer, 1997); for German law, Adolff, above n 54.

[80] B Grunewald, 'Die Haftung des Experten für seine Expertise gegenüber Dritten' (1987) 187 *Archiv für die civilistische Praxis* 285, 301; Adolff, above n 54, 122ff; Neuner, above n 54, 135.

towards a third party. And the closer research institutions are to governmental institutions (subsidies, public role), the stronger the argument for holding them liable. However, there is a case to be made for the virtue of partisan advice here. Consider an example of 'People's Institute of Mother Gaia Autopoiesis', which is financially supported by members of the ecological movement. If their advice is sought in a legal and/or political controversy on ecological issues where both parties present scientific evidence to corroborate their claims, their expertise is part of an adversary institution of truth-seeking. In such a context, they are supposed to deliver advocacy expertise, and liability towards a third party would be a threat to their necessarily partisan, one-sided, interest-bound inquiry. And the argument for advocacy expertise—exploiting any knowledge available to drive an explicitly one-sided partisan view to its limits—will be stronger than that for independence, disinterestedness and neutrality.

Exclusion of Liability and Contractual Defences

This is the Achilles' heel of contractual doctrines, particularly of a contract for the benefit of a third party beneficiary.[81] *Nemo potest transferre* provides the argument for exposing the third party to all the defences that the expert could raise against the mandator. It is especially true for exclusion of liability. The third party cannot have more rights than the mandator, that is what logic dictates. The results are rather strange. In cases where expert liability toward third parties is most urgently needed, it becomes dependent upon the collusion of mandator and expert. The courts try to avoid (some of) these undesirable results by inventing just another contractual fiction: not only do they base expert liability on the fiction of the parties' implicit intention to expand the range of liability to the third party, now they create a second fiction according to which the expert implicitly agrees not to raise contractual defences against the third party.[82]

The weak spot of this analysis vanishes once an institutional perspective is taken. As soon as implicit dimensions are no longer interpreted as referring either to the parties' intentions or to their wider relation, but as referring to those economic and social institutions in

[81] Canaris (1995), above n 24, 444f; Canaris (1999), above n 24, 216ff.
[82] BGH 127,378,385; BGH JZ 1998, 624, 625.

which their contract participates, then third party liability is no longer a derivative liability of a bilateral contract but an original liability of a trilateral nature arising from the relation between the expert and his clients. This liability need not be derived from the mandators' rights and duties. It is not exposed to the defences that the expert could raise against the mandator.[83] It cannot be influenced by their contractual exclusions of liability.[84] Rather, liability towards the third party, which has its roots in the expert's membership in the scientific community, is a direct responsibility to the third party.[85] It comes into life at the moment when the contract between mandator and expert enters the private institution.

[83] This is the dominant opinion independent of the particular construction, see particularly BGH 127, 378—Dachstuhl.

[84] Minority opinion: Esser and Schmidt, above n 16, § 34 IV 2c. The dominant opinion allows exclusion of liability: Gernhuber, above n 16, 533f; Canaris (1999), above n 24, 230f; Schneider, above n 51, 273.

[85] Esser and Schmidt, above n 16, § 34 IV 2c.

12

*Implicit Dimensions of Contract and the Oppression of Minority Shareholders**

CHRISTOPHER RILEY

INTRODUCTION

MUCH CONTEMPORARY LITERATURE on companies emphasises their contractual basis. From this, influential, perspective companies are properly understood as a 'nexus' of both explicit and implicit contracts between shareholders, creditors, employees, suppliers, consumers and so on.[1] Intra-corporate relationships, then, seem to offer a potentially rich terrain for examining the implicit dimensions of contract. The focus in this chapter is upon one particular set of corporate contracts, namely those between shareholders in small, private companies. Company law in the UK has long struggled to develop an appropriate regulatory approach to these relationships. And its difficulties have been thrown into sharp relief by the introduction, and popularity, of a statutory remedy against 'unfair prejudice'.[2] This

* Thanks to David Campbell, and to other participants at the 'Implicit Dimensions of Contract' seminar for comments on an earlier version of this paper. The usual disclaimer applies.

[1] The contractarian literature on firms, corporations and corporate law, has become too voluminous to cite in full. We can follow Michael Klausner, 'Corporate Law and Networks of Contracts' (1995) 81 *Virginia Law Review* 757, 759, n 1 by citing Barry Adler's 'Finance's Theoretical Divide and the Proper Role of Insolvency Rules' (1994) 67 *Southern California Law Review* 1107, 1108 n 1 for 'lists of articles that list other articles'.

[2] ss 459–61 of the Companies Act 1985. Under s 459, a member is entitled to relief where 'the company's affairs are being or have been conducted in a manner which is unfairly prejudicial to the interests of its members generally or some part of its members . . .' s 461 sets out the (wide) range of remedies that the court can order. The remedy is not restricted to minority shareholders, but the overwhelming majority of petitioners have been such.

remedy is now the basis of a substantial proportion of the civil litigation within companies.[3] Reflecting this practical importance, it has enjoyed considerable academic comment, where the interplay between the remedy and the parties' contractual relationship has been a recurrent theme.[4]

This chapter examines two competing explanatory accounts of the nature of inter-shareholder contractual relationships, and two related prescriptions for their regulation. The first account emphasises the importance of social context, and in particular of the embeddedness of contracting in social relations. The second is essentially economic, emphasising the rational pursuit of 'self-interest' (with a nod to trust and reputation) as the motivational driving force behind our contractual practices.

These competing accounts of shareholder contracting are then used to explore the developing jurisprudence surrounding the unfair prejudice regime. It suggests that we might identify three phases therein. In the first phase, which predates the introduction of that regime, courts tend to privilege majority rule and thereby seek to marginalise implicit dimensions of the parties' relationship. The second phase follows the introduction of the unfair prejudice regime itself. It sees a much more interventionist judicial practice, ready to discover and give effect to the parties' informal agreements, and to supplement (and constrain) their contracts by reference to implicit terms. The third phase marks a judicial retreat to a 'middle ground', in which informal understandings are recognised, but courts are otherwise discouraged from delving too far into implicit dimensions. Some generalised implicit expectations, however, are effectively raised to the status of 'default rules', applicable to

[3] For some (now slightly dated) statistics on the filing of s 459 petitions, see Law Commission Consultation Paper No 142, *Shareholder Remedies* (London, The Stationery Office, 1996), Appendix E.

[4] See eg D Prentice, 'The Theory of the Firm: Minority Shareholder Oppression: Sections 459–461 of the Companies Act 1985' (1988) 8 *Oxford Journal of Legal Studies* 55; M Clark, 'Unfair Prejudice and the Corporate Quasi-Partnership' (1989) 10 *The Company Lawyer* 153; CARiley, 'Contracting out of Company Law: Section 459 of the Companies Act 1985 and the Role of the Courts' (1992) 55 *Modern Law Review* 782; BRCheffins, *Company Law: Theory, Structure and Operation* (Oxford, Clarendon Press, 1997) esp chs 6 and 10; R Goddard, 'Enforcing the Hypothetical Bargain: Sections 459–461 of the Companies Act 1985 (1999) 20 *The Company Lawyer* 66. As to other jurisdictions, see SK Miller, 'Minority Shareholder Oppression in the Private Company in the European Community: A Comparative Analysis of the German, United Kingdom, and French "Close Corporation Problem" ' (1997) 30 *Cornell International Law Journal* 381; SK Miller, 'How Should UK and US Minority Shareholder Remedies for Unfairly Prejudicial or Oppressive Conduct be Reformed?' (1999) 36 *American Business Law Journal* 579.

inter-shareholder relationships in smaller companies unless otherwise excluded.

The chapter concludes by arguing, tentatively, that this judicial retreat might best be explained by reference to the economic account of inter-shareholder contracting. Formal economic analysis is, predictably, usually absent from the courts' reasoning. However, it may be that more robust economic analysis would indeed support—as efficient—the sort of position that the courts now seem to have arrived at.

THE CONTRACTUAL LANDSCAPE IN SMALL, PRIVATE COMPANIES

Small companies are distinguishable from large ones on a variety of axes. One is the level of their turnover and likely profits. Another—more relevant to the present enquiry—is the number of, and relationship between, their shareholders. Small companies typically have just a handful of shareholders, who will also be the company's directors. And between these shareholders there will often be a clear division between those who own a minority, and those who own a majority, of the company's shares.[5]

Disputes within such companies tend to arise along this majority—minority fault line.[6] The minority becomes unhappy about the way the company is being controlled by the majority. She may complain that she has been forced out of any active role in management (probably having been removed as a director, and finding that her minority shareholding gives her little say in company affairs).[7] To make matters worse, she now receives little income from the company, its profits being either reinvested or paid out as salary to the remaining directors. Finally, she may be unhappy about some of the managerial decisions being taken in her absence, alleging, say, that these are incompetent, or designed to divert profits into others' pockets.

What contractual arrangements are we likely to find in small companies? First, there will be some express, and relatively formal, agreements. Most familiar are the company's constitutional documents—its

[5] Sometimes, there may be a single shareholder with effective control, other times several members may form a cohesive, and controlling, group.

[6] Contrast the larger company, where the conflict is typically seen as between, on the one hand, the executives and, on the other, the shareholders as a group.

[7] *Ebrahimi v Westbourne Galleries Ltd* [1973] AC 360 provides a classic example of this 'squeeze out' of the minority by the majority shareholders.

memorandum and articles of association. These may be bespoke documents, expressly negotiated by the shareholders with the advice of lawyers. Or, rather more likely, they may follow standard precedents, such as the lawyers' or company formation agents' own office standards,[8] or the *pro forma* articles of Table A.[9] Nevertheless, section 14 of the Companies Act 1985 declares that the memorandum and articles 'when registered, bind the company and its members to the same extent as if they respectively had been signed and sealed by each member . . .'. Beyond the memorandum and articles, there may be other formal 'shareholder agreements' that give minority shareholders additional protected rights within the company. Finally, if shareholders are also to act as directors, service contracts may be entered into.

The Inevitability of Contractual Incompleteness

Whilst these formal agreements are likely to be expansive, still they cannot realistically constitute a set of 'complete contingent claims contracts' dealing with the shareholders' rights and liabilities in *all* future states of the world. This inevitable incompleteness arises for a number of reasons. First, no contract can logically provide complete definitions of its every term.[10] Secondly, it seems likely to be impossible, and certainly economically impractical, for shareholders to spell out all the assumptions they hold relative to the contract into which they are entering. Thirdly, the parties cannot foresee all the 'future states of the world'—all those events that will actually come to pass. Nor, realistically, can they envisage all possible future states of the world and their relative probabilities. They cannot therefore spell out what the obligations of the parties would be in each of these possible future states. And, even if they could envisage them all, it would hardly be economical to contract around

[8] See for example *The Encyclopaedia of Forms and Precedents*, 5th edn (London, Butterworths, 1994) Part 3.

[9] The Companies (Tables A to F) Regulations 1985 (SI 1985/805).

[10] As Charny observes, 'no text can completely specify its own means of interpretation. A contractual statement that purported to be such a complete specification would itself have to be interpreted by some set of rules of interpretation. If the text purported to supply those rules, then those rules would have to be interpreted, and so on, ad infinitum.' D Charny, 'Hypothetical Bargains: The Normative Structure of Contract Interpretation' (1991) 89 *Michigan Law Review* 1815, 1819.

them expressly in this way. Some may be judged possible, but so unlikely as not to warrant contracting around.[11]

One response to these difficulties is 'contractual informality'. It costs time and money to record agreements in the formal constitutional and extra-constitutional documentation described above. Shareholders might, then, agree much between themselves that remains outside these formal contracts. It may be agreed, for example, that all shareholders will have a right to participate in management, or that a certain level of income will be payable to shareholders, yet these shared understandings remain outside the written documents of the company.

A second response to contractual incompleteness is to allow the contract itself to change and develop over time. Instead of being cast in stone at the outset of the relationship, the parties take it as an organic, ongoing set of obligations which are modified and extended as circumstances change. Many of the cases dealing with the 'unfair prejudice' regime evidence just this sort of rich, ongoing, but informal, contracting.[12] Yet the corporate constitution embraces this sort of dynamic approach by creating its own machinery for contractual gap filling and contractual change in response to new contingencies. So, agents (directors) are appointed to run the company, with substantial authority to determine its future direction and policy. And the machinery of 'majority rule' is created to permit shareholders to fill gaps in the constitutional contract (or, in some cases, to alter the contract itself).[13] As a result, the formal contractual structure of private companies typically gives each shareholder a right to participate in majoritarian decision-making, but otherwise few rights individually to direct how the company, or fellow shareholders, shall behave.

Therein, or course, lies the danger for minorities. Majorities may use the power that majority rule gives them to act in opportunistic ways, taking decisions that promote their (the majority's), but not the minority's, interests. This risk of majoritarian opportunism[14] is exacerbated,

[11] For a useful discussion of these problems in the corporate context, see I MacNeil, 'Company Law Rules: An Assessment from the Perspective of Incomplete Contract Theory' (2001) 1 *Journal of Corporate Law Studies* 107 esp 112–17.

[12] For a discussion of some of the earlier case law, see Riley, n 4 above, 792–94.

[13] In particular, under s 9 of the Companies Act 1985, shareholders can, by special resolution alter the articles.

[14] Note that, insofar as contractual rights are given to minority shareholders, the problem of minority opportunism might arise. Thus, minorities might use their rights to block changes that the majority would not, with greater foresight, have agreed fell within the ambit of the contractual right. See SK Miller, ' How Should . . .', n 4 above.

moreover, by the problem of 'lock-in' that minority members typically face. A minority shareholder who wishes to escape from the behaviour of the majority by selling her shares will likely find there is little market for them. She will be able to sell only, if at all, by accepting a large discount on the pro-rata valuation of her shareholding.[15]

Implicit Terms: Four Meanings

Beyond the contractual landmarks described above, we now begin to move more clearly into the territory of *implicit* contracts or terms. However, this idea of the 'implicit' is a broad one, and we might usefully distinguish amongst at least four different meanings thereof. First, there might be understandings that are *articulated* and *shared* but that, unlike legal contracts, are *not* intended to confer rights enforceable by law. So, a majority shareholder might agree that a minority shareholder may have a seat on the board, or that she (the majority shareholder) will buy the other's shares if their relationship breaks down. But it might also be understood that legal sanctions will not follow if she fails to honour her agreement. There is, then, an appeal to trust and an acceptance only of non-legal sanctions (such as loss of reputation or loss of future co-operation) if the agreement is not honoured. This seems to be the sense in which 'implicit contracts' is often used in the economic literature and, in particular, in labour economics.[16]

Second, there may be what Barnett refers to as shared *tacit* assumptions. Again, because these assumptions are *shared*, there is intersubjective agreement between the parties. However, these are assumptions that the parties do not articulate, and may not be consciously addressing at the moment of agreement.[17] All shareholders might assume, for example, that all will be entitled to an equal say in the company's management. This is something they had each, at some

[15] Ie on the valuation that would be arrived at by multiplying the total net value of the company as a whole by the proportion of the shares the minority owns.

[16] For a brief discussion of these in relation to labour economics, see MA Eisenberg, 'The Structure of Corporation Law' (1989) 89 *Columbia Law Review* 1461, 1487.

[17] See RE Barnett, 'The Sound of Silence: Default Rules and Contractual Consent' (1992) 78 *Virginia Law Review* 821.

point, consciously thought about. However, none expressed the point, perhaps because all thought it too obvious to need stating.[18]

Third, different shareholders may have different, and conflicting, expectations. A minority shareholder may understand that, in return for her investment, she will be entitled to remain a director, or at least that other shareholders will acquire her shares at a fair price if they are no longer prepared to permit her a seat on the board. The other shareholders, by contrast, might understand that she is to be merely a sleeping investor, locked into the company with no rights to participate in management. Now, these various and conflicting understandings may be more, or less, reflective of *conventionalist* understandings of the meaning to be attributed to the parties' contractual language/conduct, and conventionalist understandings of how the parties ought to behave during their contractual relationship. It might, for example, now be commonly accepted amongst shareholders in small companies that members are entitled to participate in the management of the company, or at least to have their shares purchased from them if such participation is denied. A shareholder who holds that expectation in any particular small company will be closer to the conventionalist understanding of the appropriate behaviour of shareholders.

Fourth, intertwined with the above we have the body of legal rules that will be implied into the parties' contracts. Some of these rules may be mandatory. Others will operate as 'default rules' that are implied unless they have been expressly excluded.[19] It is tempting to describe these as part of the parties' implicit bargain. However, we need to draw a distinction within such terms. On the one hand, terms might be implied in an effort to capture just those implicit elements *already* discussed above. So, terms might be implied in order to give effect to the parties' *tacit* assumptions—assumptions that the parties *share*, but do not articulate. Or terms might be implied to capture those expectations that reflect conventionalist norms and linguistic usage. In such cases,

[18] In UK contract law, the 'officious bystander' test might be seen as concerned with such understandings. See, for example, *Chitty on Contract*, 28th edn (London, Sweet & Maxwell, 1999) vol 1, paras 13-004–13-007; *Shirlaw v Southern Foundries (1926) Ltd* [1939] 2 KB 206. Crucially, if the courts were to recognise such agreements, its justification for so doing would not be the reasonableness of one party's expectation, in the face of a contrary expectation by other parties. It would be precisely the consensus (albeit unarticulated) between the parties.

[19] Note, however, that express exclusion might be rendered difficult if courts raise a strong presumption that parties did not intend to exclude implied terms. See CJ Goetz and RE Scott, 'The Limits of Expanded Choice: An Analysis of the Interactions Between Express and Implied Contract Terms' (1985) 73 *California Law Review* 261.

these implied terms are an implicit part of the parties' agreement in just the same sense as the underlying expectations—tacit or conventionalist—can be described as implicit.

On the other hand, terms might be implied for some reason other than to catch what is already (prior to the law's intervention) an implicit element of the parties' agreement. Take, for example, the implied duty of care and skill owed by a company director. This has recently been subject to some refinement and extension by the courts, as they have sought to give the duty a more 'objective' content. It is possible—perhaps likely—that in so doing the courts were aiming not to capture, say, prevalent expectations within the parties' community, but were instead driven by some consequentialist judicial reasoning about the economic benefits of a more demanding duty. Now, an implied term based on such consequentialist reasoning cannot claim merely to reflect what is already implicit in the parties' agreement. To be sure, once such an implied term has *been* promulgated, we might then say such a term becomes 'implicit' in the parties' agreement just in virtue of its 'default' status. But they are implicit in a very particular sense: parties contract against them, and are bound by them unless they trouble themselves to avoid them. Their silence in the face of some such terms may or may not indicate their awareness of them, or their willingness to be bound by them.

TWO ACCOUNTS OF CONTRACTING

In this section, we consider two competing explanations for the pattern of inter-shareholder contracting in small companies. Note that what these accounts seek to explain is the contracting practices of shareholders. We are not—yet—concerned to explain, nor to evaluate, the law's response to those practices.

The first account is economic in method. It starts from the assumption that contracting parties act 'rationally'. Rationality here is conceived of in an instrumental sense—action that is calculated to pursue the parties' self-interest, meaning essentially to maximise their future expected utility (or, in some versions, the satisfaction of their preferences).[20] We should, then, understand the contractual relationships

[20] S Hargreaves Heap, M Hollis, B Lyons, R Sugden and A Weale, *The Theory of Choice: A Critical Guide* (Oxford, Blackwell Publishers, 1992) ch 1; JL Schroeder, 'Rationality in Law and Economics Scholarship' (2000) 79 *University of Oregon Law Review* 147.

that parties enter into, and the governance structures they thereby create to regulate their future affairs, as rational in this sense.[21] The form of companies' constitutions, the problems of contractual incompleteness, the reliance on open-ended terms and so on are all to be explained by reference to the pursuit of self-interest in the context of the conditions—transaction costs, bounded rationality and the like—against which contracting must take place. As Easterbrook and Fischel argue,

> it is a mistake to conclude that shareholders in closely held corporations face unique risks of oppression . . . Each organizational form presents its own problems, for which people have designed different mechanisms of control.[22]

Besides explaining the initial contracting process which shareholders undertake, the economic account also offers an explanation for the parties' subsequent, *intra*-contractual, behaviour. As we have seen, contractual relationships between shareholders are characterised by incompleteness, and by reliance upon managerial authority and majority rule to fill the gaps inevitably left in the parties' contracts. This leaves the minority open to the danger of majority oppression, where the majority opportunistically exploit the minority's lack of contractual protection. We might expect to see, then, fairly widespread oppression of minorities, as well as a pervasive reluctance to become a minority shareholder in the first place. Yet, we know that in the United Kingdom there are almost a million private companies, and in many of those companies shareholders have, presumably, accepted these great risks. And whilst sometimes majority shareholders do undoubtedly act in oppressive ways, there are very many more companies where reasonable harmony is preserved and the majority forego the chance to act opportunistically. Perhaps a consequence of our lawyerly preoccupation with litigation is that we focus on the few icebergs of shareholder disputes, ignoring the vast and relatively calm ocean of shareholder co-operation. This co-operation, however, then seems deeply problematic for the economic account of inter-shareholder contracting, for it suggests a widespread failure to act as self-interest recommends.

The economic account, in response, offers a number of reasons why, just out of self-interest, majority shareholders do indeed choose not to

[21] See, for example, OE Williamson, *The Mechanisms of Governance* (New York, OUP, 1996).

[22] FH Easterbrook and DR Fischel, *The Economic Structure of Corporate Law* (Cambridge, Mass, Harvard University Press, 1991) 231.

exploit their minority fellows. For one thing, since the law itself gives some protection to minorities, perhaps majority shareholders prudently forego oppressive behaviour out of fear of the legal consequences of doing otherwise. For another, much is made of the role played by reputation in convincing economic agents that it is in their own prudential self-interest to treat others well. Majority shareholders may calculate that if they exploit the minority today, tomorrow they will suffer as they lose their trust and co-operation. And minority shareholders, seeing how majorities have good prudential reasons to treat them well, are prepared to trust majorities even where their own self-interest initially urged caution. In this economic way, then, the apparent trustworthiness of majority shareholders, and the apparent co-operativeness of minority shareholders, form a virtuous circle that can still be explained by self-interest.[23]

Although the economic account, and the concept of self-interest on which it builds, goes some way towards explaining shareholders' contractual practices, it does not, I think, wholly succeed.[24] There must be something stronger than the glue of self-interest to hold contractual relationships together. As Durkheim put it, '[t]here is nothing less constant than interest. Today, it unites me to you; tomorrow, it will make me your enemy. Such a cause can only give rise to transient relations and passing associations.'[25] Reputation, on which the economic account relies so heavily to explain why some may choose to act co-operatively, and others then find them trustworthy, cannot plausibly bear the weight of this explanation. To put the point very briefly, to be concerned about establishing a 'good reputation' must entail being concerned to have a reputation as someone other than a self-interested economic agent. One must, logically, be concerned to establish a reputation as someone who acts in a trustworthy way without calculating

[23] For a good account of this 'self-interested' notion of trust, see B Lyons and J Mehta, 'Contracts, Opportunism and Trust: Self-interest and Social Orientation' (1997) 21 *Cambridge Journal of Economics* 239. Williamson has argued that, given this economic account of trust, we ought to stick with the terminology of calculation and risk, and avoid the confusion brought by talking in terms of 'trust': 'calculative relations should be described in calculative terms, to which the language of risk is exactly suited.' See OE Williamson, 'Calculativeness, Trust, and Economic Organization' (1993) 36 *Journal of Law and Economics* 453, 485–6.

[24] For a recent compelling critique of the attempt to ground trust in economic self-interest, see M Hollis, *Trust Within Reason* (Cambridge, Cambridge University Press, 1998).

[25] E Durkheim, *The Division of Labour in Society* (London, Macmillan, 1984, first pub 1893).

whether it is in one's self-interest so to act. Now, the economic account might seek to maintain its assumption of self-interest by claiming that agents are merely *pretending* to be genuinely co-operative, in order to reap the benefits such a pretence will deliver, whilst in reality remaining entirely self-interested. But this looks quite implausible, for in a world in which everyone is (presumably known to be) entirely self-interested, it seems unlikely that anyone would ever be fooled by others' attempts to build a trustworthy reputation. It must then be that if reputations for being trustworthy work, they do so because there really are people around who *are* trustworthy.

What the economic account underplays in its explanation of shareholders' contractual practices, and the part played therein by trust and co-operation, is the *social context* within which contracting is itself embedded.[26] This emphasis on social context, which characterises our second account of inter-shareholder contracting, is prominent within 'economic sociology',[27] and central to much of the 'relational contract' literature.[28]

When parties come together to form contractual relationships, they do so as individuals who are already members of a variety of communities. These communities are the source of norms about how their members ought to behave, including how they ought to behave in their contractual relationships with others. They offer, as Collins has argued, 'a distinct normative order, which in many respects exists prior to the contractual relation and establishes a different point of reference for behaviour.'[29] The economic account asks us to imagine contracting between asocial agents who come together with a set of preferences and a desire to agree to whatever terms will maximise their satisfaction. The social account, by contrast, assumes that the terms that parties actually agree are likely to bear the heavy imprint of these social norms.

[26] See M Granovetter, 'Economic Action and Social Structure: The Problem of Embeddedness' (1985) 91 *American Journal of Sociology* 481.

[27] See, for example, NJ Smelser, *The Sociology of Economic Life* 2nd edn (New Jersey, Prentice-Hall, 1976) esp ch 4; NJ Smelser and R Swedburg (eds) *The Handbook of Economic Sociology* (Princeton, NJ, Princeton University Press, 1994).

[28] IR Macneil, *The New Social Contract* (New Haven, Yale University Press, 1980). On economic analysis of relational contracting, see CJ Goetz and RE Scott, 'Principles of Relational Contracts' (1981) 67 *Virginia Law Review* 1089; A Schwartz, 'Relational Contracts in the Courts: An Analysis of Incomplete Agreements and Judicial Strategies' (1992) 21 *Journal of Legal Studies* 271.

[29] H Collins, 'Competing Norms of Contractual Behaviour', in D Campbell and P Vincent-Jones (eds) *Contract and Economic Organisation* (Aldershot, Dartmouth Publishing Co, 1996).

Shareholders may agree that all investors should have a right to participate in management, or to receive as income some proportion of company profits, because these are commonly accepted as fair ways to run small companies. Equally, when disputes arise *within* the contractual relationship, shareholders are likely in part to appeal to, and play by, these norms, rather than just by some prudential calculation of their own expected future utility.

Several further points deserve emphasis. First, the communities to which the parties simultaneously belong, and which will constitute sources of norms, will be manifold. So, to be sure they may be members of the same civil society, having internalised a 'generalised morality', encompassing norms against fraud and deceit, in favour of the keeping of one's promises, and so on. They may also both be members of the same ethnic or religious group within that society, or, as is common in small companies, have shared family ties.[30] Further, and as the literature on relational contracting stresses,[31] the contractual relationship can itself mature and become an independent source of norms.[32] Of course, company law itself provides machinery for shareholders to generate new terms through majority rule. But their maturing relationship offers a richer source of normative expectations than the formal resolutions generated by the company's decision-making organs might ever capture—expectations grounded in the 'performance practices formed among the parties throughout their interaction'.[33] Secondly, there is likely to be some tension between the different norms emanating from these various sources, a tension the agents will be actively engaged in resolving as they seek to determine the proper application of compet-

[30] On the interplay between ethnic/religious groups and business sectors in the creation of commercial norms, see H Collins, *Regulating Contracts* (Oxford, OUP, 1999) 110–111.

[31] See, for example, S Macaulay, 'Non-Contractual Relations in Business' (1963) 45 *American Sociological Rev.* 28, H Beale and T Dugdale, 'Contracts Between Businessmen: Planning and the Use of Contractual Remedies' (1975) *British Journal of Law and Society* 45; IR Macneil, 'Contracts: Adjustment of Long-term Economic Relations under Classical, Neoclassical, and Relational Contract Law' (1978) 72 *Northwestern University Law Review* 854, esp 886ff; Collins, n 30 above, esp chs 5–7.

[32] Schwartz draws a distinction within relational contract theory between its proponents who urge courts to rely on 'norms that transcend the relationship: judges should be guided by society's sense of what is fair, distributionally just, and adequately participatory' and those who urge an 'internal' approach under which 'courts should derive rules from "the norms of the relationship".' Schwartz, n 28 above, 275.

[33] O Ben-Shahar, 'The Tentative Case Against Flexibility in Commercial Law' (1999) 66 *University of Chicago Law Review* 781.

ing norms to the situation now before them.[34] Third, it is not being claimed here that this normative framework precludes all self-interested calculation. For one thing, some more recent empirical research has properly warned against too ready an invocation of unambiguous commercial norms.[35] Further, norms of 'co-operation' are likely to be contingent on the circumstances under which they operate, and limited in the co-operative behaviour they demand. They are likely, perhaps, to require a rather more modest form of co-operation than the subjugation by each party of her individual interest to the parties' joint interests.[36]

HOW SHOULD COURTS REGULATE THE INTER-SHAREHOLDER RELATIONSHIP?

The two competing explanations for shareholders' contractual relationships set out in the preceding section suggest two competing prescriptions for how courts *ought* to deal with inter-shareholder disputes. Begin with the socialised account of contractual behaviour. Social context not only helps to explain why parties make the deals they do, but should also guide courts in their adjudication of contractual disputes. On the one hand, social context helps the court to interpret the parties' own contractual language. Courts should have regard to the linguistic conventions of the parties' community to interpret what the parties say and do. A nod signifies consent. A baker's dozen means 13. And so on.

We might just pause here to relate this to the 'objective' approach to contract interpretation. It is trite law that in an objective approach we are concerned not with what a contracting party actually, subjectively, understood (that a cat is a large grey mammal with a huge proboscis

[34] Granovetter, for example, warned against the dangers of an 'over-socialised' account of economic action, seeking to downplay the significance of generalised morality in guiding our actions, and 'stresses instead the role of concrete personal relations in generating trust and discouraging malfeasance.' Granovetter, n 26 above, 490.

[35] L Bernstein, 'Merchant Law in a Merchant Court: Rethinking the Code's Search for Immanent Business Norms' (1996) 144 *University of Pennsylvania Law Review* 1765; L Bernstein, 'The Questionable Empirical Basis of Article 2's Incorporation Strategy: A Preliminary Study' (1999) 66 *University of Chicago Law Review* 710; R Craswell, 'Do Trade Customs Exist?', in J Krauss and S Walt (eds) *The Jurisprudence of Corporate and Commercial Law* (Cambridge, Cambridge University Press, 2000).

[36] But compare D Campbell and D Harris, 'Flexibility in Long-term Contractual Relationships: The Role of Co-operation' (1993) 20 *Journal of Law and Society* 166.

and an astonishing memory) but with the 'objective' meaning of cat. However, *within* this objective approach, there remains a choice about whether we take the 'plain meaning' of the language used, or whether, and to what extent, we contextualise meanings by reference to the understandings of the particular community to which the parties belong. References to 'cats' in a contract between parties in the motor-industry might have a particular local meaning quite different from the wider, plain meaning of that term.

Besides interpreting what the parties have actually agreed, social context should also, on this account, guide the court in filling apparent gaps left within their agreement. Where their agreement is silent, courts should give effect to parties' *reasonable* expectations. And the reasonableness of such expectations is determined by their fit with the norms that make up the social practice of contracting.[37] Of course, this is now a normative argument. The point is no longer just that contractors often *do choose* to act in accordance with such norms. It is that the law should *require* them to do so. Why? Several arguments can be advanced for so doing.[38] Barnett, for example, urges recourse to conventionalist rules because these will 'bridge the gap' between the objective and subjective interpretations of their agreement.[39] A second argument is based on the idea of reciprocity,[40] and in particular that where one has (voluntarily) received the benefits of an institution or social practice, then so too must one bear its burdens (as defined by the rules of that institution). A third argument is typically expressed in terms of the 'reasonableness' of the expectations of those parties (call them 'majority parties') who expect society's norms to be followed. And a fourth points to the likely beneficial economic consequences—in terms of the trust and co-operation we thereby foster—if courts do indeed enforce the conventionalist way of doing business in the parties' community.

When a court is called upon to resolve a dispute between shareholders in a small company, then, the court might begin with the parties' own express terms, set out in the formal contractual documentation

[37] See, for example, JM Feinman, 'Relational Contract and Default Rules' (1993) 3 *Southern California Interdisciplinary Law Journal* 43, 57.

[38] For a fuller account of the arguments here, see CA Riley, 'Designing Default Rules in Contract Law: Consent, Conventionalism, and Efficiency' (2000) 20 *Oxford Journal of Legal Studies* 367, 377–82.

[39] See Barnett, n 17 above.

[40] J Rawls, *A Theory of Justice*, rev edn (Cambridge, Mass, Harvard University Press, 1999) 88.

alluded to above—the corporate constitution, any supplementary shareholders' agreement, service contracts with directors, and so on. This, however, marks only the start of the court's enquiry. For the court is sensitive to the likelihood that the parties may have entered into other, less formal agreements or commitments at the outset, or during the currency, of their relationship. And the court might embark upon a careful, and possibly protracted, investigation into the history of that relationship in order to discover these informal understandings. But the court should go further still. The court should be ready to hold the parties to conventionalist norms where these have not been clearly excluded by the parties' express agreement. These might include fairly specific, but commonplace, expectations—say about participation in management by shareholders or the payment of dividends where profits are available—through to more abstract norms—about honest dealing, some requirement of co-operation and good faith, and the like.

The Economic Prescription

Compare, now, the economic prescription for the regulation of inter-shareholder disputes. From an economic perspective, it is much less apparent that such an adjudicative approach, with its detailed investigation into the relational context of the parties' deal, is appropriate. On the economic account, courts should interpret and enforce contracts by reference to a body of rules that will promote *efficiency* (in the sense, say, of maximising the parties' joint wealth, or social welfare).[41] What sort of rules does this warrant in the particular context of inter-shareholder contracting? A starting point is an apparently strong commitment to freedom of contract—to upholding whatever agreements the parties expressly make. Those who become shareholders in a small company choose to do so, and are aware, to some degree, of the risks that they will face. As a result, the governance schemes they expressly contract for are likely to be ones that maximise their joint wealth. If they did not, then it would be in the parties' shared interests to choose some other constitutional arrangement that created more value. To be

[41] The notion of 'efficiency', so central to economic analysis, is itself complex. For a useful recent discussion thereof, see LA Kornhauser, 'Constrained Optimization: Corporate Law and the Maximization of Social Welfare', in JS Kraus and SD Walt (eds) *The Jurisprudential Foundations of Corporate and Commercial Law* (Cambridge, Cambridge University Press, 2000) esp 89–112.

sure, the parties may sometimes err, failing to appreciate the severity of the problems they face or misunderstanding the degree of protection their contractual regime will provide. However, the courts should be slow indeed to overrule what the parties have agreed. As Easterbrook and Fischel put it,

> [p]ersons who wager with their own money *may* be wrong, but they are less likely to be wrong than are academics and regulators, who are wagering with other peoples' money.[42]

This apparent commitment to enforcing the parties' express deal is often seen as the cornerstone of the economic analysis of corporate law. Certainly, writers such as Easterbrook and Fischel trumpet its cause loudly when condemning state attempts to impose mandatory rules (and especially *redistributory* mandatory rules) on corporate actors. In fact, however, the commitment is more modest. For one thing, merely to assert that we should enforce the parties' actual agreement begs the very question we are trying to answer: just what constitutes that agreement? Moreover, the very default rules that the law should promulgate in order to promote efficiency might themselves heavily constrain apparently express terms of the parties' bargain. This becomes apparent when we consider the efficiency of courts shunning a formalistic approach and instead undertaking a detailed factual analysis of the parties' maturing relationship to discover therein informal agreements, understandings, expectations, performance practices and the like by which the parties should be bound. Whether we should regard these informal commitments to be properly enforceable depends, from the economic standpoint, on whether a rule supporting their enforcement would be efficient.

To be sure, there are some arguments in favour of the efficiency of such a rule. Enforcing informal commitments should help to control majority (and indeed minority) opportunism.[43] If prospective shareholders are aware the law will help them in this way, then they should be readier to trust, and invest, more. We have long known that such readiness to trust is an important building block in thriving economic

[42] FH Easterbrook and DR Fischel, *The Economic Structure of Corporate Law* (Cambridge, Mass, Harvard University Press, 1991) 31 (emphasis in original).

[43] Recall again that insofar as minority shareholders do enjoy individual 'personal' contractual rights against the company there is the risk that they will enforce these rights in opportunistic ways.

systems.[44] As Mill put it, 'the advantage to mankind of being able to trust one another penetrates into every crevice and cranny of human life'.[45] A judicial refusal to enforce these commitments would push the parties themselves towards greater formalism in recording their understandings and commitments. At best, this would increase transaction costs. At worst, it would punish those shareholders who remained unaware of this judicial practice. Finally, forcing shareholders to document formally all their agreements and understandings might undermine the very process of trust building we are seeking to foster. Replacing vague commitments to co-operation, reached in a mood of optimistic goodwill, by hard-nosed bargaining and legalistic contract-writing premised on the inevitable opportunism of one's fellow shareholders seems less than conducive to building good working relationships.

On the other hand, however, there are countervailing economic costs to this relational investigation. It may be expensive—for both the parties and the courts—to undertake a long, tortuous examination into the parties' relationship, picking over the bones of their actions and conversations to unearth perhaps now long-forgotten commitments. Forcing the parties to mint their agreements in the precise coinage of formal contractual documentation or duly passed resolutions should help to avoid these problems. Further, there is the possibility of judicial error, where the court wrongly interprets ambiguous evidence to uphold an agreement never actually made, or vice versa. And this prospect might encourage speculative litigation where, in the face of clearer contractual documentation, outcomes would be more predictable. Perhaps it is more efficient to hold these informal commitments enforceable only by extra-legal sanctions, such as the adverse publicity and reputational harm that will follow their breach.

These concerns about the merits of judicial investigation into informal relational commitments have led some law and economics scholars

[44] See, for example, F Fukuyama, *Trust: The Social Virtues and the Creation of Prosperity* (New York, Free Press, 1995); BA Misztal, *Trust in Modern Societies* (Cambridge, Polity Press, 1996); MM Blair and LA Stout, 'Trust, Trustworthiness, and the Behavioral Foundations of Corporate Law' (2001) 149 *Universtiy of Pennsylvania Law Review* 1735; M Sako, 'Does Trust Improve Business Relations?' in C Lane and R Bachmann (eds) *Trust Within and Between Organizations* (Oxford, OUP 1998); E Lorenz, 'Trust, Contract and Economic Cooperation' (1999) 23 *Cambridge Journal of Economics* 301.

[45] JS Mill, *Principles of Political Economy* (London, Longmans, Green and Co, 1888) bk 1, ch 7, p 68, quoted in M Sako, *Prices, Quality and Trust: Inter-firm Relations in Britain and Japan* (Cambridge, Cambridge University Press, 1992) 30.

to add their support to calls for a return to greater formalism in contract law (or as Charny calls it, 'anti-antiformalism').[46] And these concerns increase when we move away from commitments grounded in the parties' own, albeit informal, agreements to conventionalist norms that are 'external' to the relationship—say the wider community's sense of good faith, fairness, reciprocity and the like. Once again, there are at first sight efficiency advantages in permitting minority shareholders to invoke such norms as a check on majority opportunism. It offers a fairly open-ended protection from opportunism, by reference to a body of rules that do not have to be spelt out in advance. The court fills in the details of these rules *ex post*, when called upon to adjudicate particular cases. This saves the parties themselves the effort of trying to capture, *ex ante*, all the rules by which they intend to be bound. Given the impracticality and the costs of their achieving a complete specification of all such norms, this sort of *ex post* judicial gap filling looks a much more effective protection for minorities.

However, there are also costs to such an approach. First, even if we applaud open-ended judicial control of opportunism, based on judicial *ex post* gap filling, it is doubtful, from an efficiency perspective, that filling gaps always by reference to conventionalist norms is appropriate. For one thing there is, as noted above, empirical scepticism about the existence of such norms.[47] Secondly, if we are really concerned about efficiency, we cannot simply assume that conventionalist norms themselves set efficient standards of behaviour.[48]

These two criticisms do not deny the case for an open-ended judicial control per se, but do doubt that 'conventionalist norms' should provide the criterion for such control. Suppose, then, we changed the criterion. Instead of controlling opportunism by reference to conventionalist norms, the court might do so by reference to what we might call the parties' own 'subjective hypothetical bargain'. By this is meant (here) the term the parties now before the court would themselves have agreed on had they addressed the contingency now at issue.[49] Suppose that a court finds that the parties were silent on whether all the share-

[46] D Charny, 'The New Formalism in Contract' (1999) 66 *University of Chicago Law Review* 842.

[47] See the works cited above at n 35.

[48] See, for example, EA Posner, 'Law, Economics, and Inefficient Norms' (1996) 144 *University of Pennsylvania Law Review* 1697

[49] For a useful account of the concept of the parties' hypothetical bargain, and for different conceptions of that concept, see Charny, n 10 above. For an application of these different conceptions specifically to the s 459 context, see Goddard, n 4 above.

holders were entitled to participate in management, or at least on whether a shareholder denied such participation was entitled to have her shares purchased from her. The court might try to put itself in the parties' shoes and imagine what rule they would have agreed upon had the issue in question been raised for their consideration.[50]

Once again, there seem good efficiency arguments for the courts filling the gaps left in the parties' agreements by reference to the terms they themselves would have bargained. Doing so saves the parties the costs of trying to imagine, and contract for, all future contingencies. They can happily leave gaps in their agreements safe in the knowledge that, if necessary, a judge will do what they failed to do for themselves. But problems remain. There is the danger of judicial error. As the court strives to put itself into the parties' shoes, it may simply misread their hypothetical bargain. There is also a question of timing. In a long-term relationship, should the court be concerned only with agreements that would have been made at the outset, or ask also what agreements the parties would in fact have made throughout their relationship? Finally, it hardly follows that the rule a particular pair of parties *would have agreed to* will maximise either their joint, or their individual, wealth or welfare. I might yesterday have agreed to all sorts of terms that, with better information, or more sophisticated economic reasoning, I would today reject. If we are concerned to generate a rule that will promote efficiency, implying into the parties' agreements inefficient terms they would foolishly have agreed to looks less than efficient.

Suppose, then, that the courts filled gaps in the parties' agreements not by reference to the term they would have agreed, but instead by reference to the term that 'idealised' parties like them would have agreed. This idealisation of the parties would make them into more economically rational actors—actors who had perfect information, say, and desired to maximise their joint wealth. From an efficiency perspective, this seems a more attractive way to settle the parties' disputes. The court still tailors the rules it is implying to the parties before the court.

[50] Admittedly, in practice the court's inquiry into the parties' subjective hypothetical bargain might run very close to an inquiry into what the conventionalist norm would be. The court might decide that the best evidence of what the parties before it *would have* agreed is evidence of what other like parties actually *do* agree. Nevertheless, if the court is truly to discover the parties' subjective hypothetical bargain, it is not tied to these conventionalist understandings. It can decide that the particular parties now before the court, with all their relevant characteristics, would in fact have chosen a rule very different from that favoured by most others.

However, it now seeks a rule that would be *efficient* for them, and not merely the rule those parties might, inefficiently, have chosen. Once again, however, doubts surface about the courts proceeding in this way. Whilst it might have been efficient for the shareholders to have agreed, *ex ante*, to the rule the court now imposes, it does not now follow that each is left better off *ex post* by the court's imposition of the rule now. Of course, if the parties know in advance what the wealth maximising rule will be that the court will introduce into their bargain, they can each 'name their price' for accepting such a term. But where terms are first fashioned by courts *ex post*, in response to a particular dispute, this pricing-up looks implausible. A further problem in resolving shareholder disputes by reference to the idealised, efficient hypothetically bargained term is that doing so shifts costs from private actors to the state. In return, it is worth asking what public benefits arise from this expenditure. The more the court tailors the rules it implies to the particular parties now before the court, the less can it develop more general terms that might be widely applicable beyond those parties.

These various difficulties cast a general cloud over an open-ended judicial control of shareholder disputes by reference to the *ex post* discovery of efficient gap filling rules. They suggest that the efficiency prescription for resolving such disputes should be much more modest. In place of open-ended judicial control, a more limited solution entails reliance on the law promulgating, and then enforcing, a body of 'micro default rules' that will apply generally to all like cases.[51] These rules can specify particular rights or expectations—to management participation, to the distribution of income, and so on—that will, in most cases, be efficient for typical shareholders in the types of company to which the rules apply. Those whom the rules do not fit can contract out, and specify their own rules. The rest are saved the trouble of spelling out what the law presumes to be the efficient rule in their case. Most importantly, once these norms are promulgated, they exist '*ex ante*'—prior to any new contractual relationship into which they will then be implied.

There is, however, a difficulty even in this modest prescription for shareholder disputes. It assumes the generation of a body of efficient

[51] Herein lies the argument for so-called 'majoritarian defaults'—defaults mimicking the rule most contractors would choose. However, the total saving of transaction costs depends both upon the number of pairs picking the rule and the costs for each pair of replacing the default with a rule of their choosing.

micro defaults, yet how are these to be generated? The obvious answer is by the courts themselves. Called on to hear disputes between shareholders, courts can begin to grasp the sorts of problems shareholders are facing, and the sorts of terms the most sophisticated of them reach to protect their interests. The court can use this raw material—this experience of commercial life—to crystallise out the rules that are likely to be efficient for most similar agents. Yet the very point of this modest efficiency prescription was to avoid the costs, and distributional unfairness, of courts fashioning and implying efficient defaults in particular cases. It seems likely, however, that in practice we do need a period of voluminous litigation in order to generate the micro default rules that, over time, serve to reduce the volume of litigation and render the system more efficient!

THE UNFAIR PREJUDICE REGIME: SECTIONS 459–61 OF THE COMPANIES ACT 1985

Traditionally, UK company law adopted an approach to the construction of the contractual relationships between shareholders that strongly privileged majority rule over the protection of minority or 'personal' rights within the company. Disputes were to be kept out of the courts, and resolved 'internally' by shareholders, using the machinery they had themselves created for that purpose—majority rule. This satisfied a judicial policy of limiting the courts' involvement in contractual disputes between shareholders.[52] It also, it was argued, minimised the disruption to corporate life.

This approach did, to be sure, entail a very narrow construction of the personal contractual rights that a shareholder might claim against her company or fellow shareholders.[53] And it is perhaps tempting to interpret this as bearing the hallmarks of a 'classical' approach to contract law, where the courts look only to the formal written documentation executed at the beginning of the relationship, thereby reducing to a single written source, and a single moment in time, what is in reality a much more complex, and ongoing, process of bargaining.

[52] The words of Lord Eldon are usually cited as a pointed reminder of this policy: '[t]his Court is not to be required on every Occasion to undertake the Management of every Playhouse and Brewhouse in the Kingdom.' *Carlen v Drury* (1812) 1 Ves & B 154, 158.

[53] One aspect of the courts' approach here was a refusal to permit rectification of the company's articles or memorandum where those documents failed to accord with the intention of those who signed them. *Scott v Frank F Scott (London) Ltd* [1940] Ch 794.

This interpretation would, however, be erroneous. First, company law, by its very privileging of majority rule, sought to recognise the dynamic nature of the shareholders' relationship. The relationship was not to be cast in stone at a single moment in time. It could change through appropriate decisions by appropriate organs of the company. Moreover, such change could even be effected quite *informally* if all shareholders consented.[54] Secondly, this privileging of majority rule certainly did not involve a judicial reluctance to *imply* norms into the parties' bargain. As noted already, company law is suffused with judicially developed default rules. The fiduciary and common law duties on directors are obvious examples. But through the rule in *Foss v Harbottle*[55] it would remain for the majority to decide whether or not an action should be brought for a breach of duty. Thirdly, and finally, the expansive scope given to majority rule entailed sometimes refusing to enforce *express* contractual provisions in the articles. So, for one thing, provisions in the articles fettering a company's power to alter its articles will not be enforced by injunction.[56] And in an admittedly complex and at times conflicting body of case law, the courts refused to enforce some apparently clear personal rights conferred on shareholders in the articles, arguing that the company's internal dispute resolution machinery should be employed to decide on the minority's complaint.[57]

[54] See *Cane v Jones* [1980] 1 WLR 1451. The Company Law Review Steering Group ('CLRSG'), which is leading the UK Government's current review of company law, has recommended a statutory codification of this principle, stating 'that any decision which the company has power to make may be made without observing *any* of the formalities of the [Companies] Act or the company's constitution, where the members unanimously agree.' CLRSG, *Final Report* (London, DTI, 2001) para 2.14.

[55] (1843) 2 Hare 461.

[56] See *Punt v Symmons & Co Ltd* [1903] 2 Ch 506. For a discussion of some of the ways in which shareholders might overcome this restriction on their ability to entrench the articles, see CA Riley, 'Vetoes and Voting Agreements: Some Problems of Consent and Knowledge' (1993) 44 *Northern Ireland Legal Quarterly* 34.

[57] For discussions of these lines of cases, see CR Baxter, 'The Role of the Judge in Enforcing Shareholder Rights' (1983) 42 *Cambridge Law Journal* 96; R Drury 'The Relative Nature of the Shareholder's Right to Enforce the Company Articles' [1986] *Cambridge Law Journal* 219.

The Effect of Section 459

What has now become section 459 of the Companies Act 1985 was first introduced as section 75 of the Companies Act 1980.[58] Even before then, however, there had already been signs of a relaxation in the foregoing judicial approach. Of particular note was the decision of the House of Lords in *Ebrahimi v Westbourne Galleries Ltd*, dealing with what is now section 122(1)(g) of the Insolvency Act 1986.[59] There, Lord Wilberforce had spoken of there being

> room in company law for recognition of the fact that behind [the limited company], or amongst it, there are individuals, with rights, expectations and obligations inter se which are not necessarily submerged in the company structure.[60]

This seemed to offer the potential not only for the enforcement of individual minority rights, but further for the discovery of those rights in informal commitments outwith the parties' constitutional agreements.

The enactment of the unfair prejudice regime helped to realise that potential. Admittedly, section 459 does not, on its face, indicate what principles or values ought to be instantiated in its application. It could be used as a means for enforcing only what the parties formally agreed, or to give effect to conventional understandings of appropriate behaviour in the context of small companies, or to promote efficiency. After an uncertain start,[61] section 459 received an increasingly expansive interpretation, at least insofar as the smaller company is concerned.[62] Courts stressed their desire to keep the wording broad,[63] and to

[58] The predecessor to s 75 of the Companies Act 1980 was s 210 of the Companies Act 1948. This spoke of shareholders having to prove 'oppression'. It was narrowly constructed by the courts, and gave rise to only two successful actions. See further Law Commission, Consultation Paper No 142, *Shareholder Remedies* (London, The Stationery Office, 1996) para 7.8.

[59] s 122(1)(g) allows for the winding up of the company where the court thinks it 'just and equitable'.

[60] [1973] AC 360, 379.

[61] The first case decided under the section was *Re a Company* (1983) 2 All ER 36, in which the trial judge, Lord Grantchester QC, seemed to suggest that a shareholder could only complain if affected in his capacity as a shareholder.

[62] Outside of so called 'quasi partnerships'—and especially in public companies—the courts have been much more restrictive in their recognition of a shareholder's interests.

[63] See, for example, Arden J in *Re BSB Holdings Ltd (No 2)*, '[t]he words of the section are wide and general and . . . the categories of unfair prejudice are not closed.' [1996] 1 BCLC 155, 243.

approach the section on a 'case by case' basis.[64] A recurrent theme, however, picked up from *Ebrahimi*, was that whilst the articles formed the starting point in analysing the petitioner's interests, these might not 'fully reflect the understandings upon which the shareholders [were] associated.'[65] There were, then, detailed factual investigations (and lengthy case reports) into the history of the parties' relationship, and the informal understandings and expectations that co-existed with the formal constitutional arrangements. The shared, articulated understandings of the parties about such matters as participation in management, dividend policy, pre-emption rights, future ownership of the company, and the like, could all be taken into account in actions under section 459.[66] These informal agreements became subsumed under the rubric of 'legitimate expectations'. It became clear, however, that in undertaking these sorts of investigations into the parties' expectations, the courts did stray beyond that which was agreed, albeit informally. Often, the expectations of the parties were plausibly in conflict, and the courts' holding that one set of expectations was reasonable was based on some (rarely articulated) judicial sense of what is commonplace or conventional.[67]

Moreover, it is also arguable that, in moving towards this enforcement of the 'full' or 'real' bargain between the shareholders, the courts were in fact continuing to qualify *express* provisions within the articles. This was most apparent in relation to the courts' approach to 'buy out' provisions in the company's constitution. Faced with the threat of minority actions under section 459, majorities commonly try to settle those actions by offering to purchase the minority's shares. Moreover, some shareholders expressly plan for such an eventuality by inserting provisions—in the articles or some separate shareholders' agreement—specifying the terms on which a shareholder who wants to leave should sell her shares, or even requiring her to sell her shares in particular circumstances.[68] But the courts were ready to ignore such provisions, holding that they should not apply where unfair prejudice was

64 Neill LJ, *Saul D Harrison* [1995] 1 BCLC 14, 30.

65 Hoffmann LJ, *ibid*, 19.

66 See Riley, n 4 above, 793–4.

67 See for example *Re Elgindata Ltd* [1991] BCLC 959, where the court had to decide amongst competing interpretations of reasonable expectations regarding standards of managerial competence.

68 Such as in the event of her ceasing to be a director.

proven.[69] In *Virdi v Abbey Leisure*,[70] for example, the Court of Appeal refused to apply the valuation machinery in a pre-emption provision to a minority shareholder's sale of her shares following a successful section 459 petition. The court construed the contractual pre-emption provision as not applying to a 'forced' sale under section 459. More significantly, in *Re a company (No 00330) ex p Holden*, Harman J refused to enforce a provision in the company's articles that permitted the majority to compel the minority to sell her shares.[71]

The Judicial Retreat

Whilst many welcomed this approach, others were less convinced. There are constant reminders throughout the cases that '[s]ection 459 enables the court to give full effect to the terms and understandings on which the members of the company became associated, but not to rewrite them.'[72] And recent years have seen a hardening of this judicial line. Perhaps the clearest example of this is the House of Lords' recent

[69] In a stimulating analysis of the s 459 jurisprudence, Goddard, n 4 above, 78ff, argues that it is wrong to regard the court as ignoring the articles. Rather, we should see the articles as themselves incomplete, such that the court can still be said to be merely completing, rather than rewriting, their terms. Goddard offers two reasons for calling the contract incomplete. First, he argues that it is characterised by 'situational insensitivity'. A coarse contractual term treats alike a number of distinguishable future contingencies. This analysis, which draws on the work of Ayres and Gertner, (they refer to these coarse terms as 'insufficiently state contingent': see I Ayres and R Gertner, 'Filling Gaps in Incomplete Contracts: An Economic Theory of Default Rules' (1989) 99 *Yale Law Journal* 87 and, for a similar analysis, see Schwartz, n 28 above) is essentially economic. The incompleteness is a failure to exploit all possible gains from trade by replacing a single coarse term with two (or more) more finely crafted terms. But Goddard fails to acknowledge that, even from an economic perspective, the failure to exploit all gains from trade may be a rational (efficient) response to the perceived costs and risks of developing ever more finely nuanced terms. And he also fails to show why, in any case, we should treat an economic analysis of contractual relationships as determining the correct legal way to characterise the judiciary's treatment of such contracts. Goddard's second argument does potentially focus on this legal question. His second argument claims that it is unlikely that the parties intended the over-broad rule to apply to the particular contingency now before the court. We are not presented with any empirical evidence to substantiate such a claim, however. Moreover, the proper issue should surely be what *reasonable men* would take the parties' language and conduct to mean, not whether the parties, had they known then what they know now would have agreed that their 'coarse' term did not cover the contingency that has subsequently arisen.

[70] [1990] BCLC 342.

[71] [1991] BCLC 597.

[72] Per Hoffmann J (as he then was), *Re Posgate & Denby Agencies Ltd* [1987] BCLC 8, 14.

decision in *O'Neill v Phillips*.[73] P was the sole shareholder of a private company. In January 1985, he gave O 25 per cent of the company's shares, and made him a director. In December 1985 P retired from the board, leaving O as managing director. It was understood that in return for so acting, profits would be split equally between the two shareholders. There was also some discussion about O's shareholding being increased to 50 per cent. In 1991, the company's fortunes floundered, and P resumed effective control of his company. O remained an ordinary board member, but he was paid only his salary and the dividends attributable to his 25 per cent shareholding. Moreover, it was made clear that his shareholding would not be increased to 50 per cent. O brought proceedings under section 459. He claimed that the failure to continue paying him 50 per cent of the company's profits, and the refusal to increase his shareholding to 50 per cent, amounted to unfair prejudice. The trial judge found in favour of P. The Court of Appeal reversed that decision, but the House of Lords allowed P's appeal.

Lord Hoffmann delivered the judgment of the House. He emphasised the need for the petitioner to show an actual agreement that P would behave in some way other than the articles entitled him to do. 'I think that one useful cross-check in a case like this', he argued, 'is to ask whether the exercise of the power in question would be contrary to what the parties, by word or conduct, have actually agreed.'[74] And the House of Lords accepted the trial judge's finding that there had been no concluded agreement—formal or otherwise—that P would increase O's shareholding to 50 per cent. Equally, the agreement to pay O 50 per cent of the profits was not unconditional. It depended upon O remaining managing director of the company.

Two points emerge and deserve emphasis. The first is that Lord Hoffmann's judgment seems to allow the court to continue to discover, and enforce, actual but informal agreements entered into by the shareholders. The original trial judge spent some not inconsiderable time examining the parties' past history to deal with that issue, and Lord Hoffmann himself clearly thought it right that he had done so. However, subsequent cases have suggested that the courts might become still more restrictive here. So, in *Re Guidezone Ltd* Parker J accepted that the majority might be regarded as acting unfairly where they ignored some agreement or understanding that would not itself be

[73] *O'Neill v Phillips sub nom Re a company No 00709 of 1982* [1999] 2 BCLC 1.
[74] *Ibid*, 10 h.

enforceable at law. However, where such an agreement or understanding was reached not at the time the company was formed, but during the subsequent life of the company, the minority would need to show it had acted in *reliance* on that agreement.[75] Likewise, in *Re Benfield Greig Group plc*[76] the executors of a deceased shareholder were led to understand that the company would not insist upon the application of certain buy-out machinery in the company's articles which applied on the death of a member.[77] Nevertheless, at first instance Arden J refused to accept that the breach of such an understanding could amount to unfair prejudice. Although the judgment is not entirely clear, it seems to have been based on the fact that the assurances were given by the directors rather than by the shareholders, the lack of reliance by the executors on those assurances and on the public nature of the company.[78]

The second point arising from *O'Neill* goes back to the issue of implied terms. The petitioner's need to show an *actual* agreement suggests that petitioners cannot ground unfair prejudice in the mere breach of 'conventionalist norms' or 'hypothetical bargains'. This view gains support from Lord Hoffmann's dicta about looking to what the parties had *actually* agreed, and his warning against 'legitimate expectations' enjoying a 'life of their own'. Similarly, in *Re Benfield Greig Group plc,*[79] the petitioner's claim to read into the articles an implied term requiring equal treatment of the parties, equal access to information, and a right to make submissions to the valuer was also rejected.[80]

[75] [2000] 2 BCLC 321. One obvious difficulty with this requirement, which renders the corporate case somewhat different from many other long-term relationships, is the locked-in nature of share-ownership. It becomes hard to argue that a minority shareholder is relying on a promise made to her by remaining within the company when she has little chance of leaving anyway.

[76] *Re Benfield Greig Group plc, Nugent and another v Benfield Greig Group plc and others* [2000] 2 BCLC 488.

[77] In particular, the executors were led to understand that the directors would not force a compulsory sale and any sale would be at an agreed value.

[78] *Ibid*, 507 d–508 g.

[79] n 76 above.

[80] The executors subsequently appealed, arguing that the auditors could not be regarded as independent under the terms of the articles. In support of that claim, they pointed to the fact that the auditors had acted for the company for the purposes of negotiating with the Inland Revenue about the value to be attributed to shares to be issued to the company's employees. That appeal was allowed, although it does not seem to affect Arden J's discussion of the principles governing s 459 itself. See *Re Benfield Greig Group plc, Nugent and another v Benfield Greig Group plc and others* [2002] 1 BCLC 65.

Arden J held that terms could only be implied into the articles as a matter of necessity in order to make the articles workable, and not just because it would be fair or reasonable to do so.[81]

However, against this, other dicta by Lord Hoffmann in *O'Neill* seemed to accept that there might be an implication that a shareholder in a company in which substantially all the shareholders were directors would have an expectation of remaining a director thereof, or of being bought out on fair terms if the directorship were terminated.[82] Nothing was said that would restrict such a right to cases where there was some actual, albeit informal, understanding to that effect. Rather, it seemed to be an implication of what is usual in such cases, a 'micro rule' that applies by default in this type of company unless expressly excluded by the parties, and whose breach can amount to unfair prejudice.

CONCLUSIONS

We can identify three broad phases in the courts' approach to the construction of the inter-shareholder contract, including the implicit elements of that contract. Under the pre-section 459 jurisprudence, the courts insist upon a relatively strict application of majority rule. This recognises that shareholders have created their own machinery for dealing with their disputes, and that their contractual personal rights will often be subjugated to the majority rule principle. This occurs in respect of contractual rights agreed informally, outwith the articles, but applies also even to formal rights within the articles.

The introduction of section 459 leads to a second phase, in which the courts embrace the complexity, and implicit aspects, of the parties' agreements. They are prepared to engage in detailed and thorough examinations of the parties' relationship and the course of their dealing, discovering and enforcing commitments outwith the formal contractual agreements that created the company. They begin to build up a set of legitimate expectations—particularly in relation to 'quasi partnerships'—that are often seen as legitimate by virtue of their conventionalism. Finally, these understandings and expectations are sometimes now permitted even to overrule clear express terms with which they conflict.

[81] n 76 above, 512 b.
[82] n 73 above, 16 e–f.

In the third phase, the courts draw back and insist upon showing greater fidelity to the shareholders' express agreements. They are still to look to informal agreements, including those made subsequent to the original settling of the constitutional documentation (provided, perhaps, that there is reliance).[83] Moreover, unfair prejudice might still be found in the breach of those micro default rules that have been crystallised out of past case law—such as rights of management participation, income sharing, and the like. However, section 459 does not offer a basis for judicial intervention based just on the *ex post* identification of, say, conventionalist norms or hypothetical bargains.

How might we explain this change of judicial emphasis? One explanation that might be offered would be a renewed commitment to 'freedom of contract'. To recognise and enforce what is merely implicit in the parties' bargain somehow 'rewrites' that bargain and thus undermines freedom of contract.[84] It might be suggested that *O'Neill* does no more than require us to focus upon what the parties did agree; it thus rules out attempts to invoke conventionalist norms that *conflict* with, rather than merely *supplement*, the parties' express terms. However, this looks hard to sustain. As noted already, the history of the courts' construction of the parties' contractual relationship is not one that has deferred heavily to what the parties expressly agreed. The courts were happy to ignore express provisions in the company's constitution that inconveniently interfered with the operation of majority rule. Moreover, the very process of determining what the parties 'really' agreed must, as Campbell and Collins show, have regard to these implicit dimensions.

A more compelling explanation for the judicial retreat here is this. The courts are responding to many of those pragmatic concerns that characterise the economic analysis of judicial regulation of inter-shareholder relationships, described in section III above. So, in the UK there has been a growing concern at the mounting costs of litigation. Although, so far as I am aware there has been no rigorous research into the costs such actions have incurred, there has been anecdotal evidence of the growth in litigation, which is often fairly protracted as shareholders carefully dissect the behaviour of their partners over the whole length of their relationships.

[83] See, for example, *Brownlow v G H Marshall Ltd* [2000] BCLC 655, where the court was prepared to find 'a family expectation, growing over the years, that [the petitioner] would, so far as possible and so far as personal circumstances allowed, be brought into the management of the affairs of the company.' If this expectation could not be fulfilled, then 'something would have to be done to realise the value of [her] shares.' (p 669 g–I).

[84] See Campbell and Collins, ch 2 in this volume.

Moreover, these costs are too often, it is claimed, out of all proportion to the fairly modest value of the companies involved in many such cases.[85] And such costs are being borne not just by companies (or shareholders), but also by courts. Not only does this take up court time that might be saved if disputes were sorted out internally within companies, but it also involves judges dealing with matters of business in relation to which, they say, they have little expertise. Finally, the ready availability of such actions permits, it is suggested, minorities to blackmail majorities. The mere threat of commencing proceedings, given the costs and time such an action would consume, is enough to force majorities to buy out the minority's shares at an inflated price.

From these pragmatic concerns there is developing an unfair prejudice regime somewhat closer to the (admittedly incompletely specified) economic prescription for minority shareholder protection set out above. Crucial here is the rejection of an open-ended judicial power of control over majoritarian opportunism grounded in respect for conventionalist norms. Instead, from the substantial case law generated by the earlier, expansive treatment of section 459, the courts have some data about commonplace expectations in so-called quasi-partnership companies to crystallise a set of micro default rules applicable thereto. These rules together add up to what one author has called a 'code of conduct' for such companies.[86] Their existence saves on transaction costs for parties, mitigates any failure on their part to realise the need for such rules, and provides some measure of control on opportunism.

In this regard, it is interesting, if a little disappointing, to note the response of the Company Law Review Steering Group to the Law Commission's recent proposals.[87] In its review of shareholder remedies, the Commission had expressed concern at the costs and disruption caused by the growth of section 459 actions, and of the resulting inefficiency of that regime in resolving inter-shareholder disputes. And it had proposed a set of default rules designed to provide, *ex ante*, for the resolution of inter-shareholder disputes.[88] However, after a pro-

[85] See eg *Re Rotodata Ltd* [2000] BCLC 122, 124.

[86] B Hannigan, 'Section 459 of the Companies Act 1985—A Code of Conduct for the Quasi-partnership?' [1988] *Lloyds Maritime and Commercial Law Quarterly* 60.

[87] Law Commission, esp parts 7–12 and 18; Law Commission, Report 246, *Shareholder Remedies* (London, The Stationery Office, 1997) esp part 4.

[88] These rules would do the following: first, create a presumption of unfairness in respect of certain cases of exclusion from management; second, create a presumption in favour of a pro-rata valuation on a buy-out; and third, provide a model 'buy out' article.

tracted period of consultation, the Company Law Review Steering Group declared itself unconvinced of the case for adopting the Commission's proposed rules.[89] The Group's cautious approach serves as a sharp reminder of the difficulties inevitably encountered in designing *ex ante* rules that cover a reasonably wide contracting population, whilst retaining sufficient flexibility to control future opportunism by both majority and minority shareholders.

[89] See CLRSG, *Modern Company Law for a Competitive Economy: Developing the Framework* (London, DTI, 2000) paras 4.102–4.104; *Modern Company Law for a Competitive Economy: Completing the Structure* (London, DTI, 2000) paras 5.75ff and *Modern Company Law for a Competitive Economy: Final Report* (London, DTI, 2001) para 7.41.

Index